TIM MÄLZER
GREEN BOX

mosaik

2nd edition
© 2013 **Wilhelm Goldmann Verlag**, Munich, Germany
A Division of **Verlagsgruppe Random House GmbH**
© of the German Edition 2012 **Wilhelm Goldmann Verlag,**
Munich, Germany
A Division of **Verlagsgruppe Random House GmbH**
Original Title: **Greenbox.** Tim Mälzers grüne Küche
Author: **Tim Mälzer**
Tim Mälzer's Assistant: **Frank Meyer**
Project Management: **Marcel Stut**
Texts: **Stevan Paul**
Texts for Recipes: **Stevan Paul, Marcel Stut**
Translation and Copy Editing: **Marianne Harms-Nicolai**
and **Dr. Elizabeth Schlüssel**
Copy Editing: **Meredith Hays**
Proofreading: **Meredith Hays, Becky Vinter**
Requisites Majorca: **Katrin Heinatz**
Food Styling: **Tim Mälzer, Marcel Stut,**
Stevan Paul, Felix Cordes
Photography: **Matthias Haupt**
Assistant of Photography: **Christian Velten**
Cover Design: weissraum.de(sign)°,
Lucas Buchholz, Bernd Brink
Creative Director: www.**anjalaukemper**.de
Art Director: **Anja Laukemper, Tina Hilscher**
Illustrations & Scribblings: **Rinah Lang** (www.signorinah.de)
Historical Illustrations: **www.BioLib.de**
Reproduction: **Lorenz & Zeller**, Inning am Ammersee, Germany
Print and Binding: **Mohn Media GmbH**, Gütersloh, Germany
BK – production IH
Printed in Germany
ISBN 978-3-442-39254-4

www.tim-maelzer.de

www.mosaik-verlag.de   This book is printed on fsc® certificated
Tauro provided by Sappi, Stockstadt.

INFO PAGES

Calendar of Seasons 14 | **Kitchen Aids** 22 | **UMAMI** 28

Legumes 38 | **Dairy Products** 52 | **Crumbs** 76

Rice Paper & More 88 | **Tofu & Tempeh** 114 | **Herbs** 132

Liquid Vegetables 150 | **Oil** 164 | **Nuts** 184 | **Smokey Aromas** 200

Salt Mixtures 222 | **Pesto & Vegetable Pastes** 232

GARLIC

CABBAGE

tasty!

CONTENTS:

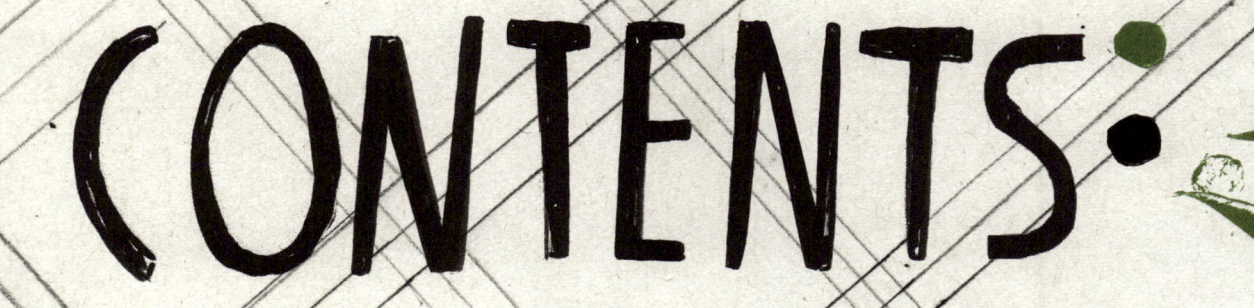

GREEN BOX — My Green Cuisine 6

Recipes 16—255

Index A—Z 256

Vegetable Index 258

Season Index 263

Easy Cooking Index 265

Quick Cooking Index 267

Cooking for Guests Index 268

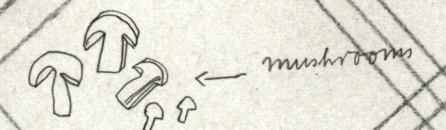

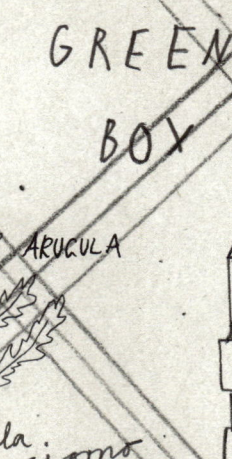

GREEN BOX
MY GREEN CUISINE

I first had the idea for the **GREEN BOX COOKBOOK** after realizing that I adored making meals with fresh, crisp and crunchy vegetables every day, despite the fact that I do love a good piece of meat! That idea came just as naturally as putting **CREATIVE, VEGETARIAN DISHES** on the menu of my restaurant "Bullerei" in Hamburg. In no time, many of those dishes became extremely popular with our guests. I love vegetables and I love challenges, so I reckoned it was **HIGH TIME** for my green cookbook!

I quickly noticed that developing a **NEW PASSION** for vegetables begins right on your doorstep. The variety of herbs, root vegetables, leafy vegetables, buds, beets, sprouts, seeds, lettuces, blossoms, nuts and fruit available in our stores and markets has never been bigger. Many farmers are now specializing in new strains of vegetables and have also begun to cultivate long-forgotten types again. **CSA's** are becoming more and more popular in big cities. Local farmers' markets are helping us to regain our **FEELING FOR THE SEASONS** and for seasonal produce. Asian grocery stores and specialized vegetable traders supplement what our local supermarkets and stores have to offer by selling fruit and vegetables from their home countries. And there is no exotic herb mixture or rare vegetable that you can't order on the Internet.

Lemon yippee!

THE FLAVOR COOKBOOK

Right from the outset of our work on the Green Box project, our team started thinking about what makes a rich and varied vegetable cuisine. We immediately agreed that it had to be **TASTY** and contain aromatic recipes with lots of flavor, ideas and "oompf" – ideally be a **VEGETABLE COOKBOOK** for confirmed meat eaters. We went shopping and bought mountains of vegetables and fruit and got started. There were no rules, no limits and no set recipes. But it was tricky! We chefs were used to thinking up recipes with fish and meat. We had to seriously change our approach. We were surprised when we realized how **QUICK, CREATIVE** and **SIMPLE** green cuisine can be when you take the time to consider the delicious potential of each ingredient. The Green Box experimental kitchen soon developed into a real school of flavor. And that's exactly what my new cookbook is: an **INVITATION, INTRODUCTION** and manual to a **GREEN VEGETARIAN CUISINE** that lacks for nothing.

VEGETABLES – FROM THE SIDELINES TO A STARRING ROLE

The taste of a crunchy carrot is unique, **SWEET SUGAR SNAP PEAS** are a little green sensation on their own, and a ripe **AVOCADO** with a sprinkling of salt can actually be a full meal.
Vegetables, fruit and herbs put lots of **VARIETY OF FLAVOR** on the plate and many of my recipes rely on the individual **CHARACTER** of the vegetables used, on the particular texture, on the **SPECIAL CONSISTENCY**, on the rich taste. You can experience pleasure by simply combining earthy beets with sweet oranges, or carrots in their own juice with spicy watercress. For the most common vegetables I have developed three to four very short and **FAST BASIC RECIPES** which can be cooked every day and which bring out the sensational flavor of each veg. You'll find them printed on a double page.

THIS IS HOW TO COOK – THE GREEN BOX VARIATIONS

Cooking has a lot to do with **GUT FEELING, INTUITION** and especially with **PERSONAL TASTE**. That's why nothing is written in stone and no recipe claims to be the only way of preparing a dish. Lots of different methods will lead to the **BEST RESULT**, that's why the variations you'll find accompanying my Green Box recipes are so important to me. They should inspire you to get creative yourself and to vary the ingredients however you like – **THAT'S REALLY HOW TO COOK!** So don't be afraid to change what the recipes say. The success or failure of a dish does not depend on whether a spoonful of sugar is heaped or leveled. Start small and then let your palate decide. That works for all measurements. Every sort of oil and every type of vinegar tastes different, and the pots and pans we use are as varied as our vegetables. That's why it is so important for cooking novices not to get discouraged: just work with the vegetables you have in front of you. A few teaspoons more or less make no difference at all. Cook and fry with your favorite oils, use the vinegar you have at hand. Pay attention to what's happening in your pots and pans; the **STEP-BY-STEP PREPARATION PHOTOS** in the book will help you with that. In any case: trust your taste! That's how things work out best.

WHERE THE "WOW" COMES FROM

While writing this cookbook we concentrated on the **VARIOUS FLAVORS INHERENT IN SOME VEGETABLES** like mushrooms, tomatoes, beans, corn, potatoes and spinach. Soy sauce or Parmesan cheese also creates a rich, round and intense taste in the green – vegetarian – kitchen. I loved using **CRUMB MIXTURES** that we developed for Green Box. Combined with fried or boiled vegetables, they are true **TASTE BOMBS**! Another simple way to get flavor and sophistication into the green kitchen is to use different pestos and salsas. Almost all the dishes in **GREEN BOX** can be made with regular kitchen equipment. But as I strived to create a "WOW"-effect with the dishes, I also used unusual cooking techniques that I want to teach you. A juicer, a vacuuming food sealer and wood smoking chips play important roles. **LET ME SURPRISE YOU!**

♡ parsley

minestrone (recipe page 254)

THE GREEN BOX FOR BEGINNERS, SHOW-OFFS AND EXPERTS

Of course, you can always manage **WITHOUT SPECIAL TOOLS** and gadgets. I really like fast, uncomplicated dishes that make you happy and fill you up without too much preparation. Green Box is full of those. However, because I (as a man) like to show off, I've also added a lot of recipes to the Green Box to **IMPRESS YOUR GUESTS**: showpieces for your eyes and your taste buds, which here and there require a little more skill and concentration. Believe me, it's worth it! In addition to a lot of **QUICK RECIPES** for people in a hurry, there are also a few that require a bit more time. Don't worry: many of them cook on their own, such as the homemade baked beans, where every single one of the 120 minutes of cooking time is worth it.

GREEN BOX – BROWSE, READ OR COOK

In addition to the many process photos, the inviting **PICTURES OF THE RECIPES** and the **RECIPES** themselves, there are many **TIPS AND PIECES OF INFORMATION** on vegetables and **PREPARATION** worth reading. You can enter into the colorful variety of my new green cuisine wherever you want. **THERE'S A LOT TO DISCOVER.** Finding your way through the **VEGETABLE JUNGLE** is easy with the unusually comprehensive index. In addition to the alphabetical listing, the recipes can also be searched for and found under the Green Box's headings, **"TYPES OF VEGETABLES," "QUICK," "SIMPLE," "FOR GUESTS"** and **"SEASONAL STUFF."**

The Green Box is an **ENJOYABLE READ**, whether you flip through the pages, read it cover to cover, or use it as a reference. It's a cookbook **THAT DEMANDS USE** – in the kitchen as well as on the sofa.

I really hope you'll **ENJOY** discovering my new flavorful vegetarian cuisine!

TIM MÄLZER

Bagna Cauda with Veggie Nibble

"Bagna cauda" (warm dressing) originates in Piedmont, Italy, but it has become a very popular warm dipping sauce all over Italy. The recipes for it vary greatly. However, traditionally, the savory dip contains huge quantities of garlic and at least one anchovy. Just a minute, did I say anchovy? We replaced it with a spoonful of Asian miso paste. That tastes great, too! But don't tell the people from Piedmont!

Ingredients (serves 2—4)

- 4 spears green asparagus
- 8 young carrots
- 1/2 cup sugar snap peas
- salt
- 8 radishes
- 1 small kohlrabi
- 1/2 fennel bulb
- 1 heart of Romaine lettuce
- 8 garlic cloves
- 1 1/3 cups milk
- 2—3 slices toast, crust removed
- 1 teaspoon miso paste
- 3 tablespoons olive oil
- pepper
- lemon juice

1. Peel off the lower third of the asparagus and cut off the stringy ends. Cut off green carrot tops. Cook the asparagus and carrots together with the sugar snap peas for 1—2 minutes in salted water, refresh in cold water and drain. Rub off the baby carrots' delicate peel.

2. Wash the radishes and cut in half. Peel the kohlrabi and slice it roughly. Wash the fennel and cut it into paperthin slices. Slice the heart of Romaine lettuce, wash it and spin it dry.

3. To make the sauce, peel the garlic and boil it in the milk for 8 minutes. Purée the garlic, toast, milk, miso paste and olive oil in a blender or food processor. Season with salt and pepper and a squeeze of lemon. Serve with the vegetables.

Preparation time: 25 minutes

> **TIP** » Usually vegetables for nibbling are served raw. But I like to blanch some types of veg in boiling salted water. That intensifies the flavor.

Beet Purée with Poached Eggs and Horseradish Bread Salad

Ingredients (serves 4)

1 pound cooked beets (see tip)
salt
apple cider vinegar
4 thin slices of white bread
1 1/2 cups mixed cress (e.g. daikon, shiso or watercress)
1 tablespoon olive oil
1 small piece of peeled, fresh horseradish
8 large eggs
3 1/2 tablespoons butter

1. Purée the beets in a blender until smooth and creamy. Put the beet purée into a pot and add salt and a dash of apple cider vinegar to taste. Toast the slices of bread for the salad and cut into bite-sized pieces. In a bowl mix together the toast, cress, olive oil and a dash of apple cider vinegar. Season to taste with salt and finely grated horseradish.
2. Bring to a boil 8 1/2 cups of water and 1 tablespoon of apple cider vinegar. Turn down the heat until the water is simmering. Crack the eggs on the edge of a cup and carefully let them slide into the water. Poach the eggs for 3 minutes, turning them gently.
3. Heat the purée in a pot and stir in the cold butter. Serve the purée with the bread salad and the poached eggs on warm plates. Add some finely grated, fresh horseradish to taste.

Preparation time: 35 minutes

TIP: You can get pre-cooked beets in well-stocked grocery stores. Or you can boil fresh, unpeeled beets in salted water or roast them until soft in the oven at 400° F and then peel them. One hour is a rough estimate for the cooking time which actually depends on the size of the beets.

TIM: "We add apple cider vinegar. That gives the beets a fruity, slightly sharp acidity."
MARCEL: "Yeah, it creates a great contrast to the earthy spiciness of the horseradish."
STEVAN: "Sensational! And then the soft egg interacting with the crisp toast and the velvety texture of the purée! People will go crazy!"
NINA: "Hey guys, do you ever listen to what you are saying? You sound like total nerds."
SALOME: "They are total nerds."

Pasta for Gals   WOMEN ARE ALWAYS RIGHT

Ingredients (serves 4)

- 1 pound broccoli
- 3 1/2 cups spinach leaves
- 1 small garlic clove
- 1 pound favorite pasta (in photo: strozzapreti)
- salt
- 3 tablespoons olive oil
- 3/4 cup frozen peas
- 2/3 cup vegetable stock
- 1 cup heavy cream
- pepper
- 1 organic lemon
- 4 stems basil
- 3 tablespoons butter

1. Wash the broccoli and cut off the florets. Wash the spinach leaves, spin them dry and chop them roughly. Peel and mince the garlic.
2. Cook the pasta in salted water according to the cooking instructions. Meanwhile, heat the olive oil in a large pot. Fry the broccoli in the olive oil for 3 minutes, add garlic after 2 minutes. Then add the peas and the spinach and let the spinach wilt.
3. Add the vegetable stock and cream and let the mixture come to a boil. Season with salt and pepper. Cook, uncovered, for 2 minutes. Drain the pasta and stir into the pasta sauce while hot. Cook again for 1–2 minutes, uncovered.
4. Finely grate the lemon peel. Mince 6 basil leaves and stir them into the sauce, together with the butter and lemon peel. Season with salt, pepper and 1 dash of lemon juice and serve with the remaining basil leaves sprinkled over it.

Preparation time: 25 minutes

"I used to think that broccoli was for girls. As I age, I am not only getting fatter, I am also getting wiser. Unfortunately, I have to admit that I really have missed out over the years."

KITCHEN UTENSILS

It's not the equipment that's crucial! The basic equipment that most kitchens already have is sufficient for all the recipes in the book.

handblender
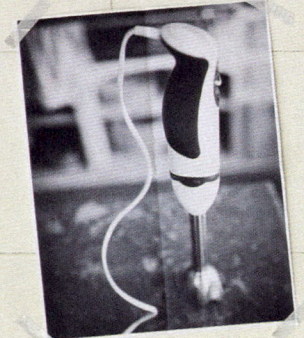

steamer baskets

sieve

chopping board

pots & pans

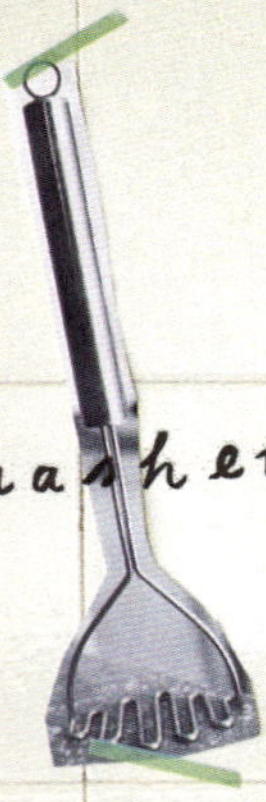

potato masher

kitchen scales

food processor

knives

4X RED: TOMATO

They're back! Tomatoes that really taste of tomato – red-fleshed, juicy, sweet and fruity, or still green, intensely aromatic and tart. Looking for these tomatoes is worth it: local farms produce fragrant wild, cherry and date tomatoes in late summer and fall. In addition, imports such as the RAF tomatoes from Spain, the large ox heart tomatoes (cuore de bue) or the green tomatoes "green zebra" or "evergreen" can be recommended.

1 Goat Cheese Calzone with Tomato Salsa and Deep-Fried Capers

Roll out **1 packet of puff pastry (approx. 1/2 pound)** and cover one half with **1/3 cup of crumbled goat cheese**. Fold in half, press the edges together tightly and drizzle with **1 tablespoon of honey**. Place the dough on a baking sheet covered with parchment and weigh it down with a baking rack. Preheat the oven to 400° F (convection: 350° F) and bake in the middle of the oven for about 15 minutes or until golden brown. Cut **1 1/2 cups of cherry tomatoes** in half, dice and drain them. Finely chop **1 small red onion** and stir into the tomatoes, together with **1 teaspoon of white wine vinegar** and **2 tablespoons of olive oil**. Season with **salt, pepper and 1 pinch of sugar**. Heat **1 inch of oil** in a deep pan. Drain **3 tablespoons of capers**, toss them in **1 tablespoon of flour** and fry them for 1–2 minutes until crunchy. Remove and drain them on a paper towel. Take the puff pastry out of the oven, cut into equal portions and immediately serve with the tomatoes and capers on top.

2 Tomato Salad "Extra Virgin"

Cut the core out of **8 ripe tomatoes**. Cut the tomatoes in slices and put into a bowl. Finely grate the peel of **half an organic lemon** and mix with the tomatoes, together with **2 tablespoons of lemon juice** and **4 tablespoons of olive oil**. Season everything with **salt, pepper** and **1 teaspoon of sugar**.

3 Igor's Tomato Soup

Chop **1 3/4 pounds of ripe tomatoes** into cubes, discarding the cores. Lay a handful of the tomato cubes aside. Put the remainder of the tomato cubes and **1 cup of tomato juice** into a blender and purée until smooth and then force through a sieve. Add **salt, pepper, 1 pinch of sugar, 1—2 dashes of tabasco sauce, 3 tablespoons of vodka** and **4 tablespoons of olive oil**. Cool for at least 2 hours in the refrigerator. Sprinkle with **chili flakes,** the remaining **tomato cubes** and **1 teaspoon of chopped fresh celery leaves** and serve.

4 The Best Oven Tomato Sauce Ever

Cut **10 tomatoes** in half, removing the cores. Sprinkle **2 tablespoons of sugar** on a baking sheet. Place the tomatoes on the sugar with the cut side facing down. Roast them in a preheated oven on the top rack at 500° F for 10—15 minutes, until the skin turns black. Take the sheet out and remove the black skin. Lower the oven to 300° F. Squash the tomatoes with a fork. Add **1 peeled and chopped garlic clove, 1 tablespoon of chopped thyme leaves, salt, pepper** and **3 tablespoons of olive oil** to the tomatoes. Let the tomato mixture simmer in the oven on the middle rack for another 60 minutes. Squash the tomatoes with your fork again, mix them and season with salt and pepper. This is the perfect topping for your favorite pasta!

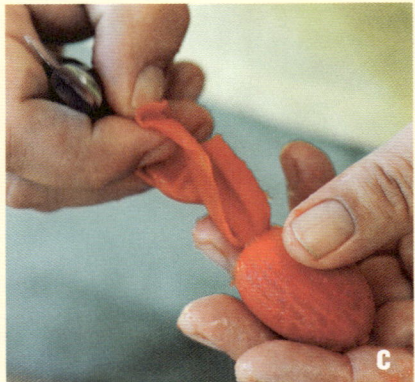

Burrata with Sweet Tomatoes and Fennel

Ingredients (serves 4)

1 cup sugar
1 garlic clove
6 bay leaves
6 black peppercorns
4 strips lemon peel (organic)
3 1/2 cups small date or cherry tomatoes
1 small fennel bulb with greens
1 teaspoon white wine vinegar
olive oil
salt
pepper
2 balls burrata (or 2—4 balls of buffalo mozzarella)

1. Bring 2 cups of water to a boil with the sugar, garlic, bay leaves, peppercorns and lemon peel. Leave to cool.

2. Place the tomatoes briefly in boiling water until the skins burst (A). Rinse them in cold water. Peel the skins off (B,C), put them into the herb stock (D) and let them soak for at least 5 hours, overnight is best (E).

3. Finely grate the fennel and marinate it in vinegar and 2 tablespoons of olive oil, season with salt and pepper and scatter over the burrata (F). Remove the tomatoes from the stock and put on the plate. Season the dish with a few drops of olive oil, salt and pepper.

Decorate with a little fennel green and serve (G).

Preparation time: 35 minutes (+ 5 hours for marinating)

"These sweet tomatoes originated in my Bullerei kitchen in Hamburg because we had the same problem every chef has: sometimes tomatoes taste good, sometimes they don't. The peeled tomatoes acquire a nice texture in our herbed stock and a perfect blend of sweet to sour. That's what intensifies the flavor of the tomato. That way we give nature a hand."

TIP This recipe is suitable for all types of tomatoes. The tomatoes will keep for up to 10 days in the refrigerator submerged in the stock.

UMAMI –
The Natural Flavor Turbocharger

In 1907, while drinking a vegetable soup made from kombu seaweed, the Japanese chemist Kikunae Ikeda, discovered the **"FIFTH" FLAVOR.** The soup he spooned wasn't salty or sweet, sour or bitter; instead it tasted very intense and "rich." Ikeda christened his newly discovered flavor "umami," which basically means **"MEATY AND SAVORY, TASTY."**

Ikeda, who had studied in Germany, later uncovered the **REASON** for the full taste: it was glutamate, a **NATURAL AMINO ACID** that can be found in the human body. Clever cooks know that **GLUTAMATE** is a **NATURAL COMPONENT** in many foods and that it gives dishes a real flavor boost – without the allergies and intolerance often caused by high-voltage, artificially produced glutamate powder. The desire for umami seems to be hereditary. **MOTHER'S MILK** contains a lot of glutamate which is perhaps why we tend to prefer food with a high percentage of vegetable-based protein or carbohydrate.

GOOD TO KNOW: the natural flavor turbocharger is found not only in kombu seaweed, but also in fresh and dried tomatoes, Parmesan cheese, mushrooms, soy sauce, beans, corn, potatoes and spinach. So you don't need any artificial powder to add the "WOW"-effect flavor to your green cooking!

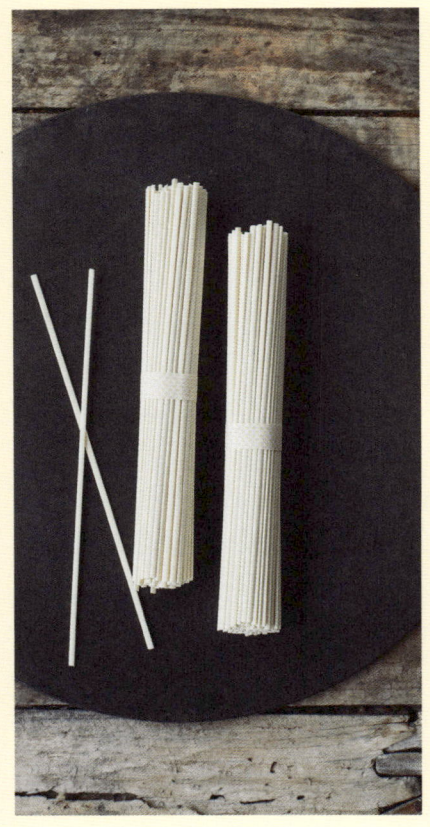

Noodle Soup "Dashi"

Ingredients (serves 4)

- 6 cups vegetable stock
- 1 piece kombu seaweed (approximately 1 1/4 x 2 1/2 inches, see note)
- 3—4 tablespoons light soy sauce
- 1/2 teaspoon Worcestershire sauce
- 1/2 garlic clove
- 1 tablespoon fresh ginger
- 1 tablespoon mirin (sweet Japanese rice wine, or 1 tablespoon sugar)
- 1 cup firm tofu
- 6 fresh shiitake mushrooms
- 2 tablespoons sesame seeds
- 2 tablespoons frying oil
- 2 scallions
- 3/4 cup soybean sprouts
- salt
- 1/2 pound udon noodles (or Asian soup noodles or glass noodles, see note)

1. Bring the stock with the seaweed, soy sauce and Worcestershire sauce to a boil. Peel and dice the garlic, peel and grate the ginger. Add the garlic, ginger and mirin to the soup and bring to a boil. Set aside.
2. Cut the tofu into bite-sized pieces. Cut the shiitake mushrooms into strips. Toast the sesame seeds in a dry frying pan then remove them and set aside. Heat the oil in the pan and fry the tofu and the shiitake mushrooms until golden brown.
3. Wash the scallions, cut them into thin strips and, together with the sprouts, mix with the tofu. Fry for another minute and season with salt.
4. Cook the noodles according to the instructions on the packet. Remove the kombu seaweed from the stock and bring to a boil. Add the tofu mixture to the soup and bring everything to a boil again. Drain and rinse the noodles and add to the soup. Serve with a sprinkling of sesame seeds.

Preparation time: 25 minutes

KOMBU SEAWEED is a very aromatic type of seaweed. You can find it in Asian grocery stores. Kombu has a very high iodine content so it should not be consumed in large quantities. In fact, people with thyroid problems should avoid it.

DASHI, a traditional and basic Japanese stock, is prepared with kombu seaweed, bonito flakes (dried tuna flakes) and water. For our green cuisine, we used Worcestershire sauce in place of the tuna flakes.

UDON NOODLES are Japanese wheat noodles. They are either cut by hand or by a machine and are normally used in Japanese soup dishes. You can find udon noodles in well-stocked supermarkets or in Asian grocery stores.

TIP: Even without extra ingredients, the soup is a great stock for Asian dishes of all kinds. You can cook it ahead and freeze portions to be used at a later date.

Lamb's Lettuce Salad with Fried Eggplants and Sweet Chestnut Purée

Ingredients (serves 4)

1 tiger eggplant (or 1 purple eggplant)
salt
1 small garlic clove
12 tablespoons olive oil
1 tablespoon butter
2 cups peeled and cooked chestnuts
4 tablespoons orange juice
pepper
4 3/4 cups lamb's lettuce
2 shallots
10 walnut kernels
3 tablespoons white wine vinegar

1. Wash the eggplant and cut it lengthwise into 1/4-inch slices. Put it on a plate, sprinkle with a lot of salt and let it sit for 15 minutes.
2. Peel and dice the garlic. In a frying pan, heat 1 tablespoon of olive oil and the butter. Sauté the chestnuts for 3—4 minutes. Remove 2/3 of the chestnuts and purée them in a blender with the orange juice, garlic and 3 tablespoons of water. Add salt and pepper to taste. Keep the rest of the chestnuts for decoration.
3. Dry the slices of eggplant with paper towels and divide them into 3 portions. Fry each portion on both sides with 2 tablespoons of olive oil per portion until golden brown. Drain them on paper towels.
4. Wash the lettuce and spin it dry. Peel and dice the shallots. Chop the walnuts into big chunks. Mix the remaining olive oil with white wine vinegar and 2 tablespoons of water. Add the walnuts and shallots to the lettuce and season with salt and pepper.
5. Arrange the chestnut purée, slices of eggplant and lettuce nicely on the plates. Drizzle the dressing over everything and serve immediately.

Preparation time: 40 minutes

  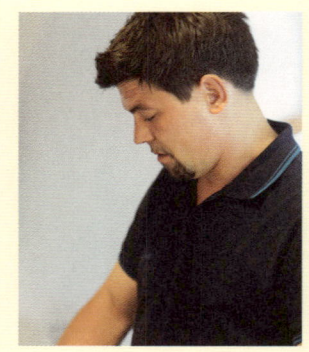

Saffron Potato Risotto with Cauliflower and Pine Nuts

Ingredients (serves 4)

1 pound red potatoes
1 small onion
1 garlic clove
1 pound cauliflower
2 tablespoons olive oil
1/2 cup white wine
1 2/3 cup vegetable stock
12 saffron threads
2/3 cup pine nuts
2 stems parsley
3 ounces Parmesan
3 tablespoons butter
salt and pepper

1. Peel and cut the potatoes into small dice, and peel and dice the onion and garlic. Divide the cauliflower into rosettes and chop them into small pieces. Heat the oil in a large nonstick frying pan and sauté the onion and garlic. Add the potato cubes and cook for 2 minutes on medium heat.

2. Deglaze with white wine. Pour in 1 cup of stock and boil for 10—12 minutes until the potatoes are al dente.

3. Add the cauliflower, saffron and pine nuts. Pour in the remainder of the stock and simmer for 5—6 minutes or until the liquid boils down to half the original amount.

4. Chop the parsley and add it to the pot. Grate the Parmesan. Add 4 tablespoons of the cheese together with the cubes of butter and let it melt, stirring constantly. Sprinkle with the remaining Parmesan. Season with salt and pepper and serve.

Preparation time: 35 minutes

Saffron can be bought either in threads or ground. It adds flavor to Spanish paella and to the famous Risotto Milanese. The stigmas of the saffron crocus are picked by hand. It takes approximately 150,000 blossoms to make 2 1/4 pounds of saffron.

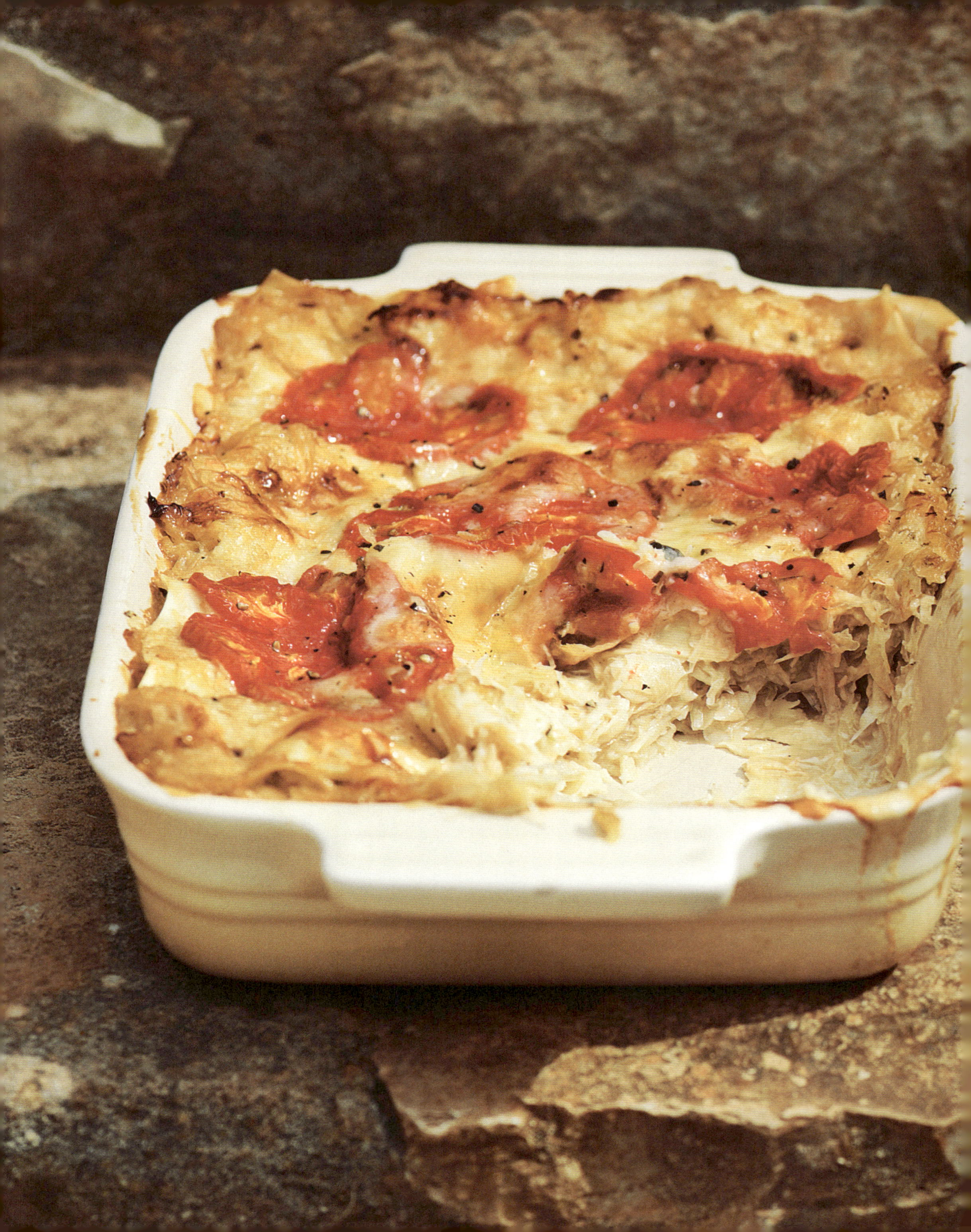

Creamy Sauerkraut Lasagne with Gruyère

Ingredients (serves 4—6)

1/4 pound shallots
1 can sauerkraut (1 1/5 pound net weight)
2 tablespoons butter
1/2 teaspoon caraway seeds
1 bay leaf
2 tablespoons honey
salt and pepper
1 cup white port wine (or white wine with 1 tablespoon sugar)
2/3 cup quince juice (or apple juice)
1 cup heavy cream
1 cup cold vegetable stock
1 tablespoon flour
4 stems fresh marjoram (or 1/2 teaspoon dried marjoram)
sugar
1 beefsteak tomato
5 ounces Gruyère cheese
9 lasagne sheets (dried not precooked)

1. Cut the shallots into thin rings. Squeeze out the sauerkraut, saving the juice, and then chop into large pieces. Melt the butter in a pot and sauté the sauerkraut and the shallots over medium heat for 5 minutes.

2. Add the caraway seeds, bay leaf and honey, season with salt and fry for another 2 minutes. Add the port and boil until all the liquid evaporates. Add the quince juice and simmer until all the liquid evaporates.

3. Mix the cream, cold stock and flour with a hand blender until smooth. Add it to the sauerkraut and boil for 2 minutes. Destem the marjoram and mix it in. Add salt, pepper and sugar to taste.

4. Wash and core the tomatoes and cut into thin slices. Finely grate the cheese. Spread the sauerkraut and cheese on top of a sheet of lasagne. Repeat layers two more times. Cover the final layer of sauerkraut with the tomato slices. Pre-heat the oven to 400° F (convection is not recommended). Bake on the second rack from the bottom for 30 minutes. Let it stand for 10 minutes before serving.

Preparation time: 1 hour and 20 minutes

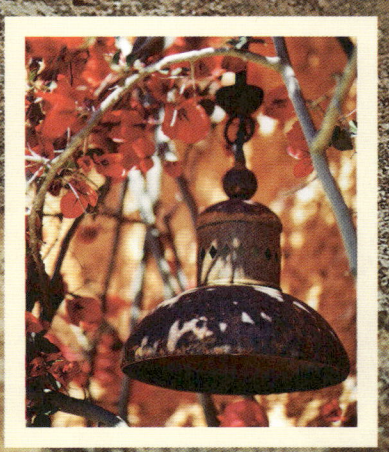

GREENBEANS

WAXBEANS

dried BEANS →

RUNNER BEANS

KIDNEY BEANS

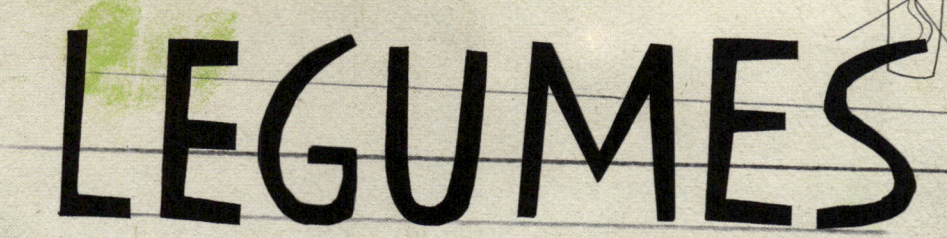

LEGUMES
A GREAT SOURCE OF FLAVOR AND ENERGY

PEA PLANT

Beans, lentils, chickpeas and peas belong to the family of legumes and pulses. Biologically speaking, so do peanuts, which also grow in pods. Something interesting for know-it-alls: if a botanist hears the terms "green bean" or "sugar snap pea," he'll frown, because the correct term is bean pod or pea pod. Pulses are a fantastic source of energy. They contain protein, minerals, carbohydrate, fiber and vitamins. They have also a wide variety of flavors.

Other members of the pulse family are green runner beans and French beans which can be eaten in their pods. Wax beans are particularly mild in flavor. Green beans are somewhat more savory and taste best cooked with fresh or dried summer savory. Green peas are tastiest when eaten fresh, but frozen peas can also be delicious. Mild-flavored white beans taste great either dried or canned and they come in various sizes. Red and black beans have more flavor and are a little bit more mealy.

Before cooking most dried beans, you need to soak them in a lot of water for several hours, at best overnight. If you are making vegetable stews, use the water you soaked the beans in for cooking – it's full of nutrients. The protein froth that appears when the beans are boiled can be skimmed off.

Dried lentils, peas and chickpeas don't have to be soaked before cooking. Black beluga lentils and red and yellow lentils cook particularly quickly. As a basic principle, always cook dried pulses without adding salt, seasoning or vinegar. Otherwise, you extend the cooking time considerably.

Pulses should only be seasoned after cooking! Roundly shaped, nutty tasting pulses love strong seasoning such as savory, thyme, oregano and garlic. To improve the taste of beans and lentils and to make them easier to digest, you can add caraway, cumin, fennel seeds or aniseed. A little vinegar, lemon and grated lemon peel round off the taste of most lentil and bean dishes.

Baked Beans *forget the canned stuff*

Ingredients (serves 6)

2 cans white beans
(16 ounces net weight)
1 can tomatoes (16 ounces net weight)
5 tablespoons Worcestershire sauce
1 tablespoon Dijon mustard
5 tablespoons maple syrup
1 clove
2 tablespoons brown sugar
1 onion
1 garlic clove
salt
cayenne pepper

1. Drain the beans and rinse in cold water. Place them in an ovenproof dish with a tight-fitting lid and mix with 4 1/4 cups of water, the peeled tomatoes, Worcestershire sauce, Dijon mustard, maple syrup, the clove and brown sugar. Peel and dice the onion and garlic and mix in.
2. Cover and cook the beans at 350°F on the second rack from the bottom for 90 minutes. Simmer for another 45 minutes, uncovered. Season with salt and cayenne pepper and serve.

Preparation time: 2 hours and 30 minutes

TIP Basically, the beans cook on their own. You can prepare them a day in advance of a big breakfast. They taste best reheated!

VARIATIONS: Baked beans taste best of all with fried eggs on buttered pumpernickel toast. But they also go very well with:
- Sheep's cheese (feta)
- Tortilla chips with spicy jalapeños
- Grilled vegetables
- Or as a filling for warm tortillas with tomato, cucumber and red onions

» Used to eat them right out of the can. Soulfood at its best! It's not much work to cook them yourself. Only takes a little time, but tastes so much better. Yum! Just thinking about it makes my mouth water! «

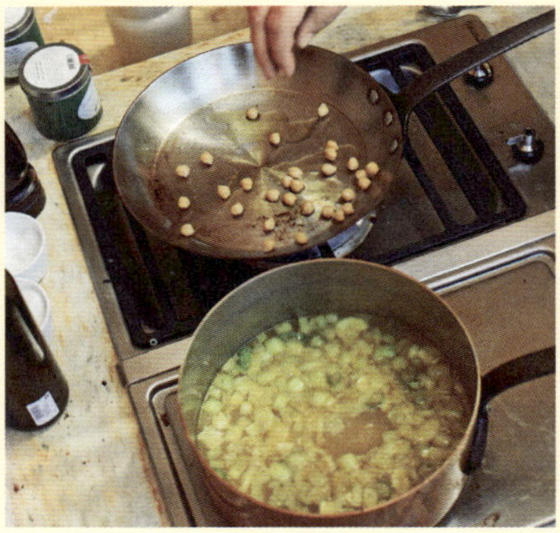
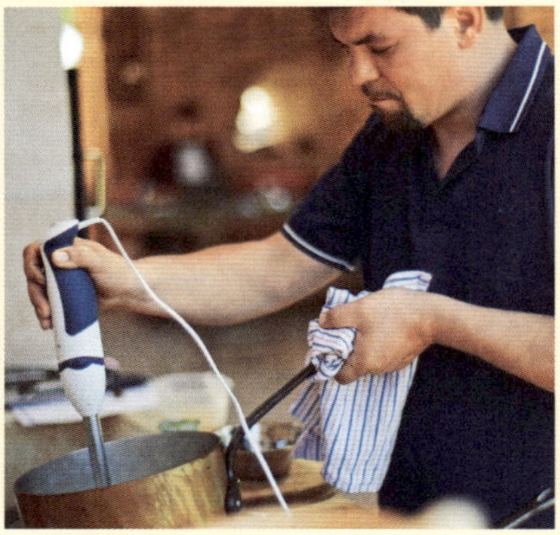
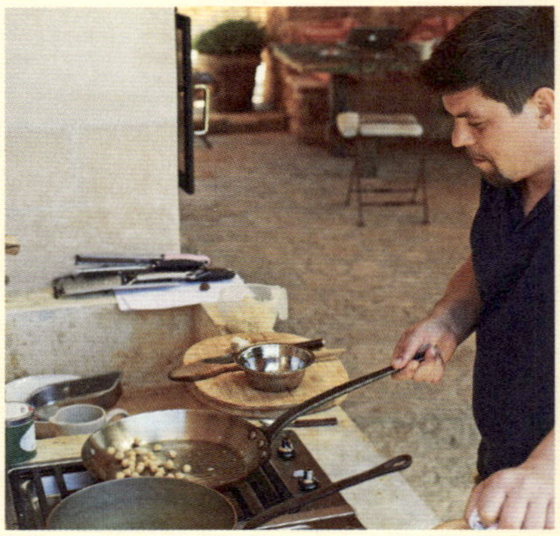
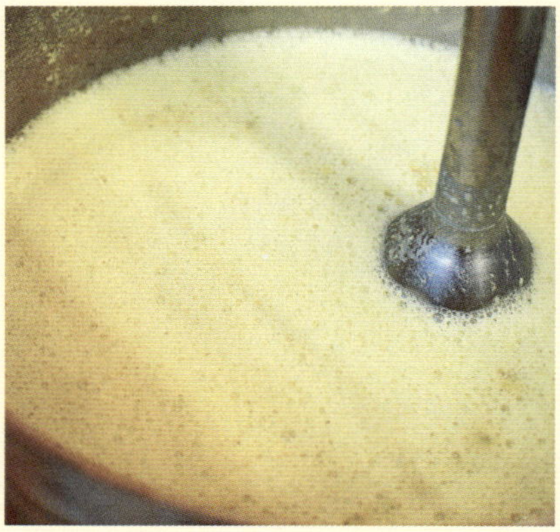
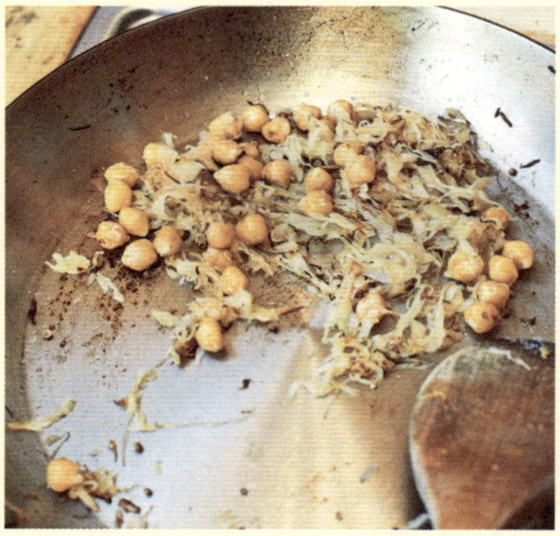
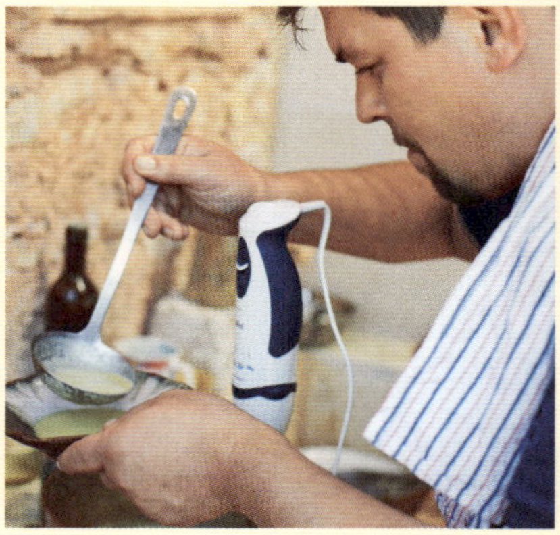
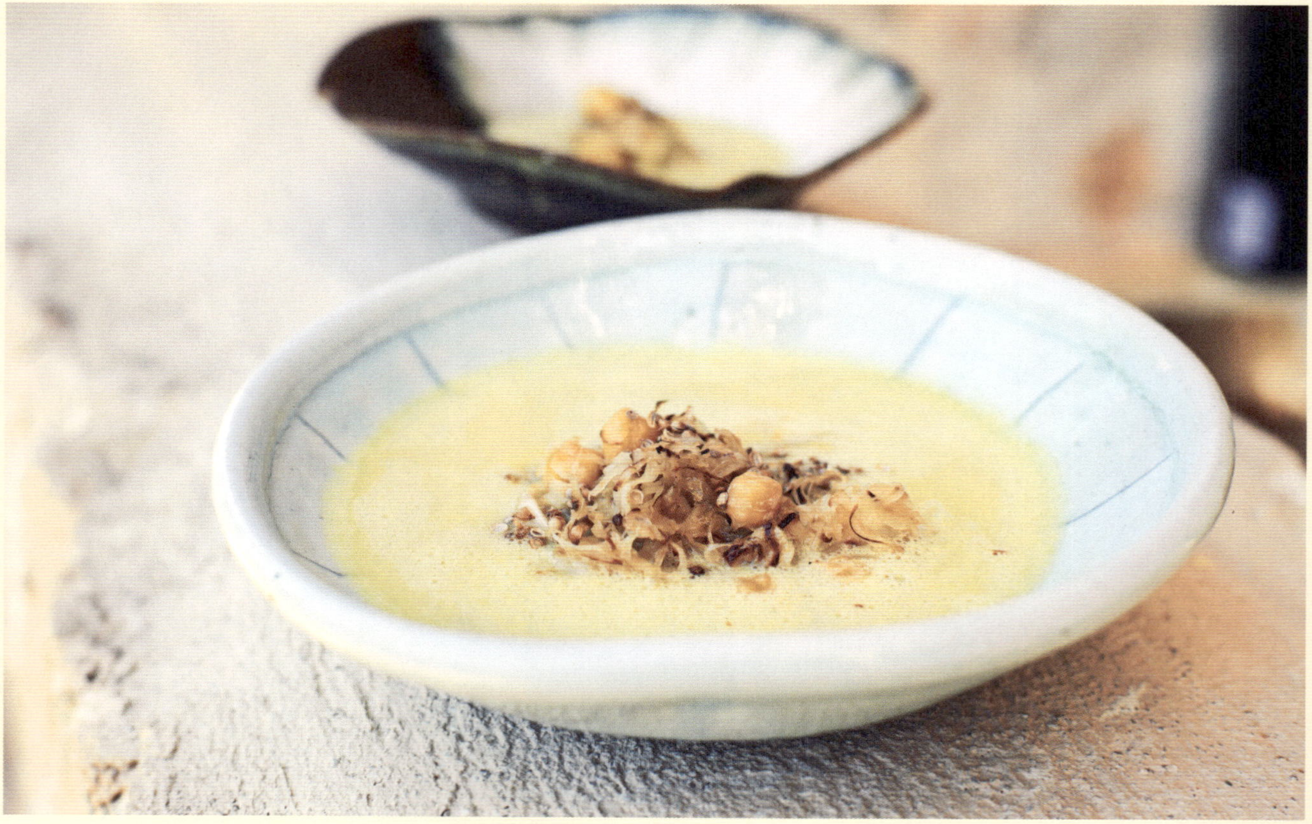

Chickpea Soup with Fried Sauerkraut

Ingredients (serves 4)

1 leek (only the white part is needed)
1 garlic clove
1 green chili pepper
5 tablespoons olive oil
1 can chickpeas (16 ounces net weight)
1 teaspoon mild curry powder
4 1/4 cups vegetable stock
1 can sauerkraut (10 ounces net weight)
1 teaspoon coarsely ground coriander seeds
sugar
salt
1/2 cup whole-milk yogurt

1. Cut the leek in half, rinse and slice. Peel the garlic, cut into slices and dice the green chili. Heat 3 tablespoons of olive oil in a pot. Drain and rinse the chickpeas. Put 2 tablespoons of chickpeas aside. In a pot, mix the rest of the chickpeas with the leek, garlic, green pepper and curry powder and cook for 1 minute. Pour in the stock. Simmer for 10 minutes, uncovered.

2. Squeeze out the sauerkraut until it's dry, and brown it together with the rest of the chickpeas and the coriander seeds in 2 tablespoons of olive oil. Season with a pinch of sugar and salt. Finely purée the soup with a hand blender, season with salt. Serve with the sauerkraut mixture and yogurt.

Preparation time: 30 minutes

VARIATIONS: Fresh rustic bread or baguette goes really well with this soup. If you prefer, you can use curry paste instead of curry powder as a seasoning. Instead of the yogurt, you can use sour cream, crème fraîche or a dollop of cottage cheese in your soup.

Pan-Fried Flatbread with Lentils, Coconut and Chickpeas (serves 4)

1 Flatbread

Mix **4 stems** of chopped **cilantro** with **2 1/2 cups of flour**, **2 teaspoons of salt** and **2/3 cup of lukewarm water**. Knead to a smooth dough. Wrap in cling wrap and chill in the refrigerator for 20 minutes. Cut the dough into 12 equal-sized slices and roll out on a floured surface. Heat an ungreased, nonstick pan until very hot and fry the flatbread for 2—3 minutes on each side.

Preparation time: 45 minutes

2 Lentil Date Salad

Boil **1/2 cup of brown lentils** for 15 minutes in salted water with **1 small piece of a cinnamon stick**. Drain, remove the cinnamon stick and marinate while warm in **3 teaspoons of sherry vinegar** and **4 tablespoons of oil**. Chop **1/3 cup of pitted dates**, peel and chop **2 shallots**, rinse and finely chop a **stalk of celery**, including the leaves. Mix it all into the lentil salad. Season with **salt** and freshly ground **black pepper**.

Preparation time: 30 minutes

TIP Flatbread is a lovely side dish for other dips and salads. It tastes great with quark (or strained Greek yogurt) mixed with herbs or cottage cheese or with any kind of soup.

one

3 Coconut Relish

Finely grate **1 cup freshly peeled coconut flesh** in your food processor or with a grater. Peel and dice **2 red onions (medium size)**. Mix with the coconut. Toast **1 tablespoon of black mustard seeds** and **1 tablespoon of cumin seeds** in an ungreased pan until the seeds start to jump. Add the roasted seeds plus the **juice of 1/2 lime and 5 tablespoons of sunflower oil** to the coconut relish. Peel and finely chop **3/4 inch of fresh ginger** and stir in. Dice **1/2—1 green chili**, coarsely chop **4 stems of cilantro** and mix them both into the relish. Season with **salt** and **sugar**.

Preparation time: 20 minutes

4 Chickpea Mousse

Drain **1 can of chickpeas (1 pound net weight)** and rinse in cold water. Purée until smooth with **4 tablespoons of yogurt, 1 peeled clove of garlic, 1 pinch of cinnamon** and the **juice of 1 lemon**. Season with **salt** and **cayenne pepper**. Sprinkle **1 tablespoon of freshly chopped parsley** over it and serve.

Preparation time: 10 minutes

4x CUCUMBER
FRESH, CRUNCHY

1 Cold Cucumber Soup

Cut **1/8 of a cucumber** into fine slices. Marinate **3/4 cup of raspberries** and the cucumber slices in **2 tablespoons of apple cider vinegar** and **2 teaspoons of sugar**. Mix in the leaves from **1 stem of dill** and a little **salt**. Peel the rest of the cucumber, chop and puree with **2/3 cup of whole yogurt** (or **silken tofu**), **1 teaspoon of canola oil, 1 dash of apple cider vinegar** and **1 stem of dill leaves**. Season with **salt** and **pepper**. Serve the cucumber soup with the raspberries and cucumber slices.

2 Tzatziki

Mix **1 3/4 cup quark** (or strained Greek yogurt), **1–2 tablespoons of lemon juice, 1/2 teaspoon dried mint** (or dried oregano) and **1 peeled and pressed garlic clove** until creamy. Season with **salt** and **pepper**. Cut **1 peeled cucumber** lengthwise, scrape out the seeds with a teaspoon, chop the cucumber and place in boiling water for 1 minute. Drain, rinse in cold water and season with **salt** and **a pinch of sugar**. Wash **1 scallion,** cut diagonally into long, thin slices and arrange on the quark with the chopped cucumber.

Cucumbers are one of the vegetables that are best to buy organic. Organic cucumbers taste much more intense and are crunchier than non-organic ones. You can actually smell the difference as soon as you slice into the cucumber. Cucumber salad and tzatziki made with organic cucumbers won't get so watery and will have much more taste overall. Cucumbers are in season in late summer.

3 Quick Stewed Cucumbers

Soften **3 1/2 tablespoons of wakame seaweed** in lukewarm water. Peel **1 cucumber,** cut it in half lengthwise and scrape out the seeds with a teaspoon. Cut the cucumber into 1/2-inch slices. Melt **1 1/2 tablespoons of butter** in a pot, add the cucumber, sprinkle **1/2 teaspoon of sugar** on it and cook for 2 minutes. Season with **salt** and **pepper.** Squeeze the wakame seaweed dry, roughly chop and add to the cucumber. Pour in 1/2 cup of water and simmer for 2 minutes. (Alternative: mix in 1 cup of baby spinach instead of the wakame seaweed.) Cut **1 1/2 tablespoons of butter** into cubes and mix them in. Bring to a boil and season with salt. Chop **1/3 cup of roasted, salted peanuts** and sprinkle them over the stewed cucumber.

4 Cucumber Salad

Peel **2 cucumbers,** cut them in half lengthwise, scrape out the seeds with a teaspoon. Cut the cucumbers into slices 1/4—1/2 inch thick and season with **salt** and a **pinch of sugar.** Let sit for 15 minutes. Peel **2 shallots** and cut into thin slices. Wash **1 bunch of watercress,** spin it dry and pull off the leaves. Mix **2—3 tablespoons of apple cider vinegar** (or white wine vinegar) and **6 tablespoons of olive oil.** Salt to taste. Drain the liquid off the cucumbers and stir them into the rest of the ingredients and the vinaigrette. If you wish, grate **some peeled horseradish** over the salad.

"I like things to be quick and easy, but I am also a guy who likes to show off and let everyone know what great technical skills I have. This is actually a simple Greek salad. By vacuuming the aroma in the cucumber beforehand, and also by the way we arrange it on the plate, it turns into a truly impressive dish."

Greek Salad with Cucumbers "Sous-vide"

Ingredients (serves 2—4)

1 cucumber
2 teaspoons white wine vinegar
3 teaspoons sugar
2 stems dill
12 small date or cherry tomatoes
2 tablespoons olive oil
1/2 pound feta cheese
1/2 small red onion, peeled
12 black olives

1. Peel the cucumber the day before and cut into thirds. Put the pieces into a freezer bag together with white wine vinegar, sugar and dill and press all the air out of the bag and close it tightly. Let sit in the refrigerator for 24 hours.
2. Remove the core of the tomatoes and dunk into boiling water until the skins burst open. Rinse in cold water. Pull the skins off, cut in half, take the seeds out and put aside. Mix the tomatoes with the olive oil.
3. Take the cucumber out of the freezer bag and cut it and the feta cheese into equal-sized pieces. Layer the ingredients on the plate and place freshly cut, wafer-thin strips of onion on top. Decorate with olives and the tomato seeds.

Preparation time: 20 minutes (+ 24 hours marinating)

SOUS-VIDE is a kitchen technique that means food is cooked in a vacuum. The cucumber for this recipe doesn't actually get cooked, it gets pickled with a little vinegar, sugar and dill in the refrigerator. The result after 24 hours is pretty spectacular: the cucumber has turned bright green and its own particular "cucumbery" taste has multiplied thanks to the mild seasoning.

Beet Tabouleh

Ingredients (serves 4—6)

- 1 pound young beets
- salt
- 1 cucumber
- 2 lemons
- 1 1/2 cups bulgur
- 3 scallions
- 1 bunch cilantro
- 1 chili pepper
- 4 tablespoons olive oil
- pepper
- sugar

1. Peel the beets and cut into thin slices (1/4 inch). Cook in 2 cups of salted water with the lid on.
2. Peel the cucumber, cut in half lengthwise and remove the seeds with a spoon. Cut into 1/4-inch slices, add to the beets and cook for another 5 minutes.
3. Remove the vegetables from the liquid and place them in a second bowl and mix with the juice of 1 lemon. Pour bulgur into a bowl. Bring the liquid from the vegetables to a boil again, add the juice of the other lemon, and stir into the bulgur. Leave it to absorb the liquid for 20 minutes.
4. Wash the scallions and cut into fine slices. Roughly chop the cilantro, including the stems. Dice the chili pepper. Mix together the vegetables, bulgur, cilantro, chili pepper and scallions. Season with olive oil, salt, pepper and 1 pinch of sugar and serve.

Preparation time: 60 minutes

TIP

COOKING CUCUMBERS – yes, you can do it! Preferably use a large cucumber with firm and not too watery flesh.

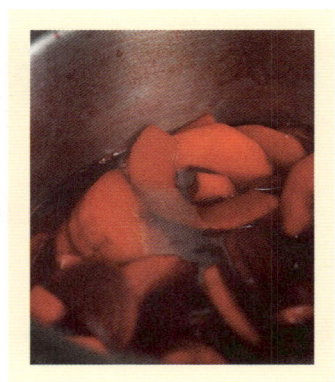

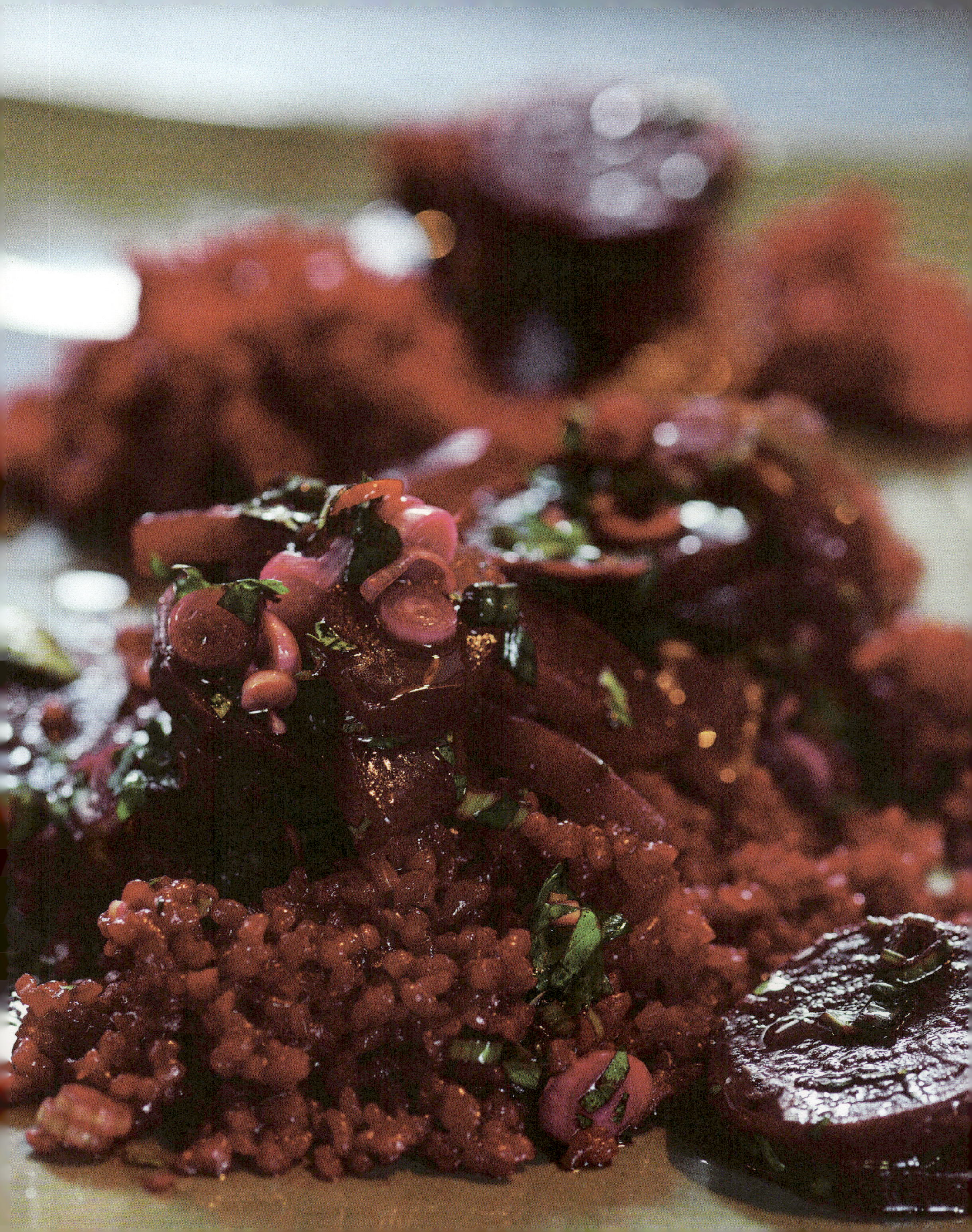

THIS IS HOW YOU DO IT:

DAIRY PRODUCTS

The following cooking adage is true for green cuisine too: with a decent slab of butter and a dash of cream, whole milk or buttermilk, dishes often taste better. Here's an overview of all the creamy, dairy-based flavor enhancers:

There's Milk in all of them!

MILK generally comes from cows. Its fat content is variable. For cooking purposes, fresh milk with a high fat content tastes best. For fluffing up the milky top of a cafe latte or cappuccino, long life milk is best. Try to buy milk from local dairies – that way you support the agriculture industry in your region.

FARMER CHEESE is edible straight after being made. It is 70% water. Ricotta cheese, quark, mascarpone and cottage cheese belong to this group.

YOGURT is milk that has been fermented and thickened by milk acid bacteria. That doesn't sound too appetizing at first, but it tastes very fresh and adds a lovely tartness and creaminess to quark, sauces, dressings and shakes. The various fat levels will affect the overall taste.

"CRÈME DOUBLE", OR DOUBLE CREAM, is the yummy stuff with 44—55% fat content. It makes for extra creamy soups, sauces and purees. The cream doesn't make them heavy, but a bit tart and fresh instead. If you can't find double cream, substitute heavy cream.

CRÈME FRAÎCHE is cream that has been treated with lactic acid bacteria. It's a little thicker than regular cream, has a fat content of at least 30% and delights your palate with its subtle sour, fresh flavor and its ultra creaminess. Can be used hot and cold.

PARMESAN is a hard cheese from Emilia Romagna and derives its name from the city and province Parma (the Italian word "parmigiano" means "from Parma"). It has a fat content of 32—35% and has a particularly strong taste, even as a young cheese.

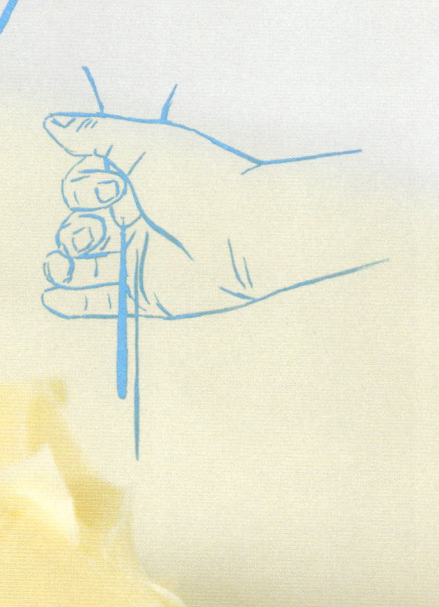

MOZZARELLA is a fresh cheese made from buffalo's or cow's milk. It matures for 1—3 days before being covered with boiling water. It is then quickly kneaded into shape. The cheese is cooled in a basin of cold water until it solidifies and then placed in whey or brine. Like many cheeses, it tastes best when it's fresh. The most famous mozzarella is the real Mozzarella di Bufala Campana DOP from the Campania region near Naples.

SOUR CREAM is related to crème fraîche. Sour cream tastes nice and tangy and has a fat content of between 10% and 18%. Heavy sour cream can contain up to 30% fat. Can be used hot and cold.

BUTTER, the scent of excellent cooking, is made from cream. It's usually obtained from cow's milk, but sometimes it's made from sheep's or goat's milk, which has a stronger flavor. The process of churning drains watery liquid (buttermilk) from the butter and what remains is the creamy deliciousness that makes us so happy. Put it on bread with some salt on top, melt it in sauces or use it to top off dishes in the frying pan just before serving.

BURRATA is a cow's milk mozzarella in the shape of a small sack. It is filled with both mozzarella and cream. The name "burrata" comes from the Italian word meaning "buttered" and refers to the time when bits of butter were kept fresh in a cheese loaf.

SHEEP'S AND GOAT'S MILK CHEESES often have a stronger taste than cow's milk cheeses. This is true for farmer cheese and especially for the more savory soft and hard cheeses. Milk and cheese from sheep and goats cannot be produced on industrial livestock farms. These animals are too smart for factory farming.

HARZ CHEESE OR HAND CHEESE is a sour milk cheese made from skimmed cow's milk and is shaped by hand. The smell can be overpowering, especially with older varieties. It is extremely tasty, despite being low in calories and fat. Apart from serving it on buttered bread, the most common way of serving it is with oil and vinegar. This is traditionally called "Hand Cheese with Music." If you can lay your hand on this delicacy, you should definitively give it a try. Alternatively, you can use Limburger cheese.

SCAMORZA is a dried mozzarella that matures in the fresh air. It's a little harder than mozzarella and has a pear shape. It is available slightly salted or smoked over beech wood, which gives it a very intense flavor.

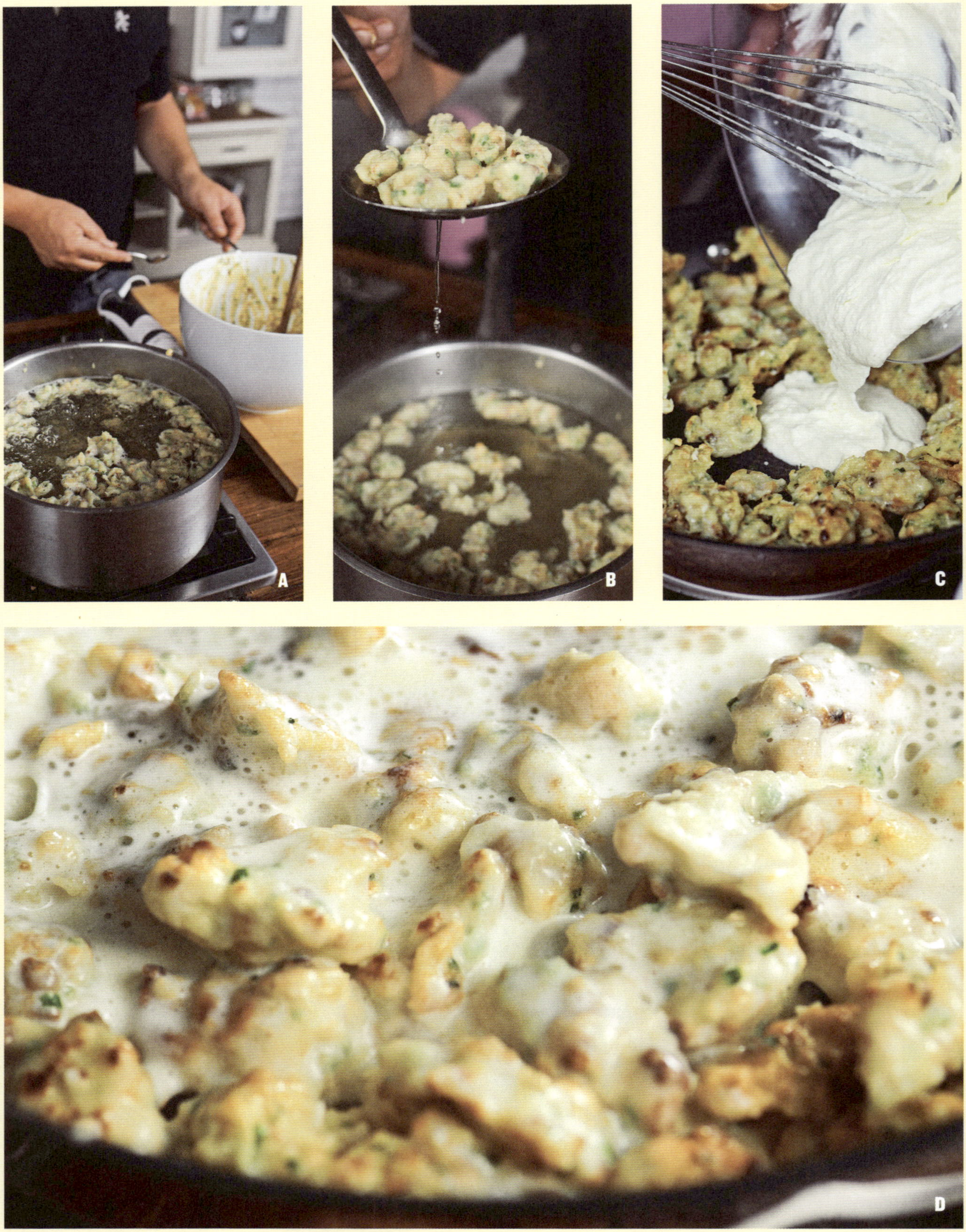
A
B
C
D

"Knoepfle" with Dried Tomatoes in Garlic Sauce

Ingredients (serves 4—6)

4 slices white bread, crust removed
6 tablespoons butter
6 large eggs
salt
3 1/2 cups flour
2/3 cup carbonated water
nutmeg
8 sundried tomatoes
1 bunch chives
2 garlic cloves
2/3 cup heavy cream
freshly ground black pepper
lemon juice

1. Dice the bread and toast it in a frying pan with 1 1/2 tablespoons of butter until golden brown. Whisk the eggs in a big bowl. Add salt, flour and water and mix until smooth for at least 5 minutes or until the mixture forms tiny bubbles. Season with a little freshly ground nutmeg.

2. Finely chop the dried tomatoes. Mince the chives and stir them with the diced bread into the batter. Boil a large pot of salted water. Using a teaspoon, break off little lumps from the batter and push them with your thumb straight into the boiling water. Cook the lumps for 5 minutes in simmering water.

3. Peel and mince the garlic. Beat the cream until stiff. Lightly brown the remaining butter in a pan. Take the knoepfle out of the boiling water with a skimmer, drain them and put them into the butter while it's still hot. Fry them for 2—3 minutes, then add the garlic and fry for another 2—3 minutes. Add the cream, salt, pepper and a dash of lemon juice and serve immediately.

Preparation time: 35 minutes

VARIATIONS: "Knoepfle" also taste great with a sauce made with 2 tablespoons of mascarpone mixed together with 2 tablespoons of water and 4 tablespoons of gorgonzola and then brought to a boil.
The "knoepfle" can also be covered with Gruyère, raclette cheese or Parmesan and baked in the oven. Endive goes really well with it!
Without the bread cubes, tomatoes or chives, the batter is the basic recipe for classic "spaezle" or "knoepfle." Using a spaezle press, potato ricer or potato press, simply press, grate or rub the batter into a big pot of boiling salted water and leave it to cook for 5 minutes. The traditional method for "spaezle specialists" is to scrape the dough straight off of a wooden board.

Ooooh: delicious! very delicious.

Avocado with Grapefruit Caramel and Farmer Cheese

Ingredients (serves 4)

4 1/3 cups yogurt
1/2 pound farmer cheese
salt
1/2 bunch parsley
1/2 bunch dill
1/2 bunch chives
1 tablespoon breadcrumbs
2 tablespoons sugar
4 tablespoons white port wine (or apple juice)
1 1/2 pink grapefruits
2 tablespoons olive oil
2 ripe avocados
2 tablespoons lemon juice
some leaves of arugula

1. Spoon the yogurt and farmer cheese onto a tea towel and place in a colander. Place a plate weighted down with a stone or a can for at least 6 hours to drain. Whisk until smooth and season with salt. Mince the parsley, dill and chives and mix them with the breadcrumbs. Moisten your hands with water and form 12 balls out of the farmer cheese. Roll the balls in the herb breadcrumbs and put them in the fridge.

2. Boil the sugar with 2 tablespoons of water until it caramelizes to a light blonde color. Deglaze with the port and remove from the heat. Add the juice of half of a grapefruit, leave to cool for a bit and then stir in the olive oil. Peel the rest of the grapefruit, removing all the white skin. Cut the grapefruit crosswise into slices and place in the port mixture.

3. Cut the avocados in half, remove the pits and lift out the flesh with a large spoon. Marinate the avocado halves with the lemon juice and a little salt. Arrange on a plate with fresh cheese balls, grapefruit slices, caramel liquid and arugula.

Preparation time: 25 minutes (+ 6 hours of draining)

VARIATIONS: You can use white grapefruits or blood oranges instead of pink grapefruits for this dish.
The herbs for the fresh cheese balls can be varied, too, for example with chervil, basil or sorrel.

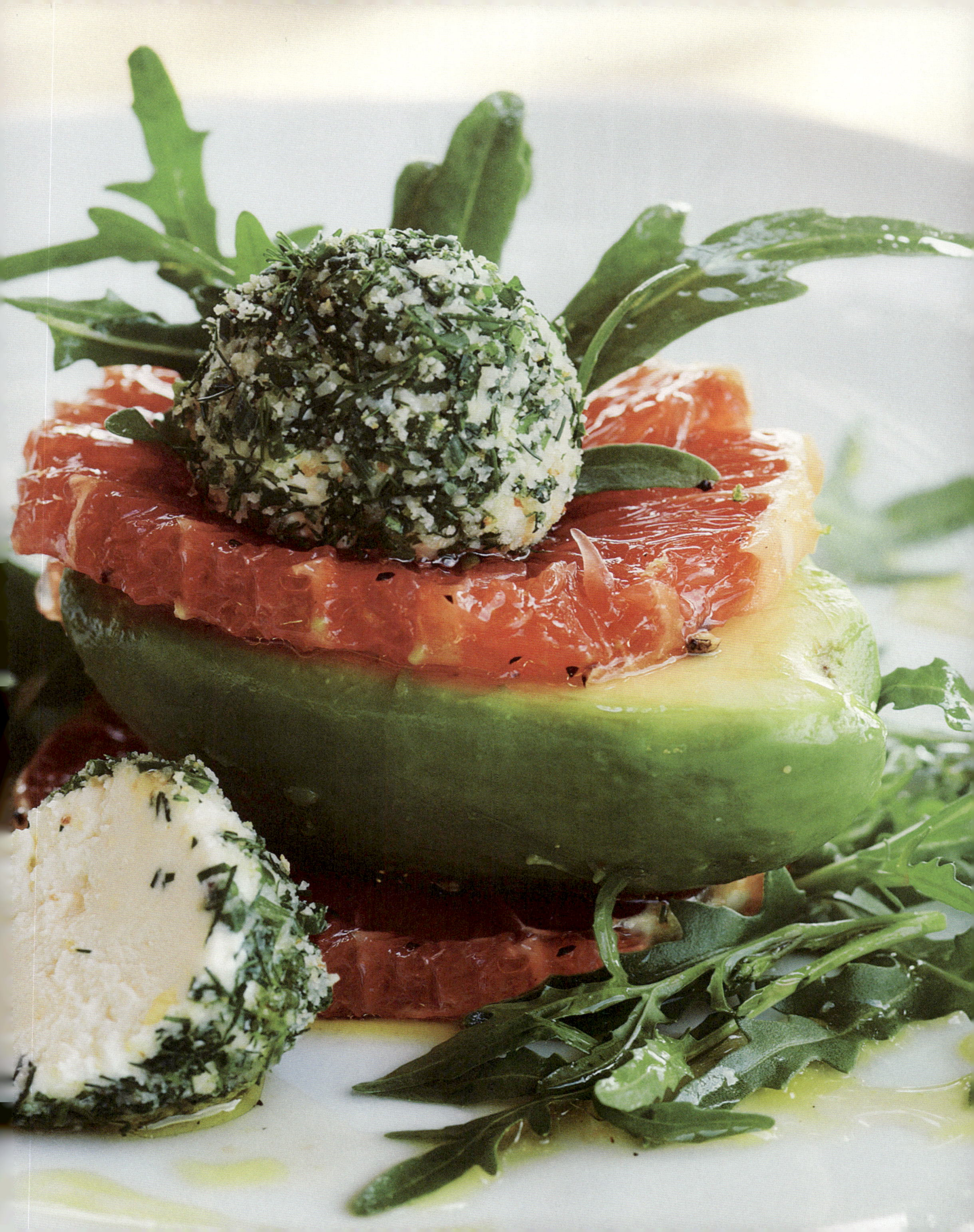

3 X SIMPLY AVOCADO

The most popular types of avocado on the market are called Fuerte, Nabal, Hass, Ettinger and Bacon. The light green flesh tastes best fresh and eaten raw. Its buttery, creamy taste develops best when eaten with fruity acid and a little salt.

1 Guacamole Panamericana

Roughly chop **1 bunch of cilantro** including the stems. Reserve a few of the leaves. Wash **1 scallion** and cut it diagonally into slices. Peel and dice **1 red onion**. Dice **1—2 chili peppers**. Dice **1 tomato**. Roast **1 teaspoon of cumin seeds** in a pan without oil and crush **1 pinch of sea salt** in a mortar. Cut **2 ripe avocados** in half and remove the pits. Lift the flesh out of the peel, squash it with a fork and mix with the **onions, chili peppers, tomato, cumin** and **cilantro**. Add **salt** and **2—3 tablespoons of lime juice** to taste. Serve decorated with cilantro leaves and scallions.

TIP: hard avocados can be ripened at home at room temperature in a few days.

2 Avocado Spread

Peel and dice 2 onions. Heat **4 tablespoons of oil** in a pan and fry the onions on medium heat for 10—15 minutes until golden brown. Dry the onions on paper towels. Cut **2 ripe Hass avocados** in half, peel and remove the pits. Roughly chop the avocado and place in a high-sided bowl with **2—3 tablespoons of lemon juice, salt** and **pepper.** Purée with a hand blender until smooth. Stir in the onions and season with salt, pepper and **1 pinch of sugar.** Wash **2 scallions** and cut diagonally into slices. Distribute the avocado spread evenly on **slices of bread** and serve sprinkled with the scallions and **freshly ground pepper.**

3 Avocado with Goat Cheese and Passion Fruit Dressing

Cut **4 passion fruits** in half, scrape out the pulp and whisk together with **3 tablespoons of olive oil.** Season with **salt** and **1/2 chopped green chili pepper.** Peel **1 firm Hass avocado,** cut in half lengthwise and remove the pit. Fill the hole where the pit was with **5 tablespoons of goat cheese** and smooth flat with a knife. Heat **1 tablespoon of oil** in a non-stick frying pan and fry the avocado halves for 30 seconds on their cut side. Serve drizzled with the dressing.

THREE SALSAS

These 3 salsas go well with crisp oven-cooked vegetables or veggies from the grill. They taste fabulous with asparagus. Season the peeled asparagus stalks with salt and pepper and cook for 25 minutes in the oven at 400°F. Then serve them with the three sauces.

Mango Pepper Salsa

Cut **1/2 of a red pepper** and **1/2 of a green pepper** into quarters, take out the seeds and dice. Peel **1 mango**, cut the pulp off the pit and then dice. Peel and dice **1/2 red onion**. Chop **1 small red chili pepper** and mix with **1—2 teaspoons of freshly chopped cilantro**. Mix with the juice of **1 lime** and **2—3 tablespoons of olive oil** and season with **salt** and **1 teaspoon of sugar**. Marinate for 10 minutes.

Müller Marquard Mälzer Salsa

In a food processor, put **1 bunch of parsley, 1 bunch of mint, 3 bunches of cilantro, 2 garlic cloves** and the **finely grated peel of 1 organic lime**. Peel the lime, removing the white part of the skin as well. Chop the pulp and add to the food processor. Purée the ingredients with **2—3 tablespoons of olive oil** and **2—3 tablespoons of water**. Wash **1 scallion**, cut into fine strips and then dice. Chop **1 green chili** pepper and stir it into the salsa along with the scallion. Season with **salt** and **pepper**.

Cucumber Nectarine Salsa

Peel **1 small cucumber**, then cut lengthwise in half, take out the seeds with a teaspoon and finely dice the pulp. Mix with **1 pinch of salt** and place aside. Peel and dice **1/2 of red onion**. Cut up the flesh of **1 nectarine**. Mix all of that with **2 tablespoons of chopped dill, 3 tablespoons of olive oil** and **1 tablespoon white wine vinegar**. Season with **2 teaspoons of sugar**, salt and freshly ground **pepper**. Marinate for 10 minutes.

Baked Potato with Salsa Verde

Ingredients (serves 4—8)

8 medium-sized red or new potatoes
8 tablespoons olive oil
5 cups of sea salt
1 bunch parsley
1/2 bunch basil
1/2 bunch mint
1 tablespoon capers
2 teaspoons mustard
1—2 tablespoons red wine vinegar
4 cornichons
salt and pepper
sugar

1. Wash the potatoes thoroughly and pat them dry. Rub the potatoes with 3 tablespoons olive oil in a bowl. Line a baking sheet with parchment paper, cover with the salt and place the potatoes on top. Sprinkle with more salt. Preheat the oven to 350°F and roast for 75 minutes.

2. Meanwhile, strip the leaves off the parsley, basil and mint. Finely chop the herbs and capers. Whisk together mustard, 5 tablespoons olive oil and red wine vinegar and mix with the herbs. Dice the cornichons and add them to the mix. Season the salsa with salt, pepper and a pinch of sugar.

3. Take the potatoes out of the oven and switch on the broiler. Cut a cross into the potatoes with a knife and, with the help of a dish towel, squeeze the sides until they burst open a little. Put the potatoes back on the sheet and broil for 8—10 minutes, until crisp. Serve with the salsa verde.

Preparation time: 1 hour and 35 minutes

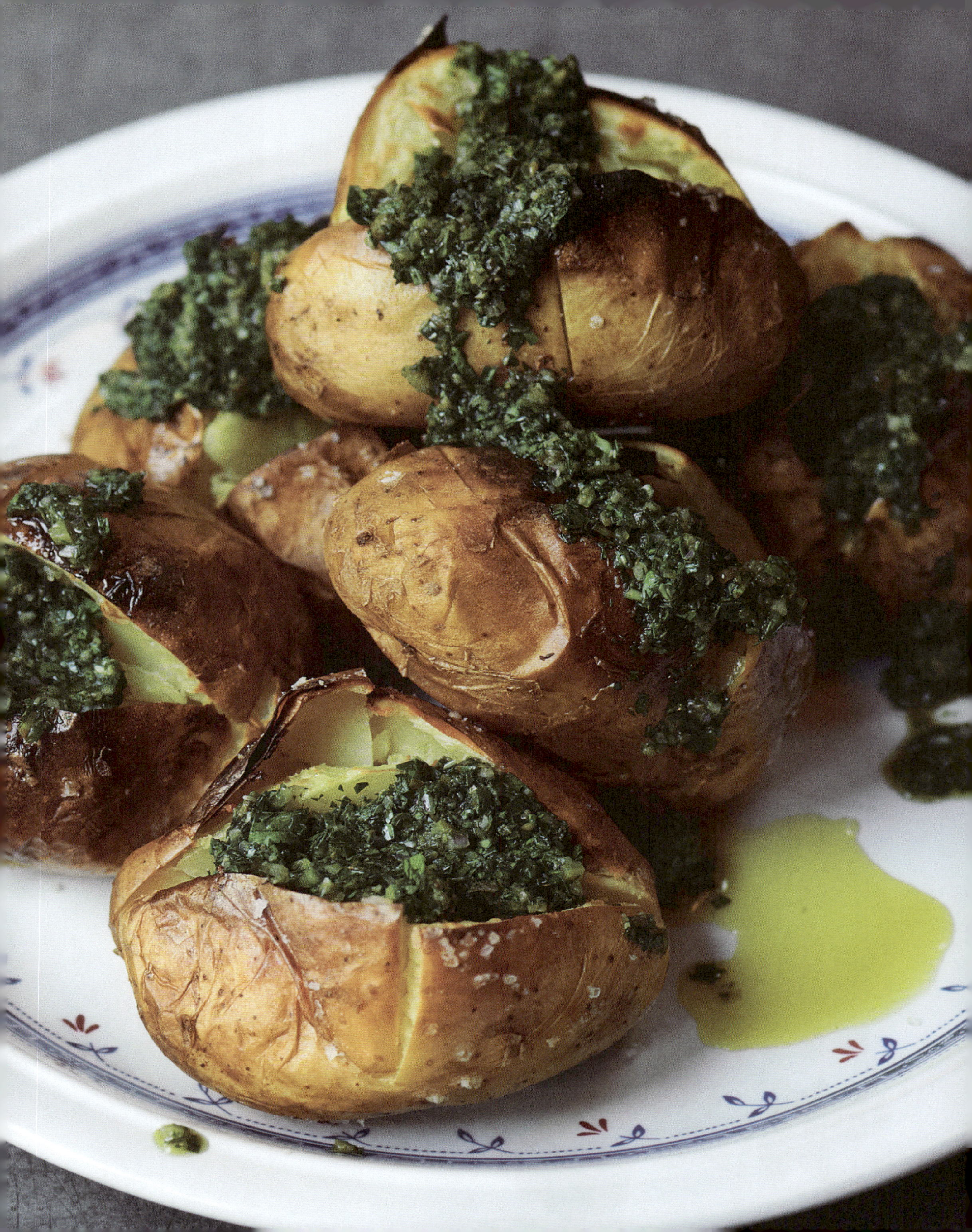

Home Fries for 2

Ingredients (serves 2)

1 1/4 pounds waxy potatoes, boiled on the previous day
1 white onion
4 1/2 tablespoons clarified butter
1/2 bunch parsley
salt and pepper
1/2 teaspoon ground sweet paprika

1. Remove the skin of the potatoes and cut them into slices. Peel and dice the onion. Heat butter in a large frying pan (see tip) and sauté the onions until translucent. Take them out and put them aside.
2. Add the potato slices to the pan and fry for 3–4 minutes. Turning them occasionally, fry for another 8–12 minutes until they are golden brown.
3. Chop the parsley and mix the onions with the potatoes. Season with salt, pepper and paprika and serve immediately.

Preparation time: 30 minutes

TIP It's best to fry potatoes over medium to high heat. If you double the recipe (serves 4), you should use 2 frying pans.

Potatoes have various cooking properties: floury potatoes are suited to making mashed potatoes, gnocchi and soups; waxy potatoes keep their shape as a side dish, in salads, gratins and as fried potatoes.

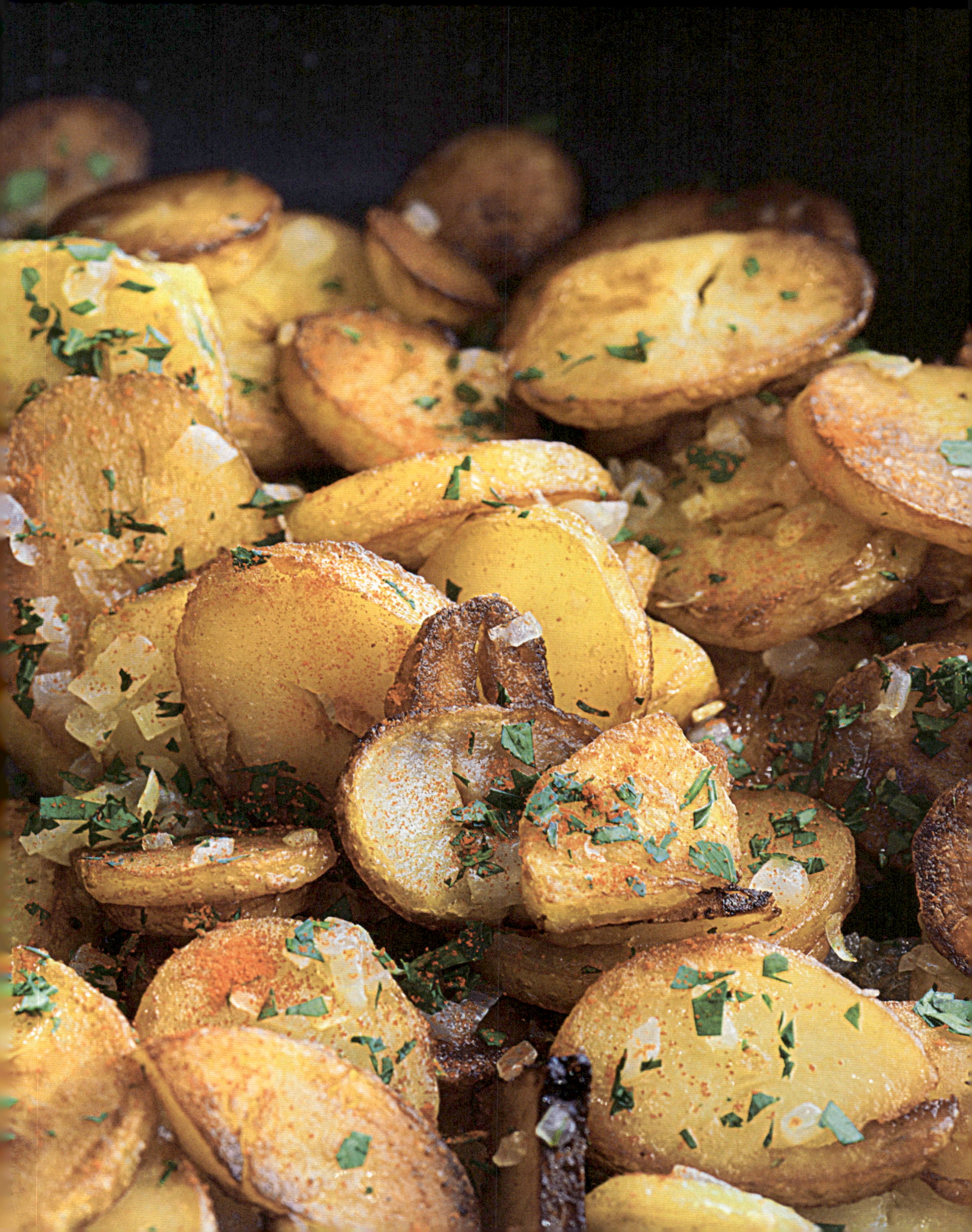

Fried Noodles "Take away!"

Ingredients (serves 4)

- 3/4 inch fresh ginger
- 7 tablespoons soy sauce
- 2 tablespoons honey
- 5 tablespoons dry sherry
- 1 cup snow peas (or peas in the pod)
- 5 ounces broccoli
- 1 carrot
- 1 parsley root
- 1/2 pound quick cooking noodles (Asian noodles to fry)
- 1/2 bunch chives
- 5 stems cilantro
- 1 garlic clove
- 5 tablespoons sunflower or peanut oil

1. To make the sauce, peel the ginger, cut into fine slices and bring to a boil with the soy sauce, honey and sherry.
2. Wash the snow peas and slice them diagonally into thirds. Wash the broccoli and cut off rosettes. Peel the carrot and parsley root, then grate into long strips.
3. Cook the pasta for 4 minutes until al dente, drain in a sieve, rinse under cold water and let drain. Mince chives and roughly chop the cilantro.
4. Peel and dice the garlic. Heat 2 tablespoons of oil in a wok or any other large non-stick pan until it smokes. Sauté the broccoli for 3 minutes. Add the snow peas, carrot, parsley root and garlic. Stir for another 2 minutes.
5. Transfer the vegetables from the wok or pan into a bowl and cover to keep warm. Heat another 3 tablespoons of oil in the wok or a pan until it smokes. Fry the pasta for 2—3 minutes until the noodles are dry. Add half of the sauce and boil it down almost completely.
6. Stir in the vegetables. Add the remaining sauce, chives and cilantro and serve immediately.

Preparation time: 30 minutes

VARIATIONS: you can fry the noodles with lots of different chopped vegetables, for example:
- It takes approximately 5 minutes to fry with cauliflower, kohlrabi, white cabbage, peppers and mushrooms.
- It takes approximately 2 minutes to fry with corn, bok choy, leeks and sprouts.

TIP: the vegetables and noodles should be sautéed over very high heat. If your frying pan or wok is small, it's better to fry them in two batches.

PRECIOUS 4X EGGPLANT

The spicy, tasty eggplant only requires a few ingredients: a splash of oil, a little garlic, some spices while frying. Grilling and stewing will boost its distinctive aromatic taste. Some people enjoy the hint of bitterness in the classic eggplant; however, if you prefer a milder taste, the striped tiger eggplant might be for you. You can get eggplants locally from July to October.

1 Eggplant Carpaccio

With a fork, poke **4 tiger eggplants (or purple eggplants)** all over. Cook them in a pot of boiling salted water for 5 minutes. Drain them. Brush a few **drops of olive oil** on cling wrap and wrap the eggplants in it while warm. Place them in the freezer for 25 minutes. Cut the frozen eggplants into thin slices and arrange on plates. Drizzle with a little **lemon juice** and **olive oil** and season with salt and **freshly cracked pepper.** Decorate with a few **arugula** leaves and 3 1/2—4 tablespoons of roughly grated Parmesan.

2 Zucchini with Eggplant Vinaigrette

Peel **1 eggplant,** cut it in half lengthwise, remove the seeds and finely dice the flesh. Cook it in boiling water for 30 seconds and drain in a sieve. Peel and dice **1/2 of a red onion.** Chop half of a bunch of parsley. Mix all the ingredients with **1 tablespoon of white wine vinegar** and **4 tablespoons of olive oil.** Season with **salt, pepper** and **1 pinch of sugar.** Cut **1 zucchini** into 1/4-inch thick slices, dress with **3 tablespoons of olive oil** and fry for 3—5 minutes on each side. Season with **salt.** Arrange on plates with vinaigrette.

4 Ajvar

Quarter and seed **2 firm red peppers,** peel them with a potato peeler and chop into rough pieces. Peel and chop **3 medium-sized eggplants.** Peel **1 onion** and cut into large pieces. Sauté all the ingredients in a pot with **4 tablespoons of olive oil.** Peel **3 garlic cloves** and add them to the mixture. Season with **salt** and cook for 10 minutes on a low heat while stirring. Deglaze with **1 cup of water** and cook for another 10 minutes in a covered pot. Purée the vegetables in a blender with **1/2 teaspoon of Piment d'Espelette** (smoked paprika) and **1 dash of white wine vinegar.** Season with **salt.** Pour into canning jar and leave to cool in the refrigerator.

3 Melanzane

Cut **2 eggplants** in half lengthwise, make crosses deep into the cut side and season with **salt.** Place in an ovenproof dish with their cut side up. In a blender, purée **2 peeled garlic cloves** with **1 diced tomato, 1/2 bunch of parsley** and **6 tablespoons of olive oil.** Season with **salt** and **pepper.** Pour the sauce over the eggplants and roast in an oven preheated to 400°F for 20—25 minutes.

1

2

3

4

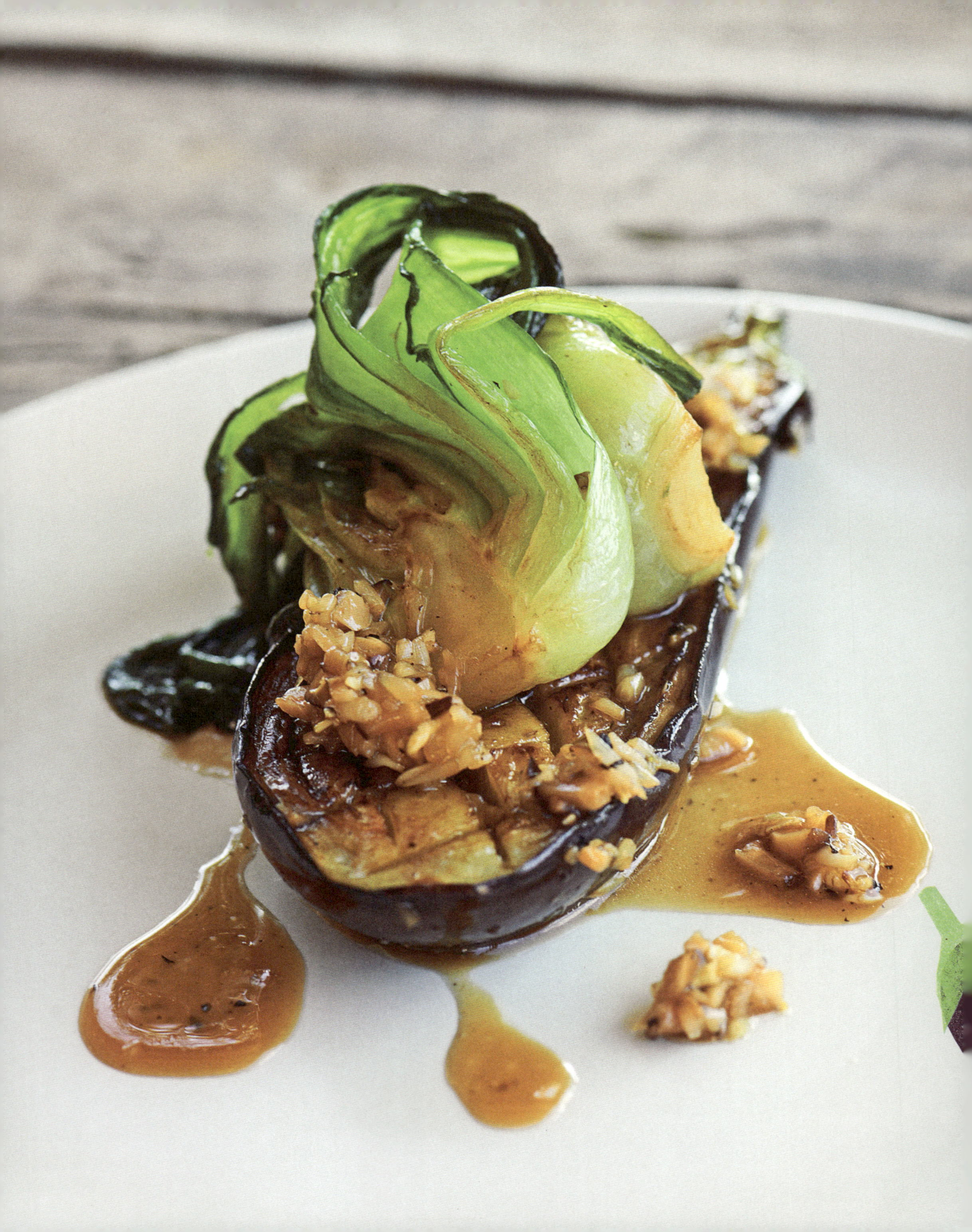

Eggplant and Bok Choy "Asian Style"

Ingredients (serves 4)
4 small bok choy (see note)
salt
3 dried shiitake mushrooms
4 small eggplants or
2 regular eggplants
8 tablespoons olive oil
1 cup bean sprouts
6 tablespoons mirin (or
6 teaspoons sugar)
5 tablespoons soy sauce
2 tablespoons rice vinegar
freshly ground black pepper
1 teaspoon sesame oil
1 tablespoon honey

1. Wash the bok choy, cut in half and boil in salted water for 1 minute. Rinse in cold water and leave to dry on paper towels. Pour hot water over the shiitake mushrooms and leave them to soak.

2. Wash the eggplants, cut them in half lengthwise and make crosses deep into the cut side. Heat up 6 tablespoons of olive oil in a pan. Season the eggplants with salt and fry in the hot oil until golden brown on a medium heat for 6—8 minutes, turning occasionally. Season with salt.

3. To make the vinaigrette, dice the shiitake mushrooms and the sprouts. Mix together with mirin, 4 tablespoons of soy sauce and rice vinegar. Season with salt and pepper. Fry the bok choy on a high heat with 2 tablespoons of olive oil and the sesame oil.

4. Add salt, honey and 1 tablespoon of soy sauce. Bring to a boil and remove from the heat. Arrange the eggplants and bok choy on a plate, drizzle with shiitake sprout vinaigrette and serve immediately.

Preparation time: 25 minutes

BOK CHOY (also called pok choi or bok choi) is related to Chinese cabbage and similiar to Swiss chard. This delicate mustard cabbage originally comes from Asia, but is now cultivated and grown successfully in green houses and can therefore be found in many supermarkets. Like spinach, it can be stewed or steamed briefly, and it can be pan-fried as a part of Asian wok dishes.

71

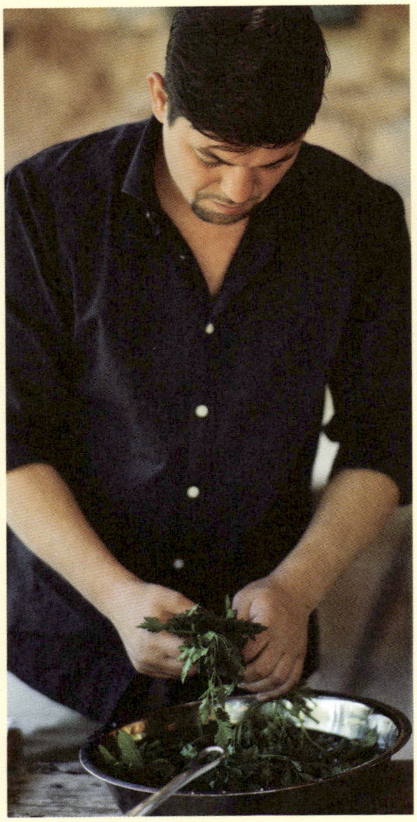
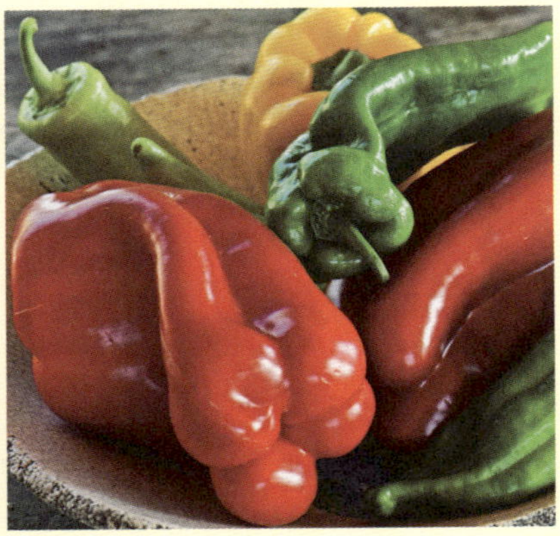
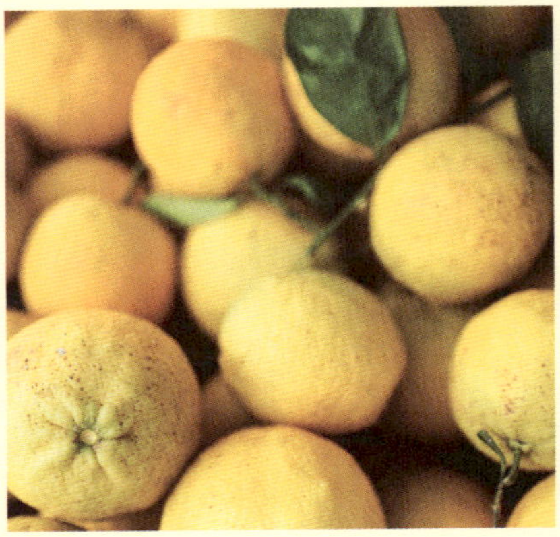
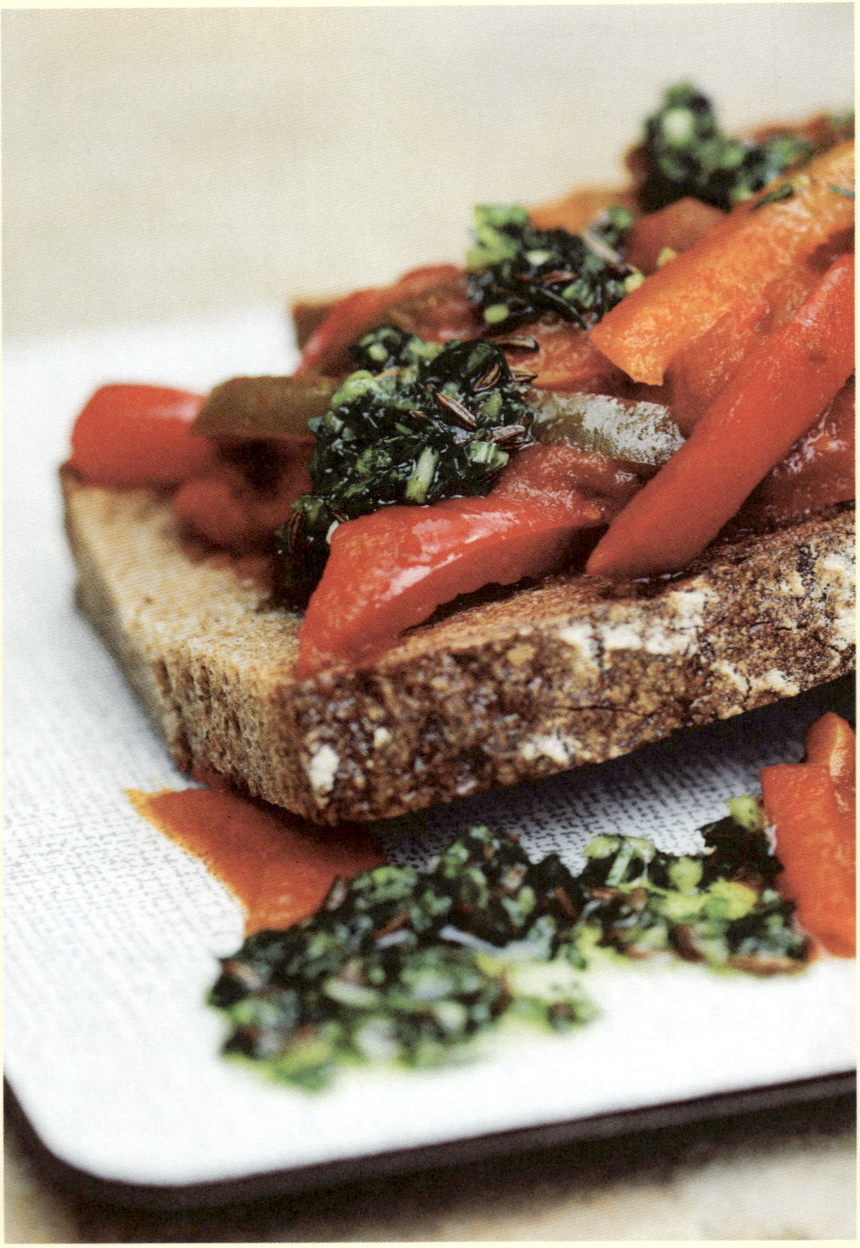
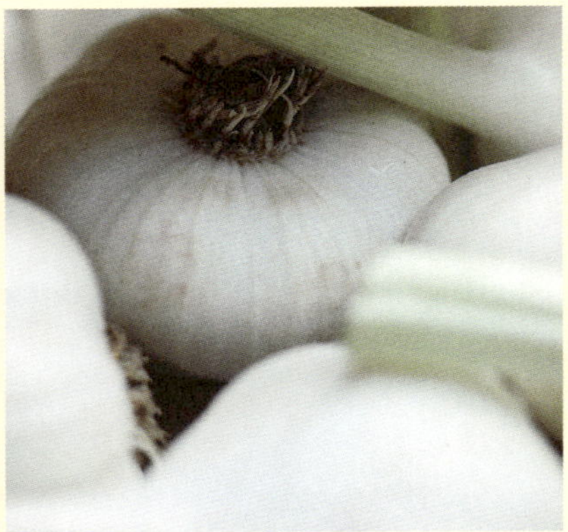
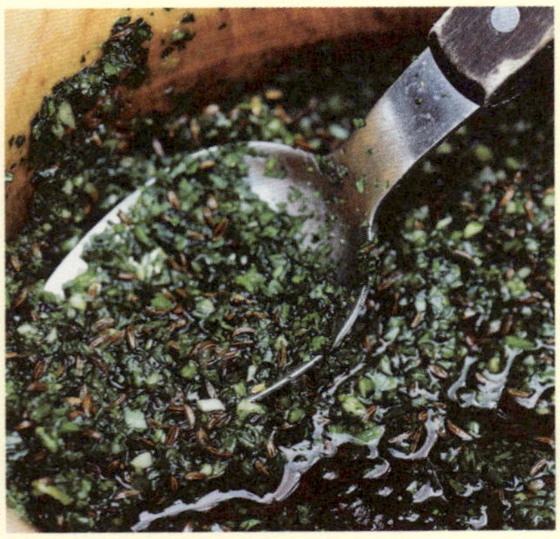

Hot Bell Pepper Pan "Juliška"

Ingredients (serves 4—6)
6 mixed bell peppers (red, green and yellow)
3 Spanish onions
5—6 garlic cloves
6 tablespoons olive oil
2 tablespoons extra hot ground paprika
1 tablespoon ground sweet paprika
sugar
1 teaspoon tomato paste
1 can crushed tomatoes (16 ounces net weight)
salt and pepper
1 teaspoon caraway seeds
1 organic lemon
4 stems oregano
1 small bunch parsley
1/2 loaf peasant bread

1. Wash the peppers, quarter them, remove the seeds and cut into strips. Peel the onions and cut into strips. Peel the garlic and cut into slices. Sauté the garlic in 2 tablespoons of olive oil until transparent.
2. Dust with paprika. Mix in 1 tablespoon of sugar and the tomato paste and cook for 1 minute. Pour in the crushed tomatoes plus 1 can of water. Season with salt and simmer for 30 minutes, uncovered.
3. To make the spiced oil, grind the caraway seeds in a mortar, finely grate the lemon peel and chop the oregano and parsley. Mix together with 4 tablespoons of olive oil plus a pinch of salt and pepper. Cut the peasant bread into slices, toast them and arrange the peppers on top. Drizzle with spiced oil and serve immediately.

Preparation time: 60 minutes

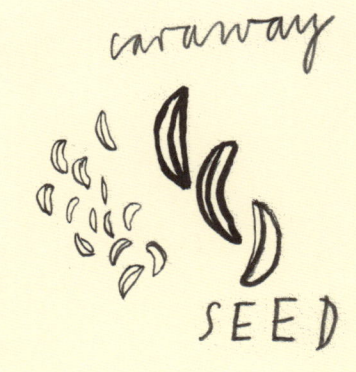

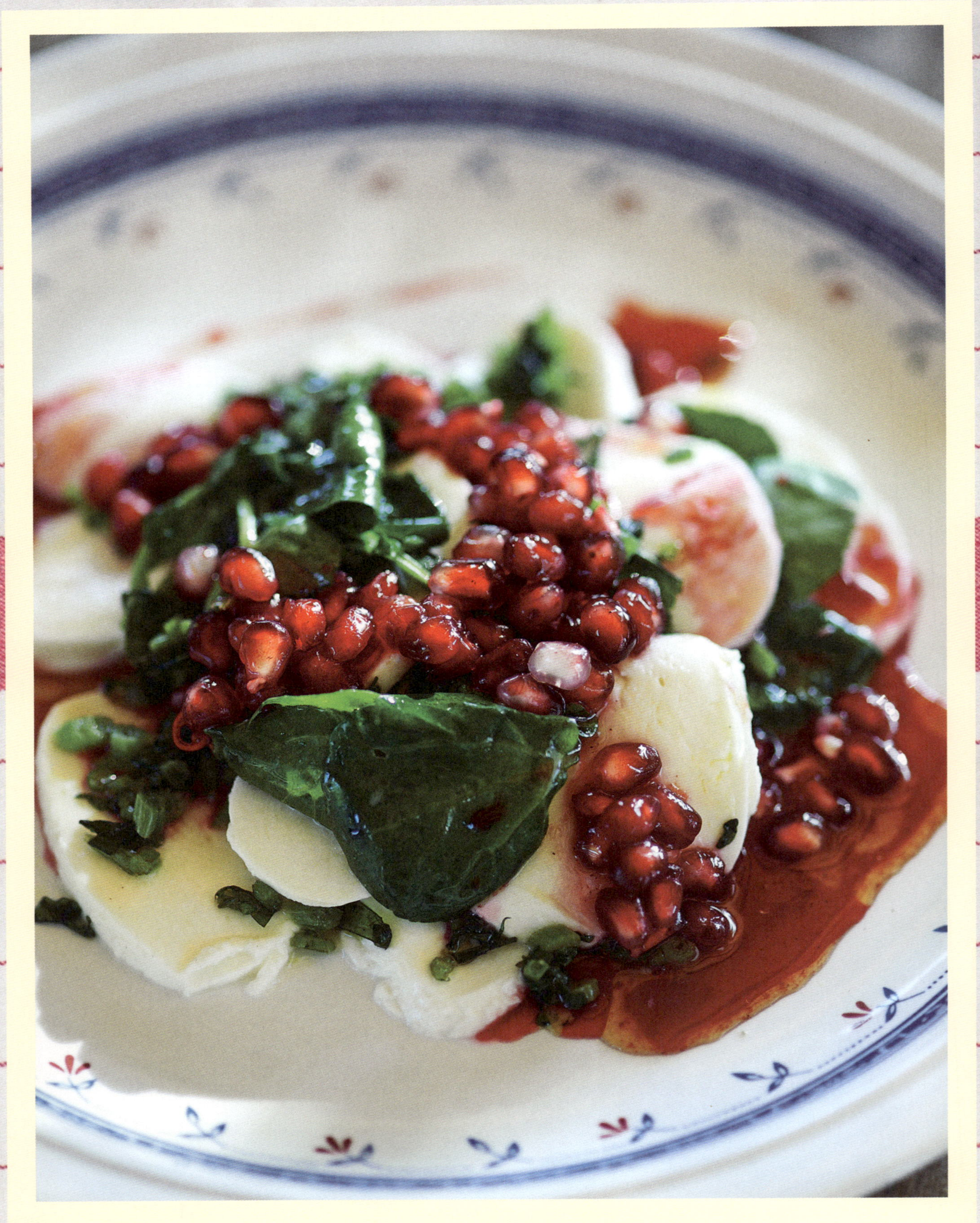

Mozzarella with Watercress Pomegranate Vinaigrette

Ingredients (serves 4—6)

1 small pomegranate
3 cups watercress
2 balls buffalo mozzarella
6 tablespoons olive oil
1 tablespoon lemon juice
salt and pepper
sugar

1. Cut the pomegranate in half and remove the seeds. Wash the watercress and spin it dry. Strip off the leaves and chop the stems into small pieces. Drain the mozzarella, cut into slices and arrange on a plate.
2. Heat 3 tablespoons of olive oil in a pan. Fry the watercress stems for 1—2 minutes. Add the pomegranate seeds and the watercress leaves and fry for another minute. Season to taste with lemon juice, salt, pepper and 1 pinch of sugar. Leave briefly to cool.
3. Sprinkle the watercress mixture over the mozzarella and drizzle with the remaining olive oil. Serve.

Preparation time: 30 minutes

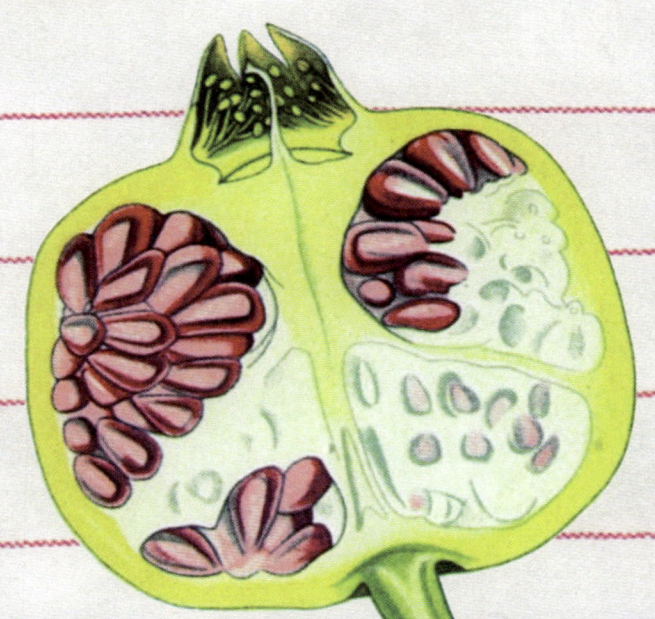

The juicy seeds of the pomegranate are sweet, but they also go really well with savory dishes. The bright red color is a delight to the eye. A fun fact: Some Oriental carpets are colored with pomegranate juice!

crumb

a quick attack on your taste buds with a crunchy crisp effect.

- bread
- lemon peel
- peanut noodles & potato chips
- Butter

Polish **CAULIFLOWER** is a dish in which old bread or dried rolls become a **DELICACY.** You cover cauliflower rosettes in breadcrumbs that are toasted in brown butter until they are golden brown. The fragrant **COMBINATION** of crumbs, butter and salt works with all other kinds of vegetables as well. You can make **BREADCRUMBS** out of any kind of **DRY BREAD** – white, brown, whole wheat, pumpernickel or even soft pretzels. **HOMEMADE** breadcrumbs taste the best.

PANKO, originally from Japan, are particularly crunchy breadcrumbs made from crustless white bread. They are bigger and less dense than regular breadcrumbs. Panko can be found in well-stocked grocery stores or Asian grocery stores.

Old bread isn't the only thing that will make good crumbs. You can also use crumbs from **CRISP BREAD,** pretzel sticks, rice crackers and so on. Grains of rice and couscous can be toasted until crisp. It's really easy to make savory crumbs too, by adding fresh, chopped or dried herbs and spices such as curry powder or chili flakes. The finely grated peel of organic **LEMONS, LIMES** or **ORANGES** provides a fresh, fruity aroma. For even more flavor, throw in some toasted **NUTS** or sesame **SEEDS**. Fried onions and roasted garlic are very effective **FLAVOR ENHANCERS** in a breadcrumb mixture.

Last but not least, a bit of **SALT** may provide a boost to your special breadcrumb mixture. Lovely **SALT FLAKES** such as Maldon sea salt from England or fleur de sel from the French Atlantic coast are particularly suited to increase flavors. Breadcrumb mixtures are not only good as crunchy **TOPPINGS,** they can also be used for topping breaded **VEGETABLE CUTLETS.** If you mix them with a little oil or knead them with some **BUTTER**, they are great as a topping for vegetable gratin. The crisp topping turns **GOLDEN BROWN** in the **OVEN.**

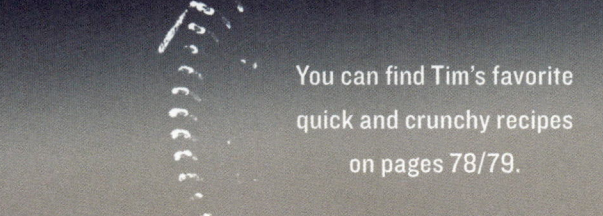

You can find Tim's favorite quick and crunchy recipes on pages 78/79.

VARIATION OF CRUMBS

Olive and Thyme Crumbs

Dice **3 slices of white bread** and fry in a pan with **4 tablespoons of olive oil** until golden brown. Dice **4 tablespoons of pitted black olives** (or green olives) and mix with the finely grated peel of **1/2 of an organic lemon** and **1 tablespoon of thyme leaves**. Toss the olives with the fried pieces of bread. Add **pepper** to taste.

Curry Crumbs

Toast **3 tablespoons of basmati rice** in an ungreased pan for 3—4 minutes and leave to cool. Roughly grind in a mortar. Toast **4 tablespoons of bread crumbs** in a pan with **3 tablespoons of olive oil, 1 pinch of brown sugar** and **1 pinch of mild curry powder**. Finely grate the peel of **1 organic lime** and add it to the crumb mixture. Add **1 pinch of fleur de sel** and **chili flakes** to taste.

THE CRUMBS ARE SO FABULOUS, YOUR TASTE BUDS WILL EXPLODE!

Asian Crumbs

Toast **2 tablespoons of white sesame seeds** and **2 tablespoons of black sesame seeds** in a pan with **1 cup Panko** (see page 77) and **4 tablespoons of olive oil** until the breadcrumbs are golden brown. Stir in **1 tablespoon of roasted garlic** (canned or homemade), **1 tablespoon of chopped chives, 1 teaspoon of sugar, 2 teaspoons of yeast flakes** (found in health food shops) and **1 teaspoon of Aleppo pepper** (or, if not available, red pepper) and roast for another minute. Season with **1 pinch of salt** and **1 teaspoon of sesame oil**.

Middle Eastern Crumbs

Toast **5 tablespoons of couscous** in an ungreased pan for 3–4 minutes until brown. Add **1 teaspoon of honey** and leave to cool. Roughly chop **2 tablespoons of salted, roasted almonds**. Heat **3 tablespoons of olive oil** in a pan and fry **4 tablespoons of breadcrumbs** until golden brown. Mix together with the couscous. Stir in **1 pinch of cinnamon, 1 pinch of salt, 1 level teaspoon of harissa spice blend**. Chop **2 tablespoons of barberries (or cranberries)** and fold them into the mixture.

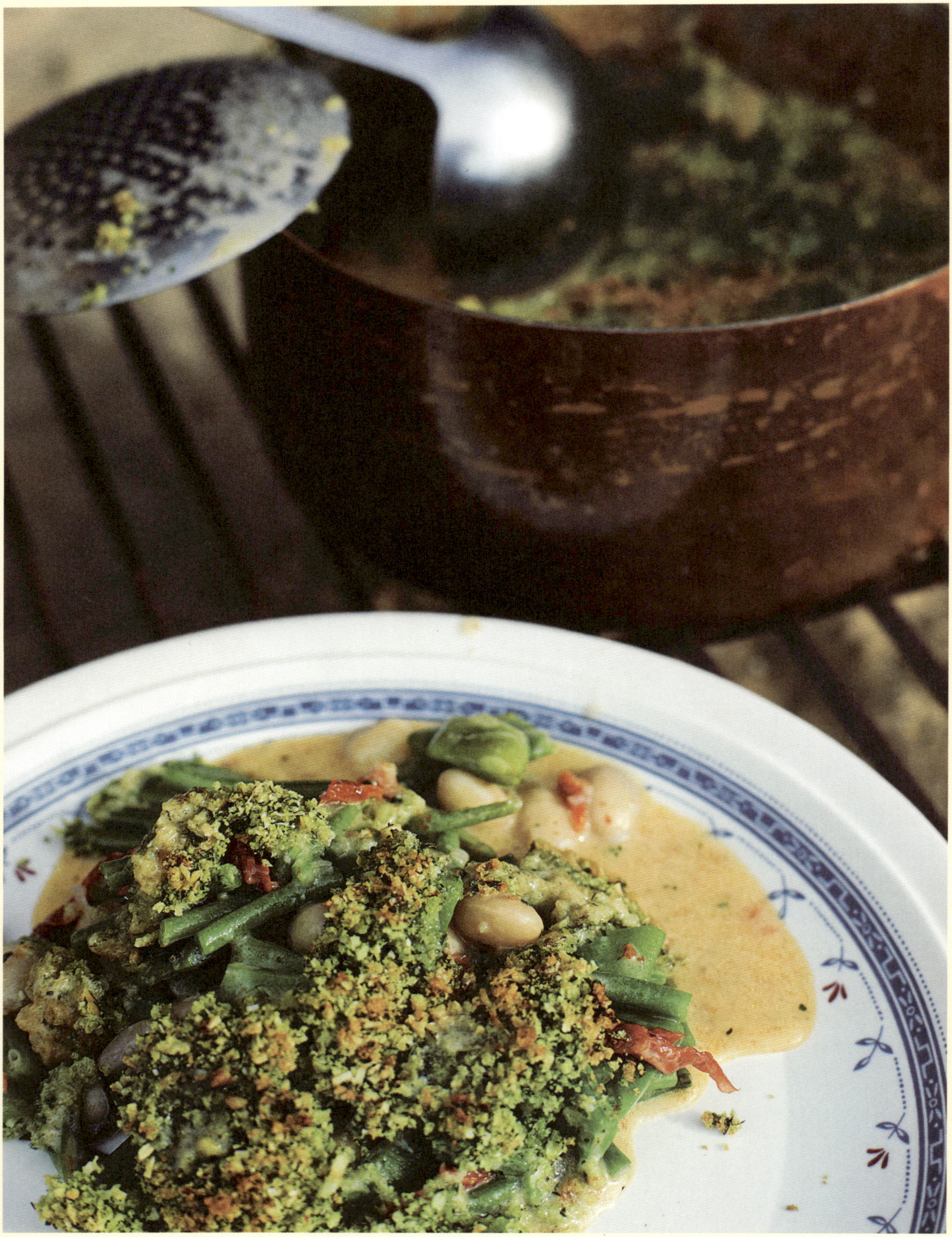

Creamy "Cassoulet" with 3 Types of Beans and Savory Crumbs

Ingredients (serves 4)

- 1/2 pound green beans
- 2/3 pound runner beans
- salt
- 1 can white beans (16 ounces net weight)
- 1 onion
- 3 garlic cloves
- 8 sundried tomatoes
- 3 1/2 tablespoons butter
- 8 stems summer savory
- 1/4 cup flour
- 1 2/3 cups vegetable stock
- 1 2/3 cups milk
- 6 stems parsley
- 1/2 organic lemon
- 2/3 cup breadcrumbs
- 1 tablespoon olive oil

1. Cut the green beans and the runner beans into bite-sized pieces and cook in boiling, salted water for 8—10 minutes. Drain and rinse off in cold water. Drain the white beans and rinse in cold water.

2. Peel the onion and 1 garlic clove and dice with the sundried tomatoes. Cook with 2 tablespoons of butter and 2 stems of savory in an ovenproof dish until transparent. Dust lightly with flour and then slowly add the rest of the flour and mix. Stir in the stock and milk with a whisk and leave it to cook, uncovered, for 5 minutes. Remove the savory, add the white beans and cook for another 5 minutes. Add the green and runner beans.

3. To make the breadcrumb crust, chop the parsley with the rest of the savory, grate the lemon peel and, in a blender, purée with the breadcrumbs the remaining peeled garlic cloves, 1 tablespoon of olive oil and 1 1/2 tablespoons of butter. Season with salt.

4. Sprinkle the crumb crust over the beans. Preheat the oven to 415°F (convection 400°F) and bake on the bottom rack for 20—25 minutes until golden brown.

Preparation time: 45 minutes

Savory is intensely peppery and spicy. Its aroma is reminiscent of thyme. You can flavor bean dishes, egg dishes and stews with fresh savory during its July to October season.

Peperonata French Fries

Ingredients (serves 4)

1 3/4 pounds waxy potatoes (red or new potatoes)
8 1/2 cups frying oil or frying fat
1 3/4 cups quark (or strained Greek yogurt)
5 tablespoons olive oil
1 bunch chives
salt and pepper
sugar
1 red bell pepper
1 green bell pepper
1 green chili pepper
1 bulb garlic
2 stems rosemary
sea salt

1. Peel the potatoes, cut lengthwise into four pieces and pat dry with paper towels. Put the frying fat and the potatoes into a pot with high sides (A). Stirring constantly, heat for 25–30 minutes (B) until potatoes are crispy and golden brown on the outside (C) and soft inside (D).

2. Then stir the quark until creamy and gradually mix in the olive oil. Mince the chives and fold them in. Season the quark with salt, pepper and 1 pinch of sugar. Set aside.

3. Just before the potatoes wedges are done, wash the peppers, cut them into quarters, remove the seeds and slice them into 1/2-inch wide strips. Peel the garlic bulb and cut in half. Add the vegetables with the rosemary stems (E) and deep fry it all for another 10 minutes (F). Remove everything with a skimmer (H), drain on paper towels and season with sea salt. Serve with chive quark (G).

Preparation time: 50 minutes

"Lots of people are really scared of deep frying without a deep fat fryer and they have good reason to be. If the food is too damp, then the fat splatters, spills over or can catch on fire. We put the cold potatoes into cold oil and slowly bring them to a boil – that way it is unlikely that anything will spill over or burn. The potatoes get nice and crispy and taste very sophisticated with garlic and rosemary."

A B C
D E F
G H

Special No. 1 (Very Hot)

Ingredients (serves 4)
- 8 dried shiitake mushrooms
- 2 tablespoons maple syrup
- 5 tablespoons soy sauce
- 1 garlic clove
- 3/4 inch fresh ginger
- 1–2 red chili peppers
- 3 tablespoons oil
- 1 teaspoon sesame oil
- 1 carrot
- 1 red bell pepper
- 1 stalk celery
- 5 spears green asparagus
- 3 scallions
- 3 1/2 cups baby spinach
- 2/3 cup mung bean sprouts

1. To make the mushroom stock, pour 1 cup of boiling water over the shiitake mushrooms. Blend together the maple syrup and soy sauce until smooth.
2. Peel the garlic and ginger and chop into very small pieces. Finely chop the chili pepper. Heat 1 tablespoon of olive oil with sesame oil and sauté the garlic and ginger until light brown. Add the maple syrup and soy sauce mixture. Add the chili peppers and bring to a boil.
3. Drain the shiitake mushrooms and cut into strips. Peel the carrot and cut into strips. Wash the pepper, quarter it, remove the seeds and cut into strips. Clean the celery and cut diagonally into long, thin slices. Peel the bottom third of the asparagus, cut the ends and cut the spears and the scallions into diagonal slices.
4. In a wok or other large, nonstick pan, heat 2 tablespoons of olive oil and fry the carrots and peppers for 3 minutes. Add the celery and the asparagus and fry for another 2 minutes. Mix the scallions and the washed baby spinach and mung bean sprouts and fry for another minute. Add the shiitake mushrooms and the sauce and cook for 1 minute, stirring constantly.

Preparation time: 40 minutes

VARIATIONS: 1. Other types of vegetables are suited to spicy Asian cuisine. Rosettes of cauliflower and broccoli, pumpkin or kohlrabi cubes take about 5 minutes to fry. Chopped or sliced mushrooms, peas, corn, sugar snap peas, chickpeas, leeks and various sprouts should be fried for 2 minutes.
2. The spicy sauce can be seasoned with chili sauce instead of fresh chili peppers.

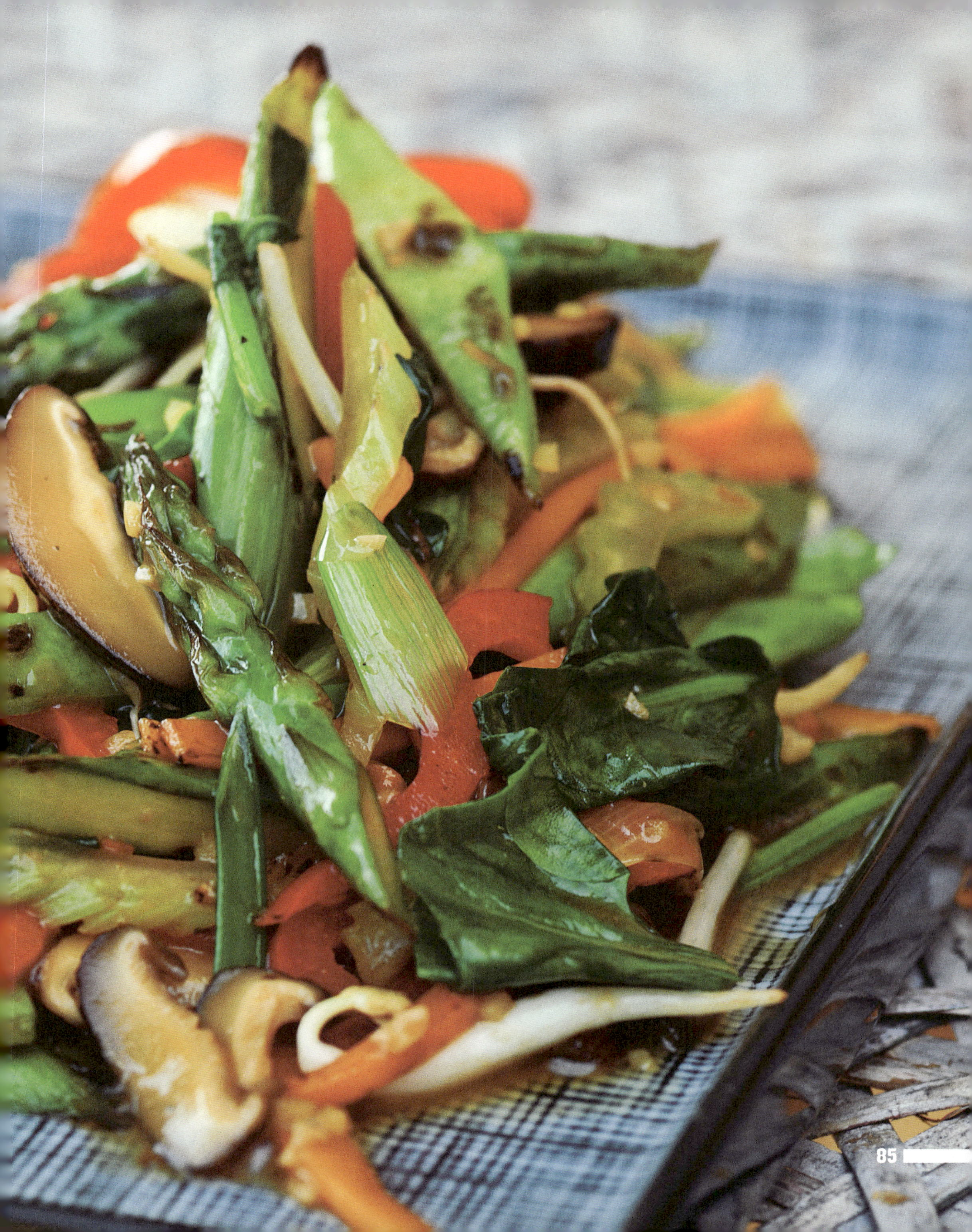

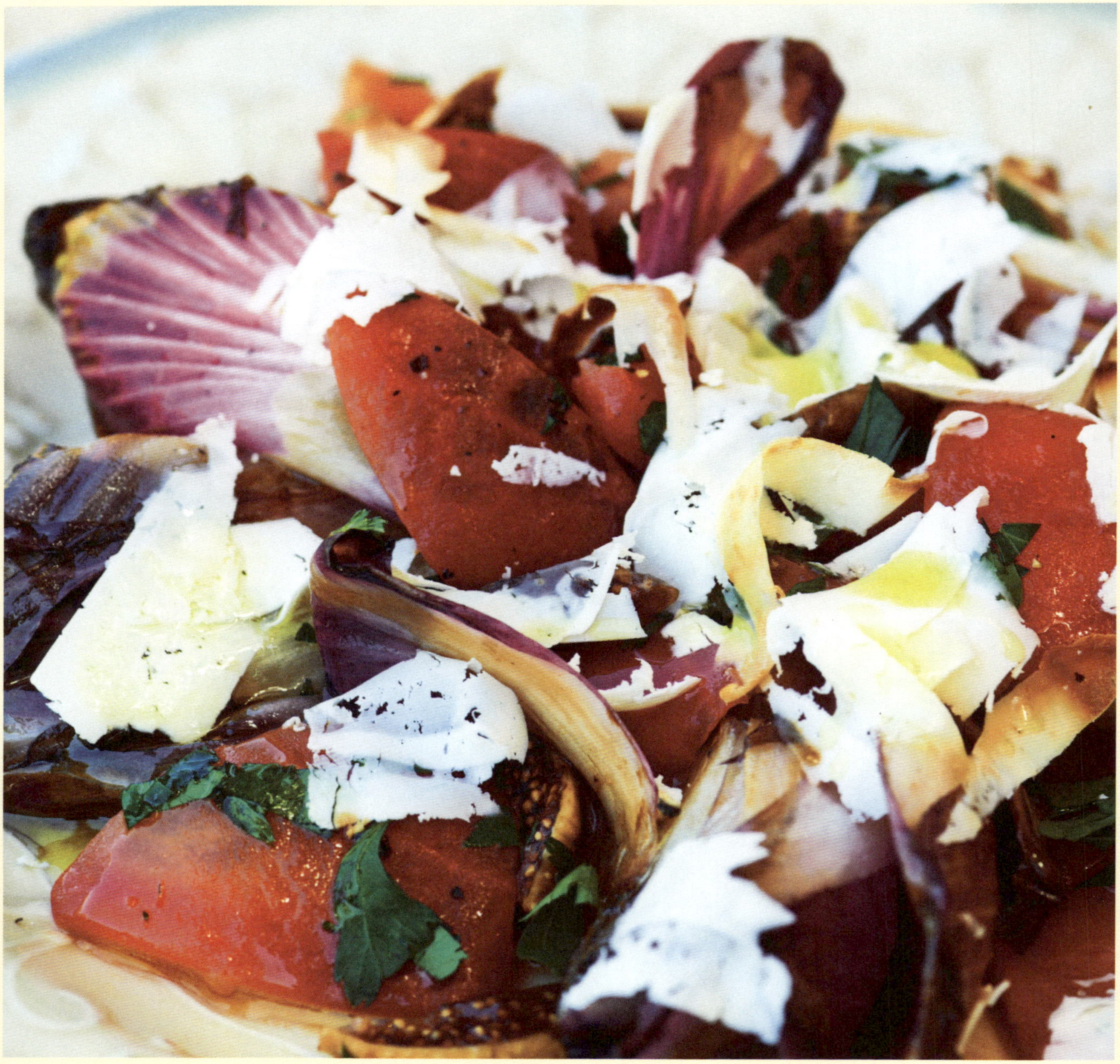

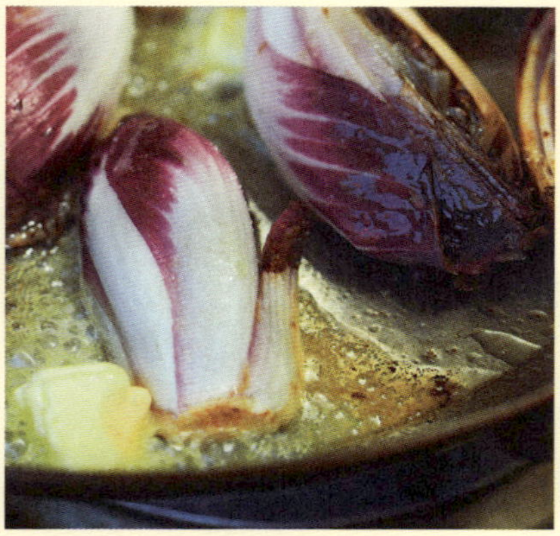

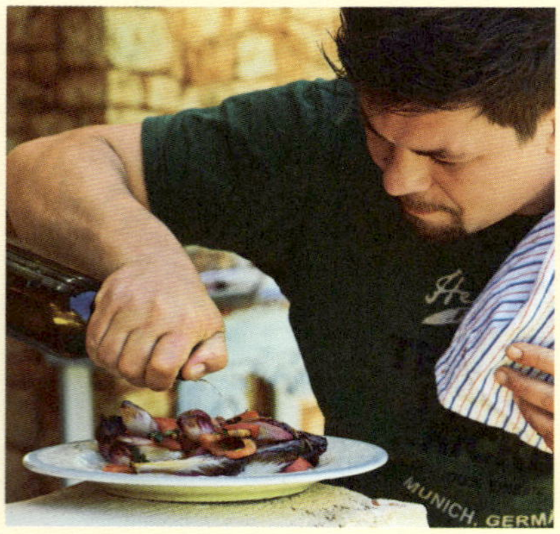

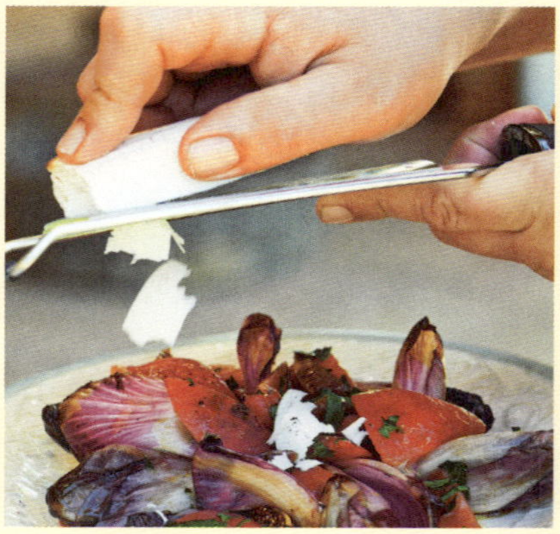

Pot-Roasted Radicchio with Warm Tomato Fig Salad and Smoked Cheese

Ingredients (serves 4)

4 beefsteak tomatoes
4 dried figs
1/2 bunch parsley
4 radicchio heads (or 8 mini-radicchio)
5 tablespoons olive oil
1 tablespoon butter
salt and pepper
1 teaspoon sugar
1 teaspoon white wine vinegar
1 piece of smoked cheese, approximately 3 ounces (e.g. ricotta affumicata, scamorza or manchego)

1. Remove the cores of the tomatoes and place tomatoes in boiling water until the skins burst. Peel off the skins, quarter them, remove the seeds and cut into bite-sized pieces. Cut the figs into thin strips. Roughly chop the parsley.
2. Cut the radicchio in half. Heat 3 tablespoons of olive oil and the butter in a frying pan and fry the radicchio for 1—2 minutes. Season with a little salt and sugar. Cook for 1 more minute, remove from the pan and keep warm.
3. Fry the tomatoes with the figs for 1 minute. Take the frying pan off the heat. Add 2 tablespoons of olive oil and the white wine vinegar. Season with salt and pepper and fold in the parsley. Arrange the radicchio, tomatoes and figs on plates and serve sprinkled with grated smoked cheese.

Preparation time: 30 minutes

RICE PAPER & MORE –
lightly wrapped

Whether as a crunchy covering, spicy wrapping or practical finger food, wraps, rice paper, strudel dough and nori leaves get the flavor rolling in vegetarian cooking. Here's a little lesson in wrapping:

You can find edible **RICE PAPER** (also **RICE SHEETS**) in square and round shapes in a well-stocked Asian grocery store. You have to **SOAK THE SHEETS IN WATER** to make them soft and smooth. There are many great **FILLINGS,** such as crunchy vegetable strips, fresh shoots or sprouts, strips of tofu and strong-tasting fried mushrooms. Sweet and sour chili sauce or soy sauce with wasabi can add just the right amount of spiciness.

PUFF PASTRY is often sold **FROZEN** in packs of 4—6 rectangular sheets that you can **DEFROST,** layer on top of each other and then roll out to the desired size on a floured surface. (Remember to remove the plastic between the pastry sheets!) You can make life easier by buying puff pastry that's already been rolled out at a bakery, or else by buying a roll of puff pastry from the **FREEZER SECTION** in the grocery store. Puff pastry is a delicate, crispy wrap for both spicy and sweet fillings. The pastry sheets mustn't be too damp, or else the finished pastry won't be crisp. Puff pastry turns golden brown after being in the oven for 20—25 minutes at 400°F.

Filo dough

FLAKY PASTRY

Ricepaper

NORI SHEETS

Wonton dough

STRUDEL DOUGH is a very smooth dough made of water, wheat flour and melted butter or oil which is stretched out until it is very thin and can be wrapped around the filling a couple of times. The dough turns golden brown and flaky **IN THE OVEN**. It's difficult to make and requires **PRACTICE**. Greek **FILO PASTRY** or Turkish **YUFKA DOUGH** are great alternatives.

SHORT PASTRY

strudel dough

Salty, crisp **SEAWEED LEAVES** are called **NORI** in Japanese. They mainly cover sushi rolls and rice balls, but are also good at enhancing strong-tasting **ASIAN SOUPS**. If you soften them in hot stock, they release a delicate **TASTE OF THE SEA** and can then be removed. You can also break up nori leaves into bits and add them to breadcrumb or salt mixtures.

spring rolls

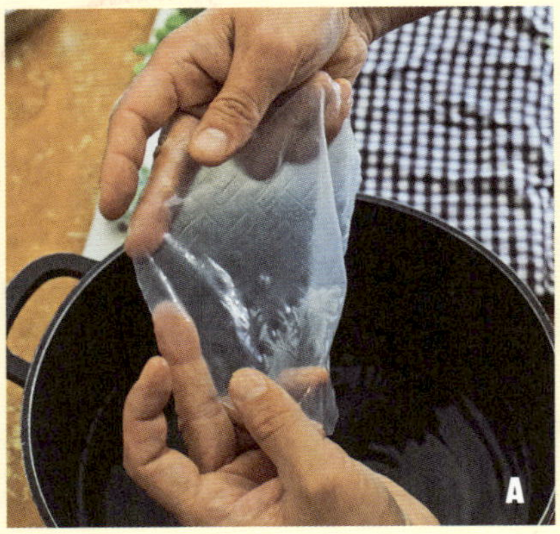
A

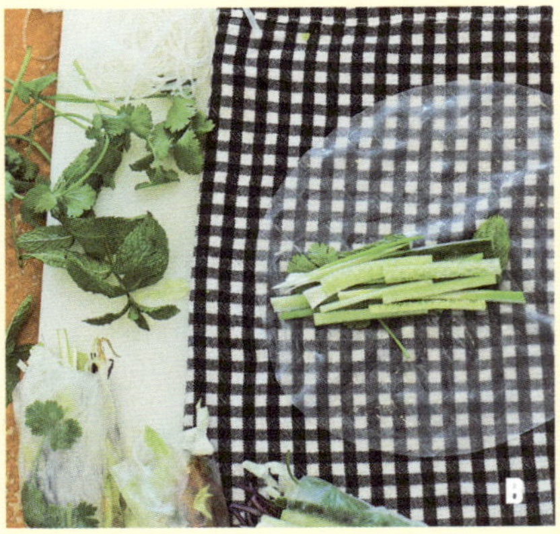
B

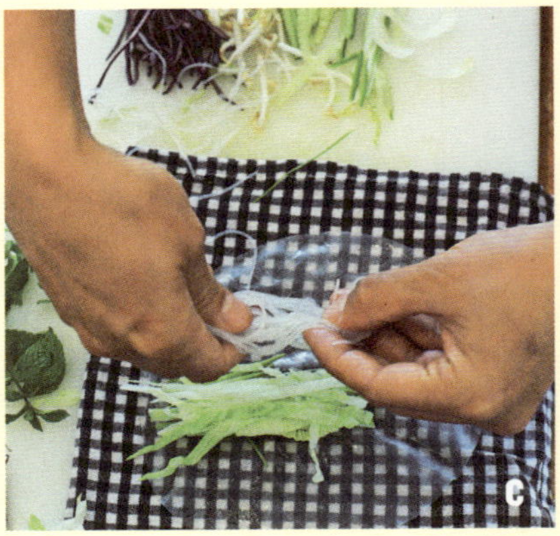
C

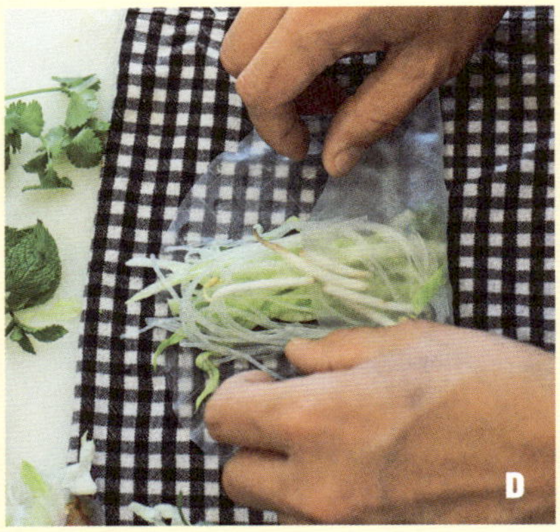
D

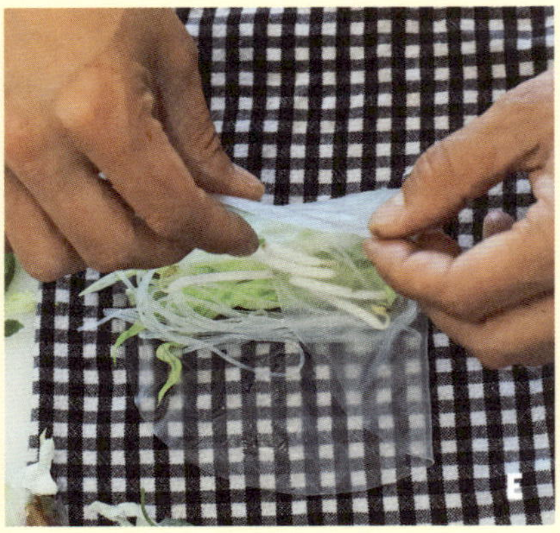
E

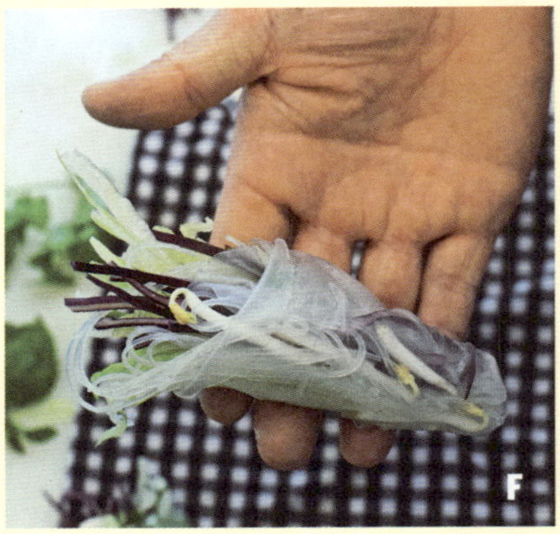
F

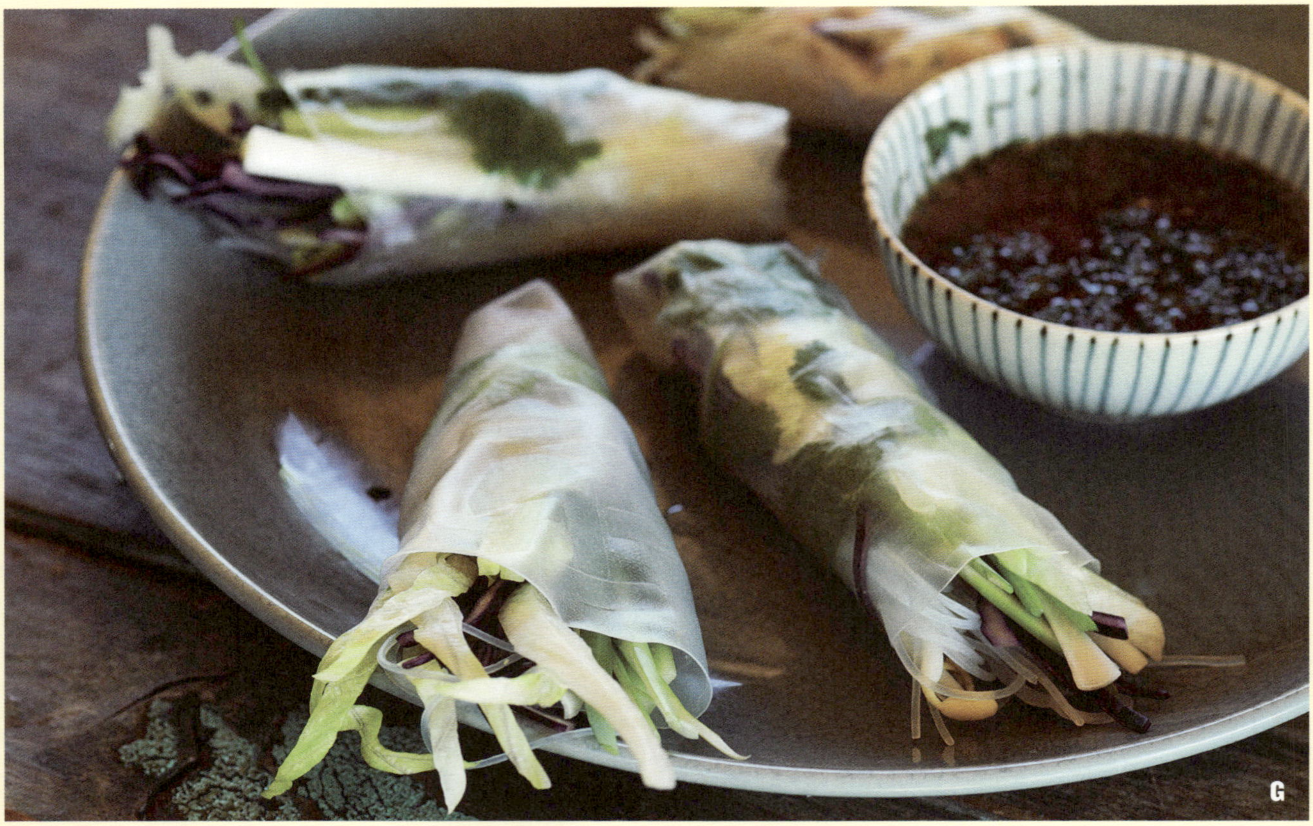
G

Summer Rolls

Ingredients (makes 8 rolls)

1/8 pound glass noodles
1/4 pound iceberg lettuce
1/4 pound red cabbage
1/4 pound cucumber
4 scallions
1/3 cup bean sprouts
4 stems mint
5 stems Thai basil
8 sheets edible rice paper
4 tablespoons sweet and spicy chili sauce
2 smoked garlic cloves (recipe see page 202)
1 red chili pepper
1 small carrot
5 stems cilantro
1 organic lime
2 tablespoons maple syrup (or honey)
salt

1. Cook the glass noodles according to the package instructions, rinse in cold water and drain. Wash the iceberg lettuce and cut into thin strips. Cut the red cabbage into very thin strips. Wash the cucumber and cut into sticks. Rinse the scallions and cut diagonally into slices. Under hot water, rinse the sprouts. Strip off the mint and Thai basil leaves.

2. For each roll, place 1 sheet of rice paper in lukewarm water (A), then drain on a dish towel or paper towel (B). Lay some of the prepared vegetables and the noodles in the middle of the sheets (C), drizzle with a teaspoon of sweet and spicy chili sauce. Fold the rice sheets in from the left and right sides (D) and then roll up (E). Cover the rolls with a damp cloth or paper towel.

3. For the dip, cut the smoked garlic into slices, dice the red chili pepper, peel and grate the carrot, chop the cilantro. Mix together with the juice of 1 lime, maple syrup and 3 1/2 tablespoons of water. Season with salt and serve with the rolls.

Preparation time: 45 minutes

Bell Pepper Pastilla

Ingredients (serves 2—4)

1 red bell pepper
1 green bell pepper
2 garlic cloves
2/3 cups dried, pitted dates
2 teaspoons fresh ginger
1 1/4 cup vermicelli
salt
3 tablespoons olive oil
1 teaspoon harissa paste (see note) or Ajvar (on page 68)
1/2 teaspoon cumin seeds
turmeric (or mild curry powder)
4 stems cilantro
4 stems parsley
2—3 tablespoons lemon juice
3 tablespoons butter
6 slices filo pastry (see page 89)
6 tablespoons sunflower oil

1. Wash the bell peppers, cut them into quarters and remove the seeds before cutting into fine strips. Peel and dice the garlic. Cut the dates into thin strips. Peel and grate the ginger. Boil the vermicelli according to the instructions on the package, rinse with cold water and chop roughly.

2. Heat the olive oil in a large pan. Fry the peppers, garlic and dates for 4 minutes. Add the noodles and season with the harissa paste, cumin, 1 pinch of turmeric and the grated ginger. Fry for 1 minute and season with salt. Chop the cilantro and the parsley and fold in. Add lemon juice to taste. Set aside.

3. Melt the butter in a small pan. Spread a thin layer of butter on 1 sheet of yufka dough. Lay another sheet on top of that, brush it with a thin layer of butter. Arrange half of the filling in the middle of the sheet. Place a corner of the dough over the filling and brush it with a thin layer of butter. Continue doing the same thing until the filling is completely covered. Prepare another pastille with the remainder of the ingredients.

4. Heat the oil in large nonstick frying pan. On medium heat, fry the pastillas on the folded sides for 2—3 minutes, then flip over and fry for 2—3 minutes more.

Preparation time: 35 minutes

PASTILLA (also called Bastilla or b'stilla, pronounced "bastiya") is originally a Moroccan dish. Warka, filo or yufka dough is a crispy wrapping for the various, spicy fillings.
HARISSA is a Middle Eastern spicy paste made of chili, garlic, cumin, cilantro and other spices. It can be found in well-stocked grocery stores.

Onion Tart

Ingredients (serves 2—4)
8 white onions, approximately 1 pound
4 red onions, approximately 1/2 pound
3 tablespoons olive oil
salt and pepper
2 stems thyme
2 stems marjoram
1 package refrigerated puff pastry
(10 ounces)
3 tablespoons crème fraîche
1 tablespoon honey
1/2 teaspoon ground sweet paprika
cayenne pepper

1. Peel the onions and slice thinly. Heat the olive oil in a frying pan. Add salt to the onions and cook them for 10 minutes on a medium heat. Chop the thyme and marjoram and fold in. Season with pepper.

2. Lay the puff pastry on a baking sheet covered in parchment paper. With a fork, poke the dough several times. Season the crème fraîche with salt and pepper and spread on the pastry, leaving an edge of 3/4 inch. Spread the onions on the pastry and drizzle with honey. Season with ground paprika and cayenne pepper. Preheat oven to 425°F (convection: 360°) and bake on the middle rack for 20—25 minutes.

Preparation time: 60 minutes

Sweet and mild, hot and spicy – onions have an amazing range of aromas. As a modest member of the Allium family, the onion is the most used ingredient in vegetarian cooking.

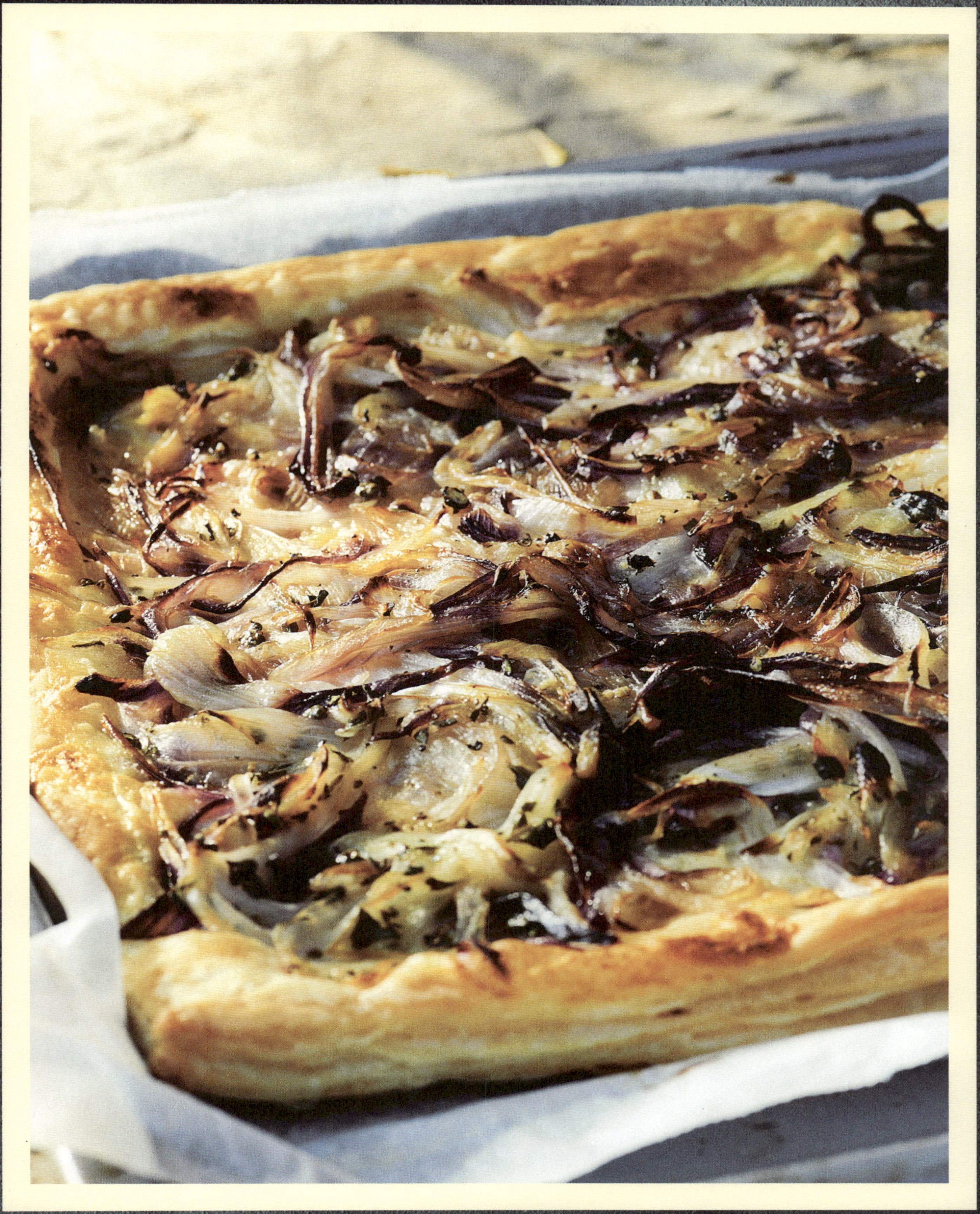

Ragú "Especial"

Ingredients (serves 4—6)

Approximately 1 pound mixed mushrooms (e.g. white mushrooms, shiitakes, oysters)
2 carrots
2 celery sticks
1 Spanish onion
1 clove garlic
3 tablespoons olive oil
1 tablespoon tomato paste
1/2 cup dry white wine
2 cans diced tomatoes (1 pound net weight)
1 teaspoon dried thyme
1 teaspoon dried oregano
2 bay leaves
1 teaspoon ground sweet paprika
sugar
salt and pepper
3—5 ounces (per person) of favorite pasta (photo: linguine)
1 cup freshly grated Parmesan

1. Clean the mushrooms and chop roughly in a food processor. Spread them out on a tray and let them turn dark for 30 minutes (they will ferment and acquire a wonderful aroma). Meanwhile, peel the carrots, celery sticks and onion. Finely dice all three vegetables (A).

2. Peel the garlic clove, chop and sauté with the mushrooms in olive oil (B). Add the vegetables and sauté for another 5 minutes (C). Mix in the tomato paste. Add the white wine (D) and bring to a boil. Add the cans of tomatoes and 1/2 can of water (E).

3. Mix in the thyme, oregano, bay leaves and paprika. Season with 1 tablespoon of sugar, salt and pepper. Cook in an open pot for 25 minutes.

4. Meanwhile, cook the pasta according to the package instructions, drain (F) and mix in with the sauce while hot (G). Sprinkle with Parmesan and serve.

Preparation time: 1 hour and 20 minutes

» This vegetarian ragú is an awesome discovery! It doesn't just look like Bolognese; it also tastes like it. I know for sure that noone, not even fanatic meateaters, will be able to tell the difference. This sauce has everything a good ragú needs. «

GARLIC

Broccoli Cannelloni in a Spicy Tomato Sauce

Ingredients (serves 2—4)

1 head broccoli (approximately 1 pound)
salt and pepper
2 large eggs
2/3 cup goats quark (or ricotta)
nutmeg
12—14 cannelloni
butter (for greasing the baking dish)
2 cans of diced tomatoes (16 ounces net weight each)
1/2 teaspoon chili flakes
1/2 teaspoon cinnamon
2 tablespoons raisins
2 tablespoons olive oil
1/2 cup smoked scamorza (see page 53)

1. Wash the broccoli and cut into rosettes. Peel the stems and chop into pieces. Put 3—4 rosettes aside. Cook the rest of the broccoli for 2 minutes in salted water until al dente. Drain and rinse under cold water. In a food processor, chop into big pieces. Beat the eggs and the quark in a bowl. Mix in the pieces of broccoli. Season with salt, pepper and a pinch of freshly grated nutmeg.

2. Using a piping bag or freezer bag, fill the cannelloni with the mixture. Butter an ovenproof dish and put in the cannelloni.

3. With a fork, squash the tomatoes with the chili flakes, cinnamon and raisins. Season with salt and spread over the cannelloni. Cut the rest of the broccoli into slices and sprinkle over the top. Drizzle with olive oil.

4. Bake the cannelloni at 375°F (convection oven: 350°F) on the second bottom rack for 35 minutes. Sprinkle with roughly chopped scamorza 10 minutes before they are finished cooking.

Preparation time: 50 minutes

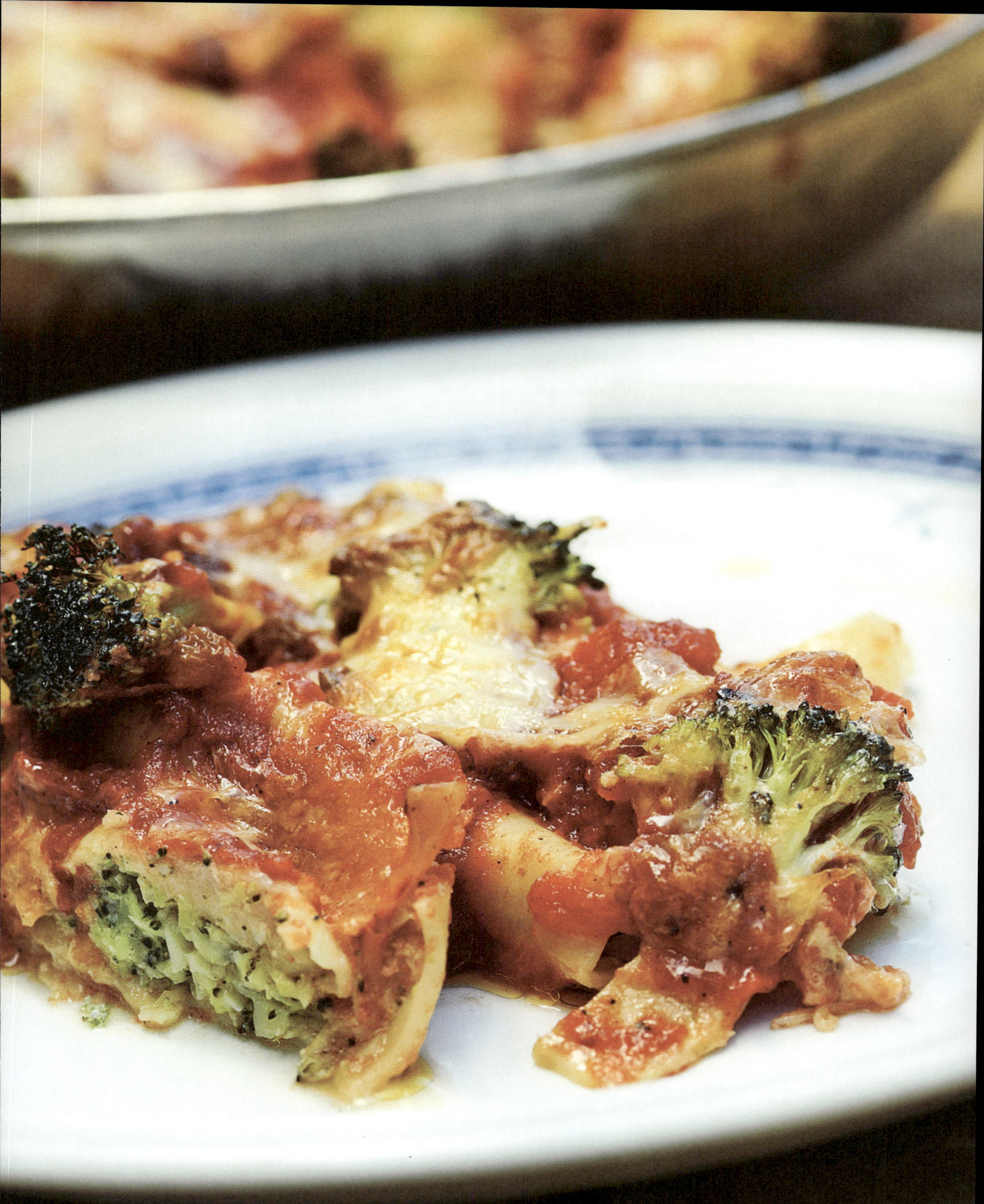

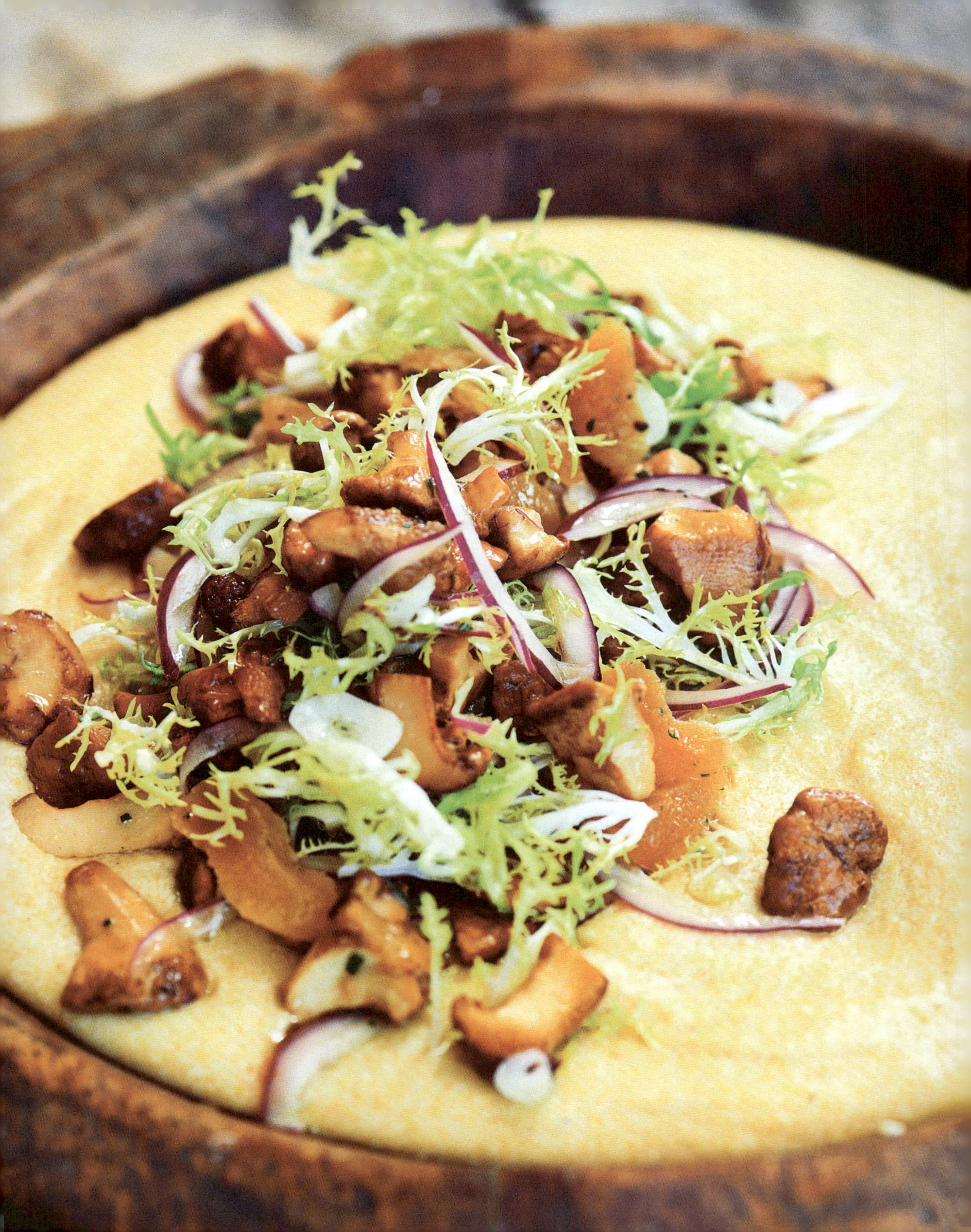

Creamy Cheese Polenta with Chanterelles

Ingredients (serves 4)

1 pound chanterelle mushrooms
1/2 head frisée lettuce
8 dried apricots
1/2 red onion
4 tablespoons olive oil
1 tablespoon red wine vinegar
1 teaspoon chopped fresh rosemary
salt and pepper
2 1/2 cups vegetable stock
1/2 cup heavy cream
nutmeg
1 1/4 cups polenta (cornmeal)
1/2 cup freshly grated fontina cheese
(or Gruyère or Parmesan)
1 tablespoon butter

1. Clean the chanterelles, halving the bigger ones. Wash the frisée lettuce and spin it dry. Set mushrooms and lettuce aside. Cut the apricots diagonally into fine slices. Peel the onion and slice into thin strips. Make a vinaigrette out of the onion, 2 tablespoons of olive oil, red wine vinegar and rosemary. Season with salt and pepper. Add the apricots.

2. To make the polenta, boil the vegetable stock with the cream. Season with salt, pepper and a pinch of nutmeg. Slowly pour in the polenta, stirring continuously with a whisk for 10 minutes allowing the mixture to expand. Fold fontina and butter into the polenta and pour into a serving dish.

3. On high heat, sauté the chanterelles in 2 tablespoons of olive oil for 2–3 minutes. Add salt and pepper and toss them with the frisée in the vinaigrette. Serve the salad on the polenta.

Preparation time: 30 minutes

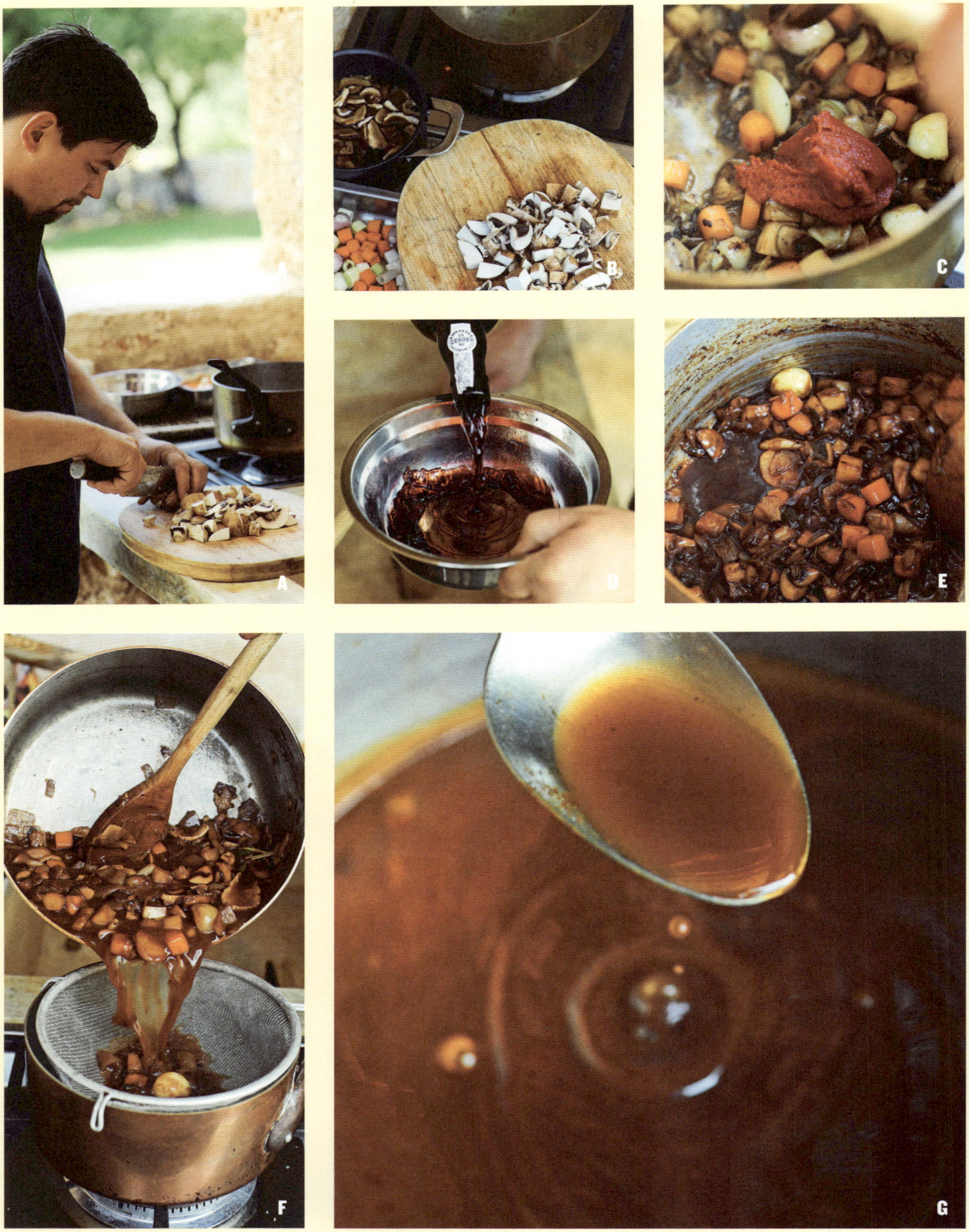
A
B
C
D
E
F
G

Gravy *intense, deep, strong*

Makes approx. 2 cups

4 1/2 tablespoons dried porcini mushrooms
mixed greens for soup (e.g. 1 carrot, 1/4 celery root, 1/2 leek, 2 stems of parsley)
8 shallots
10 brown mushrooms
2 tablespoons olive oil
2 garlic cloves
1 teaspoon black peppercorns
1 tablespoon tomato paste
1/2 cup red wine
1/2 cup red port (or 1/2 cup red wine and 1 teaspoon sugar)
2 stems thyme
3 bay leaves
1 tablespoon soy sauce

1. Soften the porcini mushrooms in 4 1/2 cups of hot water. Wash and dice the mixed soup greens. Peel the shallots and cut them in half. Clean the brown mushrooms, chop into chunks (A) and sauté on a high heat with 1 tablespoon of olive oil. Remove and set aside (B). Put the soup greens with the shallots and the rest of the oil into a pot and sear it.
2. Pour in 3 1/2 tablespoons of water to deglaze the contents in the bottom of the pot. Let the water evaporate and now fry the vegetables until dark brown. Peel the garlic cloves and add along with the black peppercorns and tomato purée to the pot (C). Continue sautéing until a new crust forms on the bottom of the pan.
3. Pour in red wine and deglaze again, stirring all the time. Cook until the liquid has reduced and thickened. Add the port (D) and reduce again (E). Add thyme and bay leaves. Pour in the porcini mushrooms with the water they have soaked in. Reduce for 20 minutes, uncovered. Then strain the juice through a sieve, reserving the liquid.
4. Mix the stewed vegetables with 2/3 cup of fresh water, sieve again (F) and add to the juice. Season with soy sauce and cook, uncovered, for another 10 minutes

Preparation time: 50 minutes

VARIATIONS: You can vary the gravy with all sorts of seasonings and extra ingredients, for example: chopped fresh herbs, roasted nuts, cranberries, chopped olives or fried mushrooms. If you add heavy cream, you will create a lovely, creamy sauce.

"This is incredible! As a cook, over the years I was taught that stock can only be made out of bones, that I have to roast a dead animal to get flavor. We cooks make a huge fuss about this. After all, stock is the signature of a chef. So we thought about how we could develop a really dark, intensely flavored 'stock' for our green kitchen. We sure outdid ourselves on this one."

Grilled Asparagus with Parmesan-Polenta and Pine Nut Gravy

Ingredients (serves 2—4)

1 3/4 cups milk
salt
2/3 cup polenta (cornmeal)
2 ounces Parmesan
1 bunch green asparagus
olive oil
2 tablespoons pine nuts
1/2 cup gravy (page 103)
1 teaspoon raisins

1. Boil the milk with 1 pinch of salt. Stir in the polenta. Cook for 2—3 minutes. Finely grate the Parmesan and stir into the polenta. Between 2 sheets of oiled parchment paper, pour out the polenta to a thickness of 1 1/4 inches. Allow to cool for 40 minutes.

2. Peel the lower third of the asparagus spears and cut off the ends (cut the fat spears in half). Cook the asparagus for 1 minute in boiling water and then rinse in cold water. Drain on paper towels and drizzle with 1 tablespoon of olive oil. Toast the pine nuts in an ungreased frying pan.

3. Cut the cooled polenta into bite-sized strips. Pour a little olive oil in a pan and fry the polenta slices for 2—3 minutes on each side. Set aside and cover with a dish towel to keep them warm. Fry the asparagus spears for 2—3 minutes. Season with salt.

4. Boil the gravy with the raisins, stir in the roasted pine nuts and serve with the asparagus and polenta.

Preparation time: 30 minutes (+ 40 minutes for cooling)

VARIATIONS: you can make polenta with grana padano cheese, pecorino or a strong-tasting mountain cheese instead of Parmesan. If you prefer, you can season the polenta with roughly ground black pepper, finely grated truffles and a few cut rosemary needles or finely chopped, sun-dried tomatoes. Instead of pine nuts, you can also use toasted sliced hazelnuts.

TIP: If you haven't made any gravy, you can serve the dish with a pine nut-raisin butter instead. Melt 4 tablespoons of butter and add the raisins and toasted pine nuts. Season with 1 tablespoon of balsamic vinegar and a little salt.

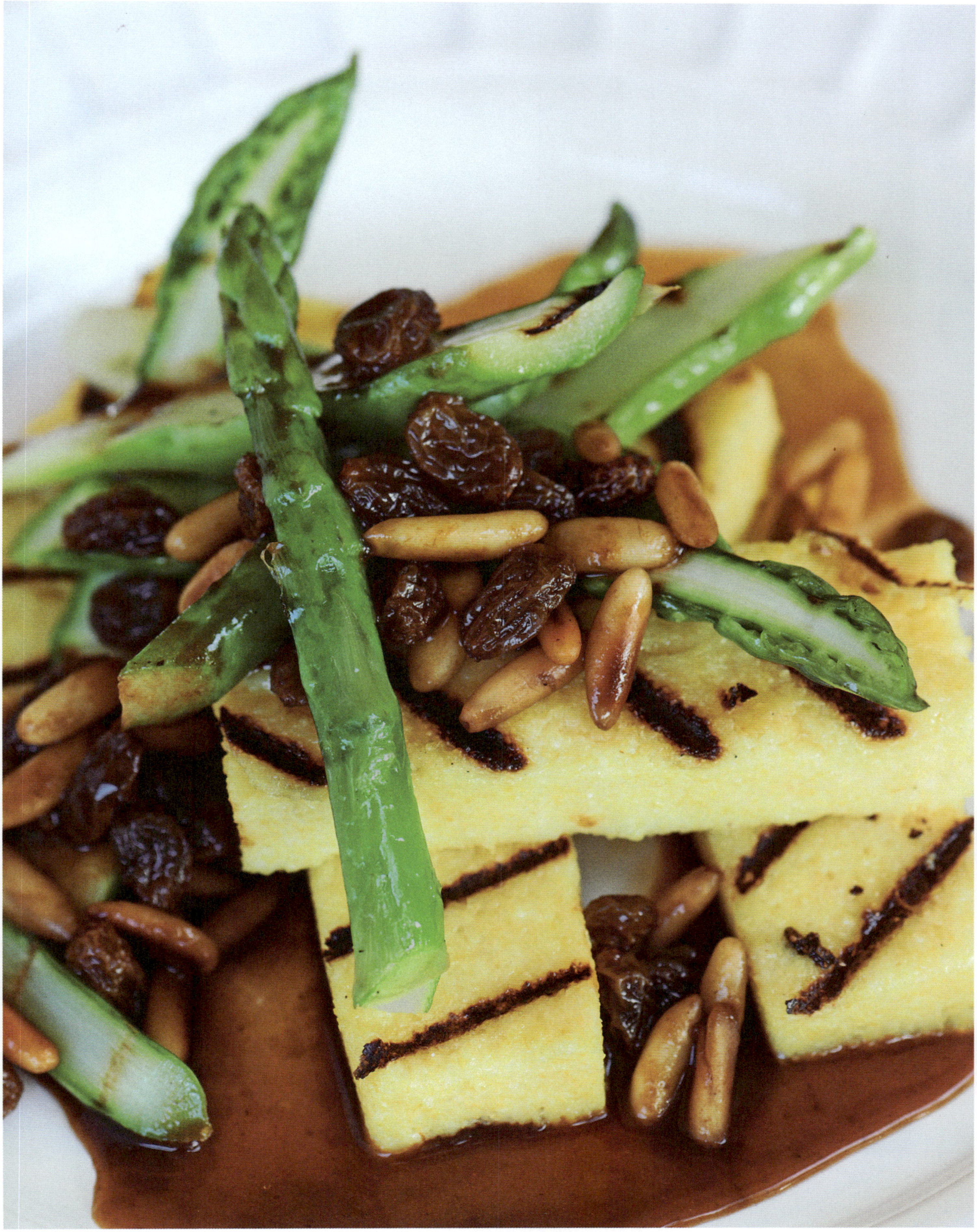

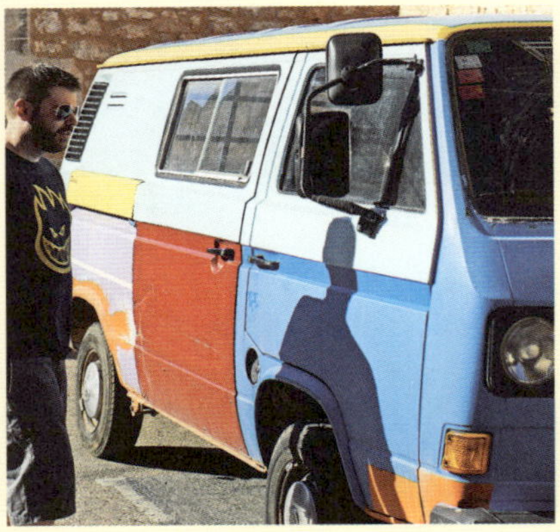
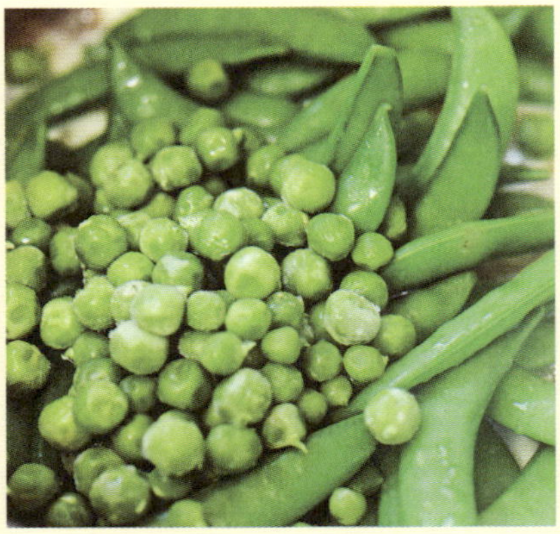
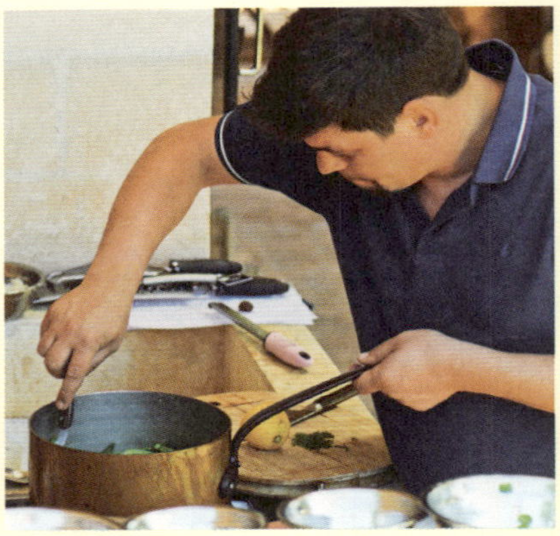
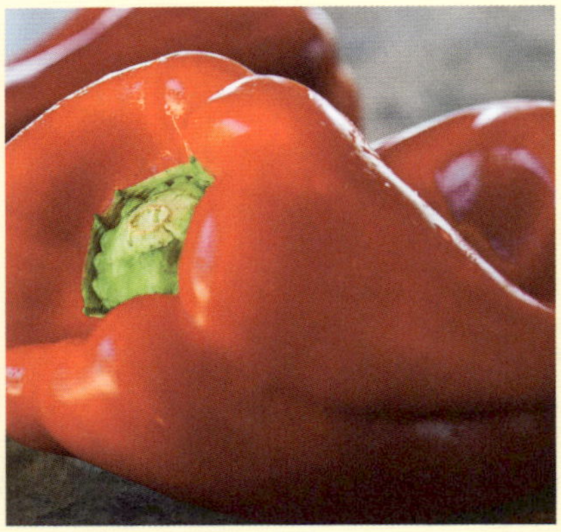
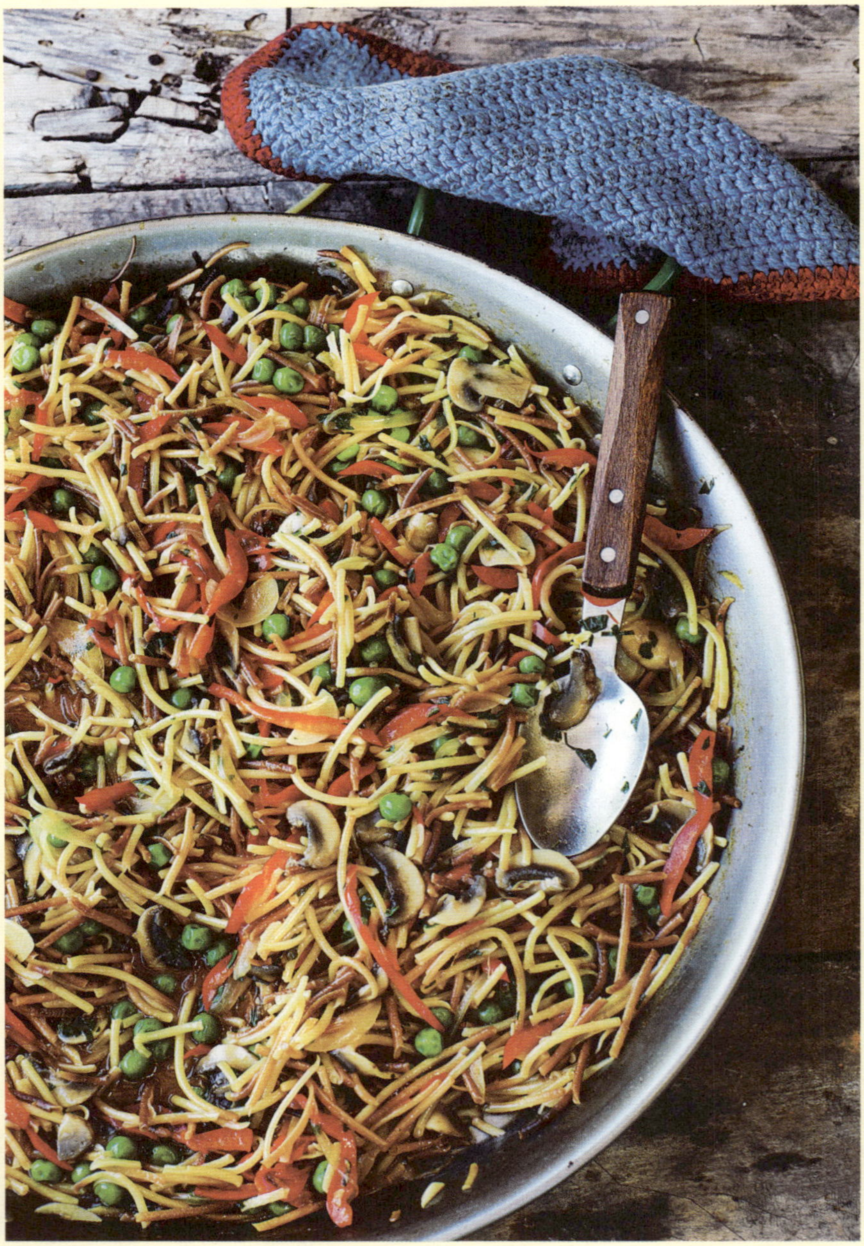
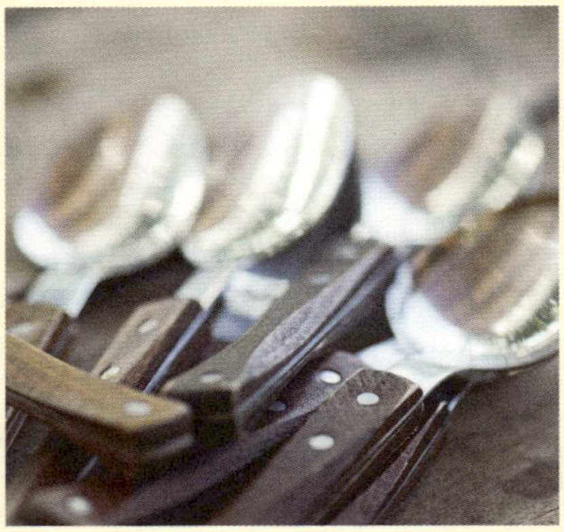
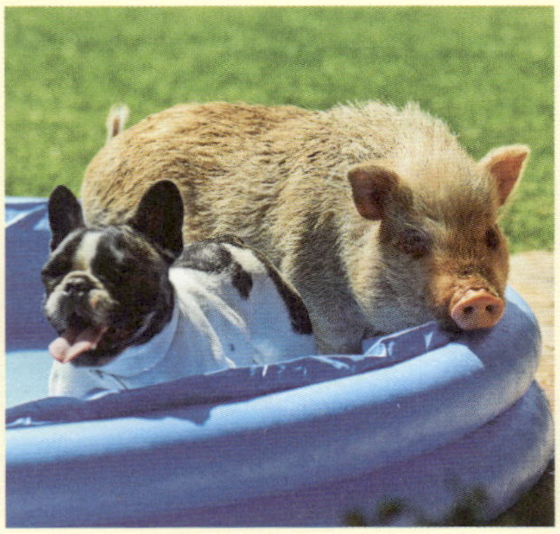

Pasta Paella

Ingredients (serves 4—6)

- 1 red bell pepper
- 1 Spanish onion
- 1/2 pound brown mushrooms
- 2 garlic cloves
- 1 1/3 cups peas (frozen)
- 20 threads of saffron (or 1 pinch of ground saffron)
- 4 1/3 cups vegetable stock
- 4 tablespoons olive oil
- 11 ounces vermicelli egg noodles
- 5 stems parsley
- salt
- 1/2—1 teaspoon sambal oelek (Indonesian chili paste; or chili sauce)

1. Wash the bell pepper, quarter it and remove the seeds and then cut into strips. Peel and dice the onion. Clean the brown mushrooms and cut into slices. Peel and chop the garlic. Lay the peas out to defrost.
2. Bring the saffron threads with the vegetable stock to the boil. Sauté the vegetables (not the peas) in hot olive oil for 5 minutes.
3. Take the vegetables out of the pan, put in the egg noodles and toast until light brown. Return the vegetables to the pan, pour in the stock little by little until the noodles are soft.
4. Stir the chopped parsley and peas in at the end. Season with salt and sambal oelek.

Preparation time: 35 minutes

» The noodles are key. You toast them in the pan until they're light brown. That way they acquire a special flavor before you cook them. «

CONNECT FOUR WITH CAULIFLOWER

In the 19th century, cauliflower was thought to be one of the kings of the vegetable garden, along with artichokes and asparagus. Cooked briefly or fried in a hot pan, it is a delicate vegetable with a firm texture and a refined taste. Cauliflower contains mustard oils that lend a sophisticated flavor to the vegetable. It tastes best fresh. Its season starts in May and lasts until fall.

1 Miguel's Raw Cauliflower Salad

Wash **1 pound of cauliflower** and break up into rosettes. Drizzle **3 tablespoons of sherry vinegar** and **5 tablespoons of smoked olive oil** (or regular extra virgin olive oil) over the cauliflower and season with **salt** and **pepper**. Cut a little **green from 1 scallion** and chop into thin strips, sprinkling over the cauliflower.

2 Cauliflower with Polish Salsa

Boil **1 small head of cauliflower** in salted water for 12–15 minutes. Boil **2 eggs** for 8–10 minutes. Remove the eggs and let cool in cold water. Keep the cauliflower warm in the boiled water. Peel the eggs and chop into small pieces. Grate the peel of an **organic lemon** and squeeze the lemon to get the juice. Chop **3 stems of thyme.** Mix all the ingredients except the cauliflower with **1 tablespoon of olive oil.** Season with **salt** and **pepper.** Lift the cauliflower out of the boiled water, drain and serve covered in the egg salsa.

4 Cauliflower Soup

Peel and slice **3 shallots.** Wash **1 pound of cauliflower** and chop into small pieces. Melt **1 1/2 tablespoons of butter** in a pot and on medium heat, sauté the shallots with **1 teaspoon of fennel seeds** for 3 minutes or until glazed. Add the cauliflower, cook for 2 minutes and season with **salt** and **1 pinch of sugar.** Add **1/4 cup of white wine** and bring to a boil. Pour in **3 1/2 cups of vegetable stock** and **1/2 cup of heavy cream.** Simmer on a low heat for 20 minutes. Purée with a hand blender. Thin with some **stock** if desired. Drizzle a **few drops of olive oil** on top before serving.

3 Fried Cauliflower with Sesame

Wash **1 pound of cauliflower,** separate into large rosettes and cut these into slices. Heat **2 tablespoons of olive oil** and **1 teaspoon of sesame oil** in a large non-stick frying pan. Fry the cauliflower on medium heat for 4 minutes. Toast **1 tablespoon of sesame seeds** in a second frying pan without oil. Add **salt** to the cauliflower and sprinkle with sesame seeds.

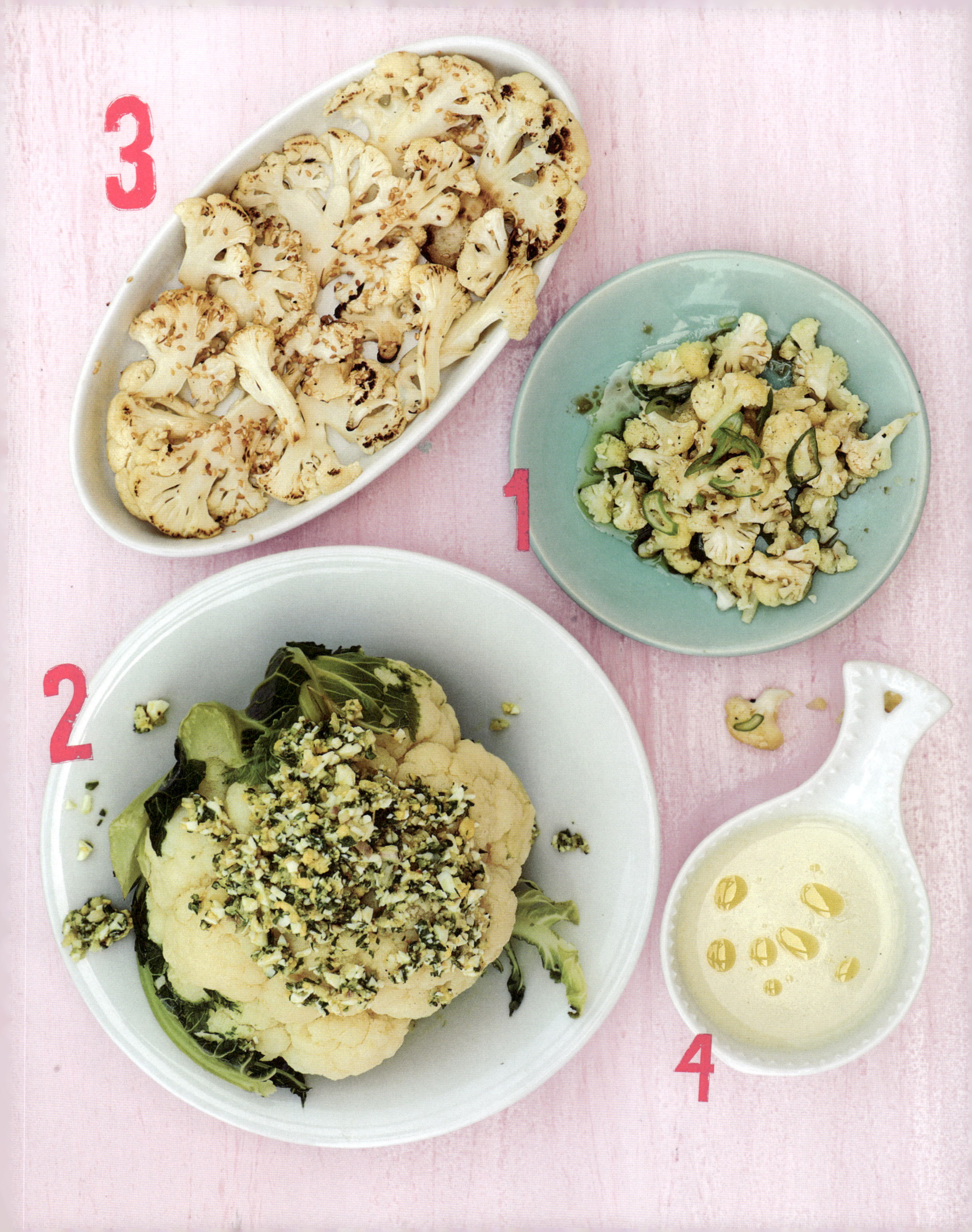
3
1
2
4

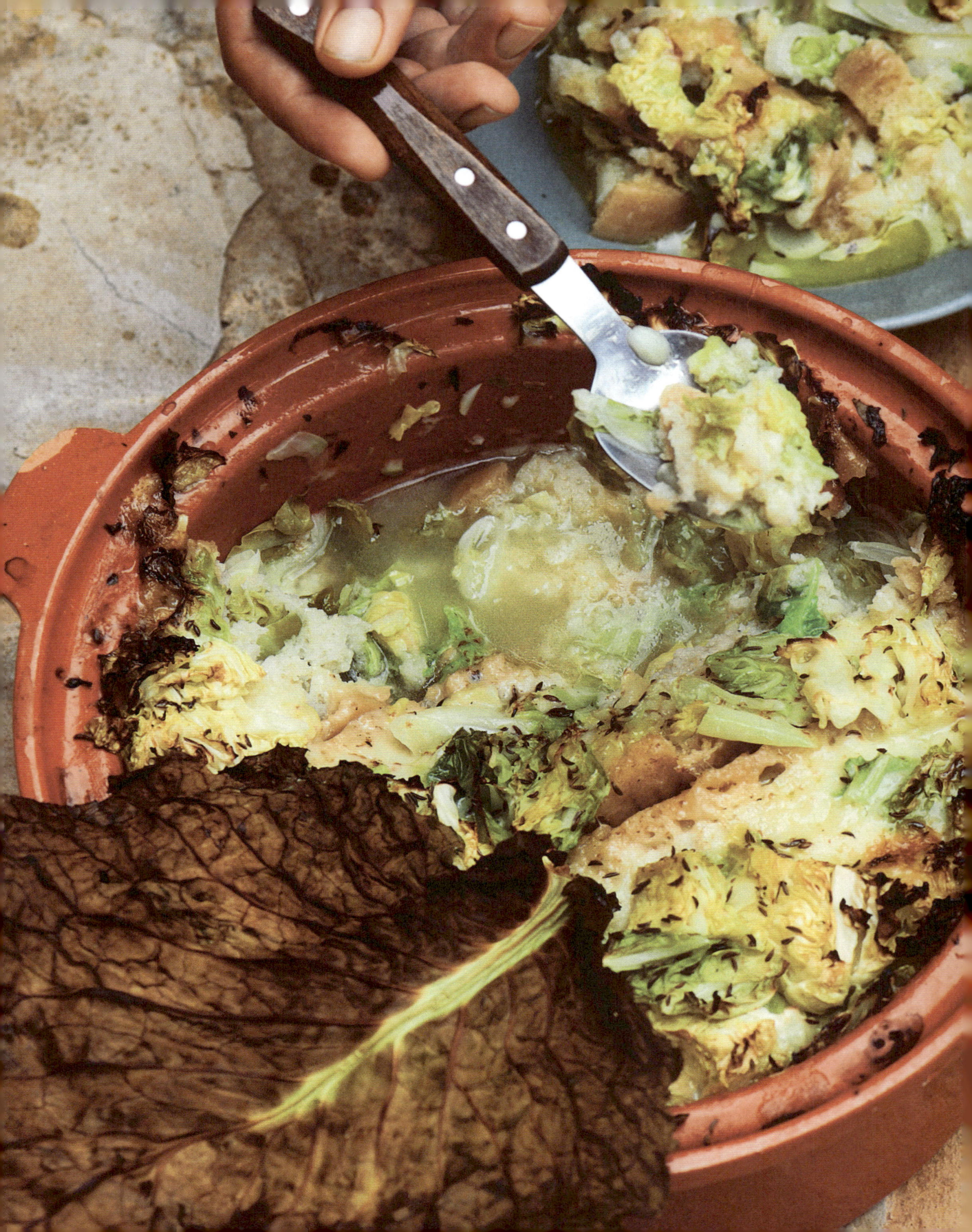

Savoy Fondue with Bread, Stock and Swiss Cheese

Ingredients (serves 6)

1 1/2 pounds savoy cabbage
2 Spanish onions
6 cloves garlic
1 1/3 pounds young/middle-aged Swiss cheese (such as Gruyère or Appenzeller)
1/2 cup white wine
1 tablespoon caraway seeds
8 1/2 cups strong vegetable stock
salt and pepper
nutmeg
8 large slices white bread
butter
olive oil

1. Quarter the savoy cabbage, remove the stem. Set aside a large leaf and cut the rest in broad strips. Peel the onions and cut into wedges. Peel the garlic and cut into thin slices. Slice the cheese. Bring the white wine to a boil with caraway seeds and add the vegetable stock. Season with salt, pepper and freshly grated nutmeg.
2. Layer the cabbage, onions, garlic and cheese with the slices of bread in a buttered, ovenproof dish. Pour the stock over it and place the large cabbage leaf on top.
3. Preheat the oven to 400°F and place the covered dish on the bottom shelf to cook for 45 minutes. Serve with freshly ground pepper and a little olive oil on top.

Preparation time: 60 minutes

VARIATIONS: This dish also tastes excellent drizzled with a little pumpkin seed oil — it's a perfect compliment to raclette cheese.

>> This is definitly not "Nouvelle Cuisine". A meal for real guys to take with them on hiking and skiing trips. <<

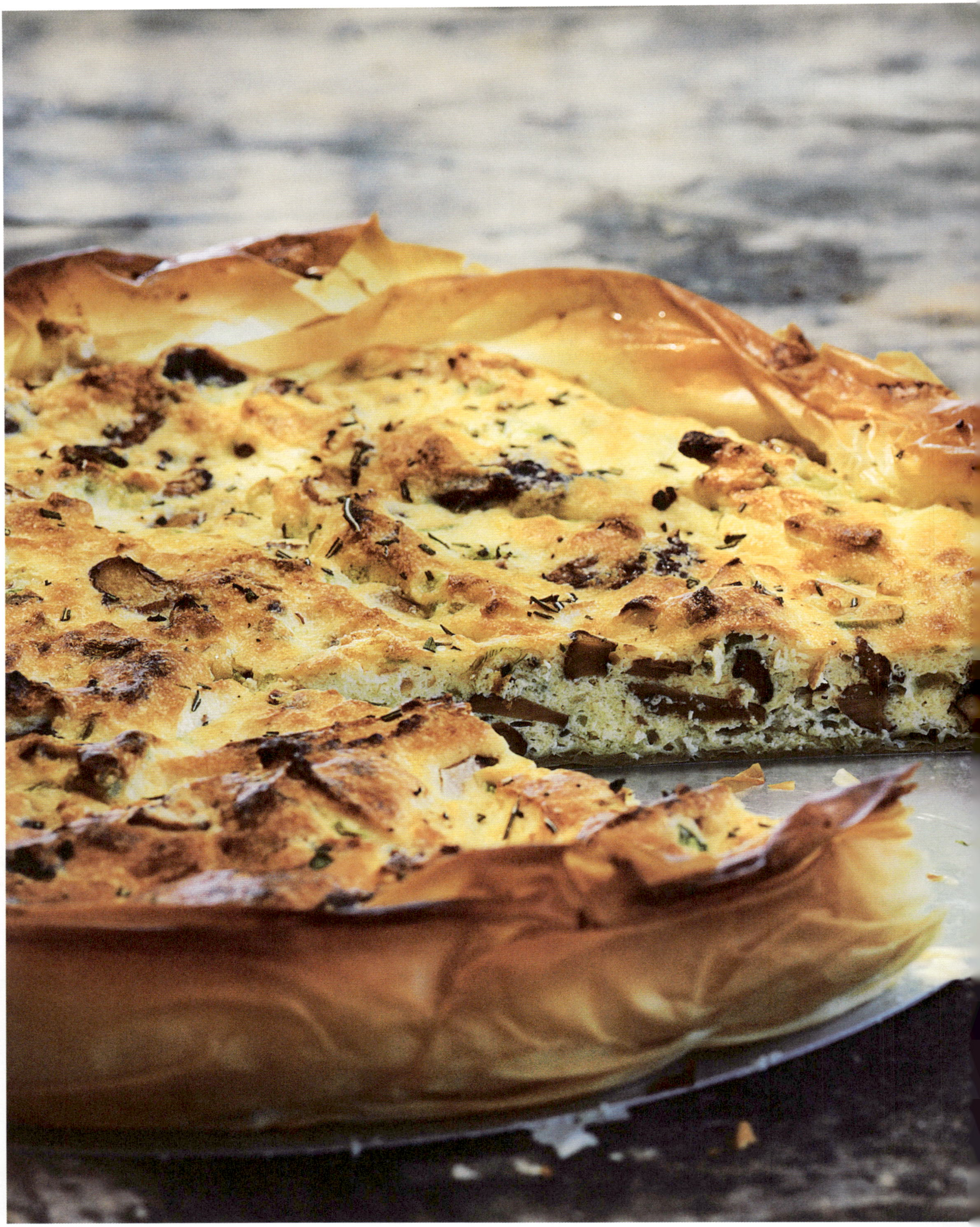

Chanterelle Ricotta Tart "Filo!"

Ingredients (serves 4—6)

- 10 ounces chanterelles
- 5 scallions
- 1 stem rosemary
- 1 garlic clove
- 3 tablespoons olive oil
- salt and pepper
- 1 1/2 cups ricotta
- 3 large eggs
- 6 tablespoons butter
- 3 sheets yufka pastry (18 x 14 inches, see note)

1. Clean the chanterelles and cut into pieces. Wash the scallions and cut into thin rings. Strip off and finely chop some rosemary needles. Peel and chop the garlic. Heat oil in a frying pan and sauté the chanterelles for 3 minutes on high heat. Add scallions, garlic and rosemary and sauté for another 2 minutes. Season with salt and pepper and put into a bowl to cool.

2. Beat the ricotta with a hand blender until creamy. Separate the eggs. Fold the yolks into the ricotta and add the cooled mushroom mixture. Season well with salt and pepper. Whisk the egg whites with a pinch of salt until stiff and then fold in.

3. Melt the butter in a pan. Cut the yufka pastry sheets lengthwise in half. Brush a little butter on a tart dish (diameter approx. 12 inches). Place a yufka sheet in the dish and fold the edges in to form a crust. Brush a little more butter on the sheet of pastry. Follow this method with all of the sheets. Fill with the ricotta and mushroom mixture and smooth the top. Preheat the oven to 400°F (convection: 360°F). Bake in the middle rack for 30—35 minutes until golden brown.

Preparation time: 60 minutes

FILO PASTRY, also called yufka dough or malsouka dough, is commonly used in Turkish, Greek and Arabic cuisine. The thin sheets of pastry are similar to strudel pastry and are very easy to work with. You can find filo pastry in well-stocked grocery stores.

TOFU & TEMPEH – Eating culture from Asia

Although many believe that seitan, tofu and tempeh are boring, uninspiring **MEAT SUBSTITUTES**, they are, in fact, food with a **VERY OLD TRADITION**, history and culture. All three have very different textures so they can be **USED IN VARIOUS WAYS** in cooking. They should not be confused with processed meat substitutes that are generally based on seitan and tofu. These chemically treated substitutes in the form of fried sausages and artificial burgers usually taste like sawdust. The real stuff has a **SUBTLE FLAVOR**, but a very interesting texture. You can heavily season seitan, tofu and tempeh, marinate them in herb oil, spread herb paste on them and fry them in tasty breadcrumb mixtures.

TOFU is made from soy bean curds that are produced when soy milk curdles. (Chinese "to" means "bean," "fu" means "curdle.") The various types of fresh tofu get their different textures when the curds are poured into a mold and the liquid is pressed out. Tender silken tofu has the highest water content; it can be eaten in a smooth puréed form and used as a cream or mayonnaise substitute. Firmer types of tofu can be fried, deep-fried and cooked. They are available plain, slightly smoked or with various seasonings.

TEMPEH originally comes from Indonesia and is made from soy beans fermented with fungal spores. The fungal spores break down the bean proteins and make the tempeh easier to digest. Tempeh is very versatile and puts up with a lot: it can be fried, baked, stewed and deep-fried. With a smear of blue cheese it tastes nutty.

TIP

Tofu and tempeh spoil very quickly so you should always buy them fresh and keep them well-refrigerated. Grocery stores and organic shops usually keep them vacuum packed.

soya beans

smoked tofu

tempeh

silken tofu

tofu

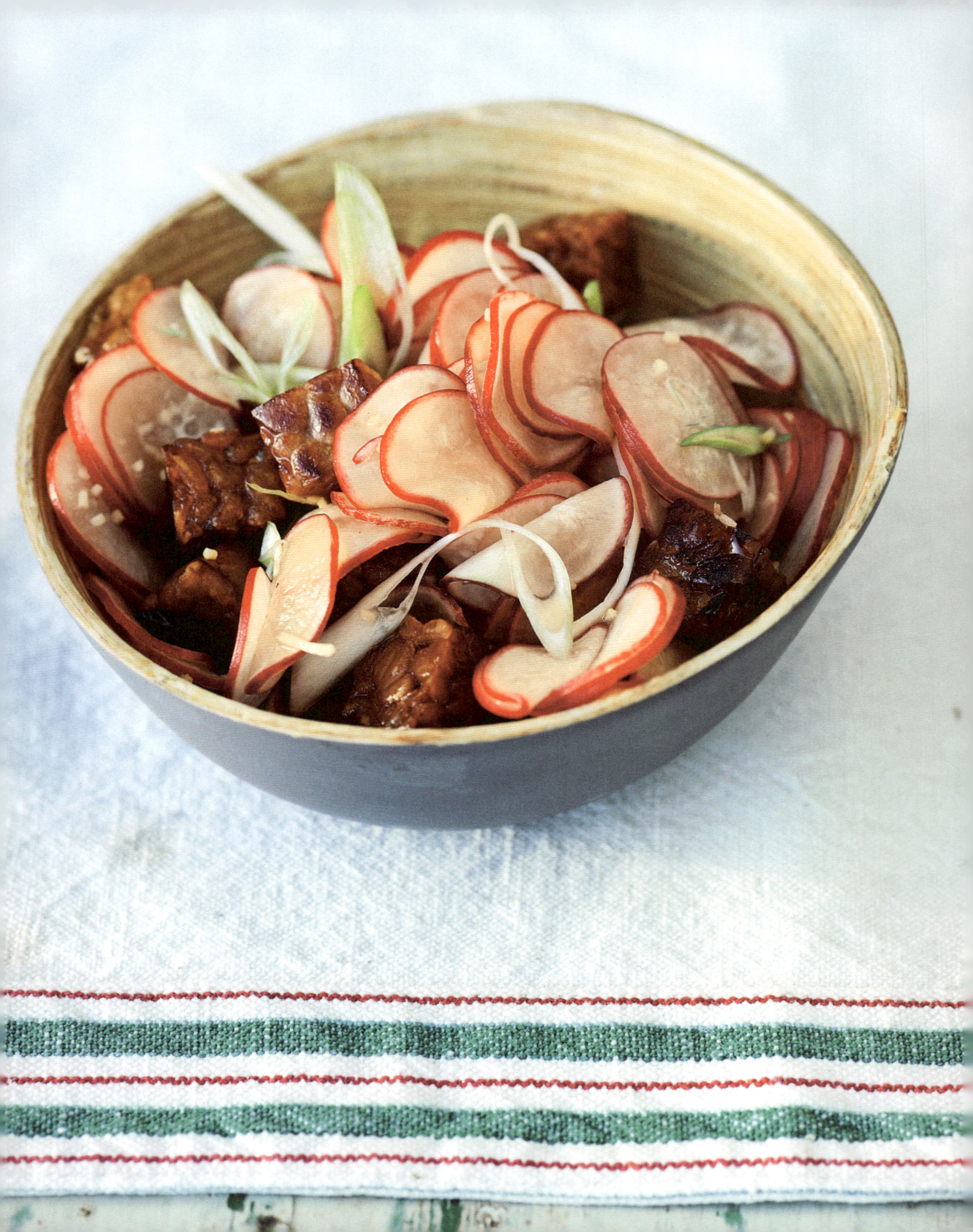

Asian Radish with Crispy Tempeh

Ingredients (serves 4)

3/4 inch fresh ginger
4 tablespoons sugar
8 tablespoons soy sauce
1 tablespoon white wine vinegar
1 tablespoon olive oil
1 teaspoon sesame oil
salt
2 bunches small radishes
6 tablespoons freshly squeezed orange juice
1 tablespoon honey
9 ounces tempeh (see note)
2 scallions

1. Peel and dice the ginger and mix with 2 tablespoons of sugar and 3 tablespoons of soy sauce, 1 tablespoon of white wine vinegar, 1 tablespoon of olive oil, sesame oil and season with salt. Wash the radishes and cut them into thin slices. Mix them with the vinaigrette and set aside.

2. To make the tempeh sauce, blend the remaining 5 tablespoons of soy sauce with orange juice and honey until smooth. Dice the tempeh into bite-sized pieces. Cover the bottom of a pan with oil and sauté the chopped tempeh on a medium heat until golden brown. Drain on paper towels. Pour off the oil from the pan. Put the tempeh cubes back into the pan with the tempeh sauce and boil just until the sauce thickens.

3. Wash the scallions, cut diagonally into thin slices and scatter them with the tempeh cubes over the radish salad.

Preparation time: 30 minutes

TEMPEH originally comes from Indonesia and is made out of soy beans fermented with fungus spores. The fungus spores break down the bean protein and make it more easy to digest. Tempeh has many uses and can put up with a lot: you can fry tempeh, bake, stew or deep fry it. You can buy the bean slices that are loaded with dietary fibers in Asian shops or natural food stores.

Steamed Silk Tofu with Carrot Butter

Ingredients (serves 4)

12 ounces firm silk tofu (see note)
salt and pepper
1 small kohlrabi
1/2–3/4 inch fresh ginger
1 firm pear
1 scallion
1–2 teaspoons lemon juice
1 tablespoon olive oil
2/3 cup carrot juice (preferably freshly juiced, or bottled)
6 tablespoons cold butter

1. Cut the tofu into 4 portions. Boil 1 1/2 inches of water with a little salt in a pan. Carefully place the tofu in the water. Take the pan off the heat and cover the tofu for 10 minutes.
2. To make the salad, peel the kohlrabi and ginger into thin slices and then into thin strips. Wash and quarter the pear, remove the core and cut the quarters into thin slices and then into thin strips. Wash the scallion and cut into thin strips. Mix with the lemon juice and olive oil and season with salt and pepper.
3. Boil the carrot juice in a small pan, uncovered, until reduced to 4 tablespoons. Dice the cold butter and stir in. Season to taste with salt and a dash of lemon juice.
4. Lift the tofu out of the pan and drain. Arrange with the salad and serve on the carrot butter.

Preparation time: 25 minutes

TOFU is obtained from white soybean dough which is produced when soy milk curdles. As opposed to the firmer types of tofu, the softer, delicate silk tofu is not drained or pressed; therefore, it is very damp. You can buy either creamy/soft or firm tofu.

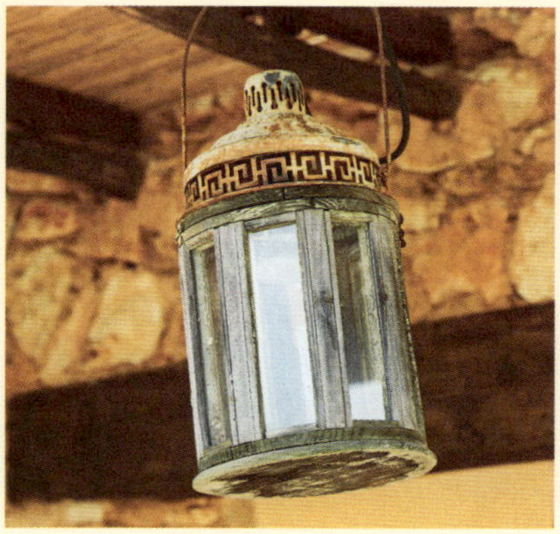
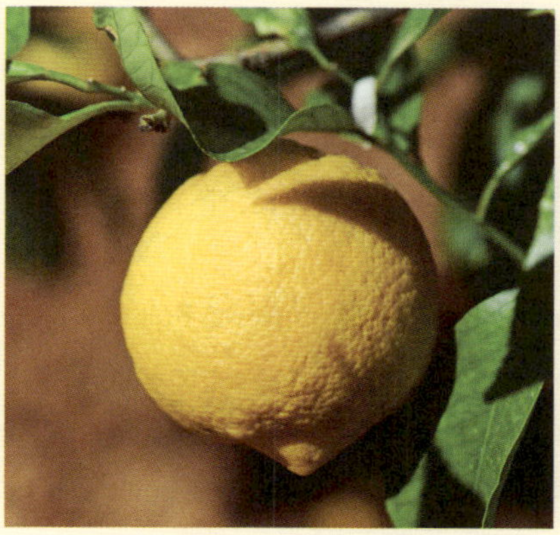
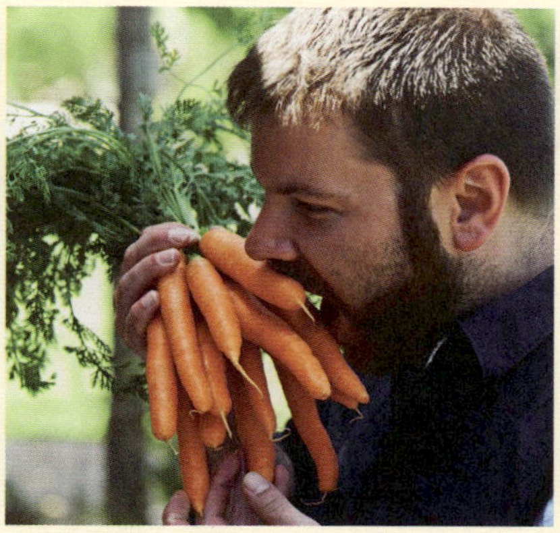
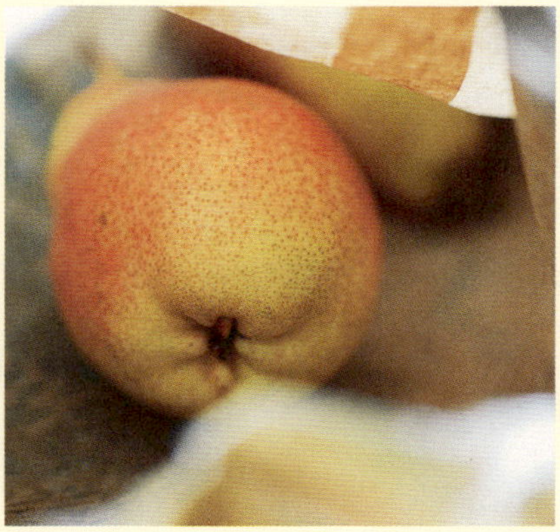
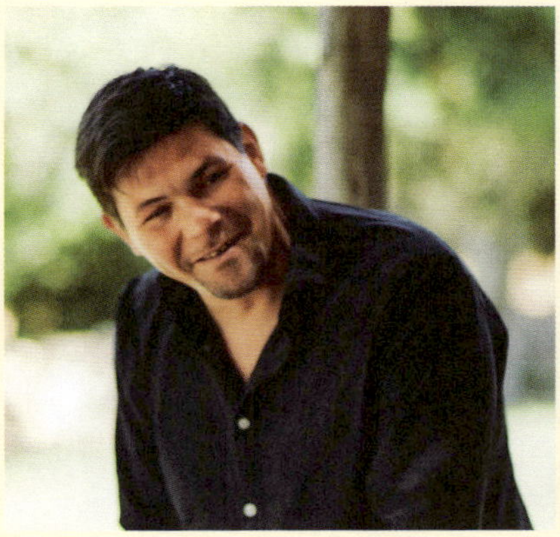
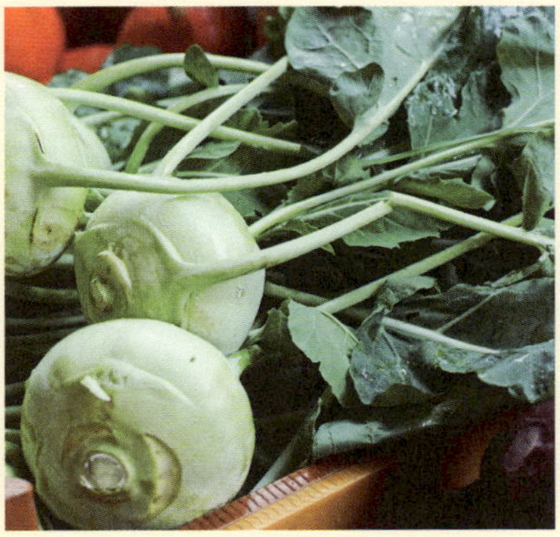
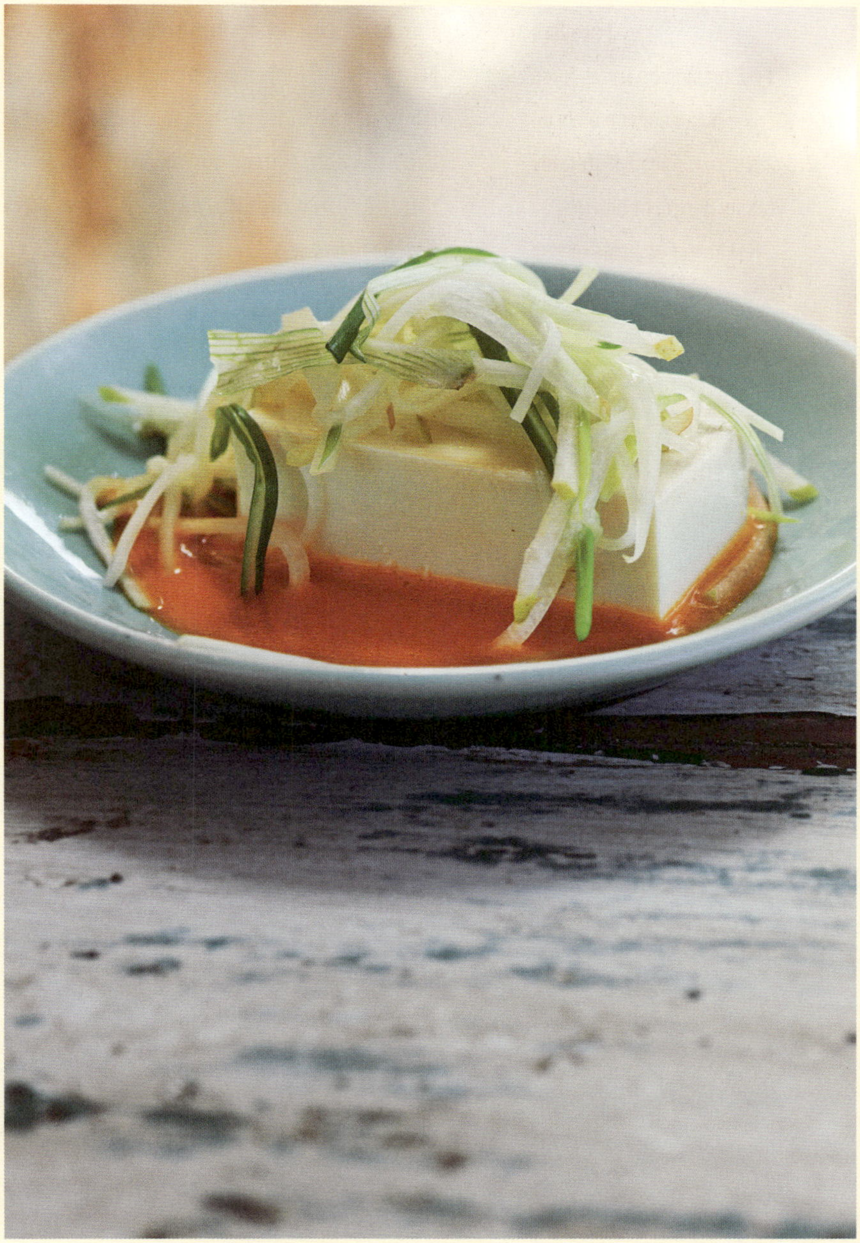

3X PESTO
PLUS THE CLASSIC ONE

Smoked Almond Pesto
Coarsely purée in a blender or food processor **1/3 cup of salted, smoked almonds** with **3—4 tablespoons of Parmesan, 1 peeled garlic clove, 4 stems of parsley** and **10 tablespoons of olive oil**. Season with **salt**.

Green Olive Pesto with Macadamia Nuts and Orange
Dice **1/2 cup of pitted green olives**. Chop **6 tablespoons of toasted macadamia nuts** in a blender and blend with the olives, **1 tablespoon of chopped cilantro greens**, the **grated peel of 1 organic orange, 8 tablespoons of olive oil** and the **juice of 1/2 of an orange** until smooth.

TIP If you are in a hurry, you can make the pesto in the blender as described above.
If you have a little more time on your hands, it is worth making the pesto in a mortar, because the flavors will come together in a more intense and aromatic way.

PESTO SAUCES are the means to create a savory vegetarian dish the fastest way possible. The only things missing are your favorite pasta, boiled potatoes or fried vegetables – and your quick, everyday soul food is ready.

Tomato Pistachio Pesto with Couscous

Roughly blend **1/4 cup of dried tomatoes** together with **9 tablespoons of green pistachios**, **1 tablespoon of couscous** and **10 tablespoons of olive oil**.

Classic Basil Pesto

Toast **4 tablespoons of pine nuts** in an ungreased pan until golden brown and allow to cool. Chop **2 bunches of basil** and blend in the blender with the pine nuts and **1 peeled garlic clove**. Pour in **8–10 tablespoons of olive oil**. Mix in **6 1/2 tablespoons of freshly grated Parmesan** and season with **salt** and **pepper**.

Green Ratatouille with Sweet Stewed Chicory

Ingredients (serves 4)

4 heads Belgian endive
4 tablespoons olive oil
3 tablespoons butter
1 tablespoon honey
juice of 1 orange
salt and pepper
1 large onion
1/4 pound celery sticks
1 green bell pepper
1/2 pound zucchini
1/2 cucumber
1 tablespoon fennel seeds
3 1/2 tablespoons cold butter
white wine vinegar
2 stems dill

1. Cut the Belgian endive in half and fry on high heat in 2 tablespoons of olive oil. Add butter until light brown. Add honey and cook for 2 minutes. Pour in orange juice and cook for another 2 minutes. Season with salt and pepper.
2. Peel the onion. Wash the celery sticks and dice with the pepper and zucchini. Chop the cucumber into large pieces and purée them with a hand blender until smooth.
3. Strain the juice through a sieve and season with salt. Sauté the diced vegetables with the fennel seeds in 2 tablespoons of olive oil. Deglaze with the cucumber juice. Reduce the mixture, uncovered, by half. Chop up the cold butter and melt it in the vegetables. Bring to a boil once, season with a dash of white wine vinegar, freshly chopped dill, salt and pepper. Arrange the green vegetables with the endives on a plate and serve immediately.

Preparation time: 30 minutes

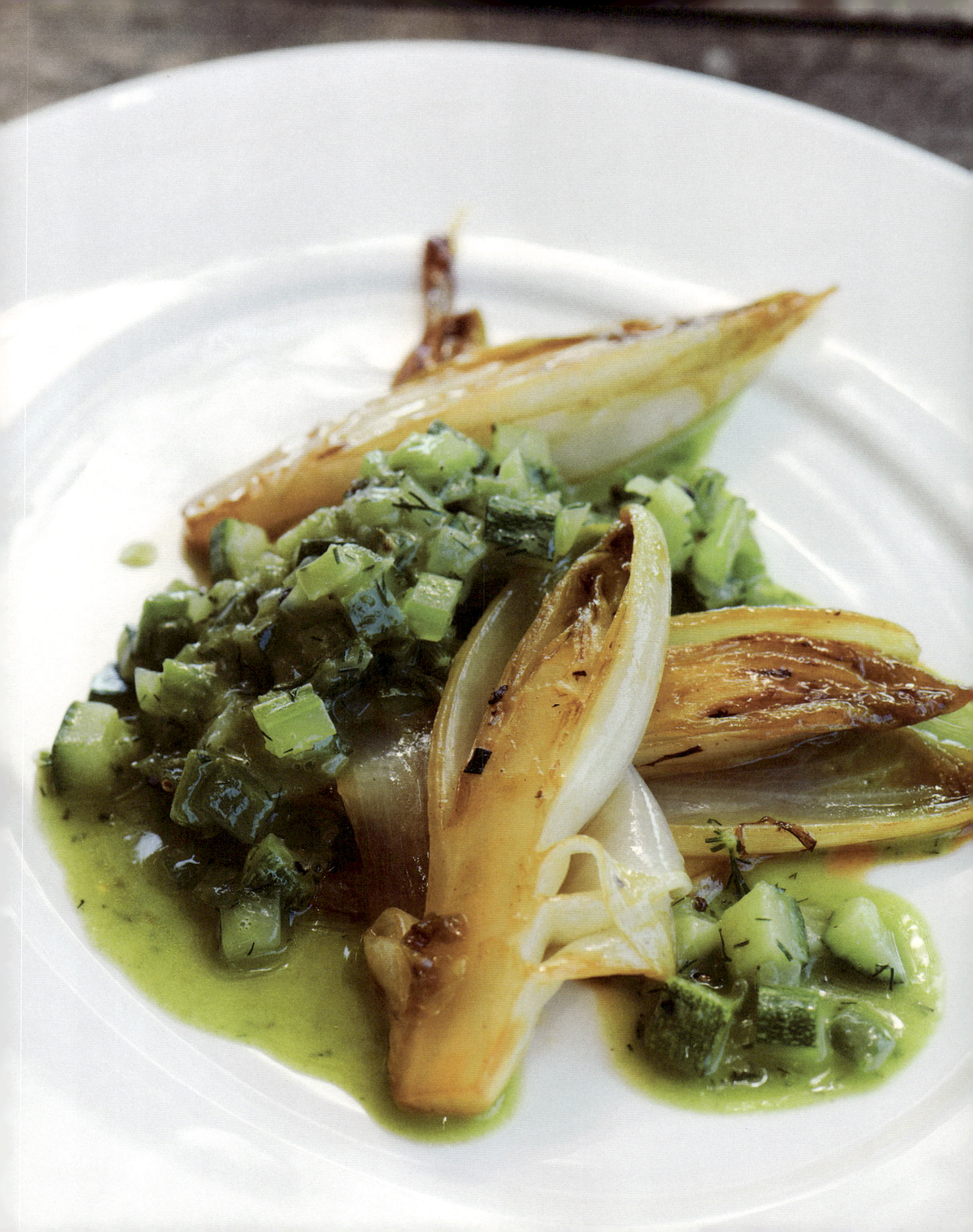

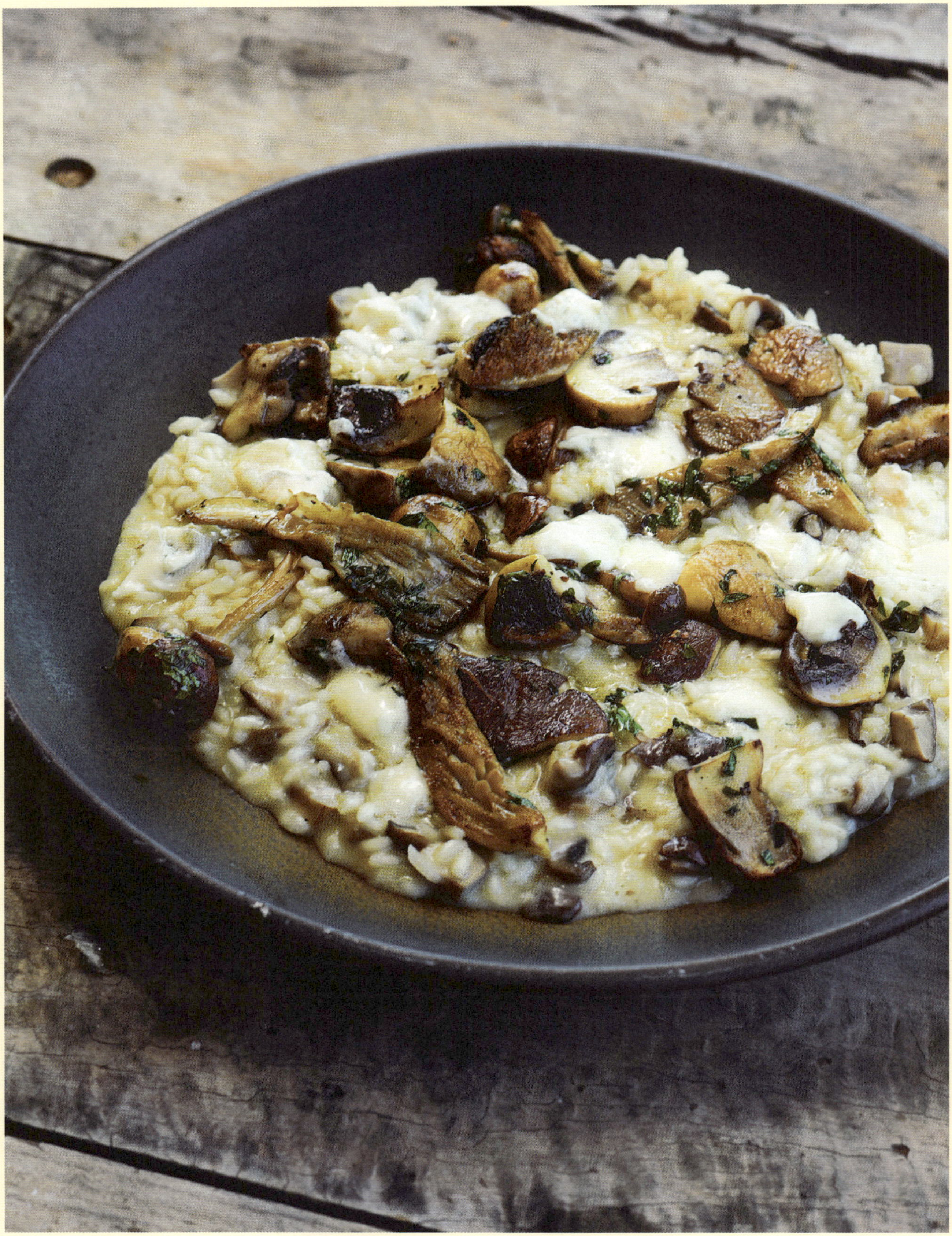

Mushroom Risotto with Gorgonzola

Ingredients (serves 4)

1 pound mixed mushrooms
(e.g. white mushrooms,
oysters, porcini)
1 onion
1 garlic clove
6 tablespoons olive oil
1 1/2 cups risotto rice
1/2 cup dry white wine
4 cups hot vegetable stock
3 tablespoons butter
3—4 tablespoons freshly
grated Parmesan
salt
freshly ground black pepper
4 stems parsley
2 ounces Gorgonzola

1. Clean the mushrooms. Set aside one third of the mushrooms. Chop the rest of them into large pieces. Peel and dice the onion and garlic.
2. Heat 4 tablespoons of olive oil in a pan and sauté the chopped mushrooms, onions and garlic for 2—3 minutes. Add the rice and stir until it is shiny. Deglaze with white wine and bring to a boil. Add a little hot stock. Cook while stirring until the liquid has almost completely evaporated. Add some more stock. Cook the risotto this way for 25—30 minutes until it is tender.
3. Stir the risotto with the butter and Parmesan cheese until smooth. Sauté the remaining mushrooms in 2 tablespoons of olive oil until golden-brown. Roughly chop the parsley and fold it in. Season the mushrooms with salt and pepper and sprinkle them over the risotto. Crumble the Gorgonzola, sprinkle the cheese over the mushrooms and serve immediately.

Preparation time: 40 minutes

TIP Read the instructions on the risotto package carefully, as cooking times vary.

Black Salsify "à la Crème"

Ingredients (serves 4)
1 pound black salsify (see note)
1 organic lemon
4 1/2 tablespoons butter
1/2 teaspoon flour
1 cup heavy cream
salt and pepper
nutmeg
2 slices pumpernickel bread
sugar

1. Put on disposable gloves and peel the salsify (see note). Place the peeled salsify in lukewarm water with a dash of lemon juice.
2. Cut the black salsify into 1/2—3/4-inch long pieces and cook in 3 tablespoons of butter over medium heat for 3—4 minutes. Dust with flour and fold it in. Pour in cream and allow the sauce to thicken. Season to taste with salt, pepper, 1 pinch of freshly grated nutmeg and a dash of lemon juice.
3. Crumble the pumpernickel in a pan with 1 1/2 tablespoons of butter. Fry until crisp. Season with a pinch of sugar and salt and spread the mixture on the salsify. Serve right away.

Preparation time: 25 minutes

BLACK SALSIFY is not really in fashion anymore because the milky juice, which dribbles out during the peeling process, doesn't just stick to your hands, it also turns them brown. If you are brave enough to peel black salsify anyway, wear disposable gloves; we promise it will be worth the trouble! This fine, savory root vegetable has a unique taste that doesn't need much besides the cream and crispy pumpernickel crumbs.

Black salsify, the "winter asparagus," tastes nutty, savory and tart. Rediscovering this forgotten vegetable is worth it!

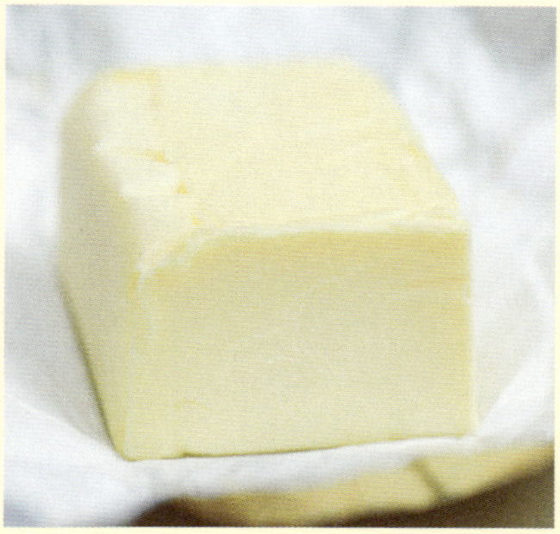
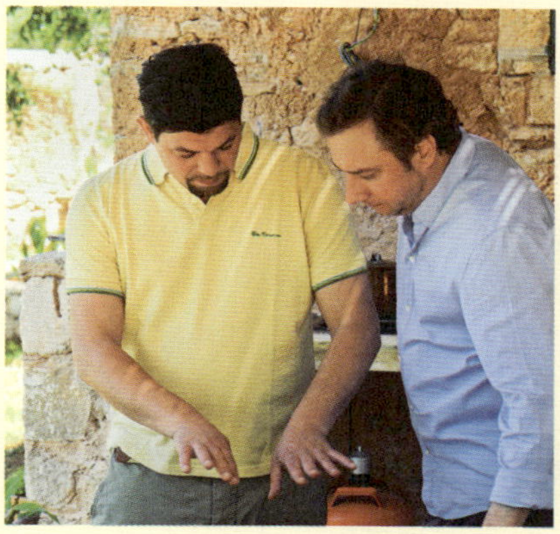
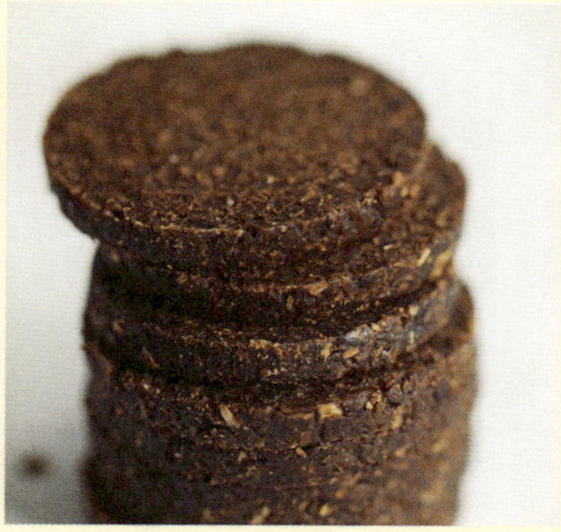
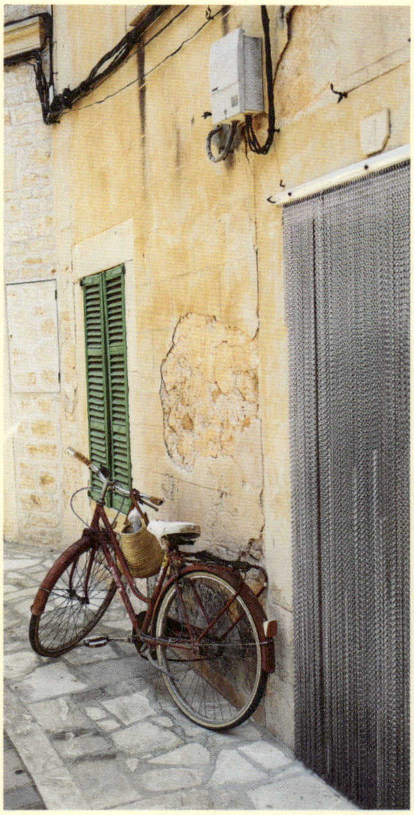
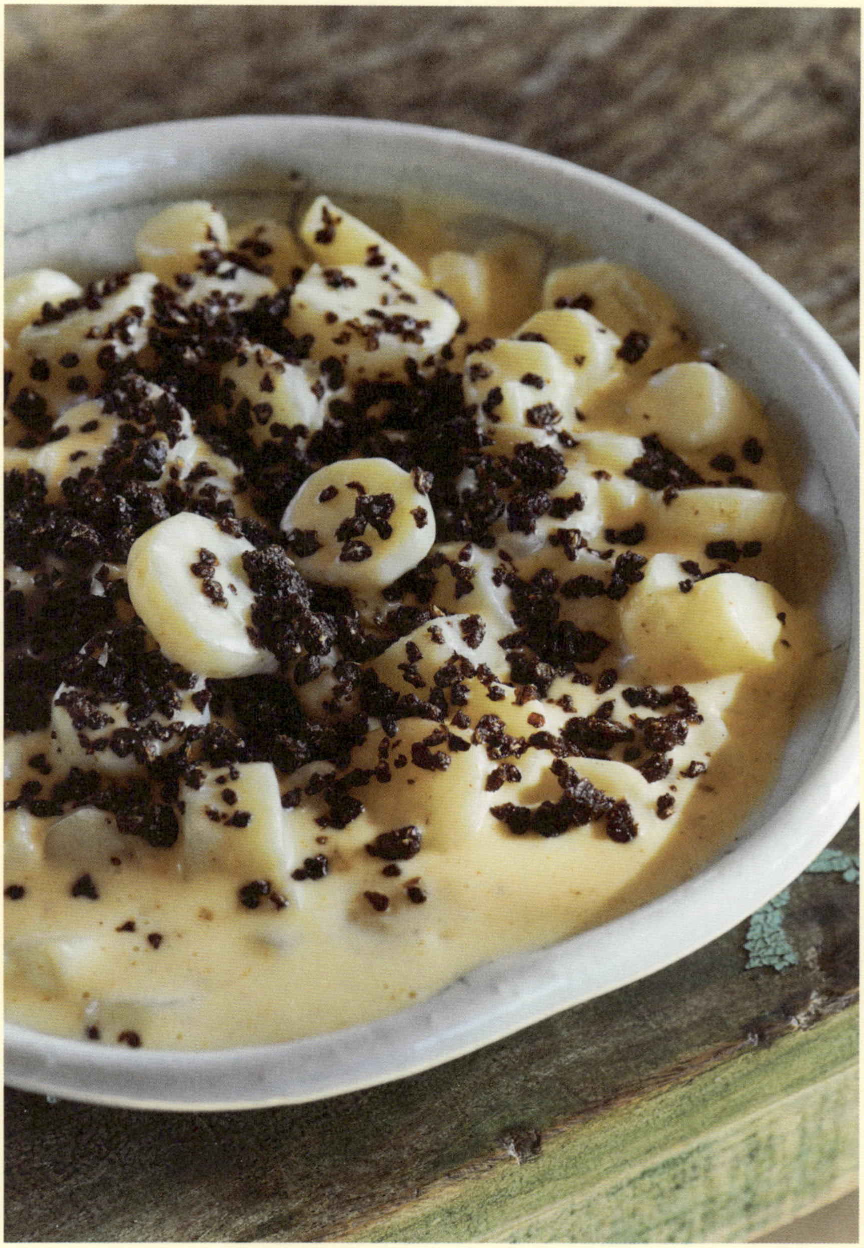
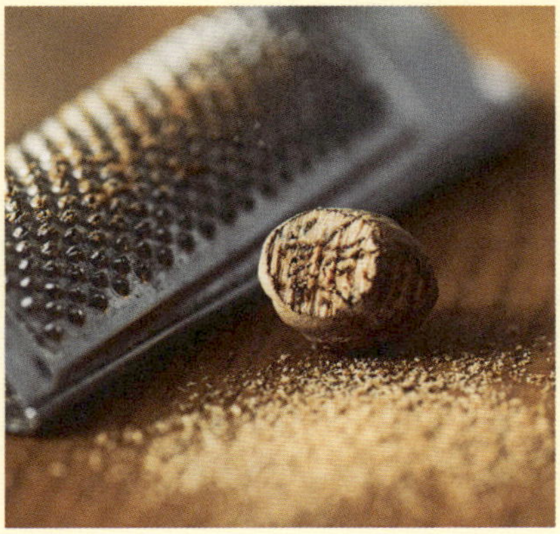

Quick Sauerkraut with Grapes and Walnuts

Ingredients (serves 4)

1 3/4 pounds white cabbage
salt
sugar
3 cups quince juice (or unsweetened apple juice)
2 tablespoons rice vinegar (or white wine vinegar)
1 1/2 tablespoons butter
3 stems parsley
1/3 cup walnuts
2 tablespoons neutral-tasting vegetable oil
2 1/3 cups red and green seedless grapes

1 Wash the cabbage and cut out the core. Cut into thin strips. Knead thoroughly with 2 teaspoons of salt and 1 teaspoon of sugar. Allow the cabbage to marinate for at least 2 hours, mixing occasionally.

2 Put the cabbage in a covered pot with quince juice and vinegar. Cook for 45 minutes over medium heat. When it is done, season with salt and a pinch of sugar and mix in 1/2 tablespoon of butter.

3 Meanwhile, strip off the parsley leaves and mince them. Roughly chop the walnuts.

4 Heat the oil and the remaining butter in a frying pan. Sauté the walnuts and the grapes for 3—4 minutes and season with salt and pepper. Arrange the cabbage and the grapes on a plate and serve.

Preparation time: 1 hour and 15 minutes (+ 2 hours for marinating)

TIP
Serve as a side or main dish, for example fried in a pan together with spaezle.

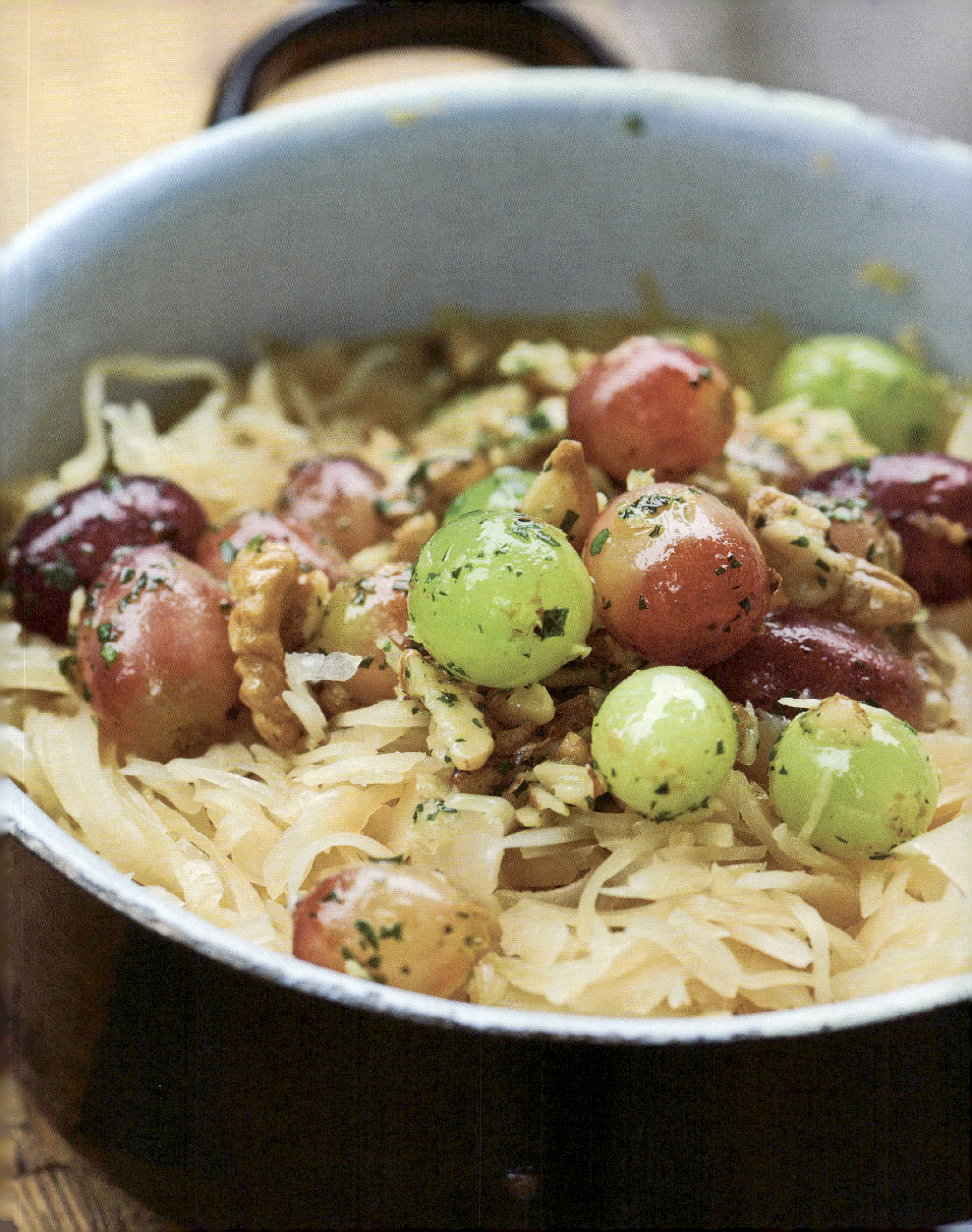

Focaccia with Grilled Vegetable Salsa

Ingredients (serves 4)

2 cups all-purpose flour
salt and pepper
1/2 cube fresh yeast (or 2 teaspoons dry active yeast)
sugar
1 red bell pepper
1 green bell pepper
olive oil
1 zucchini
4 scallions
juice of 1 lemon
1 bunch dill
1 stem rosemary
fleur de sel (or coarse sea salt)

1. Sift the flour into a bowl and mix with 1 teaspoon of salt. Dissolve the yeast with 1 pinch of sugar in 2/3 cup of lukewarm water, add to the flour and knead into a smooth dough (5 minutes). Cover with a towel and leave to rise in a warm place for 35 minutes.

2. Meanwhile, wash the peppers, cut them into quarters and remove the seeds. Drizzle the quarters with olive oil and broil them in the oven or grill on a grill pan over medium heat until the peppers are soft and the skins start to blister. Wash the zucchini and cut into thin slices and wash the scallions. Drizzle olive oil over them and put them under the broiler until soft. Season the vegetables with salt and pepper. Leave to cool.

3. Spread out the dough into a large flatbread. Line a baking sheet with parchment paper and leave the dough to rise. Meanwhile, peel off the pepper skins. Chop all the vegetables in small pieces and mix with the lemon juice and 6 tablespoons of olive oil until smooth. Chop dill and fold into the mixture.

4. Make lots of indentations in the dough with your fingertips and then sprinkle with the rosemary needles, a little fleur de sel and coarsely ground pepper. Bake in a preheated oven at 475°F (convection 440°F) on the bottom rack for 12 minutes. Then move the sheet to the top rack and bake until golden brown for another 3—5 minutes. Serve with the grilled vegetable salsa.

Preparation time: 1 hour and 45 minutes

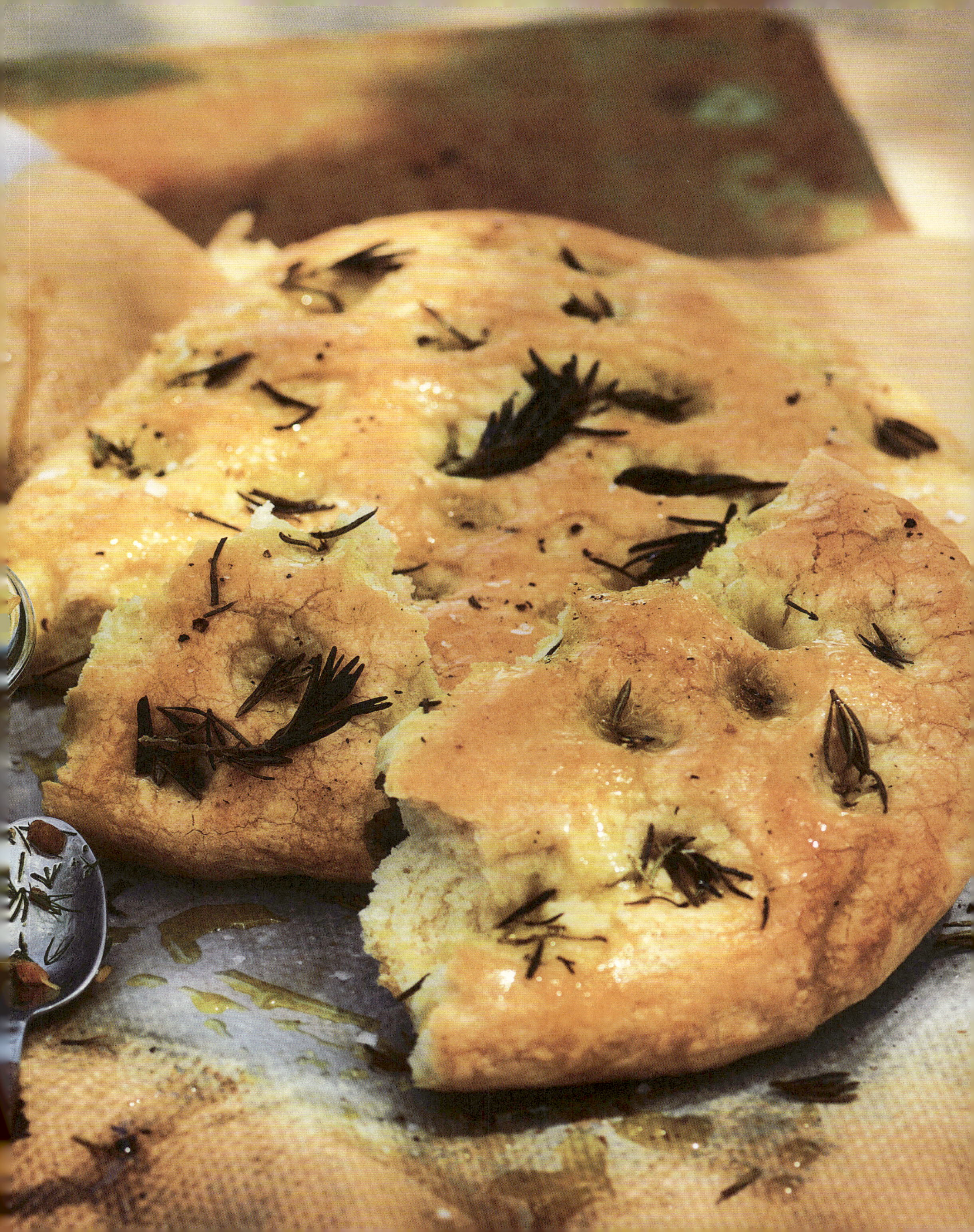

HERBS

Taste the green
In addition to seasonings, fresh herbs are the most important ingredient in green cuisine. The possibilities are endless. Herbs are real team players, but they are also great on their own anytime!

Dried herbs
Dried herbs are a big help for winter cooking and have strong aromas. You should always buy them in the smallest available portions because they lose their taste and scent after a while.

Fresh herbs on duty
Don't add fresh herbs until just before you've finished cooking your dish. That way the herbs stay green and the essential oils retain their full aromas. In uncooked recipes, you should chop the delicate herbs quickly and roughly, and they should be added to the quark, the yogurt, the vinaigrette, the sauce or salsa right away in order to capture their full flavor. Fresh herbs should encourage you to experiment. It doesn't always have to be parsley!

Leftovers
Putting fresh herbs in water like flowers doesn't work too well. Herbs wilt quickly. They keep fresh for several days if you wrap them in cling wrap or put them in a freezer bag. Dried herbs should be kept in airtight, light-resistant containers.

basil
dill
parsley
thyme
marjoram
Thai basil
CILANTRO
sage
CHERVIL
chives
bay laurel

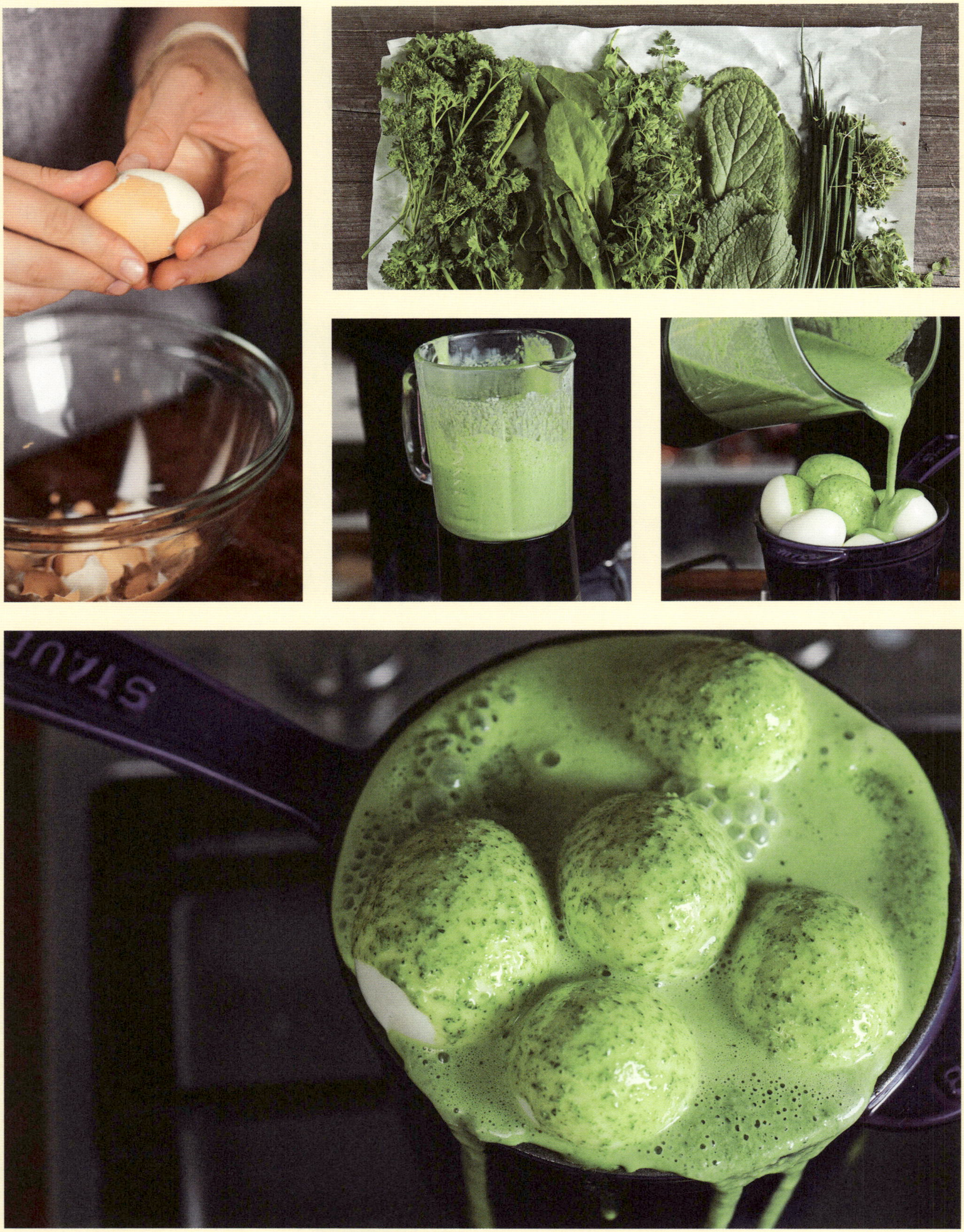

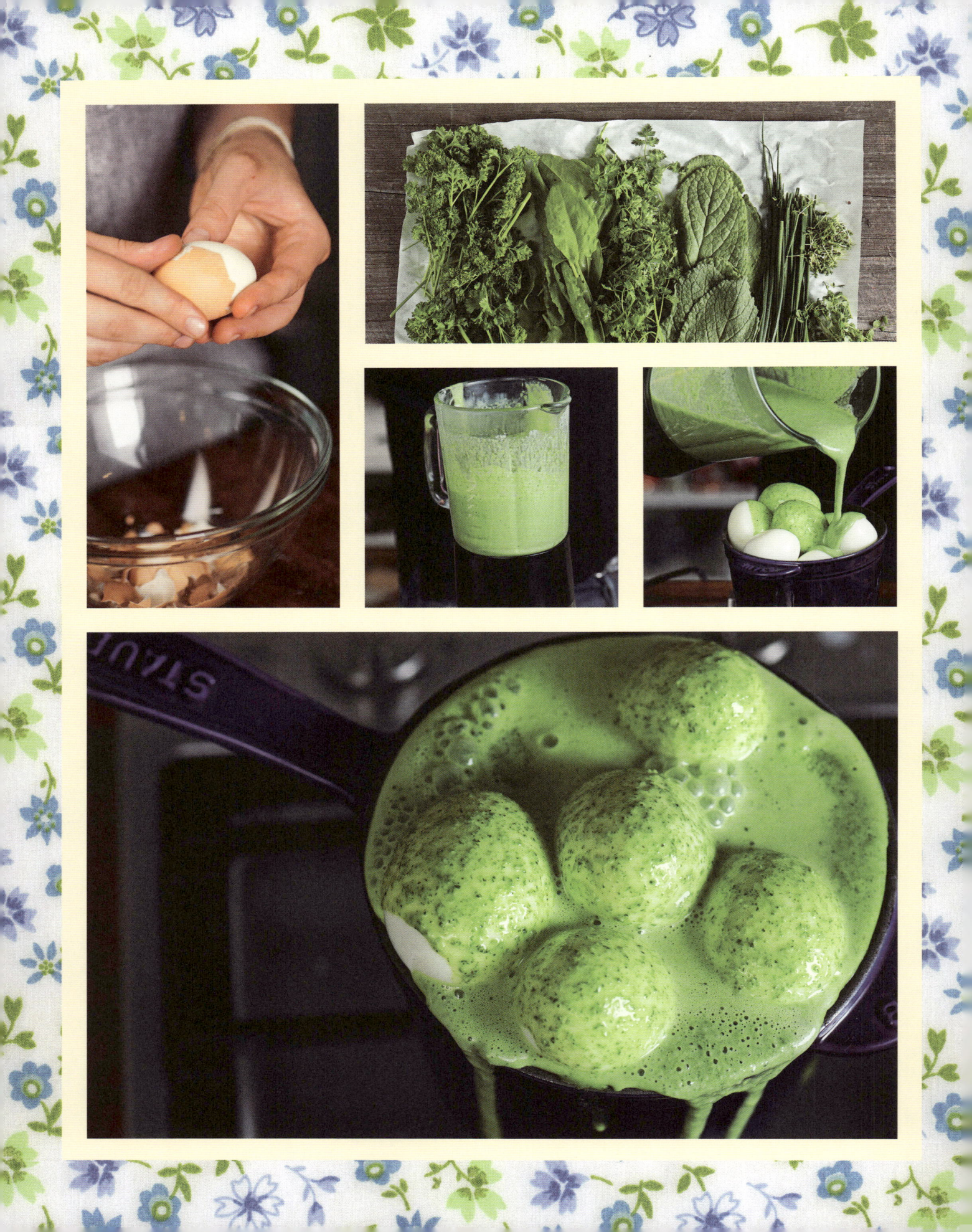

Soft-Boiled Eggs in Green Sauce

Ingredients (serves 4)

3 1/2 tablespoons butter
3 1/2 tablespoons flour
3 cups whole milk
1 bay leaf
salt and pepper
nutmeg
8 large eggs
1 bunch (4 cups) mixed herbs
(borage, chervil, cress, parsley,
salad burnet, sorrel and chives)*

1. To make the sauce, melt the butter in a pan on low heat. Sift the flour and mix in. Pour in the milk, stirring continuously. Add the bay leaf and simmer on low heat for 20—25 minutes. Season with salt and nutmeg. Remove the bay leaf.
2. Boil the eggs for 5 minutes. Rinse them in cold water and peel them.
3. Roughly chop the herbs and mix them with the sauce in a blender or food processor until very smooth. Place in a pan with the eggs and heat briefly. Season with salt and pepper and serve immediately.

Preparation time: 45 minutes

TIP: Mashed potatoes go well with this.

* If some of these herbs are not available, you can either increase the amount of the herbs you do have or get creative and substitute tarragon, dandelion, lemon verbena, lovage or arugula.

THE PEAS ROLL X 3

The garden pea belongs to one of the oldest cultivated types of vegetables in the world. It is actually very exotic: its origins are in Asia. It wasn't until the 15th century that the green pea became well known and very popular in European countries. Crunchy, sweet, home-grown peas in a pod are available in the summer months.

1 Pea Purée

Peel and dice **1 garlic clove** and braise in **1 tablespoon of melted butter** for 2 minutes. Add **3 cups of peas (frozen)** and cook for 2 minutes. Add **1/2 cup of vegetable stock** and cook over medium heat for 5 minutes, uncovered. Drain the peas, rinse in cold water and drain again. Add **2 tablespoons of crème fraîche** and **1 tablespoon of finely chopped basil leaves** and blend. Season with **salt** and **pepper**.

2 Pea Pasta

Cook **1/2 pound** of your **favorite pasta** (in the photo: corn pasta) in salted water according to the package instructions. Peel **4 garlic cloves,** cut into thin slices and sauté in 4 tablespoons of olive oil until light brown. Add **2 cups of frozen peas** and **1/2 teaspoon of dried oregano** and sauté briefly. Pour in **2/3 cup of vegetable stock,** bring it to a boil and mix in **1 cup of arugula** and **1 1/2 tablespoons of butter.** Leave it to cook for 2 minutes, uncovered. Drain the pasta and fold it into the mixture. Season with **salt** and **pepper**.

3 Mozzarella with Pea Vinaigrette

Defrost **1 cup of frozen peas**. Finely dice **2 tomatoes**. Mix **3 tablespoons of lemon juice, 6 tablespoons of olive oil** and **1 tablespoon of honey** together to make the vinaigrette and season with **salt** and **pepper**. Finely chop **2 stems of mint leaves** and fold into the peas and the tomatoes. Cut crosses into **2 balls of mozzarella,** pull them apart and serve drizzled with the vinaigrette.

"I used frozen peas in my recipes because they are handy and are available year round. Still, when they are in season, you should really go to the effort of getting them fresh and shelling them. You will get about 2 cups of fresh peas from 4 1/4 cups of peas in their pods. They only need to be cooked for 1 minute in salted water before using them in a dish."

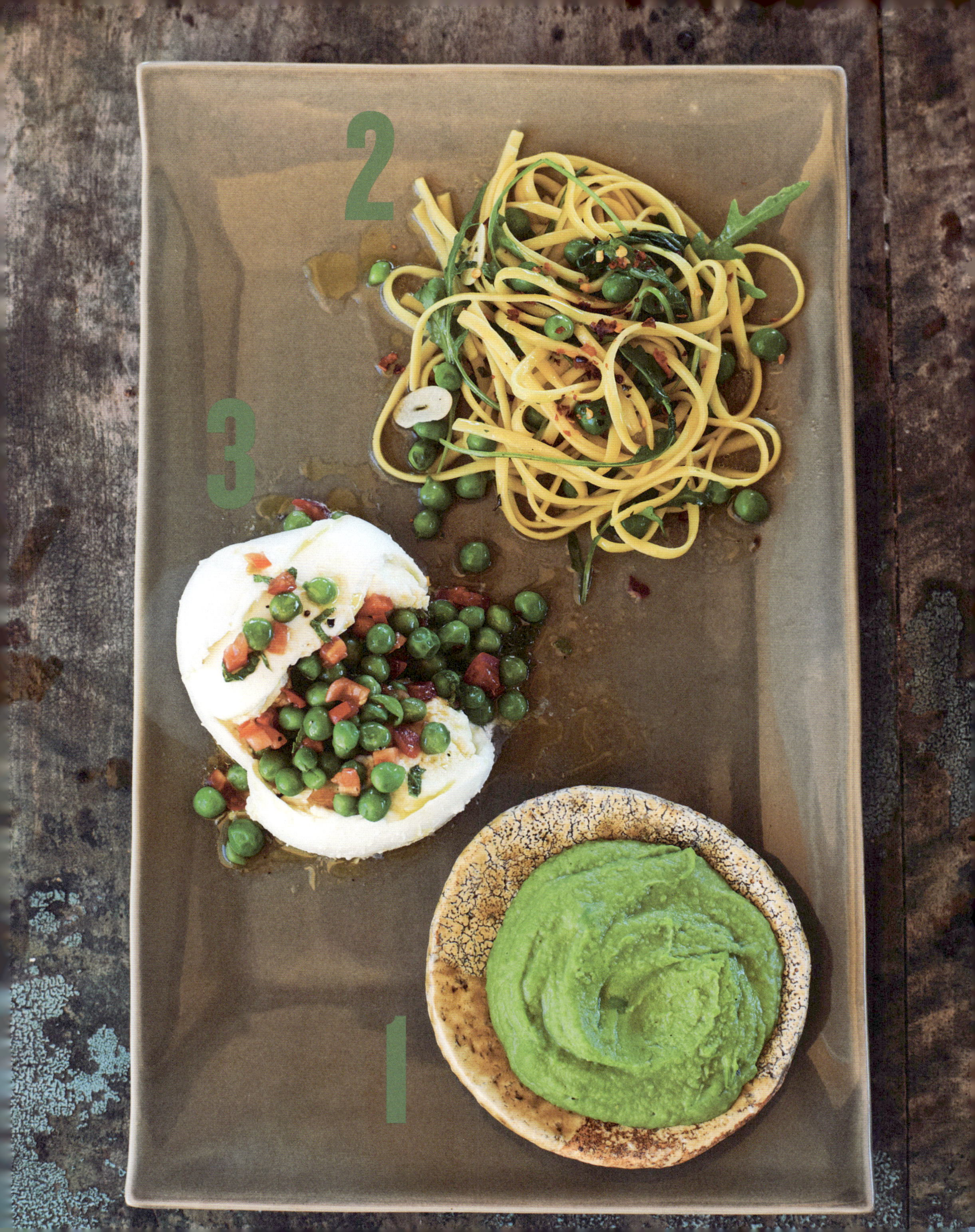
2
3
1

Lentils with Stewed Parsley Root

Ingredients (serves 4)
1 1/4 cups beluga lentils (see note)
1 tablespoon fennel seeds
1 red onion
1 inch fresh ginger
3 stems marjoram
3 tablespoons sherry vinegar
6 tablespoons olive oil
sugar
salt
1 pound small parsley root
2 tablespoons butter
1/2 bunch parsley
freshly ground black pepper
1 bunch arugula

1 Cook the lentils in unsalted water for 15 minutes. Toast the fennel seeds in an ungreased pan, let them cool and grind them coarsely in a mortar. Peel and dice the onion. Peel and finely grate the ginger. Chop the marjoram and mix everything into a vinaigrette with the vinegar, olive oil and 6 tablespoons of water. Season with sugar and salt. Drain the lentils and mix with the vinaigrette while they are still hot.

2 Peel the parsley root, quarter it lengthwise and fry in a pan with the frothy butter on medium heat for 10 minutes.

3 Chop the parsley and mix it in with the parsley root. Season with salt, a pinch of sugar and pepper. Wash the arugula and fold it into the lentils. Serve with the parsley root.

Preparation time: 35 minutes

BELUGA LENTILS, also called caviar lentils, are little black lentils with a nutty taste. They require much less cooking time than their brown and green buddies and they don't get mushy. They are available in well-stocked supermarkets, natural and health food stores.

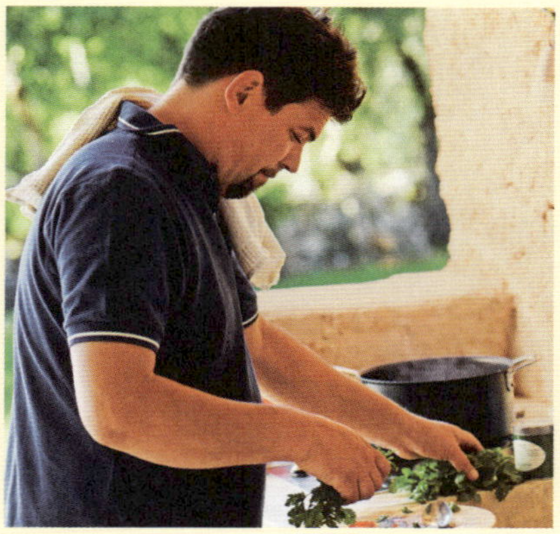
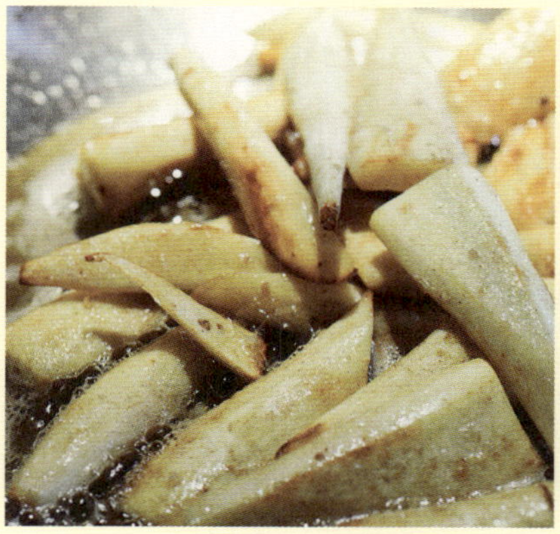
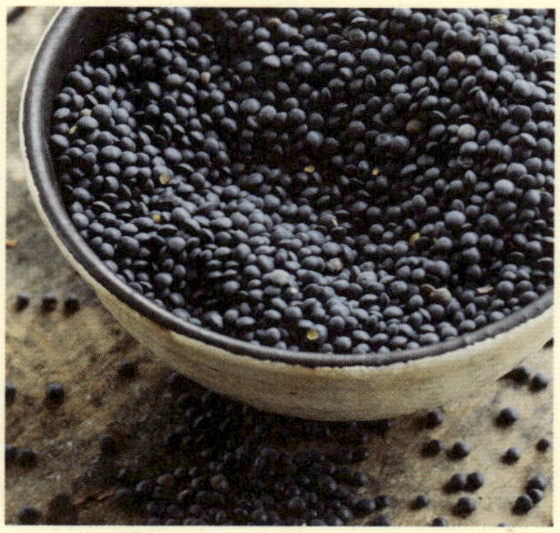
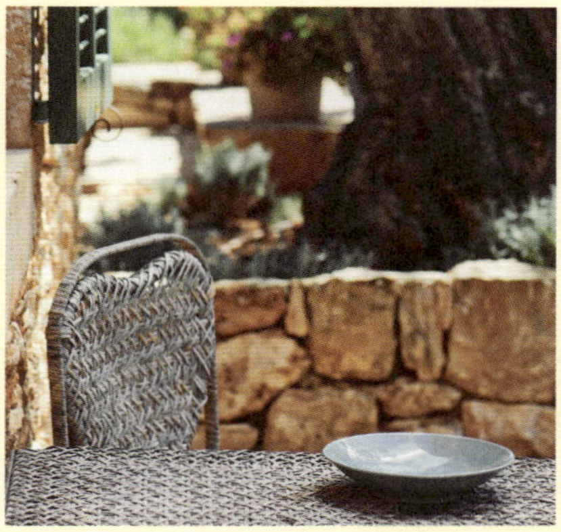
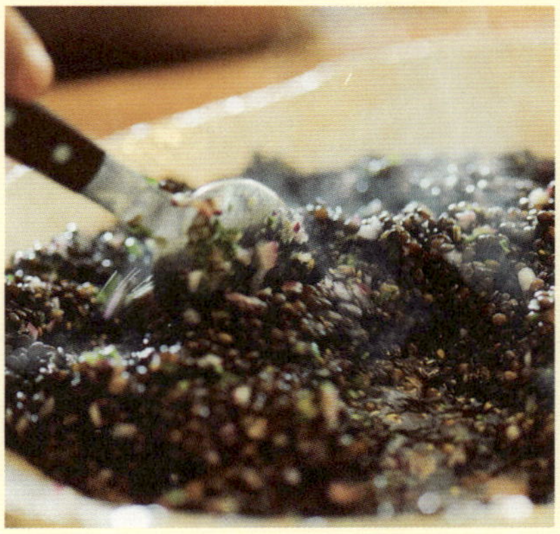
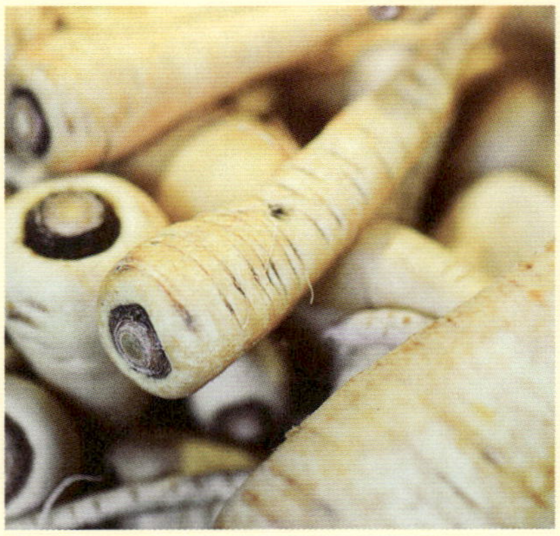
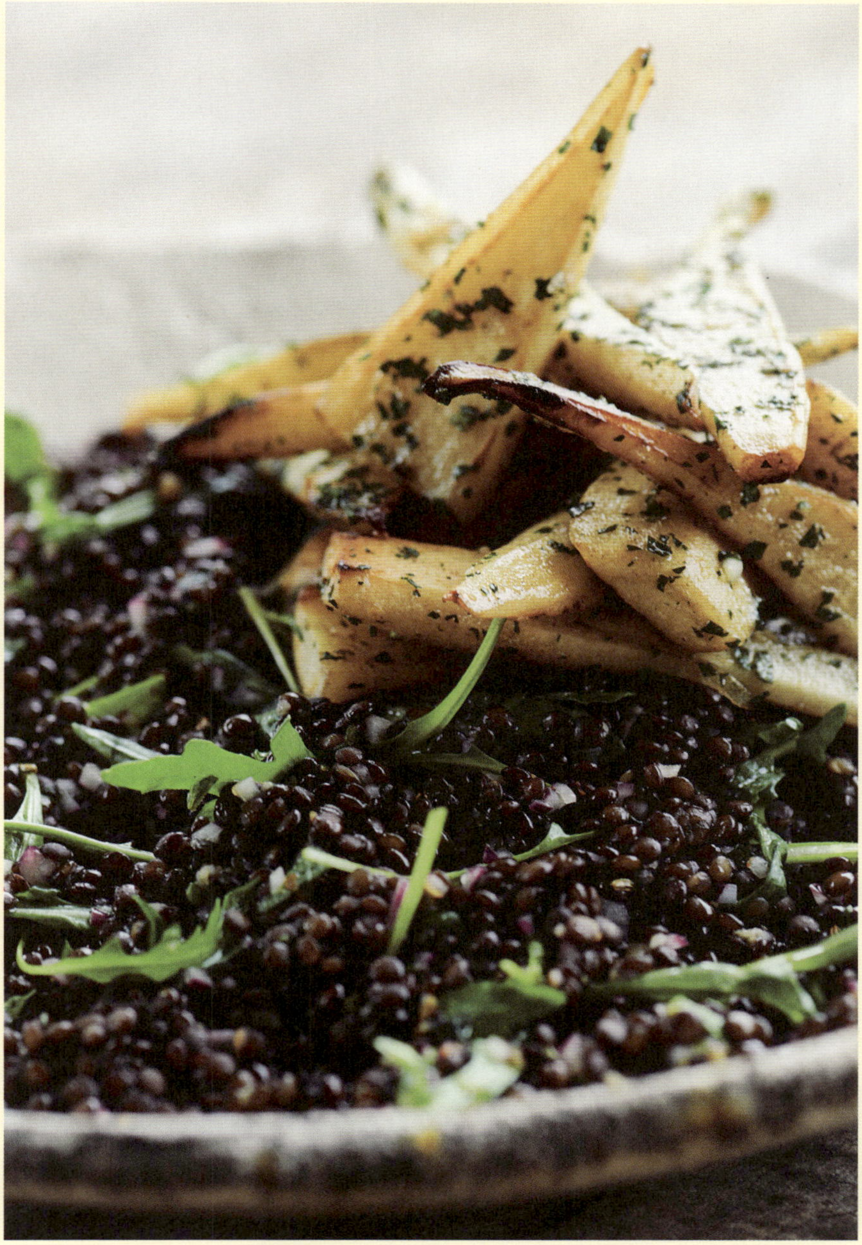

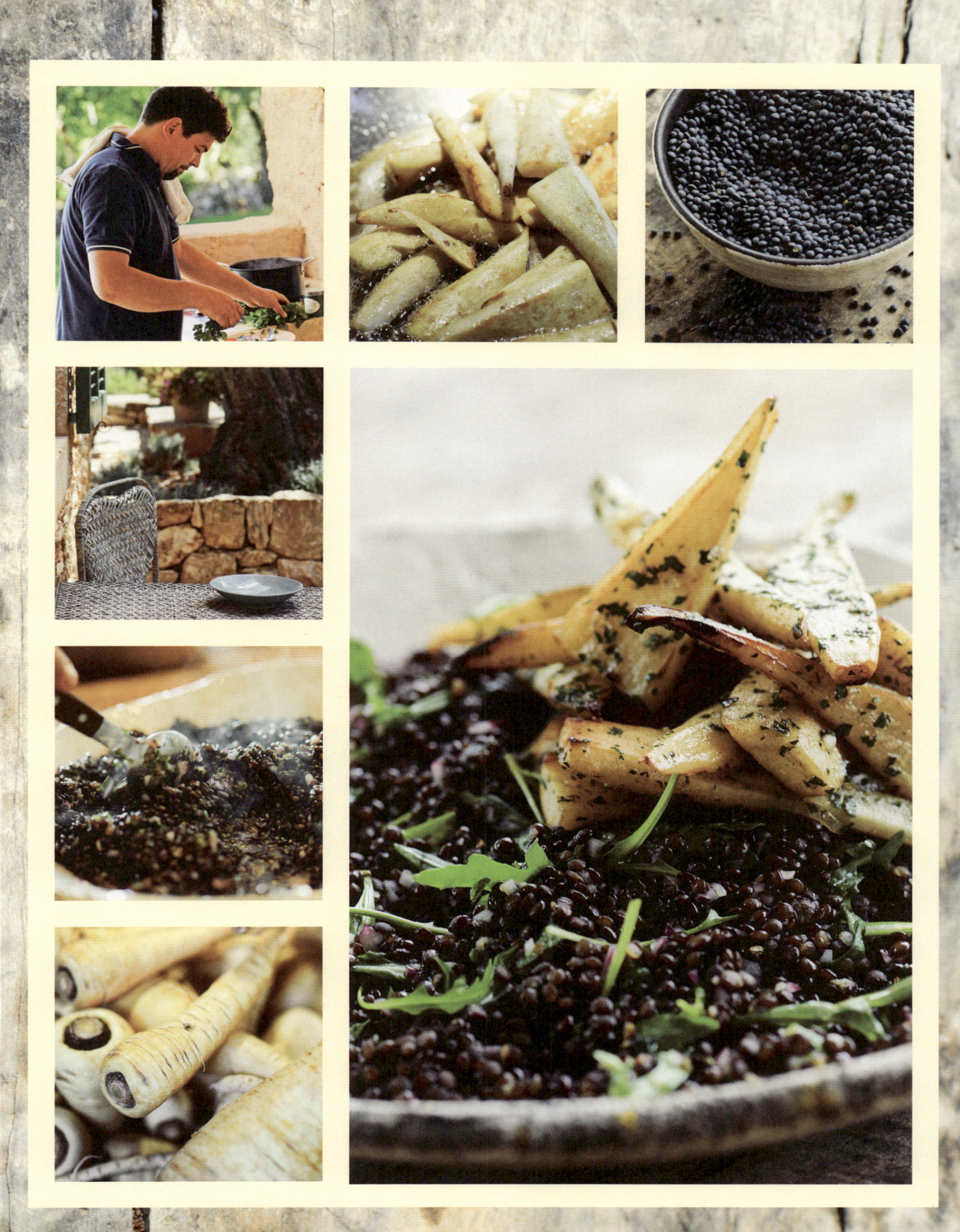

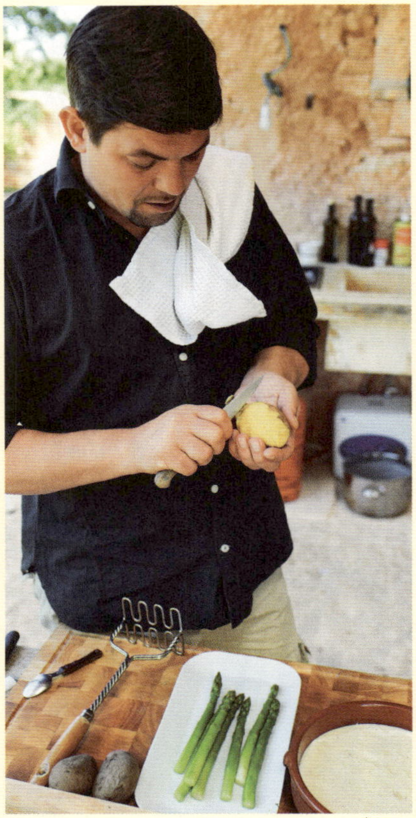
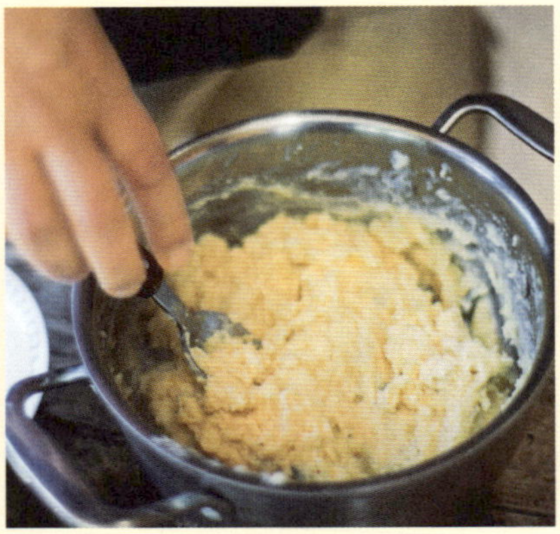
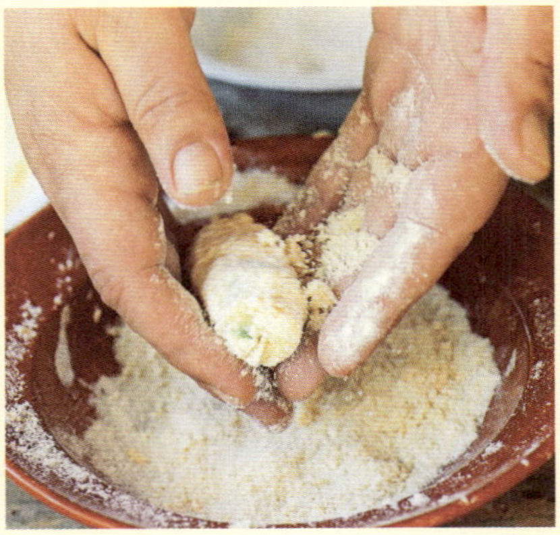
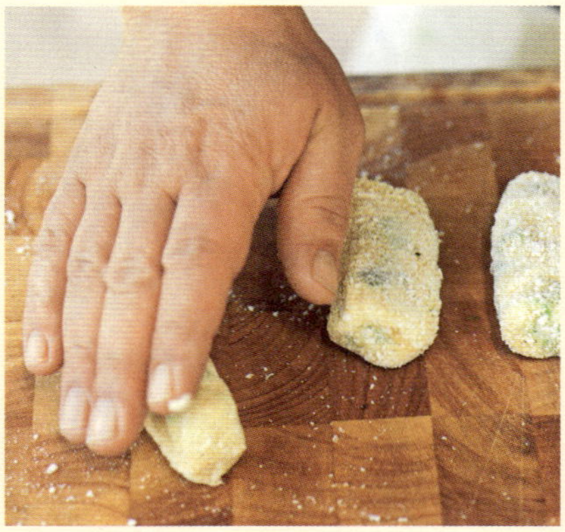
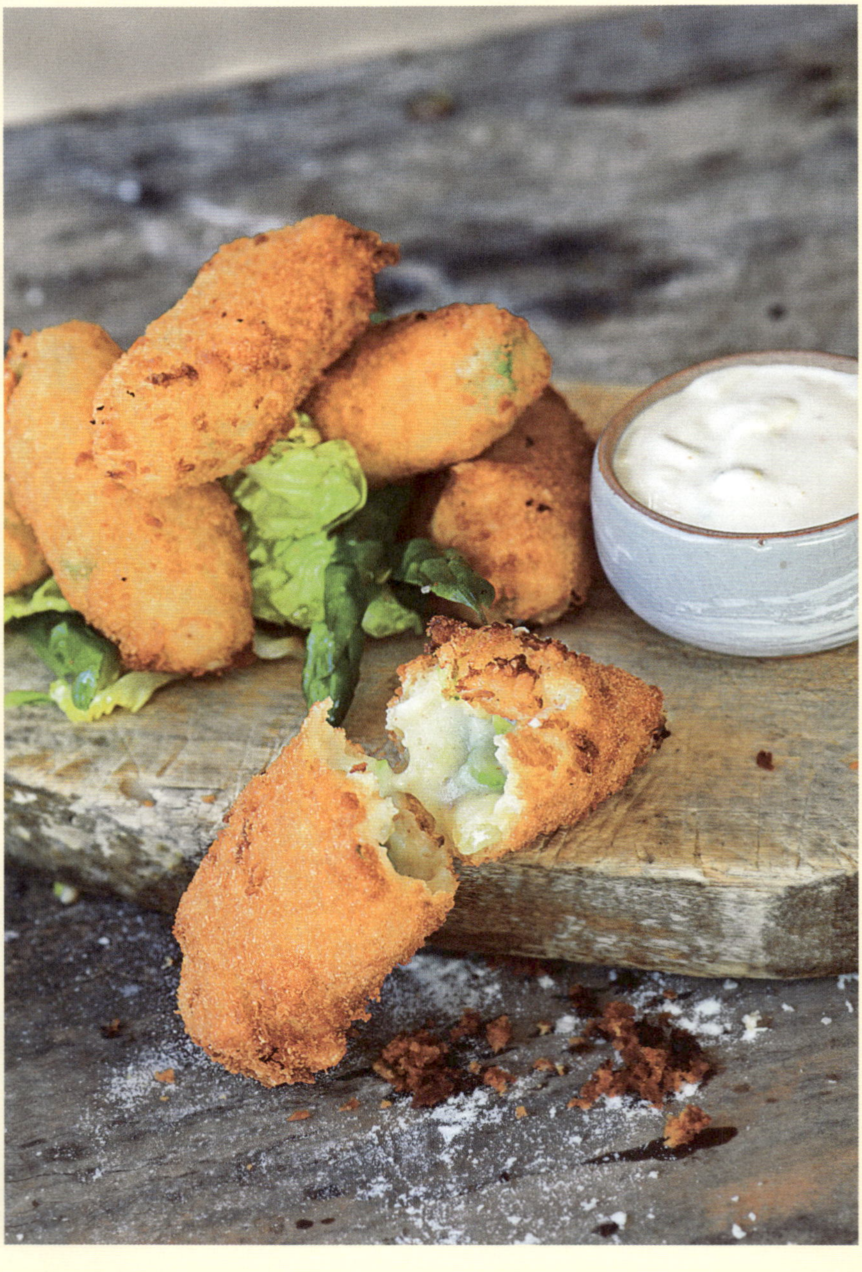
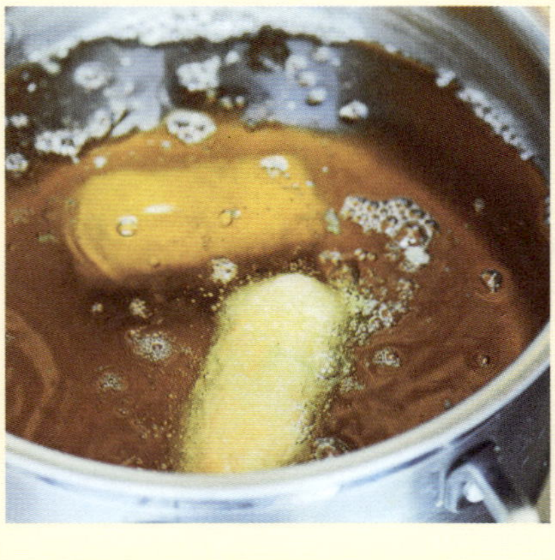

Green Asparagus Croquettes with Blood Orange Mayonnaise

Ingredients (serves 4)

2 tablespoons butter
2/3 cup flour
1 cup milk
1 bay leaf
salt
5 spears asparagus
2 potatoes (1/2 pound), cooked the previous day
1/2 organic blood orange (or juicing oranges or pink grapefruit)
1/2 teaspoon pickled green peppercorns
3 1/2 tablespoons mayonnaise
2/3 cup whole-milk yogurt
cayenne pepper
2 large eggs
2 tablespoons durum wheat semolina
1 1/3 cups breadcrumbs
oil or fat for deep frying

1. Melt butter in a nonstick pan. Whisk in 4 tablespoons of flour and continue whisking until the mixture is bubbling. Whisk in a thin stream of milk. Add the bay leaf and boil into a thick white béchamel sauce for 20—25 minutes over medium heat. Season with salt.
2. Allow the sauce to cool for 15 minutes. Peel the lower third of the asparagus spears. Boil the asparagus in salted water for 2 minutes. Rinse in cold water, drain and cut crosswise into slices.
3. Mash the potatoes with a fork and mix with the béchamel sauce and the asparagus. Refrigerate for 2 hours.
4. Meanwhile, grate the orange peel for the mayonnaise. Squeeze the oranges. Finely chop the green peppercorns and mix with the mayonnaise, yogurt, orange zest and juice until smooth. Season with salt and cayenne pepper.
5. Whisk the eggs. Mix in the semolina and the rest of the flour. Make thick croquettes out of the potato dough. Coat with the flour mixture, dip into the eggs, allow to drain, and then turn them in the breadcrumbs. Heat the oil in a high-sided pot or in a deep fryer to 350°F. Fry the croquettes for 3—4 minutes in small portions until golden brown. Drain on paper towels and serve with the blood orange mayonnaise.

Preparation time: 1 hour and 20 minutes plus time to cool

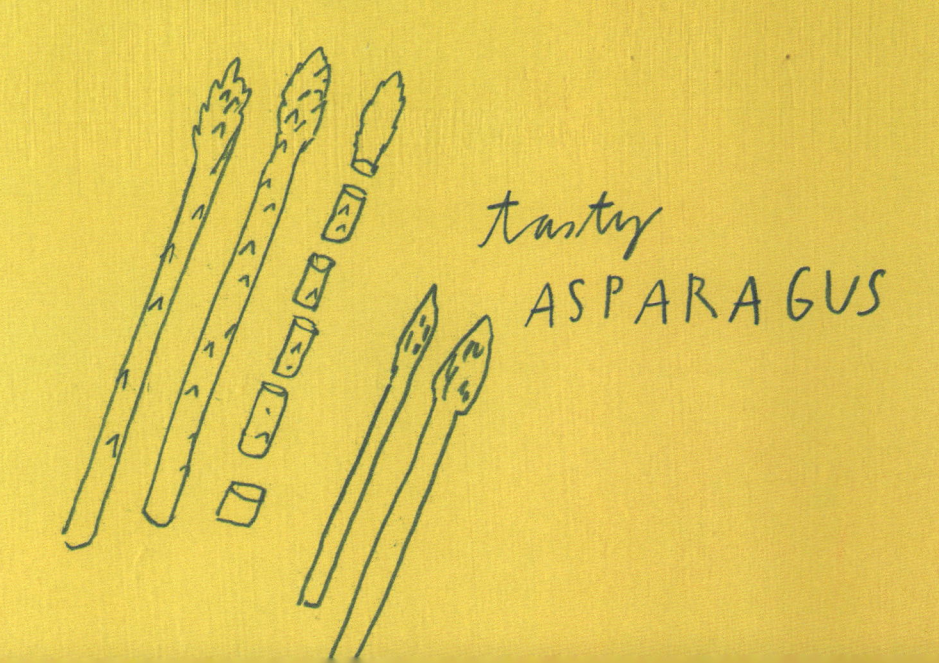

tasty ASPARAGUS

Chickpea and Fennel Salad with Apricots and Oranges

Ingredients (serves 4)

2 small fennel bulbs
8 apricots
2 organic juicing oranges
1/2 organic lemon
1 tablespoon medium-hot mustard
6 tablespoons olive oil
1 tablespoon honey
salt and pepper
1 can chickpeas (16 ounces net weight)
1 small red onion
chili flakes

1. Wash and finely slice the fennel. Cut the apricots into slices and remove the pits. Peel one of the oranges, removing the white part of the skin as well, and cut into slices. Squeeze the juice from the other orange and blend with the lemon juice, mustard, olive oil and honey until smooth. Season with salt and pepper.

2. Rinse the chickpeas under cold water, drain. Peel the onion and slice into fine rings. Stir them into the vinaigrette. Mix the chickpeas, fennel, apricots and orange slices with the vinaigrette. Arrange on a plate and sprinkle with chili flakes.

Preparation time: 20 minutes

VARIATIONS: This fruity vinaigrette also tastes great as a creamy dressing made by adding some buttermilk. You can add chopped fresh herbs that are in season (such as dill, parsley, chives, sorrel and others).

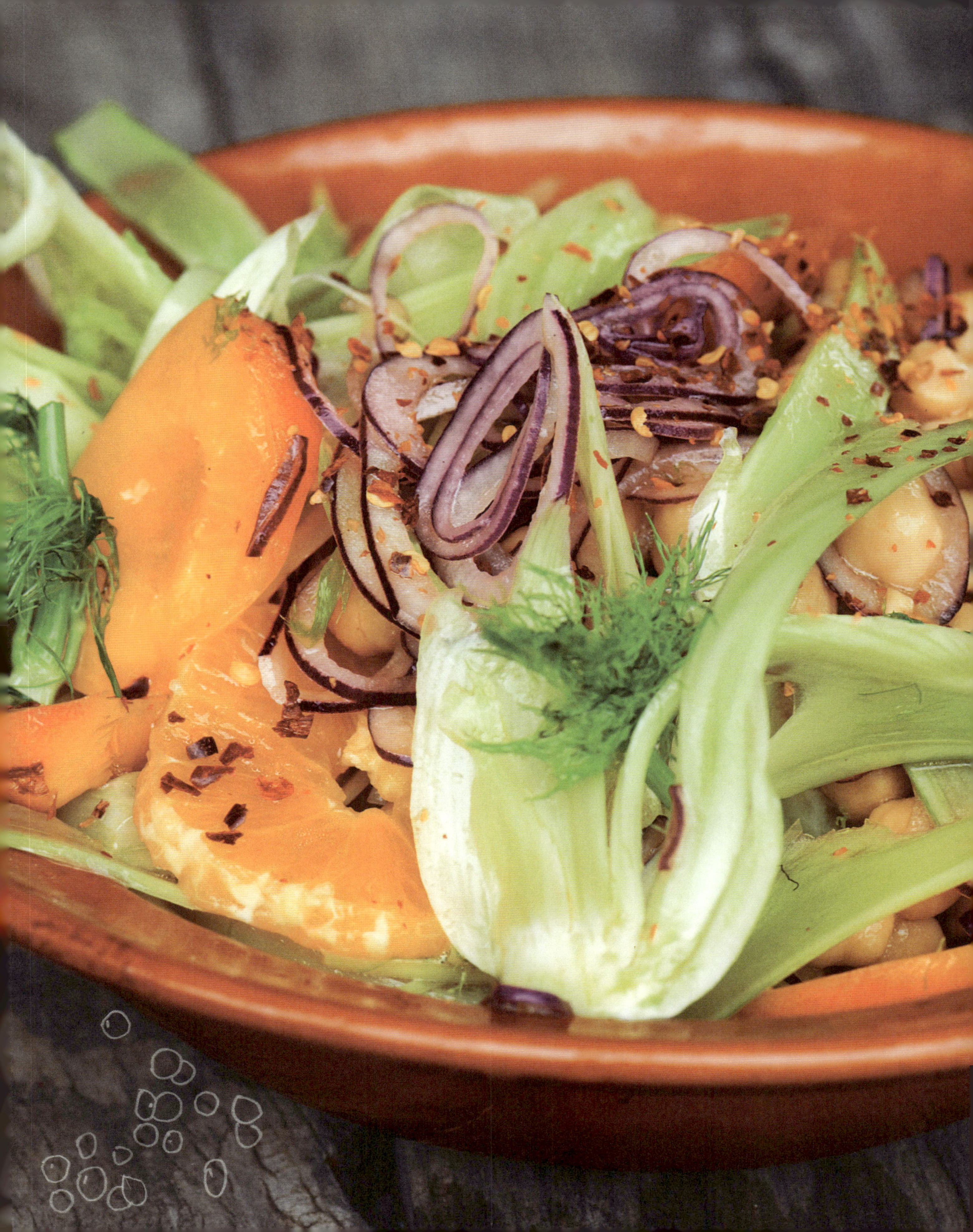

1

2

3

BELL PEPPER
TRIPLY GOOD

Bell peppers are juicy and crunchy. The red and yellow varieties are especially aromatic and sweet. Green bell peppers are not fully ripened so they have a zestier flavor. Long green peppers add spiciness. Peppers are available all year round.

1 Bell Pepper Ketchup

Wash **2 red bell peppers,** cut them into quarters, remove the seeds and then chop coarsely. Peel **2 garlic cloves** and cut into slices. Put both ingredients in a pan with **2 tablespoons of sugar, 1 star anise** and **1 chopped red chili pepper.** Cover with water and bring to a boil. Simmer on a low heat with the lid on for 1 hour. Remove the star anise. Using a skimmer, remove the pepper, chili and garlic and purée them with **1 teaspoon of tomato paste** in a blender. Add the liquid until you get a ketchup-like consistency (the ketchup will thicken slightly when cooling). Season the red bell pepper ketchup with **a few drops of lime juice** and **salt.**

2 Bell Pepper Tortilla

Wash, quarter, and remove the seeds from **1 red, 1 green** and **1 yellow bell pepper.** Cut into strips. Peel **1 onion** and **1 clove of garlic** and cut into slices. Sauté everything in a pan with **4 tablespoons of olive oil** over low heat for 20 minutes. Season **5 large eggs** with **salt** and **pepper** and beat until smooth. Pour the eggs over the bell pepper, let them thicken and then finish cooking under the hot broiler on the second rack from the top for 4–5 minutes.

TIP

The ketchup goes really well with the Crunchy Burger on page 147! It stays fresh for at least a week in the refrigerator if stored in an airtight container. You can also prepare the ketchup for a barbecue in advance.

3 Bell Pepper Antipasti

Quarter and remove the seeds from **2 red, 2 yellow** and **2 green bell peppers** and place them with their skin side facing up on a baking sheet covered with parchment paper. Preheat the oven to 450°F and broil on the top rack until the skin begins to bubble and turn black. Seal in a freezer bag and allow to cool for 10–15 minutes. Remove the skin of the bell peppers and arrange the peppers on a platter. Peel **1 garlic clove,** grate it and sprinkle over the peppers. Drizzle **3 tablespoons of olive oil** over the dish and season with **salt** and **pepper.**

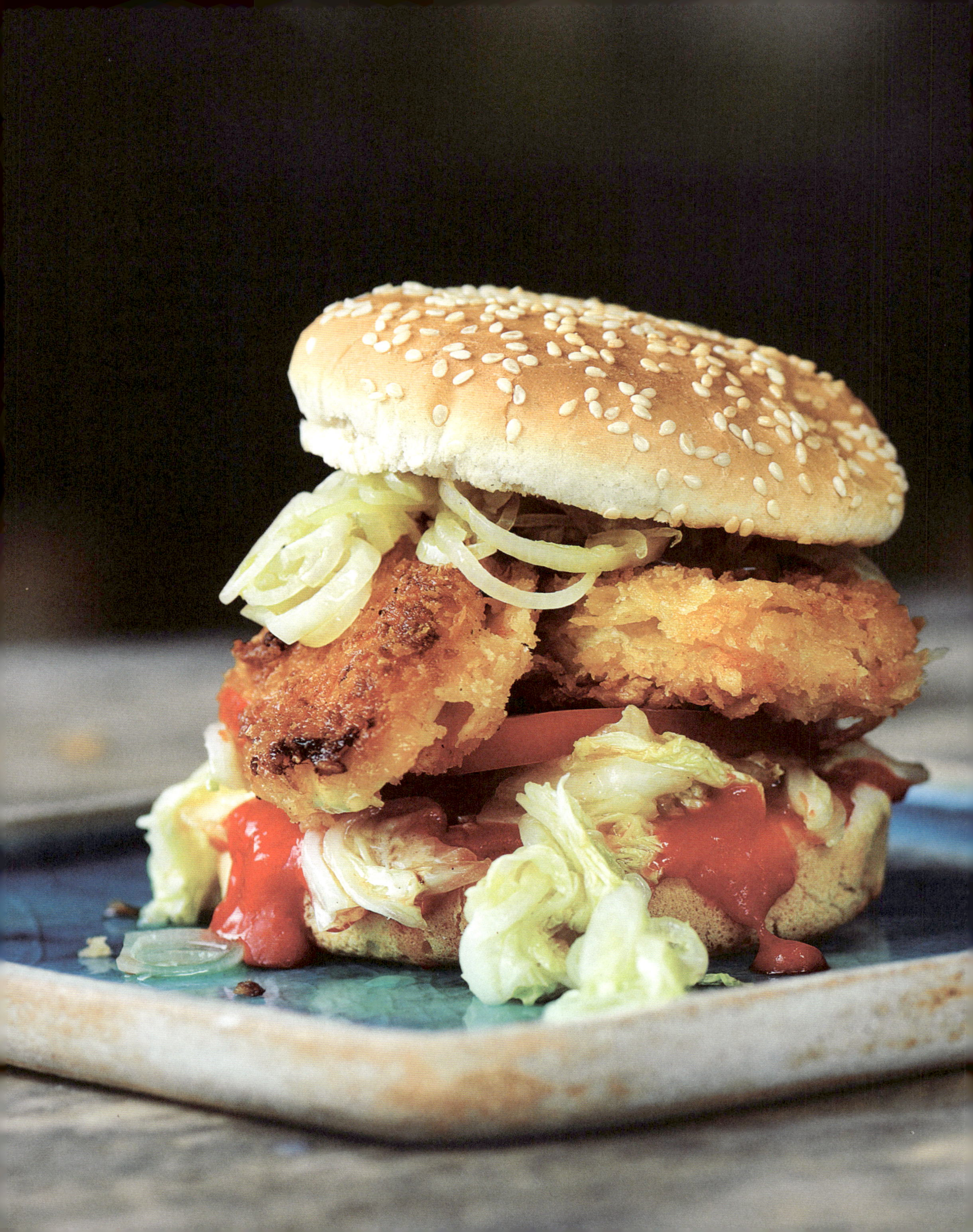

Tim's Crunchy Burger with Ginger Shallots

Ingredients (serves 2)

4 shallots
3/4 inch fresh ginger
2 tablespoons olive oil
1/2 head Napa cabbage
salt
1/2 cup buttermilk
1 teaspoon ground sweet paprika
1 large or 2 medium king oyster mushrooms
2 cups Panko breadcrumbs (or other breadcrumbs, see note)
sunflower oil
2 sesame burger buns
3 tablespoons bell pepper ketchup (recipe on page 144, or tomato ketchup)
1/2 beefsteak tomato

1. Peel the shallots and ginger and cut both into fine slices. Sauté in 1 tablespoon of olive oil until soft and then remove from the pan. Wash and dice the Napa cabbage and sear in the pan with 1 tablespoon of olive oil. Season with salt and remove from the pan.

2. Season the buttermilk with ground paprika and salt. Cut the mushrooms into 1/2-inch thick slices and dunk into the buttermilk. Take them out and immediately press them into the Panko breadcrumbs on both sides. Cover the bottom of the pan with sunflower oil and fry the mushroom slices for 2–3 minutes until golden brown. Season with salt and drain on paper towels.

3. Briefly toast the burger buns in the oven or on the grill. Spread bell pepper ketchup on the bottom of the buns. Wash the tomato, core and cut into slices. Add salt and arrange the tomatoes and the Chinese cabbage on the bottom of the buns. Add the mushrooms and use the ginger shallots as a topping. Add the top of the buns and enjoy!

Preparation time: 30 minutes

PANKO, originally from Japan, are breadcrumbs. Made from crustless white bread, Panko is more airy and coarser than regular breadcrumbs. You can find it in a well-stocked supermarket or in an Asian grocery store.

"The ginger shallots make the burger really spicy, so it can be served with regular tomato ketchup. However, it really tastes best with my homemade paprika ketchup."

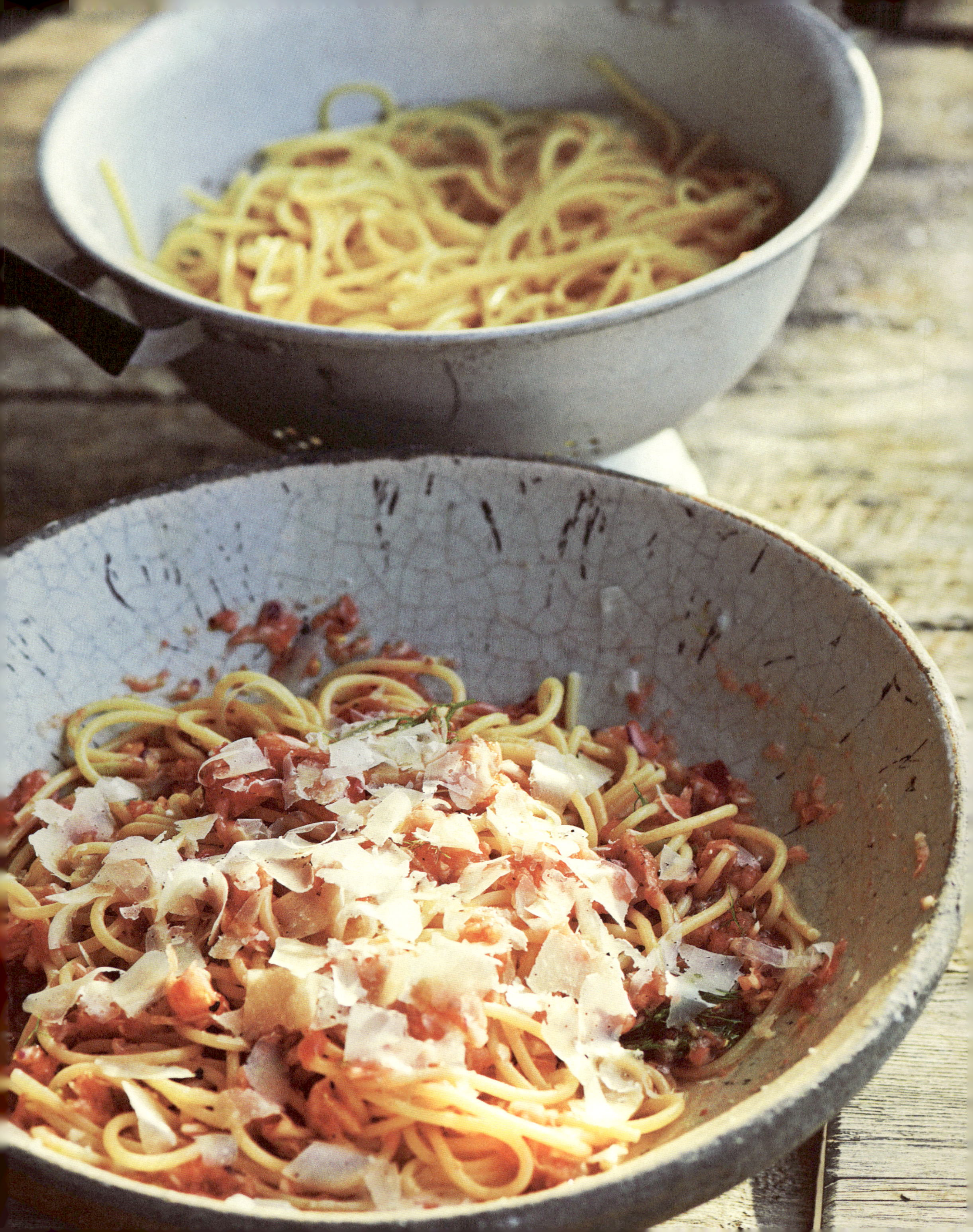

Pasta with Grated Fennel Tomato Sauce

Ingredients (serves 4)

1 pound spaghetti
salt and pepper
1 large fennel bulb (1 pound)
4 medium-sized tomatoes (3/4 pound)
1 organic lemon
8 tablespoons olive oil
sugar
1/3 cup freshly grated smoked ricotta cheese (or Parmesan or pecorino)

1. Cook the spaghetti until it is al dente according to the package instructions. Drain the spaghetti and reserve 2/3 cups of cooking water.
2. Meanwhile, wash the fennel and set aside the fennel greens. Place your grater in a large bowl. Roughly grate the fennel bulb and tomatoes. Squeeze the lemon and mix the juice with 4 tablespoons of olive oil. Season with salt, pepper and sugar.
3. Add the pasta, the remaining olive oil and cooking liquid to taste. Season with salt and pepper. Decorate with the fennel greens and cheese and serve.

Preparation time: 15 minutes

LIQUID VEGETABLES –

getting to the heart of the matter

Too lazy to chew? Not at all! Fresh vegetable juices are full of nutrients and create an intense, pure vegetable flavor in green cooking.

For vegetables to taste their best on their own, you need a **JUICER**. It's an investment worth making: you can enjoy homemade juices from crunchy carrots and peppers, full-flavored beets and sweet apples. Really juicy vegetables such as ripe tomatoes and fresh cucumbers can be pureed in the **BLENDER** and then **STRAINED**. Vegetable juices taste **JUST FABULOUS** with a little bit of salt. In summer they refresh you when they're chilled. And they can also be used as the **BASIS** for warm and cold soups, vegetable jellies, salsas, chutneys, vinaigrettes and salad dressings.

Vegetable juices can be cooked up into **TASTY SAUCES** and it's not complicated to make them! Just throw carrots, peppers or any other favorite vegetable into the juicer and collect the juice. Then boil it down to half of its original amount and add a couple of cold cubes of butter and blend it all with a **HAND BLENDER**. Add salt, pepper and a pinch of sugar to taste and you've got a **DELICIOUS VEGETABLE SAUCE** that can be varied with herbs and seasoning. On the other hand, a wonderfully aromatic vegetable stock results from a fusion of various flavors: peels and pieces of different vegetables can make a strong-tasting **CLEAR SOUP**, which becomes more complex when you add dried mushrooms, herbs and spices. You can use any **VEGETABLE AND HERB SCRAPS** kept 2–3 days in the refrigerator (just be sure they have been thoroughly washed and kept covered).

TIP

You can freeze vegetable stock in ice cube bags – it will be on hand as you need it.

Vegetable Stock

Put **1 pound of vegetable scraps** and **1 bunch of soup greens** (e.g. 1 carrot, 1/4 celery root, 1/2 leek, 2 stems of parsley), **1 teaspoon ground paprika**, **1 teaspoon of fennel seeds**, **1 teaspoon of mustard seeds**, **1 teaspoon of dried savory**, **3 dried porcini**, **10 peppercorns** and **2 bay leaves** into **8 1/2 cups of cold water**. Add **1 teaspoon of salt** and simmer gently for 10 minutes. Take off the heat, allow to cool and strain when cold.

Asian Vegetable Stock

Put **1 pound of vegetable scraps**, **1 crushed clove of garlic**, **3 tablespoons of sliced ginger**, **1/2 of a chili pepper**, **1 star anise**, **1 teaspoon of fennel seeds** with **4 tablespoons of soy sauce** into **8 1/2 cups of cold water**, add **1 teaspoon of salt** and bring it all slowly to the boil. Simmer gently for 10 minutes. Remove from the heat, allow to cool and strain when cold.

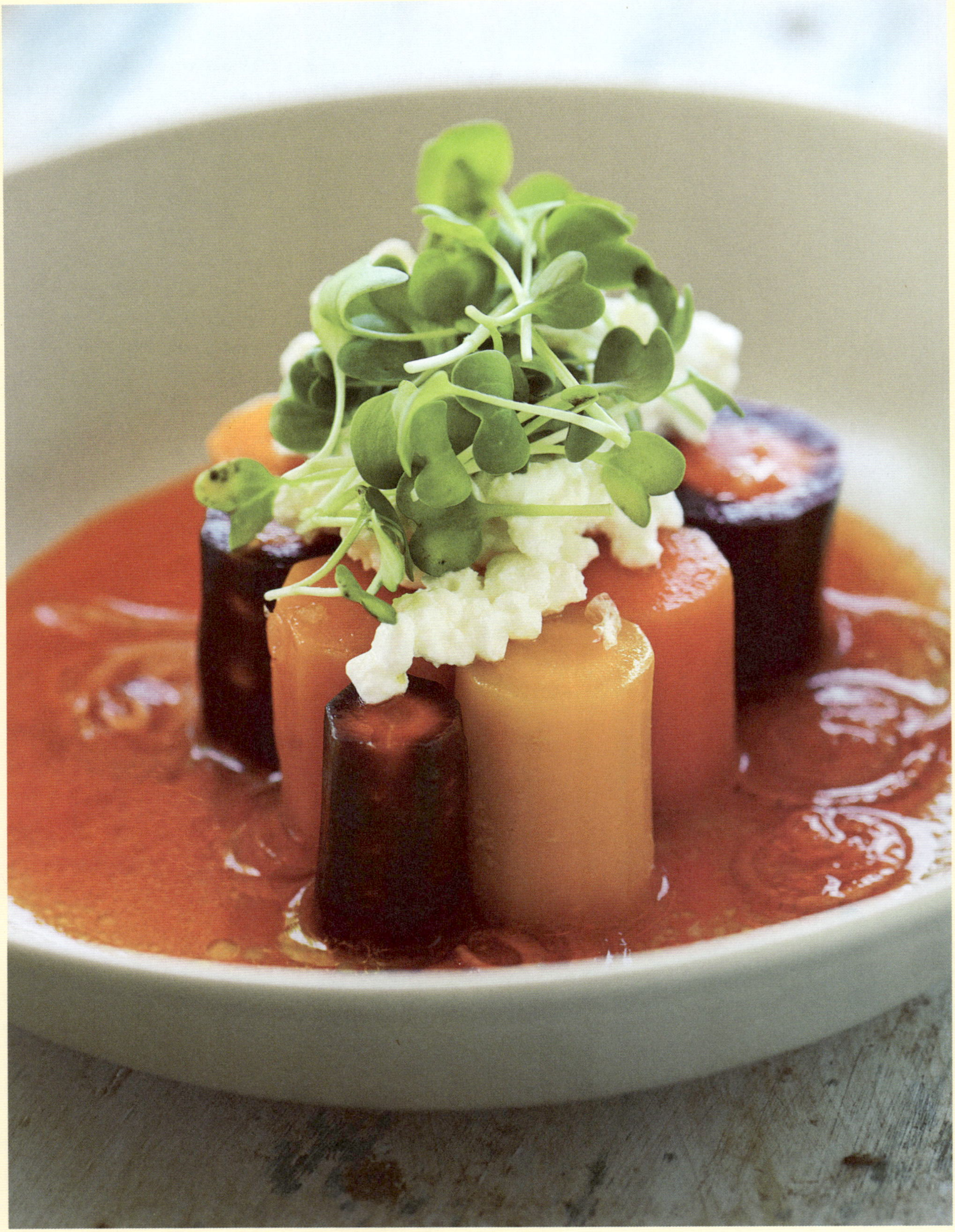

Carrot with Carrot Vinaigrette, Cottage Cheese and Daikon Cress

Ingredients (serves 4)
8 carrots (a mixture of different types, if you like)
salt and pepper
2 shallots
1/2 cup carrot juice (fresh, or from a bottle)
1 tablespoon sherry vinegar (or apple cider vinegar or white wine vinegar)
3—4 tablespoons olive oil
1 cup cottage cheese
1 cup daikon cress (or watercress)

1. Peel the carrots and cook in salted water for 10 minutes. Remove and allow to cool.
2. Peel the shallots and cut into fine rings. Mix with carrot juice and sherry vinegar. Whisk in the olive oil drop by drop. Season the vinaigrette with salt and pepper.
3. Pour the vinaigrette into 4 bowls. Cut the carrots into 1 1/2—2-inch long pieces and place them upright on the plate. Place cottage cheese and daikon cress on top.

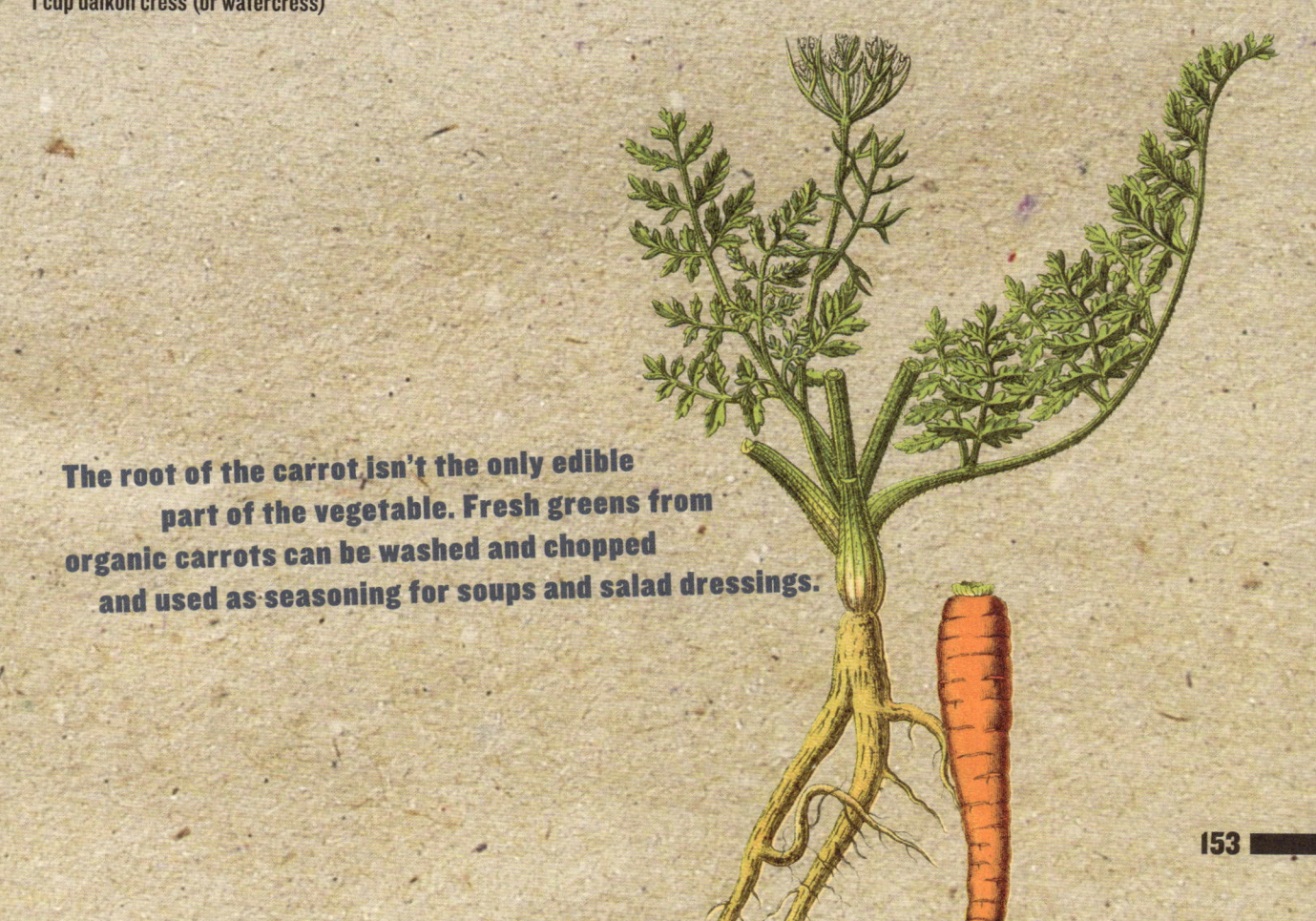

Preparation time: 20 minutes

The root of the carrot isn't the only edible part of the vegetable. Fresh greens from organic carrots can be washed and chopped and used as seasoning for soups and salad dressings.

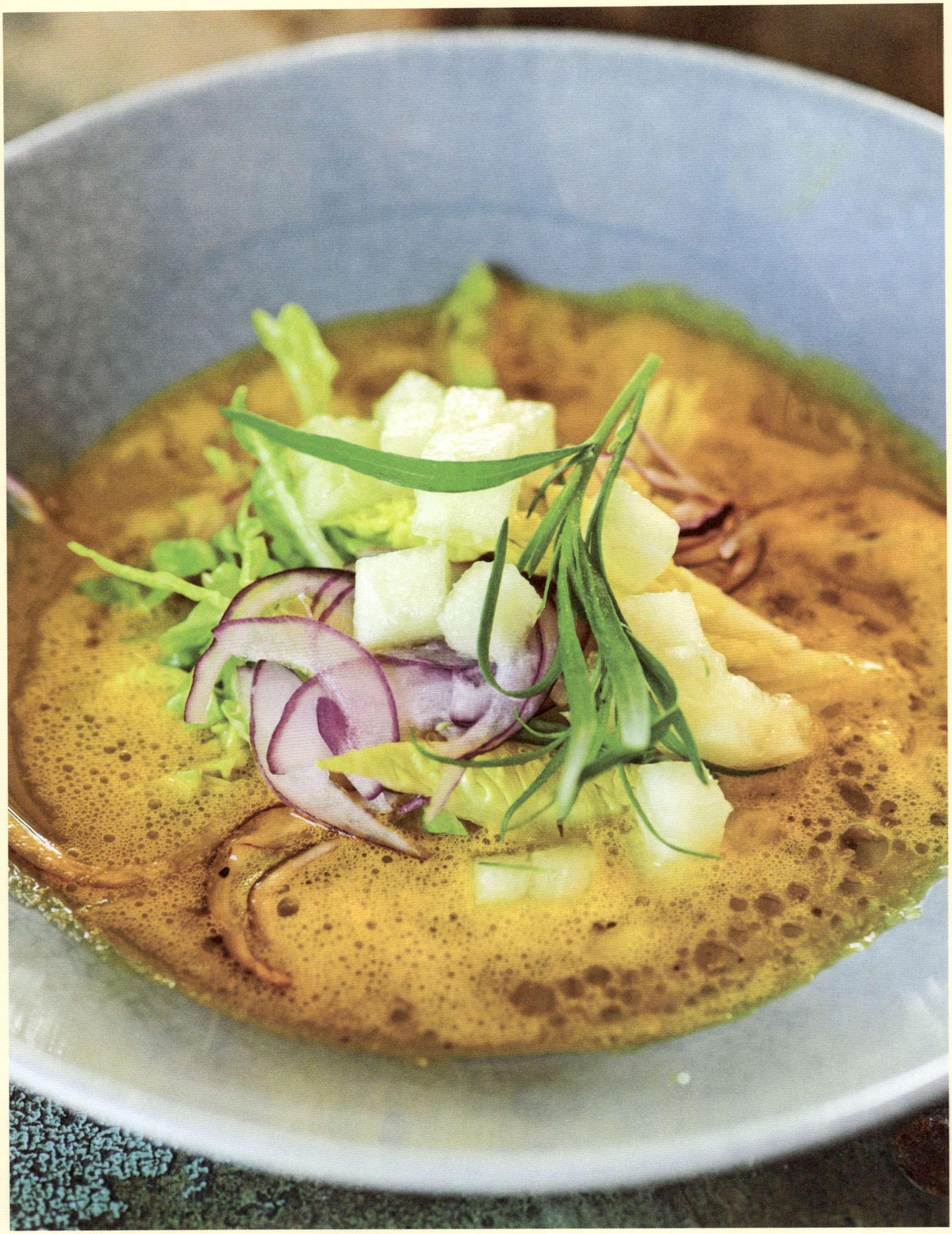

Cooled Bell Pepper Soup with Melon

Ingredients (serves 4)

- 4 yellow bell peppers
- 4 tablespoons olive oil
- 2—3 tablespoons white balsamic vinegar (or 1—2 tablespoons white wine vinegar)
- salt and pepper
- sugar
- 1 pound cantaloupe or galia melon
- 1 heart of romaine lettuce
- 1 small red onion
- 1 stem tarragon

1. Quarter the bell peppers, discard the seeds, and put the peppers through a juicer. Mix the bell pepper juice (1 3/4 cups) with the olive oil and white balsamic vinegar. Add salt, pepper and a pinch of sugar. Leave to cool.

2. Peel the melon, remove the seeds and dice. Cut the heart of romaine lettuce into quarters lengthwise and then into fine strips. Peel the onion, cut in half and then into fine stripes. Wash the lettuce and separate the leaves. Arrange the leaves in bowls with the melon and onion strips. Pour in the bell pepper soup. Sprinkle with a few tarragon leaves and serve.

Preparation time: 20 minutes

Although the crunchy bell pepper is technically a fruit, in cuisine it's considered a vegetable. Its taste is sweet and mild. Chilis and hot peppers from the same family provide spiciness.

Pineapple Apple Salad with Celery and Red Lentils

Ingredients (serves 4)

- 1 cup red lentils
- salt
- 1 small pineapple
- 3 stalks celery
- 3 stems basil
- 2 green apples (preferably Granny Smith)
- 2–3 tablespoons olive oil
- 2–3 tablespoons lemon juice

1. Rinse the lentils. Pour into boiling, salted water and cook for 5—6 minutes over low heat, uncovered. Drain in a sieve, rinse with cold water and leave them to dry.
2. Peel the pineapple and remove the "eyes." Cut it in half lengthwise, remove the core and cut the pulp into thin strips. Wash the celery sticks and cut diagonally into thin slices. Pull off the basil leaves. Wash and thinly slice the apples.
3. Mix all the prepared ingredients in a bowl with olive oil and lemon juice. Arrange on a plate and serve.

Preparation time: 20 minutes

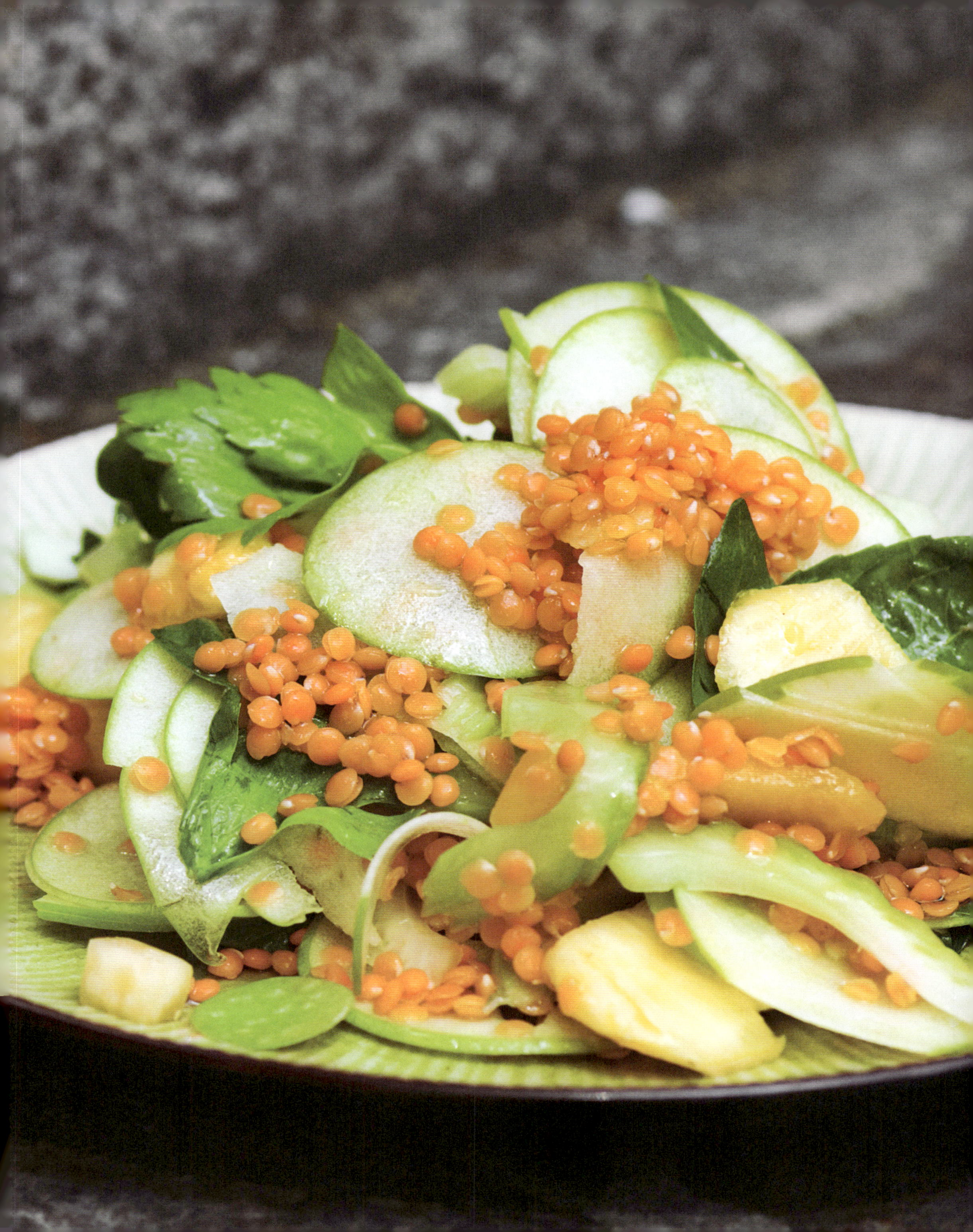

ASPARAGUS GALORE 4X

At the start of spring you can catch a first glimpse of sprouting asparagus heads. But things start livening up one or two months later. That's when the savory-sweet "asparagus officinalis" drills its way up through the warm earth towards the sun. The asparagus season is open! These recipes also work well with green asparagus.

1 Sautéed Asparagus

Peel **1 pound of white asparagus,** cut off the ends. Cut the spears diagonally into 1/2-inch long pieces. Finely chop a **small green chili pepper.** Heat **3 tablespoons of olive oil** in a pan and sauté the asparagus for 2—3 minutes, stirring all the time. Sprinkle with **1 teaspoon of sugar.** Add **1 tablespoon of butter, 1 teaspoon of sesame oil** and the **chili** and season with **salt.** Pull off the leaves from **4 stems of basil,** add to the asparagus, give it all a stir and serve immediately sprinkled with freshly ground pepper.

2 Asparagus Salad with Cilantro and Mango

Peel **1 pound of white asparagus,** cut off the ends and then cut diagonally into slices. Peel **1 mango,** separate the pulp from the pit, then cut into thin slices. Peel and dice **1 small red onion.** Pull off the leaves from **3 stems of cilantro.** Mix **2 tablespoons of lime juice** with **1 teaspoon of honey** and **4 tablespoons of olive oil** and add the cilantro leaves. Mix the asparagus, mango and onions with the salad dressing. You can spice up the salad with the help of red **chili flakes,** if desired.

3 Iced Cream of Asparagus with Yogurt

Peel **1 pound of white asparagus** and cut off the ends. Set aside 2 spears of asparagus. Roughly chop the rest of the asparagus. Peel **1/3 pound of potatoes**, dice and sauté together with the pieces of asparagus in a pan with **3 tablespoons of butter**. In an open pot, bring the ingredients to a boil barely covered in water and leave to cook on a medium heat for 20 minutes. Season with **salt, pepper** and **1 pinch of sugar**. Divide into 2 batches and purée in a blender. Strain the mixture through a sieve and leave to cool in the refrigerator for 2—3 hours. Before serving, cut the two uncooked asparagus into batons and sauté over medium heat in **1 tablespoon of butter** for 2 minutes. Season with **salt** and **sugar**. Chop the chives. Pour the cold soup into bowls. Stir **2/3 cups of yogurt** until smooth. Sprinkle the asparagus batons and the chives over the soup and serve.

4 Grilled Asparagus with Parmesan Vinaigrette

Whisk **5 tablespoons of finely grated Parmesan** with **2 tablespoons of lemon juice** and **5 tablespoons of olive oil**. Season with **salt, 1 pinch of sugar** and **pepper**. Peel **1 pound of white asparagus**, cut off the ends, cut the spears in half lengthwise and boil them in salted water for 2 minutes. Rinse off in cold water and drain on paper towels. Peel the bottom third of **1 pound of green asparagus** and cut off the ends. Wipe a thin layer of olive oil on a grill pan and heat to a maximum heat. Grill all sides of the spears in the olive oil for 2—4 minutes, portion by portion. Season with **salt** and **pepper** and serve drizzled with the vinaigrette.

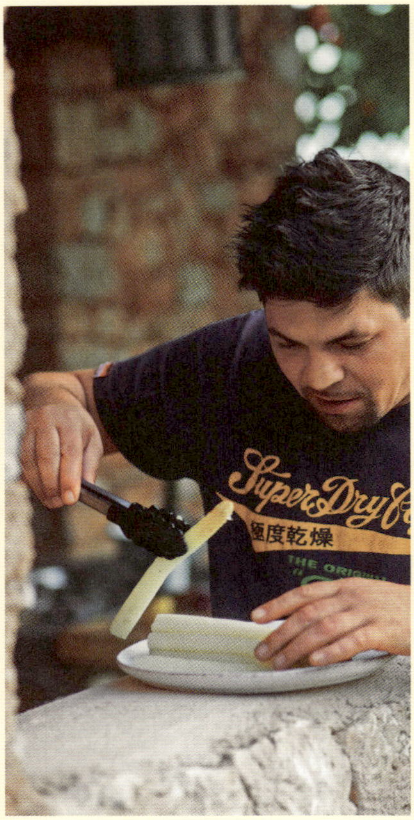
極度乾燥
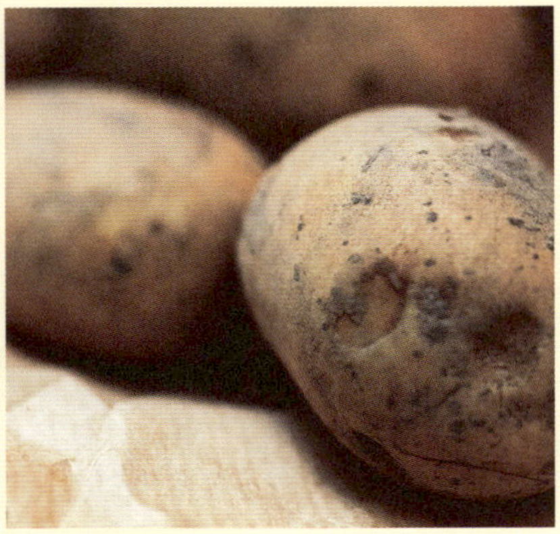
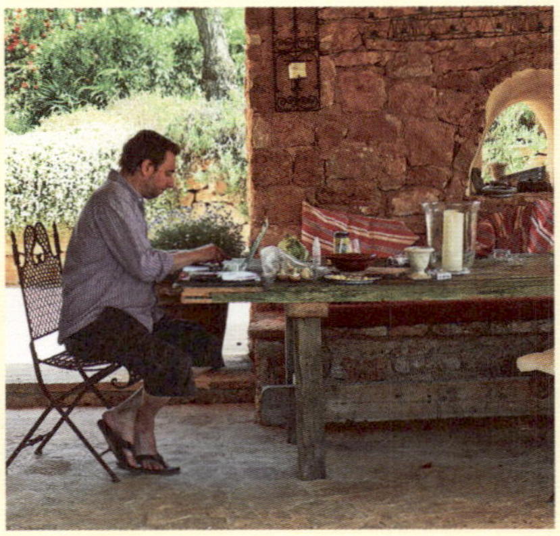
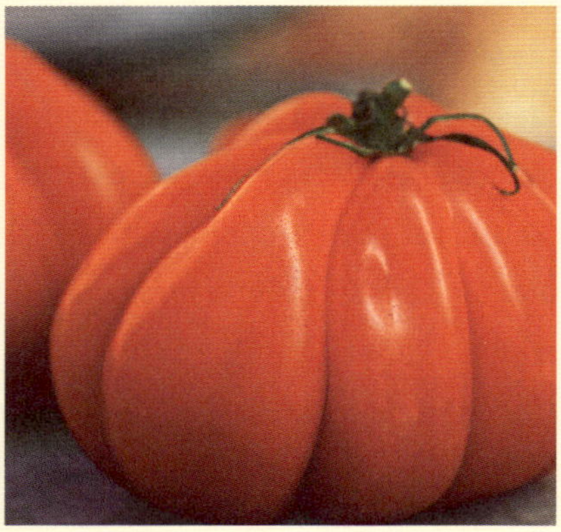
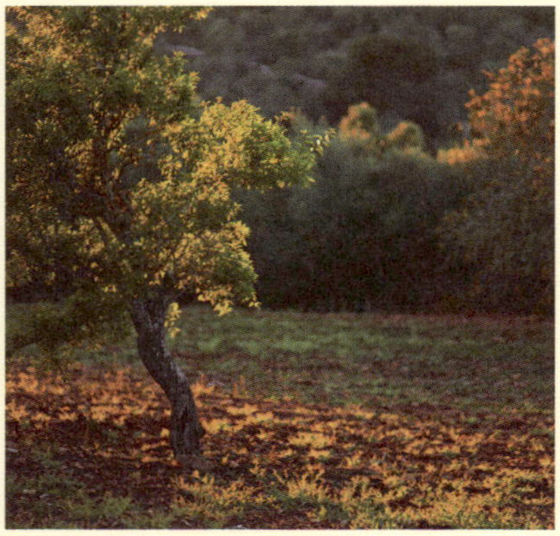
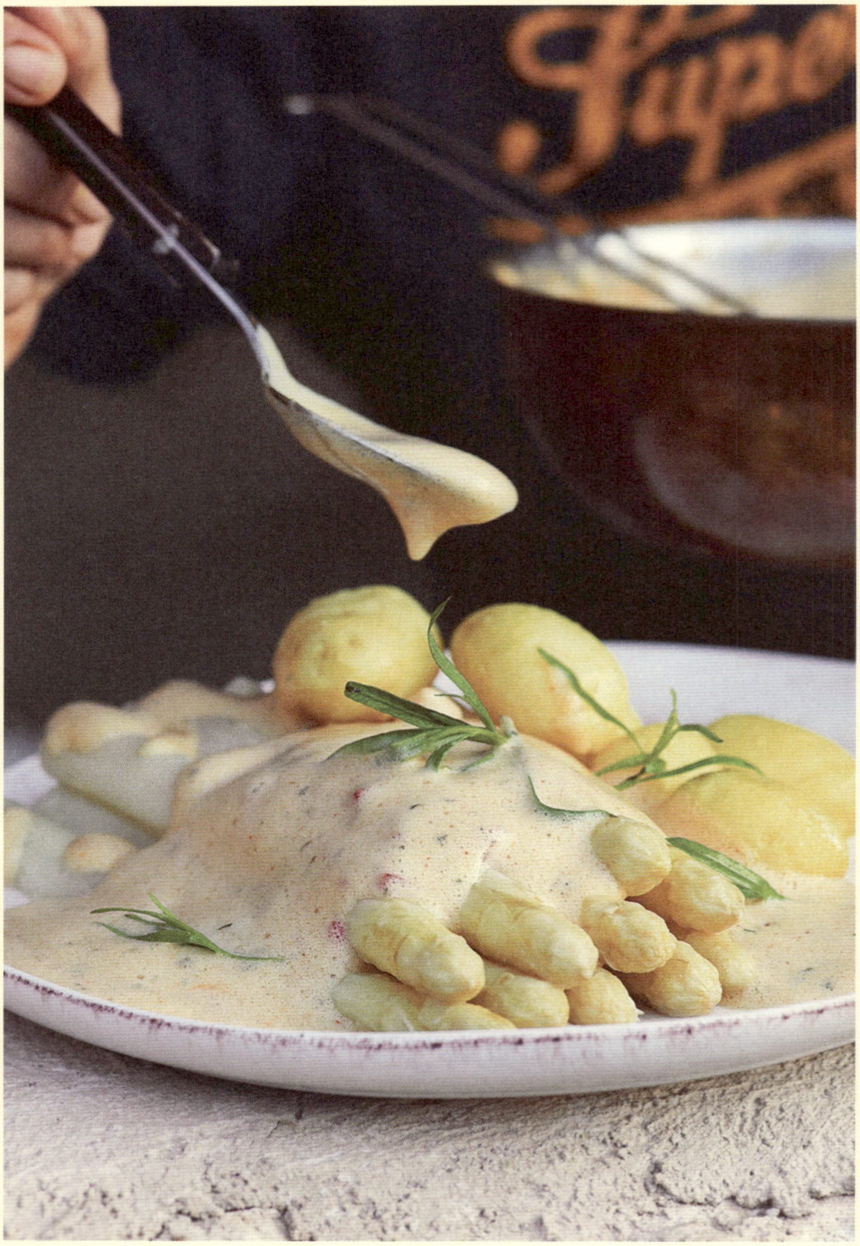

Asparagus with Tarragon Tomato Zabaglione

Ingredients (serves 4)
1 3/4 pounds small new potatoes
salt
4 1/2 pounds white asparagus
sugar
1 tablespoon butter
1 tomato
4 egg yolks (large egg)
1 teaspoon tomato paste
1/4 cup white port wine
1/4 cup vegetable stock
1/2 teaspoon dried tarragon
1 tablespoon chopped fresh tarragon
cayenne pepper
lemon juice

1. Wash the potatoes thoroughly and cook them in salted water for 15—20 minutes until just tender. Peel the asparagus and trim off the ends. Boil the asparagus in salted water with 1 tablespoon of sugar for 8 minutes. Remove from the heat, and depending on how thick the spears are, leave them to soak in the cooking liquid. Peel the potatoes and while they are still warm, stir them around in the butter until just tender. Add salt and keep warm.
2. Wash the tomato, cut it into quarters, remove the seeds and dice. Set aside. Put the egg yolks, tomato paste, port, vegetable stock and dried and fresh tarragon into a metal bowl or pan. Whisk either in a water bath or directly on the stove on low to medium heat for 10—12 minutes until thick and creamy. Stir in the tomato pieces. Season to taste with cayenne pepper, 1 pinch of sugar and lemon juice.
3. Remove the asparagus from the water, drain and arrange the hot asparagus on preheated plates. Serve immediately with potatoes.

Preparation time: 60 minutes

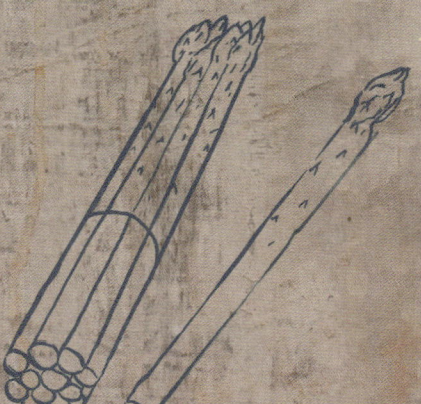

TIP If you use green asparagus instead of white, reduce the cooking time to 4 minutes.

Potato Celery Purée with Buttered Green Vegetables

Ingredients (serves 4)

1 pound russet potatoes
1/2 pound celery root
salt
8 tablespoons butter
5 ounces fava beans
1 bunch green asparagus
5 ounces snow peas
1/4 pound green peas
1 garlic clove
1 teaspoon flour
1 1/3 cups vegetable stock
6 leaves fresh mint
1 scallion
nutmeg
lemon juice
olive oil

1. To make the purée, peel the potatoes and the celery root and cut into pieces. Cook until soft in boiling salted water. Drain, allow to steam briefly and then mash with 5–6 tablespoons of butter. Season with salt. Keep warm.

2. Boil the fava beans in salted water for 1–2 minutes. Rinse under cold water. Press the beans out of the waxy skins. Peel the lower third of the green asparagus, cut off the ends and cut the spears into 3 pieces. Boil the asparagus with the snow peas and green peas for 2 minutes in salted water and then rinse in cold water.

3. Sauté the cooked vegetables in a pot with 2 tablespoons of butter for 2 minutes. Peel the garlic and cut into slices and add to the vegetables. Dust the vegetables with flour. Deglaze with vegetable stock and cook for 2 minutes. Slice the mint into fine strips and fold in.

4. Wash the scallion and cut into fine diagonal strips. Season the vegetables with a light touch of nutmeg, a dash of lemon juice and salt. Sprinkle the bits of scallion over the top. Drizzle with a few drops of olive oil and serve with the purée.

Preparation time: 45 minutes

VARIATIONS: You can use canned lima beans instead of fava beans for this dish. If you don't like celery root, you can use 1/2 pound of carrots.

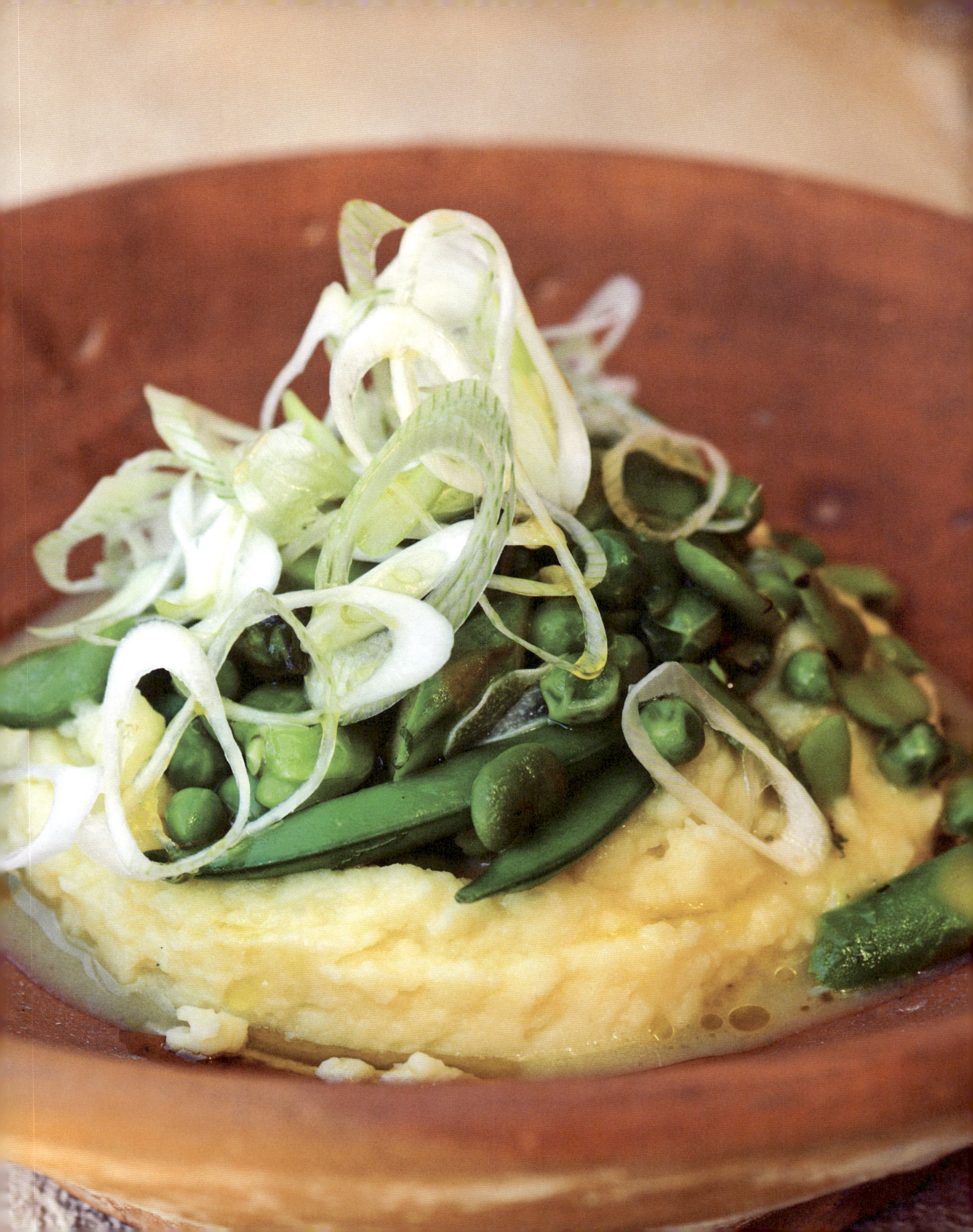

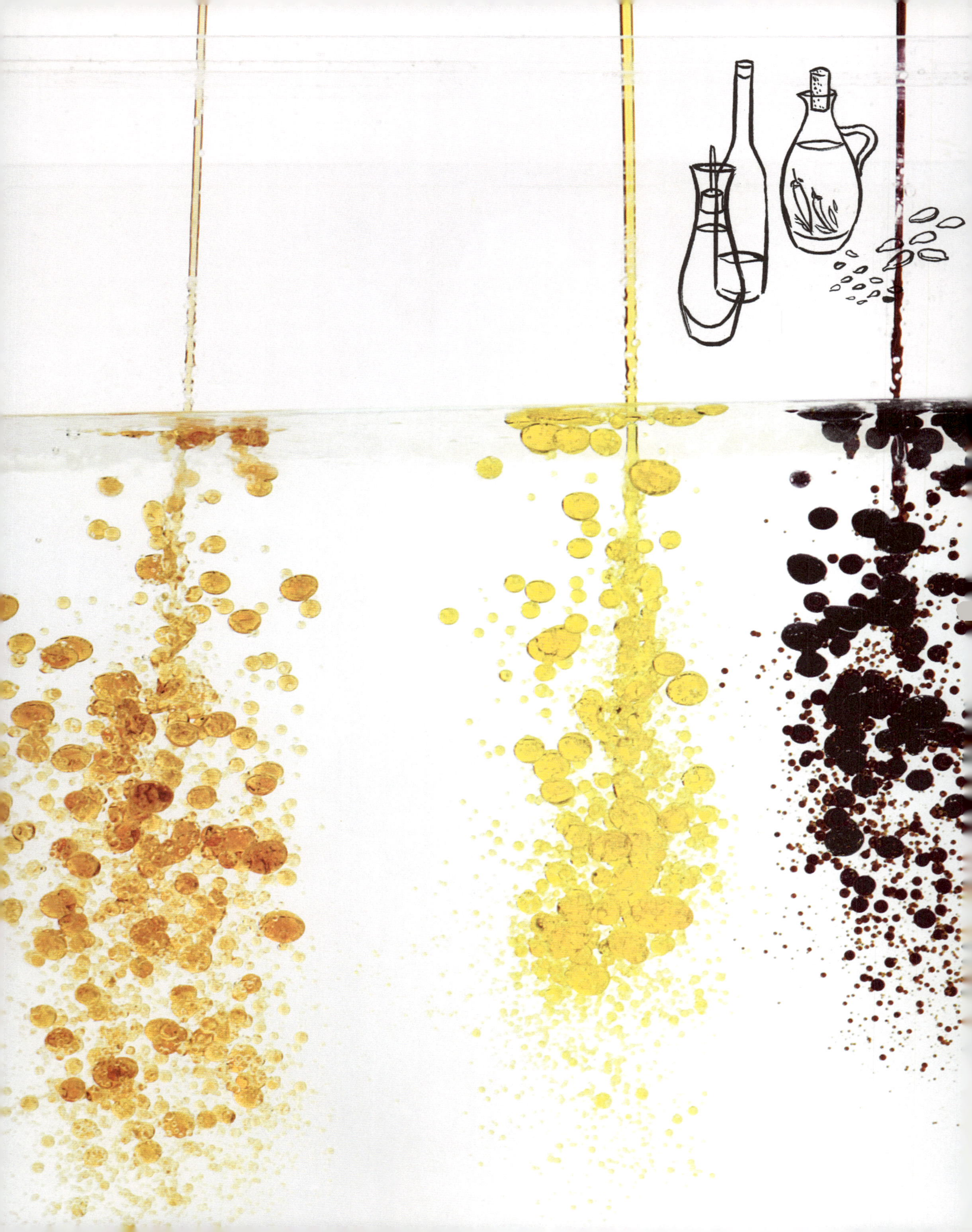

Oil

WHEN THINGS ARE WELL-OILED!

Oil adds flavor to vegetarian cooking, but not every oil is right for every occasion. Each oil has its own character and its own aroma. Here's a list of the most common ones:

OLIVE OIL is the queen of oils. There are so many different qualities and flavors of olive oil out there that it can be very confusing. Take care to buy a natural, untreated and cold pressed oil, designated "extra virgin." Test results and surveys can only give you an indication of which are the best oils; it's best to try them out yourself because, overall, it is definitely a matter of personal taste. Strong-flavored oils with a lot of character are suitable for many cold dishes. The less expensive and less complex oils are better for frying and steaming. It is possible to deep fry things in olive oil; however, the particularly "olivey" taste disappears with the smoke. If you ever try French fries made in olive oil and sprinkled with sea salt, you will definitely want more!

SESAME OIL is extracted from roasted sesame seeds and has a very strong aroma. You should use it very sparingly. It gives many Asian dishes a characteristic taste.

SUNFLOWER OIL is pretty neutral tasting and a rather reserved vegetable oil. It is ideal for frying and deep frying. Due to its mild taste, it can be used in salad dressings and vinaigrettes or as a basis for mayonnaise.

PUMPKIN SEED OIL has a unique flavor. Just a few drops of the dark green oil are enough to give a dish a wonderful toasted aroma. It goes well with cheese, radishes, on top of mashed potatoes, with vegetable quiches, and is delicious dribbled over pumpkin soup. It is not advisable to heat this oil.

WALNUT OIL should only be used cold. Its nutty aroma develops best in salad dressings and vinaigrettes. It's also delicious dribbled over cooked vegetables or cheese, and as seasoning in marinades, soups and sauces.

GOOD TO KNOW! All oils should be stored in a cool and dark place. Hazelnut, walnut and pumpkin seed oil should be kept in the fridge. You should always buy fresh olive and pumpkin seed oil and they should not be kept for too long. For many, it's better to buy small bottles.

Majorcan Coca with Rhubarb

Ingredients (serves 2—4)

- 2 teaspoons fresh yeast (or 1 teaspoon active dry yeast)
- sugar
- 2 cups plus 1 tablespoon flour
- salt and pepper
- 8 tablespoons olive oil
- 1 egg yolk (large egg)
- 2 shallots
- 1/2 pound rhubarb
- 1/2 pound spinach
- curry powder

1 Dissolve the yeast and 1 pinch of sugar in 1/3 cup plus 4 teaspoons of lukewarm water. Put the flour, 1 teaspoon of salt, 6 tablespoons of olive oil, egg yolk and yeast mixture into a bowl. Using a dough hook on a hand blender, mix thoroughly and then knead with your hands until smooth. Cover and leave in a warm place for 45 minutes.

2 Peel the shallots and cut into thin slices. Wash the rhubarb and cut into 1 1/2—2-inch long pieces. Slice these lengthwise into three equal pieces and then cut into large dice. Mix with 1 teaspoon of sugar and 1 pinch of salt. Wash the spinach, spin it dry, roughly chop and let it wilt in a pot with 2 tablespoons of hot olive oil and the curry powder. Season with salt and drain in a sieve.

3 Roll out the dough to the size of 16 x 12 inches and lay it on a sheet lined with parchment paper. Evenly distribute the spinach, rhubarb and shallots on top. Season with salt and pepper and drizzle with a few drops of olive oil. Preheat the oven to 425°F (convection: 390°F) and bake on the bottom rack for 30—35 minutes until golden brown. Serve hot or cold.

Preparation time: 30 minutes (+ 75 minutes for the dough to rest and bake)

VARIATIONS: You can, of course, use other stewed or sautéed vegetables according to taste. A quick and easy option: spread ripe slices of tomato with real buffalo mozzarella on the "coca" with a few drops of olive oil. Bake it according to the recipe. Sprinkle with fresh basil leaves and serve immediately.

"Classic pizza from the wood oven is delicious. The "coca," a Majorcan vegetable pie with a lot of olive oil in the dough, also turns out really crispy when cooked in regular household ovens."

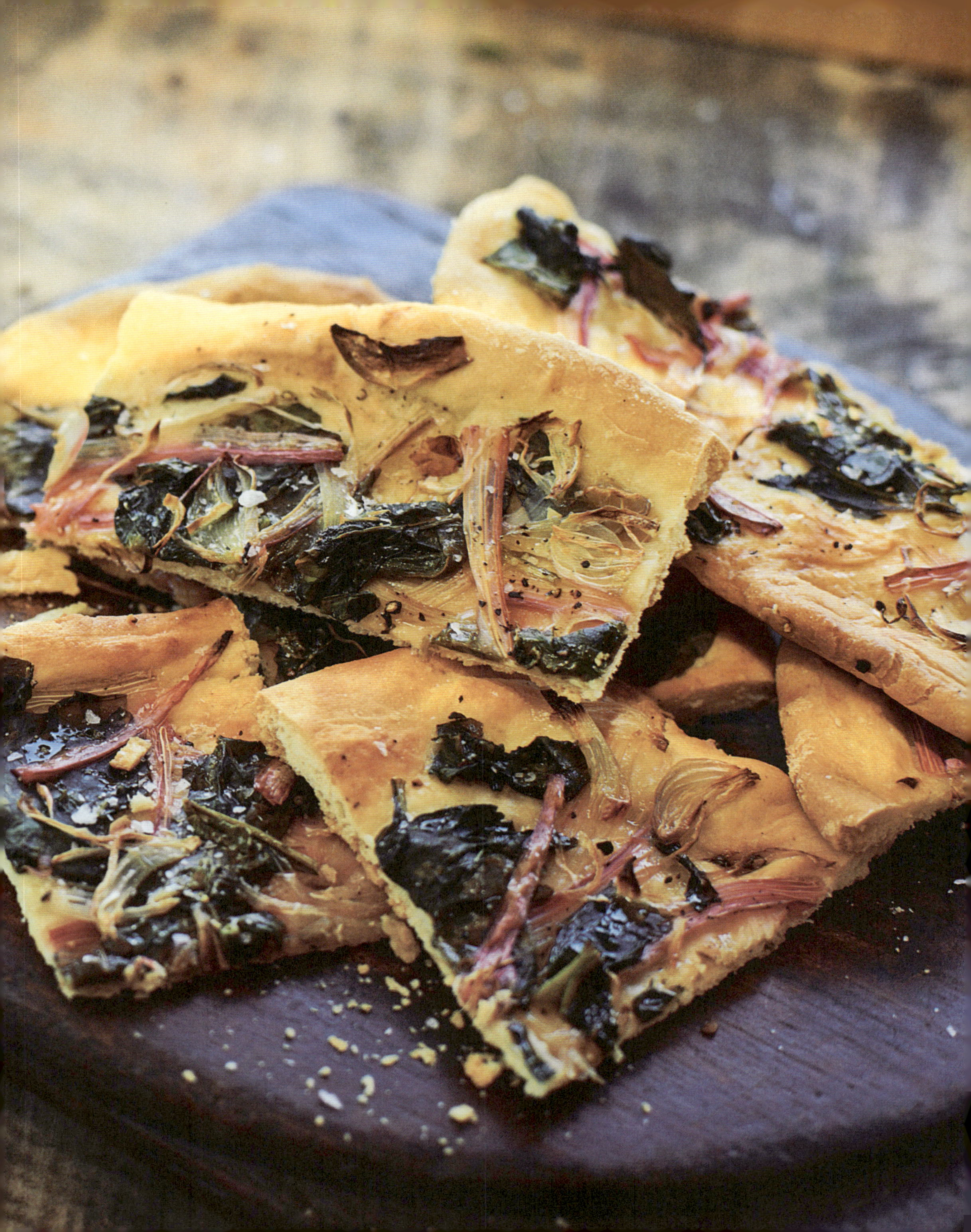

Peach Zucchini Salad with Mozzarella Dressing

Ingredients (serves 4)

1/2 pound buffalo mozzarella or burrata
1 cup lowfat yogurt
2 small zucchini
8 tablespoons olive oil
4 ounces fava beans (or peas, either fresh or frozen)
salt and pepper
4 peaches
1 red chili pepper
4 stems basil
1 organic lemon

1. Rinse the mozzarella under cold water, drain and cut into pieces. Purée it together with the yogurt until it has a smooth consistency. If the sauce isn't runny enough, add some water. Cover and place in the refrigerator for 15 minutes.

2. Meanwhile, wash the zucchini and cut into very thin slices. In 2 tablespoons of olive oil, brown the zucchini slices on both sides for 2—3 minutes. Drain dry on paper towels.

3. Cook the fava beans in boiling salted water for 1—2 minutes, rinse with cold water, drain dry and press the beans out of their waxy skins.

4. Cut the peaches into thin slices removing the pit. Slice the chili pepper. Pick off some basil leaves.

5. Mix the fava beans, zucchini slices and peach slices and season with salt, pepper and the juice of one lemon. Arrange the salad in deep plates and pour the mozzarella dressing over it. Sprinkle with sliced chili pepper, basil leaves, drizzle with the rest of the olive oil and serve.

Preparation time: 35 min

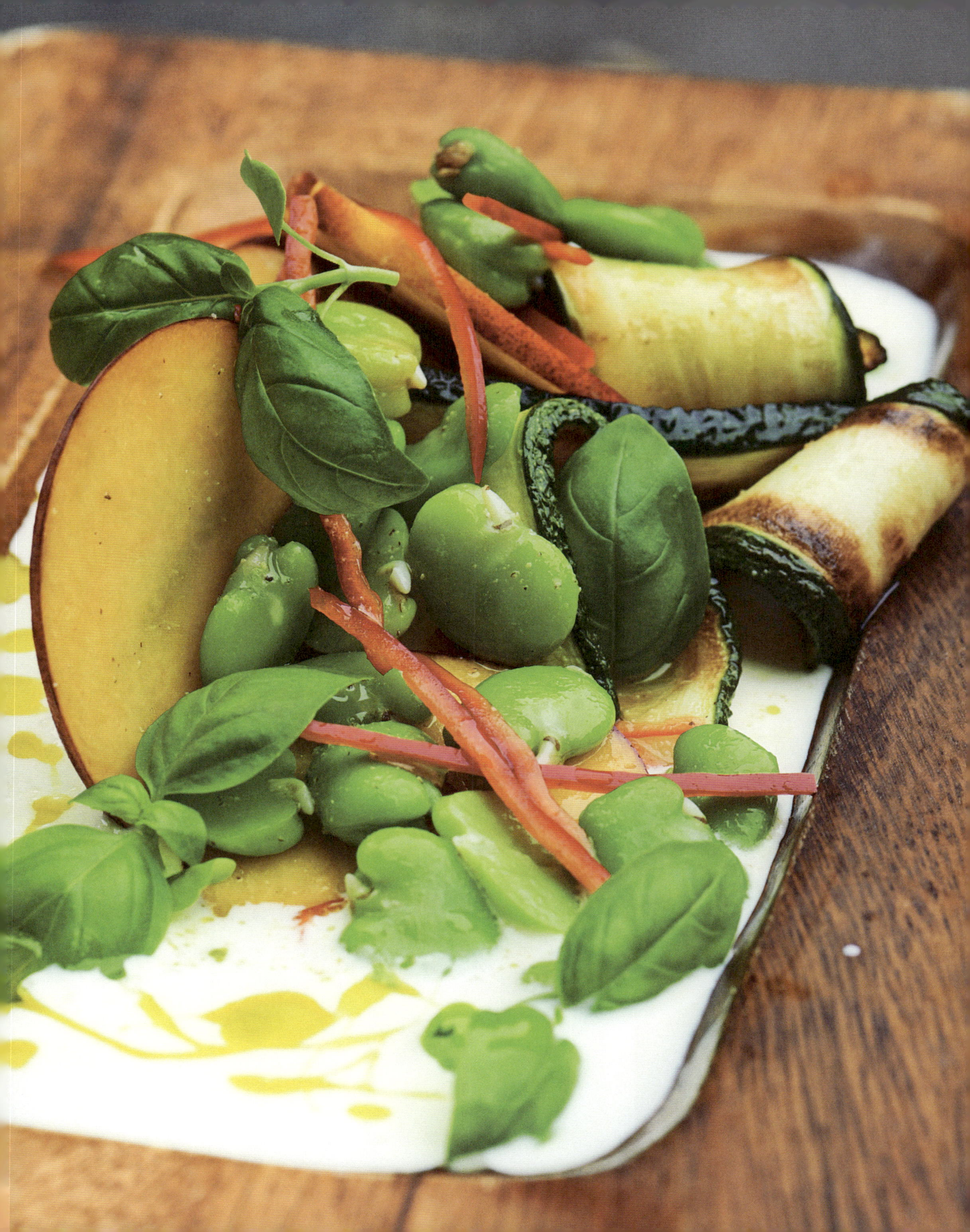

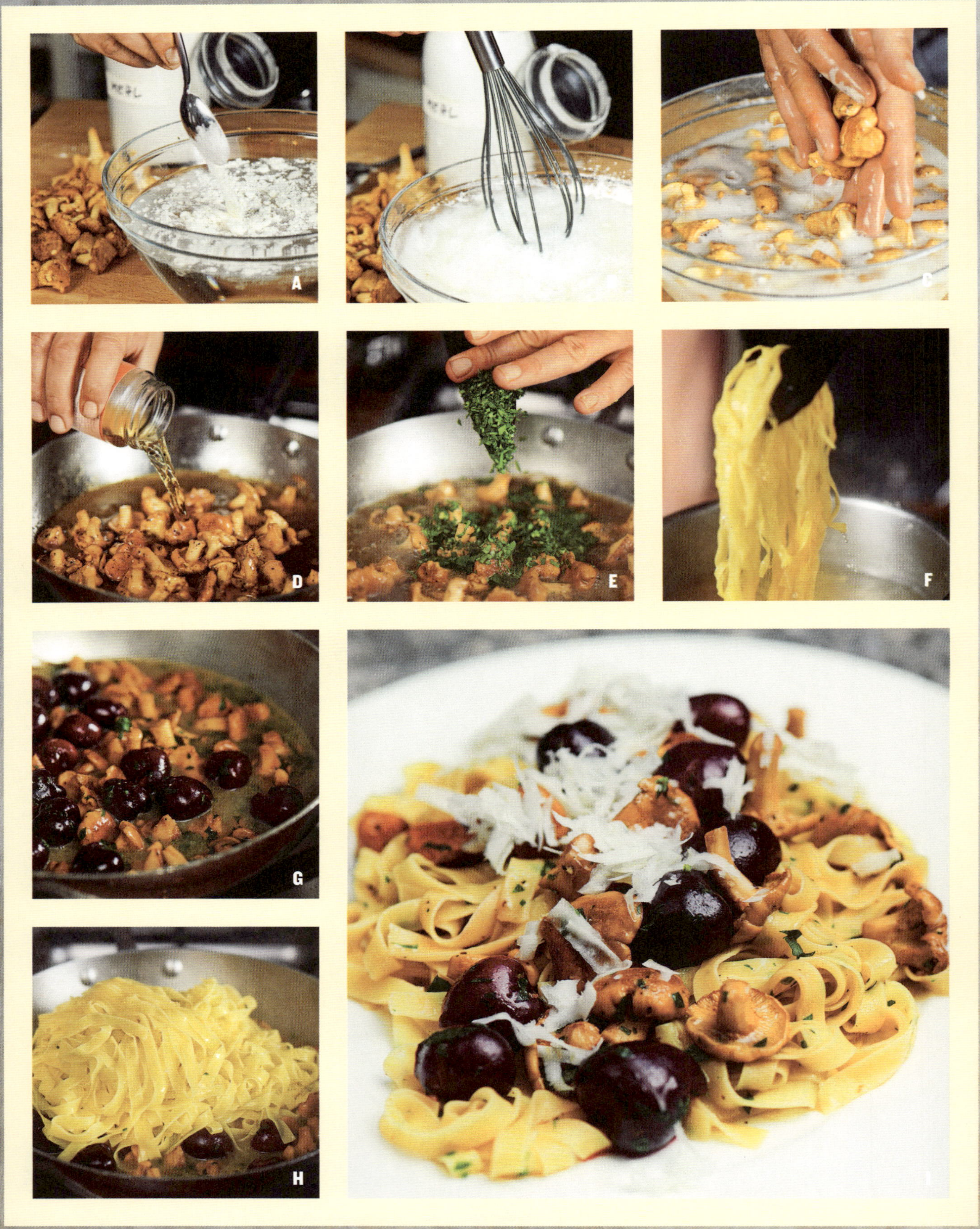
A
C
D
E
F
G
H

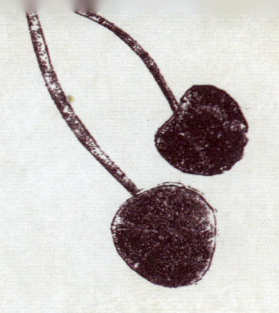

Tagliatelle with Chanterelles and Cherries

Ingredients (serves 2—4)

- 1/2 pound chanterelles
- 1/2 pound cherries
- 3 tablespoons olive oil
- 1 cup vegetable stock
- 6 stems parsley
- 1/2 pound tagliatelle all'uovo or fresh tagliatelle
- salt
- 2 tablespoons butter
- freshly ground black pepper
- fresh horseradish

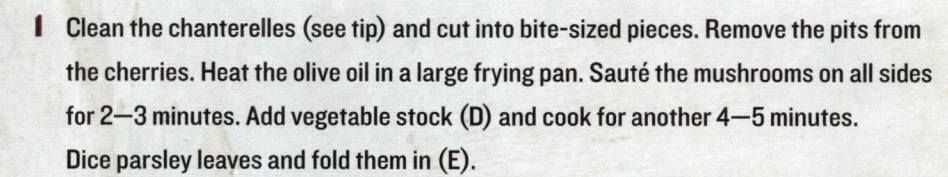

1. Clean the chanterelles (see tip) and cut into bite-sized pieces. Remove the pits from the cherries. Heat the olive oil in a large frying pan. Sauté the mushrooms on all sides for 2—3 minutes. Add vegetable stock (D) and cook for another 4—5 minutes. Dice parsley leaves and fold them in (E).
2. In the meantime, cook the tagliatelle in plenty of boiling salted water until it is al dente. Drain in a sieve (F).
3. Add the cherries, pasta and butter to the mushrooms (G, H). Season well with salt and pepper. Sprinkle with freshly grated horseradish and serve (I).

Preparation time: 30 minutes

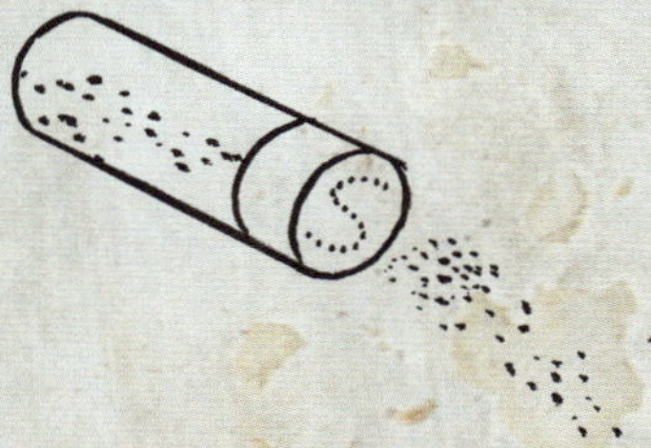

TIP If the mushrooms are really dirty and sandy, it's easy to clean them. In a bowl, whisk a few tablespoons of flour and cold water (A, B). Add a few mushrooms at a time to the flour mixture and then quickly rub them clean (C). Let them dry on paper towels or on a dish towel.

1

2

3

3X EASY CORN

In summer and late fall it is culinary paradise when a dab of well-seasoned butter melts over corn on the cob right off the grill. The sun-kissed corn is sweet and juicy and great for making soups and fresh salads. For the rest of the year, you can use canned corn...until the next summer.

1 Sautéed Corn

Drain **1 can of corn (16 ounces net weight)**, wash **2 scallions** and **3 cloves of garlic**. Cut the scallions and garlic into slices and sauté with the corn in **2 tablespoons of olive oil**. Season with **salt** and **chili flakes**.

3 Salt 'n Pepper Corn

Boil **4 cobs of corn** in a pot with salted water for 12—15 minutes. In the meantime, toast **1 tablespoon of black peppercorns** in a pan. Coarsely grind the pepper in a mortar. Cream **2/3 of a cup of butter at room temperature** with a hand blender. Mix in the pepper with **1 pinch of chili flakes** and **1 teaspoon of roasted garlic** (canned or homemade) and season with salt. Remove the cobs of corn and pat dry with paper towels. Brush the cobs with a little **oil** and roast them on the grill for 6—8 minutes. Season with **salt** and serve spread with **butter**.

2 Corn and Coconut Soup with Lime

Prepare the **Sautéed Corn** in the recipe above and set aside 2 tablespoons of corn. Cook the rest of the corn in an uncovered pot with **2 1/3 cups of vegetable stock** for 10 minutes. Add **1 cup of coconut milk** to the soup and, with a hand blender, blend until very smooth. Season with **salt** and **1—2 teaspoons of lime juice**. Mix in the rest of the sautéed corn with **cilantro leaves** and sprinkle over the soup.

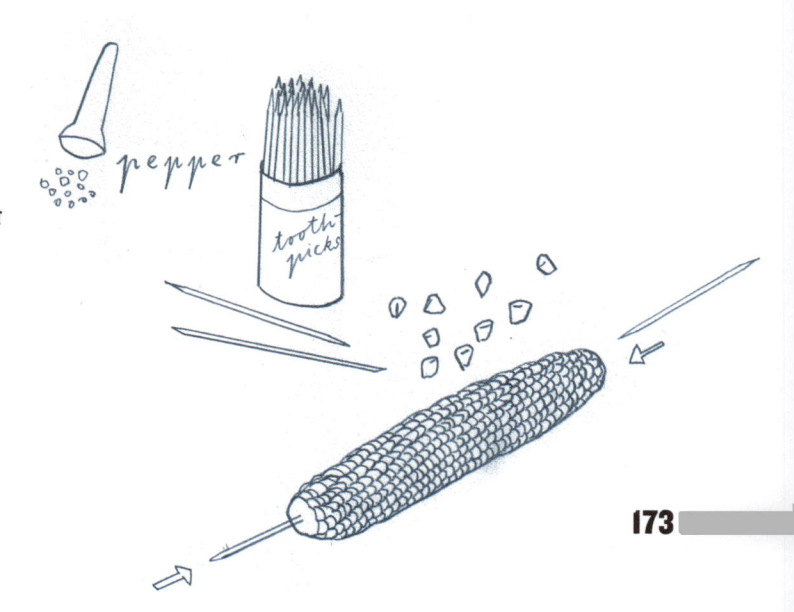

Squash Risotto with Morels and Almonds

Ingredients (serves 4)

1 ounce dried morels
4 1/3 cups hot vegetable stock
1 pound red kuri squash
6 tablespoons olive oil
1 large onion
2 garlic cloves
1 2/3 cups risotto rice
2 bay leaves
1/2 cup dry white wine
20 almonds, unpeeled
1/2 small organic lemon
1 bunch chives
6 tablespoons butter
salt
3—4 tablespoons freshly grated Parmesan
freshly ground black pepper

1 Soften the morels in the hot vegetable stock. Peel the squash, remove the seeds, dice and sauté in 4 tablespoons of olive oil. Set aside. Peel and dice the onion and 1 clove of garlic. Add to the squash with rice and bay leaves. Pour in wine and bring to a boil. Add some of the hot stock. Stirring from time to time, cook until it is reduced, then add more stock. Cook the risotto this way for 25—30 minutes until tender (see tip).

2 Meanwhile, finely chop the almonds. Trim off the lemon peel and slice into fine strips. Peel 1 clove of garlic and cut into thin slices. Mince the chives. Let 3 tablespoons of butter and 2 tablespoons of olive oil foam in a pan. Add the almonds, lemon strips, garlic and chives and allow to foam again. Season with salt.

3 Add the soft morels to the finished risotto and bring to a boil once again. Mix until smooth with 3 tablespoons of butter and Parmesan cheese. Season with the juice of the peeled lemon, salt and pepper. Serve immediately, covered in the almond lemon butter.

Preparation time: 45 minutes

TIP Different types of risotto rice have different cooking times. Please pay attention to the instructions on the packaging.

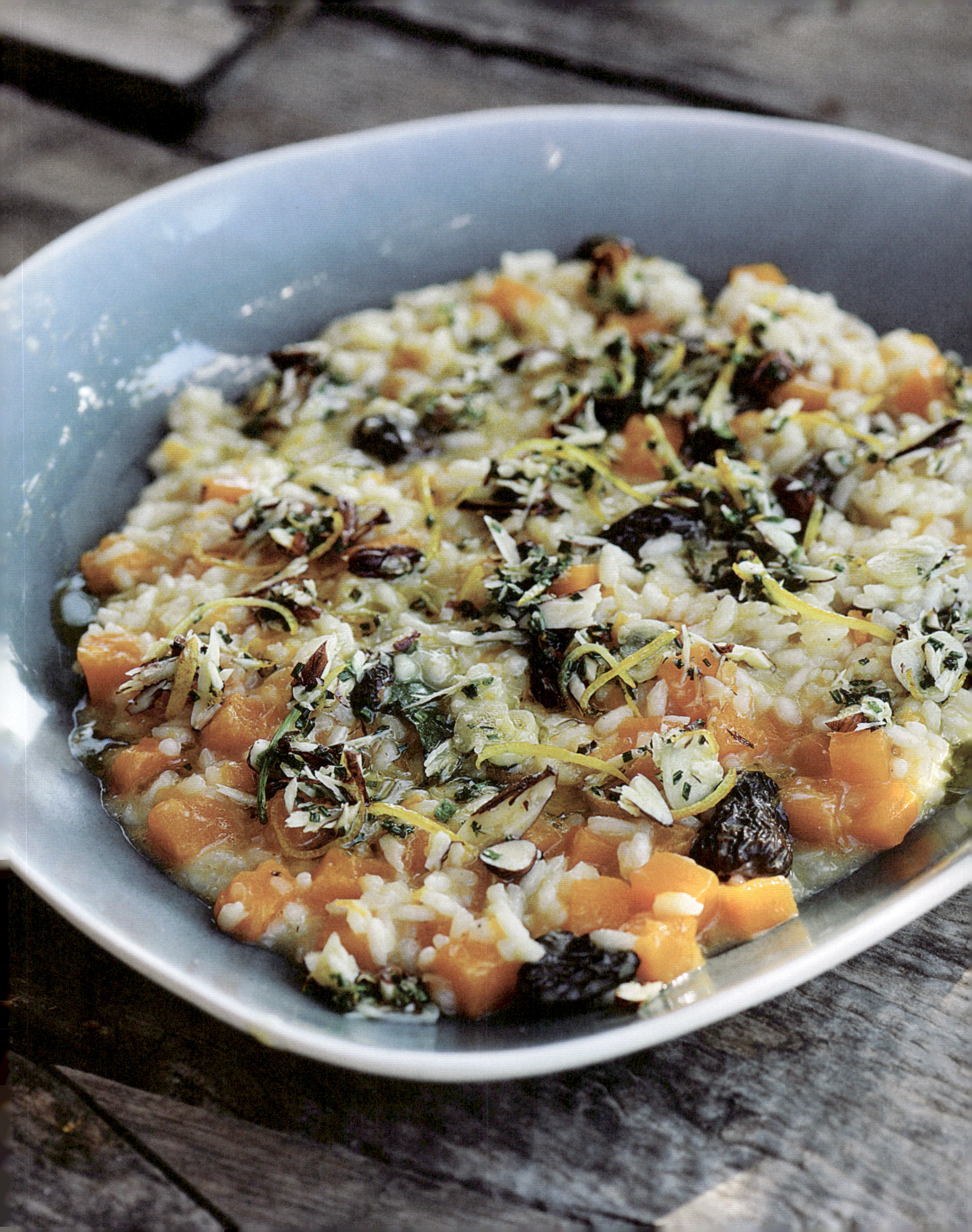

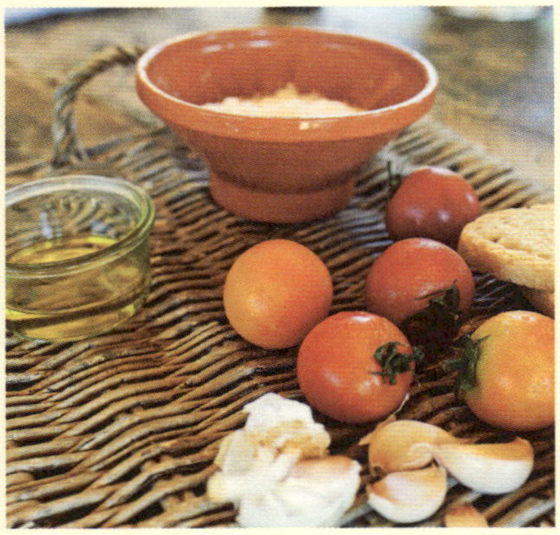
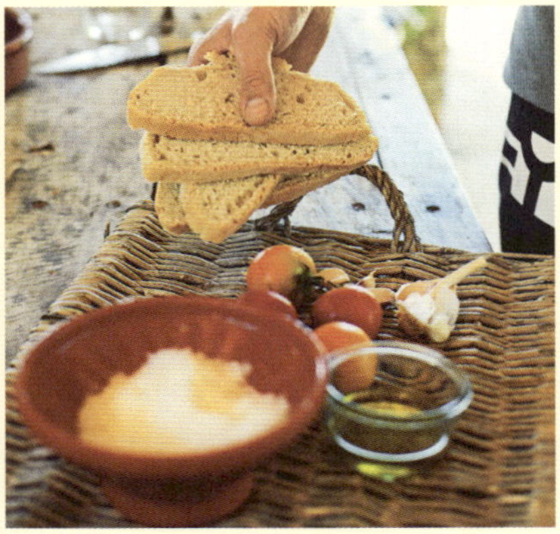
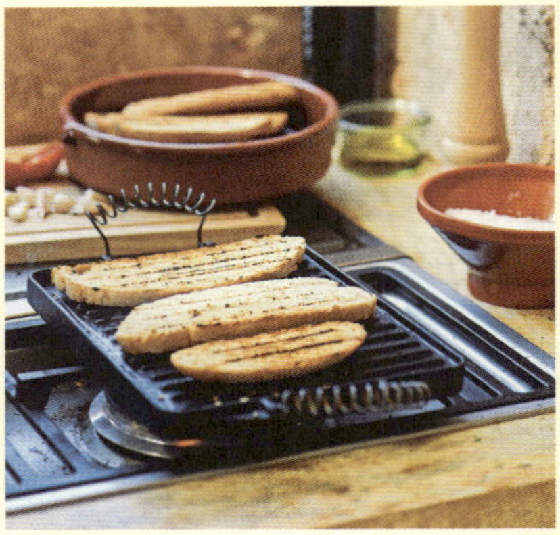
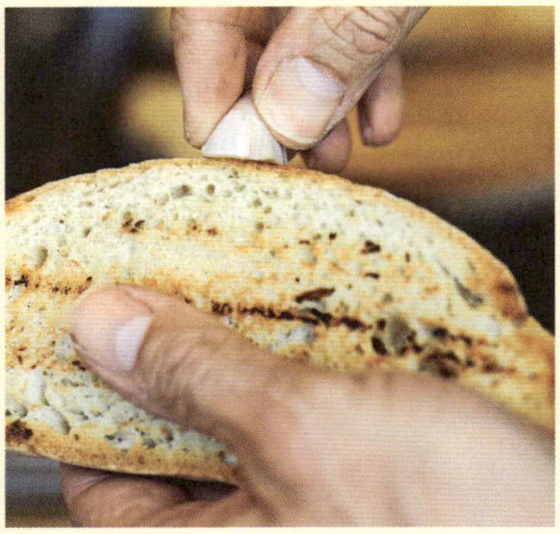
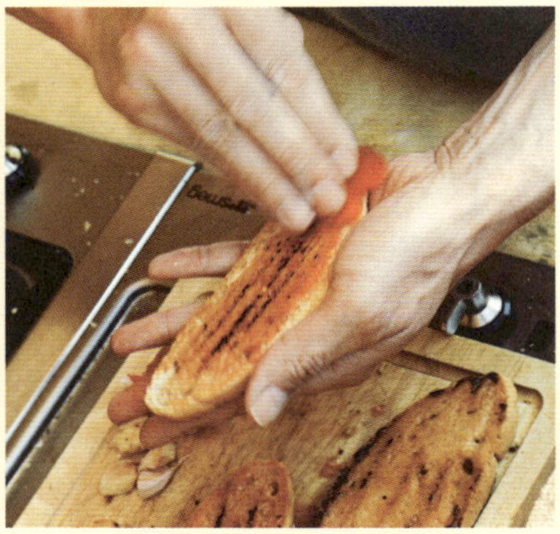
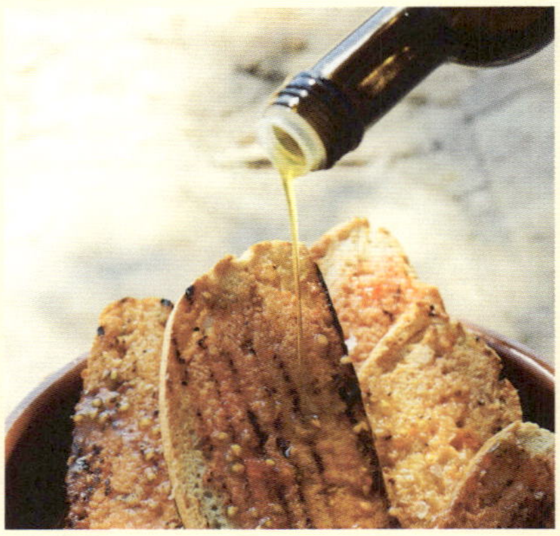
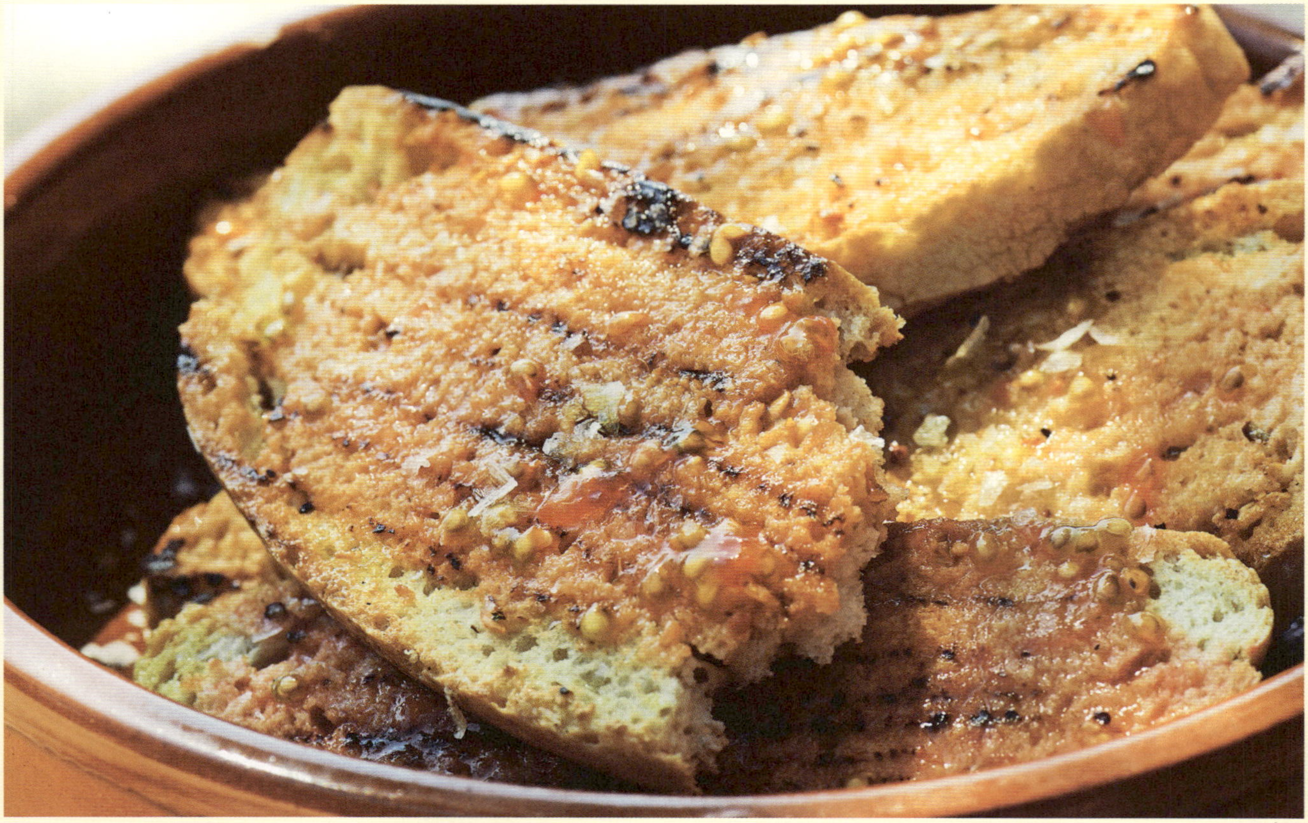

Matthias' P'amb oli

Ingredients (serves 4)
8 thick slices white bread
3—4 garlic cloves
4 tomatoes, as aromatic as possible
fleur de sel
pepper
6 tablespoons olive oil

1. Toast the white bread under the broiler or in a grill pan until light brown on both sides. Peel the garlic cloves, halve them and rub the cut sides on the grilled slices of bread.
2. Wash the tomatoes, slice them in half and rub the cut side on the bread. Sprinkle with a little fleur de sel and pepper and drizzle with olive oil. Serve immediately.

Preparation time: 20 minutes

TIP This recipe also works well with any kind of day-old bread.

P'AMB OLI is the classic Majorcan tomato bread and is the perfect complement to every table.

PRETTY HOT ONIONS X 3

They are the first step in most recipes. They can taste as light as spring or rustic; they are spicy, they are juicy, they can be mild or biting. There is only one thing that onions aren't ever, and that is boring. They melt sweetly into aromatic sauces, provide crunch and flavor in fresh salads and surprise you when hidden in crisp wrappings.

1 Grilled Scallions

Wash **8 thick scallions** thoroughly, dry them and coat in **1–2 tablespoons of olive oil.** Grill the scallions all the way round for 5 minutes until they are totally black. Pull or scrape off the burnt skin. Place the tender, cooked scallions on a platter and drizzle with **lemon juice** and **olive oil.** Season with **sea salt** and **pepper.**

2 Onion Rings

Peel **1 Spanish onion** and cut into thick rings. Soak in **2 1/4 cups of buttermilk** for 20 minutes. Mix **1 cup of flour** with **1 teaspoon of ground sweet paprika** and **1/2 teaspoon of salt.** Drain the onion rings and cover in flour. Deep fry the onions in **oil** at 350°F for 3–4 minutes until crunchy. Drain on paper towels. Mix the onion rings with a few washed and rinsed **arugula** leaves and serve with **ketchup.**

3 Shallots from the Oven

Wash **1 pound of unpeeled shallots,** pat them dry and mix with **2 tablespoons of fleur de sel** and **5 tablespoons of olive oil.** Spread on a baking sheet and cook on the middle rack in a preheated oven at 450°F for 30 minutes. Let the shallots cool a little, then cut them open at one end, squeeze them out and spread the shallot mousse on **6–8 slices of toasted bread.** Arrange on plates with freshly picked **leaves from two marjoram stems, sea salt,** a **few drops of olive oil** and **freshly ground pepper** and serve.

2

3

1

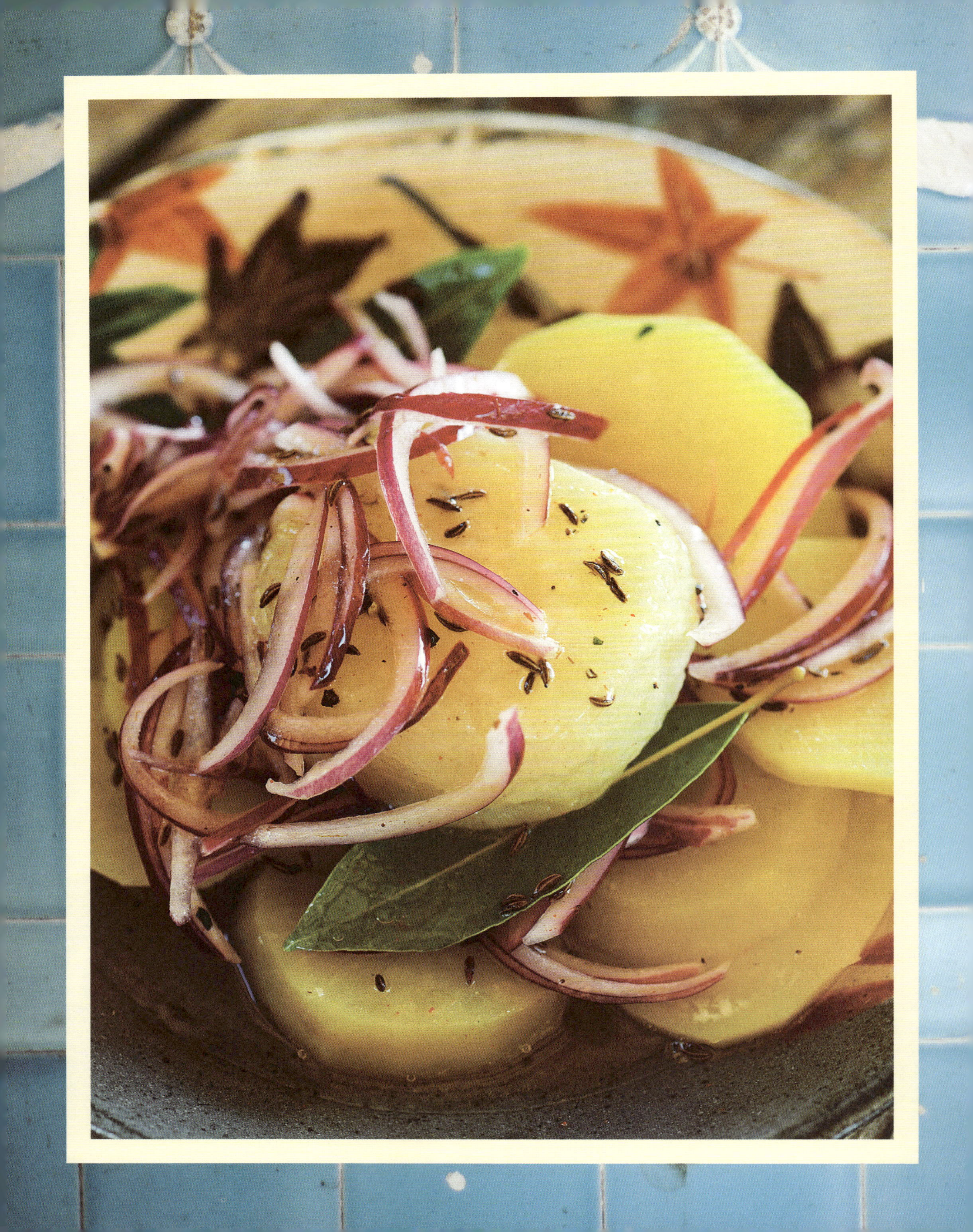

Warm Harz Cheese "with Music" and Bouillon Potatoes

Ingredients (serves 2)

2 red onions (1/4 pound)
3 bay leaves
1 teaspoon caraway seeds
1/3 cup red wine vinegar
1 teaspoon salt
1 tablespoon sugar
ground sweet paprika
2—3 tablespoons sunflower oil
pepper
2 large waxy potatoes (red or new potatoes)
2 cups vegetable stock
2 Harz cheese (or Limburger cheese)

1. Peel the onions and cut into thin rings. Snip the bay leaves with scissors. Toast the caraway seeds in an ungreased pan. Allow to cool and then roughly grind.

2. Mix 6 tablespoons of water with vinegar, salt, sugar, 1 pinch of ground paprika and the oil. Mix in the onion and the bay leaf. Season the vinaigrette with pepper and let it soak for 15 minutes.

3. Peel the potatoes and cut into slices 1/2-inch thick. Cook in the vegetable stock for 10—12 minutes until they are al dente.

4. While cooking the potatoes, add the Harz cheese and marinate it in the vinaigrette for 5 minutes. Remove the cheese, drain and lay in an ovenproof dish. Preheat the oven to 350°F and cook for 5—6 minutes. Arrange on plates with the onion vinaigrette and the drained potatoes.

Preparation time: 40 minutes

♥ tasty

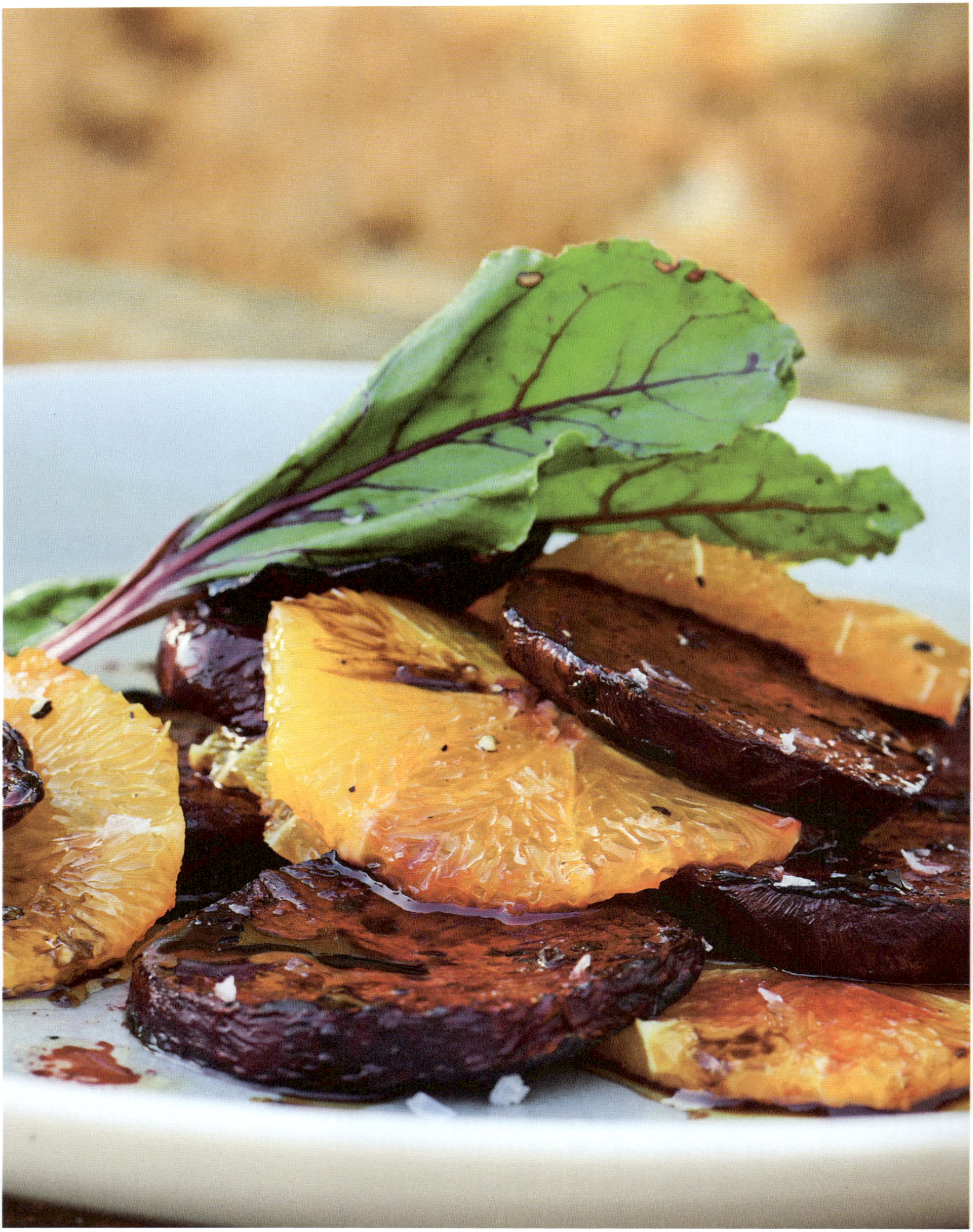

Grilled Beets with Balsamic Vinegar, Oranges and Olive Oil

This actually works! We tried various experiments before we developed our recipes – we wanted to create a beet recipe that didn't require hours of cooking time. We just peeled the beet, cut it into thin slices and tossed it onto the grill. The scent of the grilled beets on its own was incredible. We added some sweet and sour fruitiness and straight away the earthy winter root became the nicest summer salad you can imagine.

Ingredients (serves 4)

- 1 bunch young beets
- 5—6 tablespoons olive oil
- 3 organic oranges
- 3—4 teaspoons balsamic vinegar
- salt and pepper

1. Separate the beet bulbs from their greens. Set aside some of the delicate leaves. Peel the beets with a potato peeler and cut them into slices 1/2-inch thick. Mix with 2 tablespoons of olive oil and grill on a high heat on both sides for 3—4 minutes (the beets will still be quite firm).

2. Peel the oranges, making sure to get rid of the white skin. Cut the oranges into slices and arrange on plates with the grilled beet slices. Drizzle with balsamic vinegar and 3—4 tablespoons of olive oil. Season with salt and pepper. Garnish with the delicate beet leaves and serve.

Preparation time: 15 minutes

TIP These beet slices always work out – on any grill or frying pan.

walnut   pistachio   PEANUT

SESAME   ALMONDS

sunflower seeds

NUTS, SEEDS & CO
CRISPY AND CRUNCHY

HAZELNUT

Brazil nut

Nuts bring crunch and crispness to vegetarian cooking. Hazelnuts, peanuts, cashews, almonds, pine nuts and the like can give new depth to your recipes. Here are a few tips for nut crackers:

Whether with or without shells, loose or pre-packaged, nuts always taste best when they are fresh. They spoil quickly due to their high fat content, so pay attention to the sell-by date when you buy them. Most locally grown nuts such as walnuts, hazelnuts, pine nuts, pistachios and almonds are in season in late summer and fall. Imported and exotic nuts are available year round.

In cooking, nuts taste best when they are toasted before being used, because that's when they develop their full aroma. The fastest way to toast them is in the oven on a sheet at 300°F (time varies according to the type of nut) or in a nonstick, ungreased pan on a low heat. Keep your eyes on the nuts the whole time during toasting as they burn easily, especially smaller ones like pine nuts.

For quick everyday cooking, it is advisable to use pre-toasted nuts. However, you won't need as much salt if they are pre-toasted. You can buy really special nuts with added seasoning. These add new flavors to vegetarian cooking, such as spicy wasabi peanuts for Asian dishes or cashew nuts dusted with curry for Indian cuisine. It's fun to experiment!

Ground nuts are useful as a natural binder for creamy soups and sauces. You can make quick and easy pastes out of toasted nuts that can be used in pasta and pesto dishes, as seasoning in salad dressings or soups, and as spreads for bread or crackers. Nut pastes work out best when the nuts are ground in a mortar. If done in a blender or food processor, the pastes become somewhat sticky. You can add any kind of chopped herbs, grated cheese, grated citrus fruit peel, chopped or dried tomatoes or finely grated garlic.

Pommes Anna with Sautéed Onions and Hazelnut Crust

Ingredients (serves 4)

2 1/4 pounds waxy potatoes (red or new potatoes)
1 1/2 pounds onions
salt and pepper
2 tablespoons olive oil
1/2 cup sherry
2 stems thyme
1 tablespoon plum jelly
1 2/3 cups vegetable stock
2 bay leaves
3 1/2 tablespoons soft butter
3 1/2 ounces peeled, toasted hazelnuts (or other toasted nuts)
4 stems parsley

1. Peel the potatoes, slice them in the food processor. Place them in a dish and cover with cold, fresh water.
2. Peel onions, cut into fine slices and add salt. Sauté in olive oil on medium heat for 10 minutes until golden brown, stirring constantly. Pour in the sherry and bring to a boil until all of the liquid has evaporated. Pull off thyme leaves and fold into the plum jelly. Season the onions with salt and pepper and set aside.
3. Bring the stock to a boil with bay leaves and half of the butter. Add salt to taste. Take the potato slices out of the water and drain well. Layer half of the potatoes in an ovenproof dish, forming an edge with the potatoes along the inside of the dish.
4. Make a layer of sautéed onions (A). Place the remaining potatoes on top (B) and pour stock over it (C).
5. Preheat the oven to 350°F. Roughly chop the hazelnuts and knead together with the remaining butter. Distribute evenly over the potatoes (D, E) and bake on the bottom rack for 1 hour. Turn the oven up to 400°F and bake for another 20 minutes. Allow to rest before serving (F). Serve sprinkled with freshly chopped parsley.

Preparation time: 2 hours

A

B

C

D

E

F

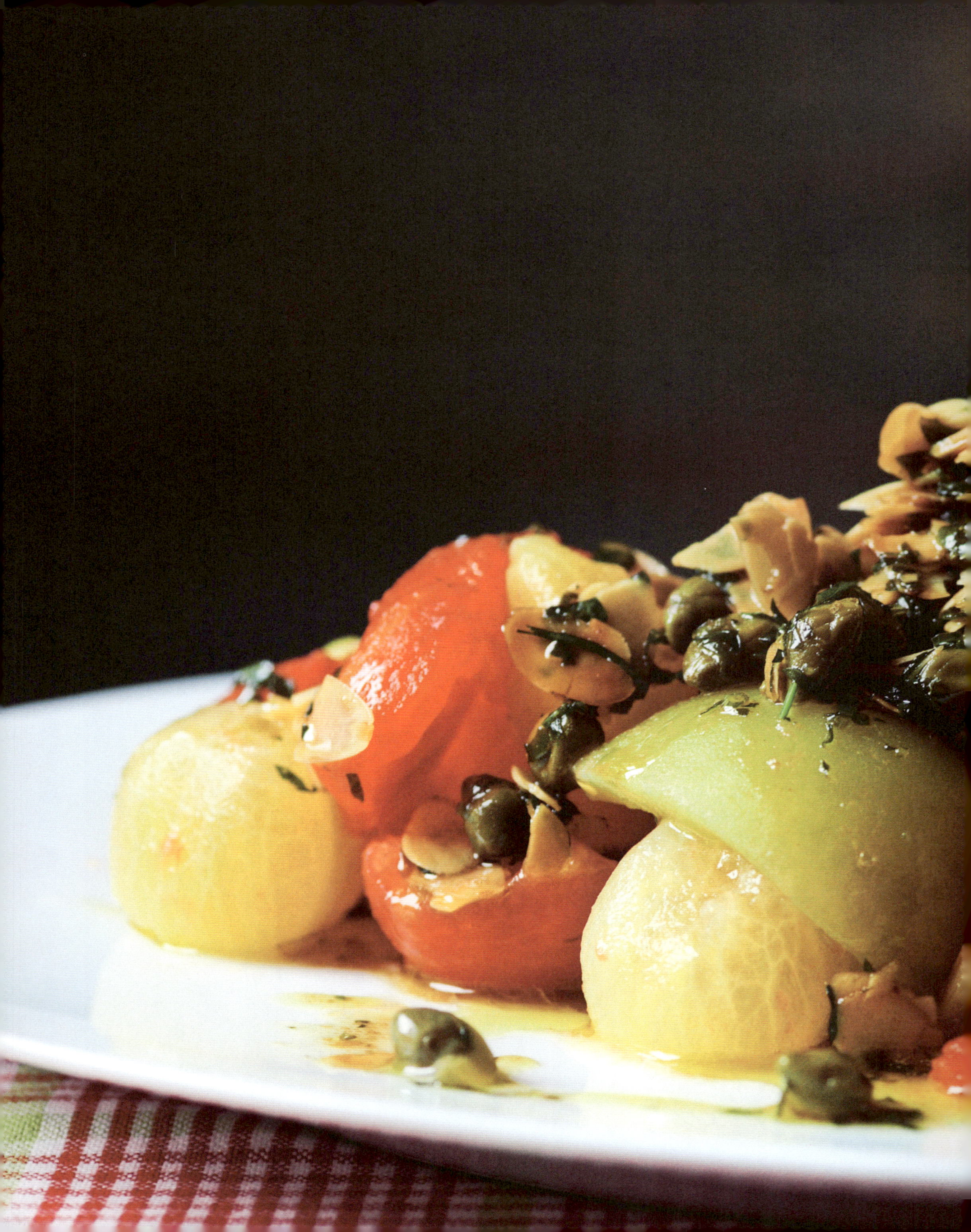

Tomato Salad with Almond and Caper Vinaigrette

Ingredients (serves 4—6)

- 1 3/4 pounds mixed tomatoes
- salt and pepper
- 6 stems parsley
- 4 tablespoons sliced almonds
- 1 tablespoon butter
- 2 tablespoons small capers (nonpareil)
- 1 tablespoon vinegar
- 6 tablespoons olive oil
- sugar

1. Remove the core of the tomatoes with a sharp knife, cutting out a good wedge. Cook the tomatoes in boiling, salted water for 20 seconds, drain, rinse in cold water and remove the skins. Cut the tomatoes into bite-sized pieces and arrange on a plate.
2. Pull off the parsley leaves and chop them coarsely. Toast the sliced almonds in an ungreased pan until golden brown. Add butter and allow to melt over low heat. Add the capers and sauté briefly. Pour in vinegar and remove from the heat. Mix in the olive oil and parsley and season with salt, pepper and a pinch of sugar.
3. Pour the almond and caper vinaigrette over the tomatoes, let them absorb the vinaigrette briefly and serve.

Preparation time: 25 minutes

Spinach has to be washed thoroughly in warm water to get all of the sand out of the folds in the leaves. But it's worth the trouble! Spinach is delicious with seasonings like cream, olive oil, butter and salt, or it can be enjoyed on its own. The more delicate baby spinach is milder in taste and can be prepared faster. In particular, it goes well with cold cuisine – or when you don't have time to clean regular spinach.

GREENS GALORE: SPINACH x3

1 Creamed Spinach

Wash and spin dry **1 pound of spinach** and cook in boiling water for 30 seconds. Rinse with cold water and squeeze dry. Peel and dice **1 medium-sized onion** and sauté in **2 tablespoons of olive oil.** Fold in spinach and add **1 cup of heavy cream**. Season with **salt, pepper** and **nutmeg** and cook for 2 minutes without a lid. Blend coarsely with a hand blender.

2 Sesame Spinach Salad

Wash and spin dry **1/2 pound of spinach** and cook in boiling water for 30 seconds. Rinse in cold water and squeeze dry. Peel **1 garlic clove,** cut into fine slices and mix with **3 tablespoons of light soy sauce, 3 tablespoons of water, 2 tablespoons of olive oil, 2 drops of sesame oil** and the **juice of 1 lime.** Toss the spinach in the spicy sauce. Toast **2 tablespoons of sesame seeds** in an ungreased pan and sprinkle over the sesame spinach.

3 Spinach Bruschetta

Cut **1 baguette** lengthwise and then into 8 pieces. Drizzle with **4 tablespoons of olive oil.** Toast the bread for 3–4 minutes in a pan until golden brown on both sides. Set the bread aside. Cut **2 tomatoes** into 1/2-inch slices and sauté on a high heat in the same pan with **1 tablespoon of olive oil.** Sprinkle the cut sides with **1 pinch of sugar,** turn them over and let them caramelize. Distribute the tomatoes on the bread. Peel **2 garlic cloves,** cut into thin slices and sauté in the same pan with **2 tablespoons of olive oil.** Add **1/4 pound of baby spinach** and allow it to wilt. Season with **salt** and **pepper.** Spread the spinach on the bread while it is warm.

1

2

3

Pretzel Dumplings with Crème Fraîche, Tomatoes and Horseradish

Ingredients (serves 4)

1/2 pound day-old white bread
1 pound soft pretzels (or pretzel sticks, pretzel rolls)
1/2 pound spinach
1 tablespoon olive oil
salt and pepper
1 onion
1 garlic clove
3 tablespoons butter
1/2 cup milk
2/3 cup heavy cream
2 large eggs
8 ripe tomatoes, preferably an assortment
1 cup crème fraîche
lemon juice
1 small piece fresh horseradish root, peeled

1. Chop the bread and pretzels into very small chunks and throw into a bowl. Wash and coarsely chop the spinach. Heat the oil in a pan and wilt the spinach in it. Add salt and set aside. Peel and dice the onion and garlic. Heat the butter in a second pan and sauté the onion and the garlic. Pour in the milk and cream and bring to a boil. Season with salt and pepper.

2. Drain the spinach by squeezing it until dry and then add it to the bread. Mix everything with the onion cream sauce and let it cool down a little. Fold in the eggs and season the mixture with salt and pepper. Knead into a smooth dumpling dough and let rest for 10 minutes. Form 16 firm dumplings. Bring a large pan of salted water to a boil. Simmer the dumplings for 15 minutes.

3. Wash the tomatoes, cut into slices and arrange on a platter. Season with salt and pepper. Blend crème fraîche with 1–2 tablespoons of water until smooth and season with salt and a squeeze of lemon juice. Distribute over the tomatoes. Sprinkle freshly grated horseradish over the dumplings and place them on top of the tomatoes. Serve immediately.

Preparation time: 40 minutes

» Quick, someone get the photographer! If something works out well for once, I sure want a picture taken of the result! «

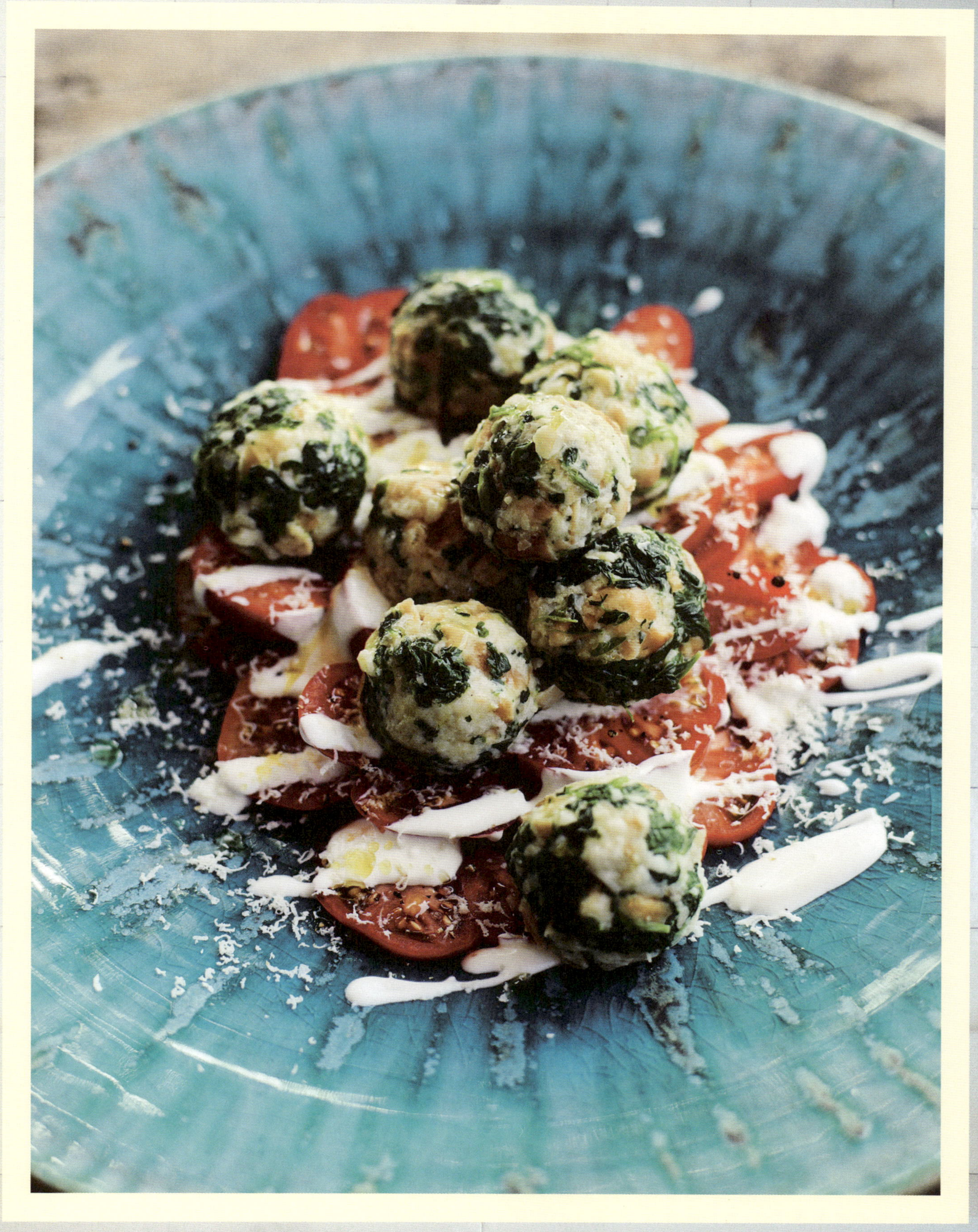

Porcini with White Bean Mousse, Spinach and Hazelnut Vinaigrette

Ingredients (serves 2–4)

- 4 stems parsley
- 2 tablespoons sliced hazelnuts
- 1–2 teaspoons white wine vinegar
- 9 tablespoons olive oil
- salt and pepper
- 1 can cannellini beans or white beans (16 ounces net weight)
- 1 garlic clove
- 1 pound small porcini
- lemon juice
- 1/2 pound baby spinach
- 1 1/2 tablespoons butter

1. Chop the parsley. Toast the hazelnuts in an ungreased pan. Fold in the parsley and mix with the white wine vinegar and 3 tablespoons of olive oil. Season the vinaigrette with salt and pepper and set aside.
2. Drain the beans and peel the garlic. Blend both in the food processor until very smooth. Wash the porcini, cut in half and sauté until golden brown in 4 teaspoons of hot olive oil. Season with salt and lemon juice.
3. Remove the porcini from the pan, but keep them warm. Wash the baby spinach leaves and spin them dry. Add 2 tablespoons of olive oil and heat the butter in the pan. Add the spinach and allow it to wilt. Season with salt.
4. Heat the bean mousse in a pot. Season with salt and drizzle with the hazelnut vinaigrette. Arrange with the spinach and the mushrooms.

Preparation time: 25 minutes

WARNING: Humans are not the only ones who like the nutty aroma of porcini: it also attracts mushroom maggots. Porcini are always served cut in half because the worms are not visible from the outside. The kings of mushrooms, the porcini, are available during the summer and fall months. You should always leave it to the experts to harvest porcini. Non-experts confuse porcini with the bitter bolete – and even the maggots don't touch those!

» Matthias! (photographer) Get closer! Crawl into the food! «

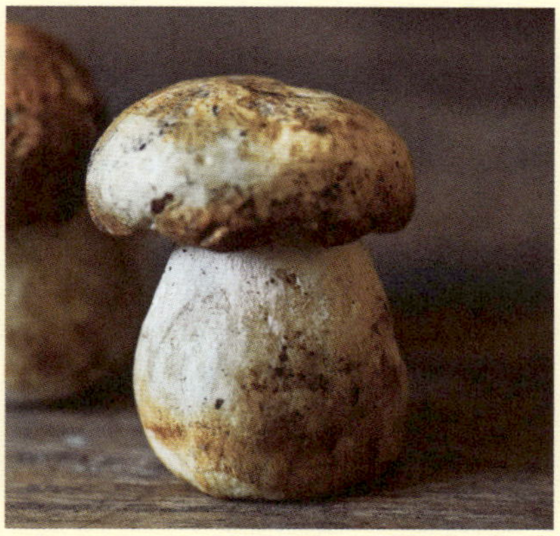
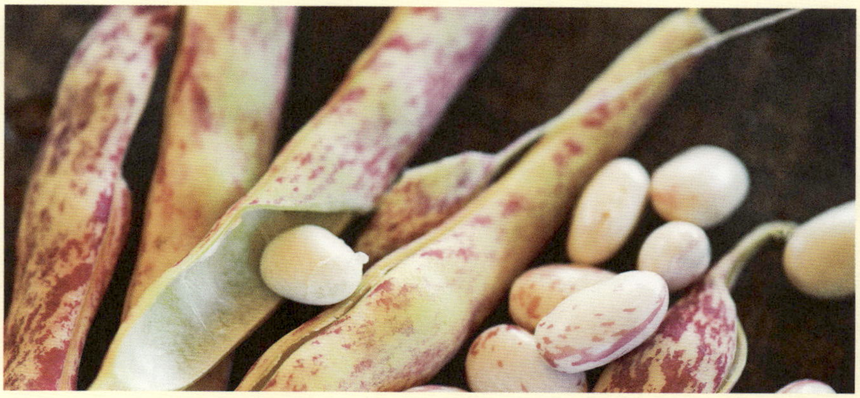
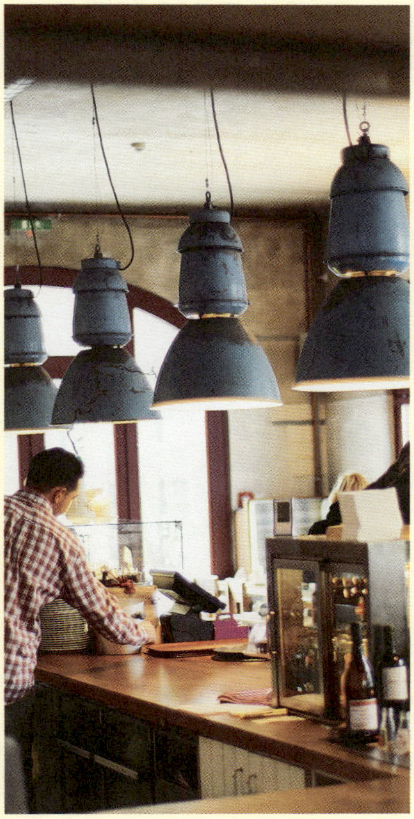
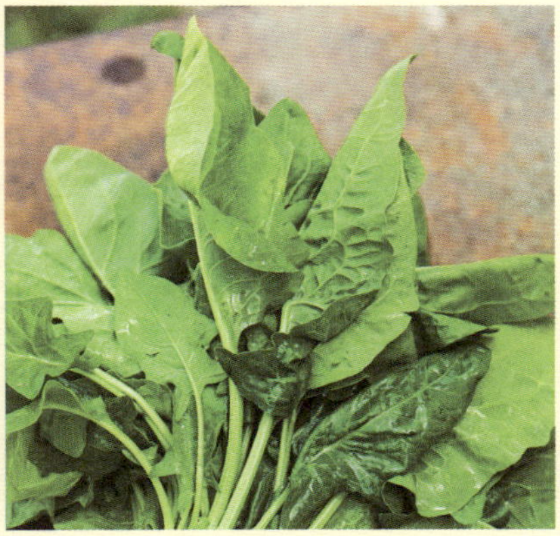
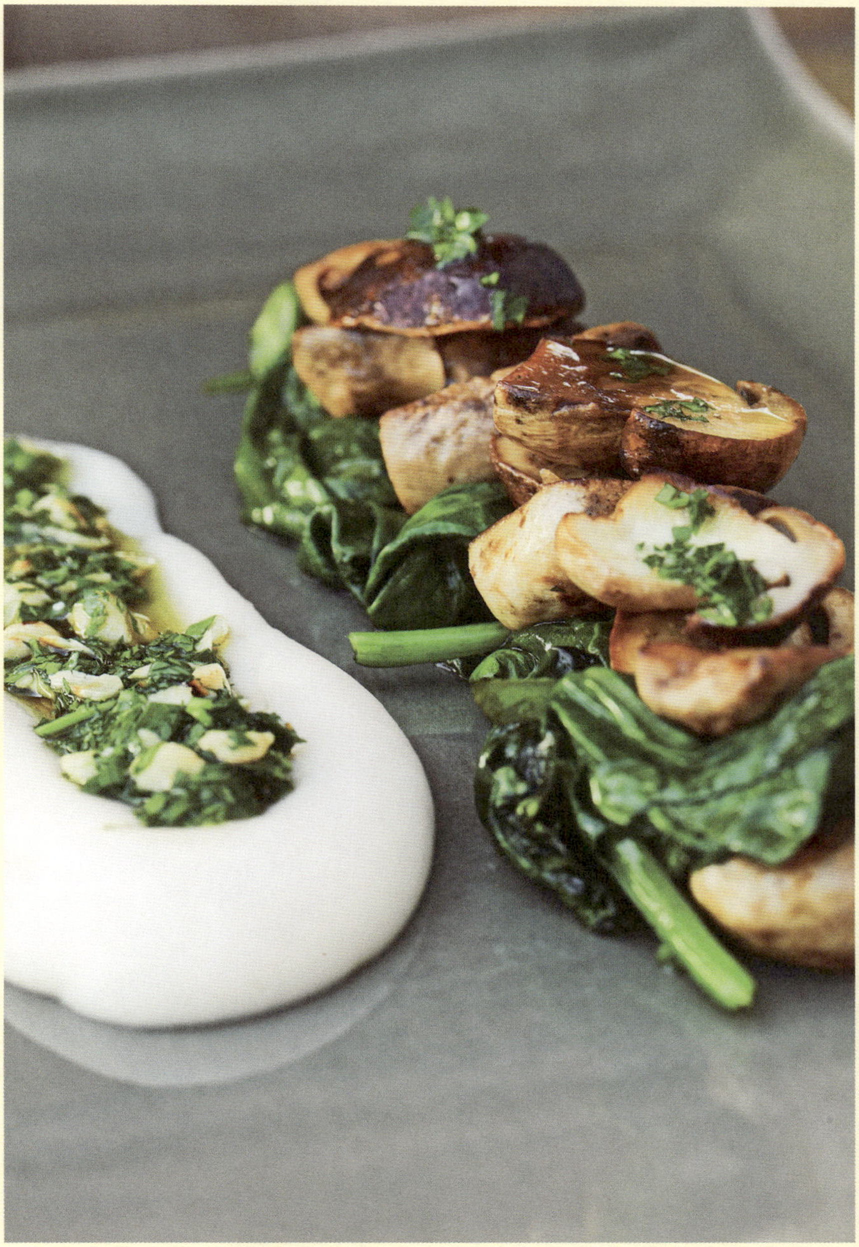

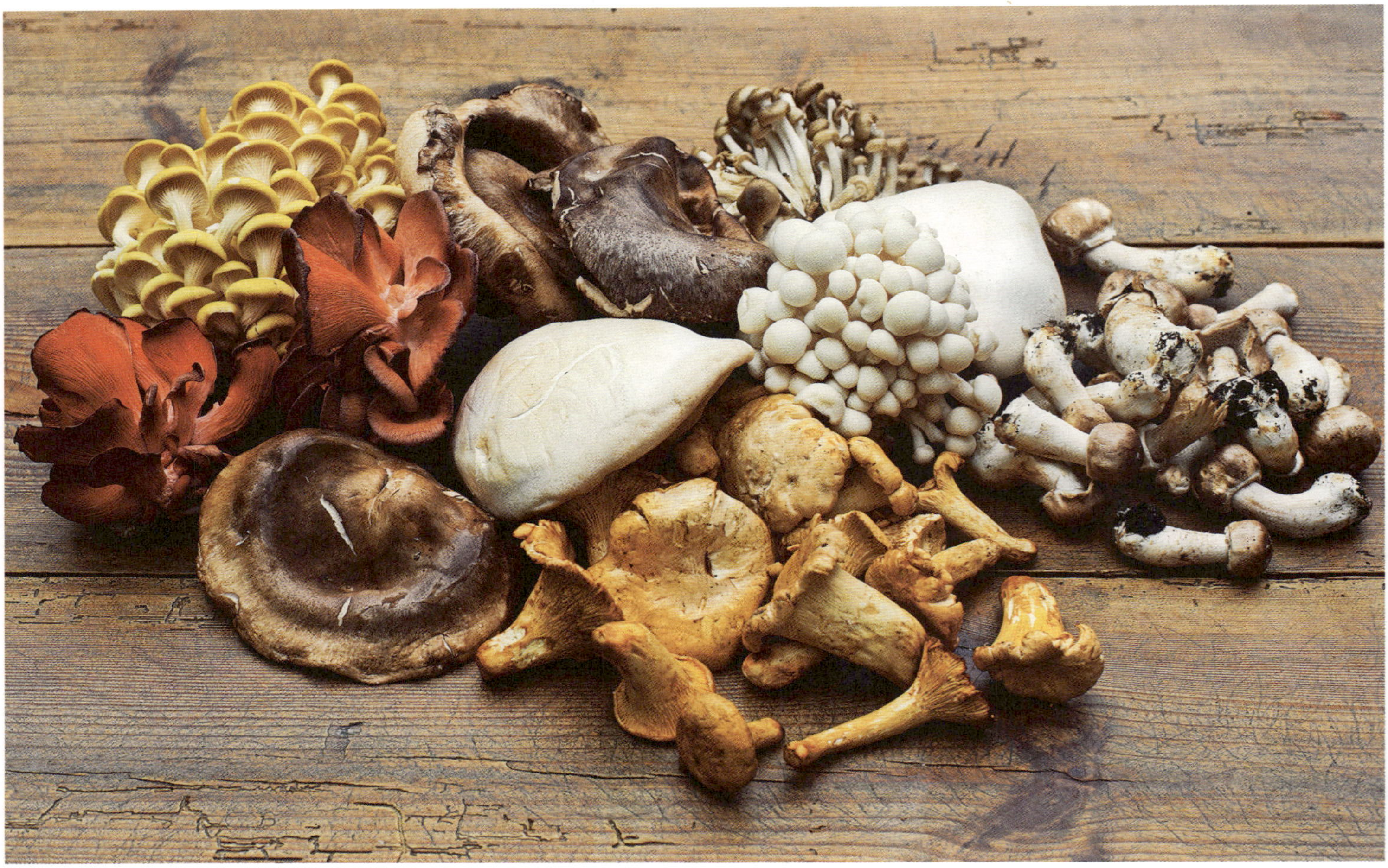

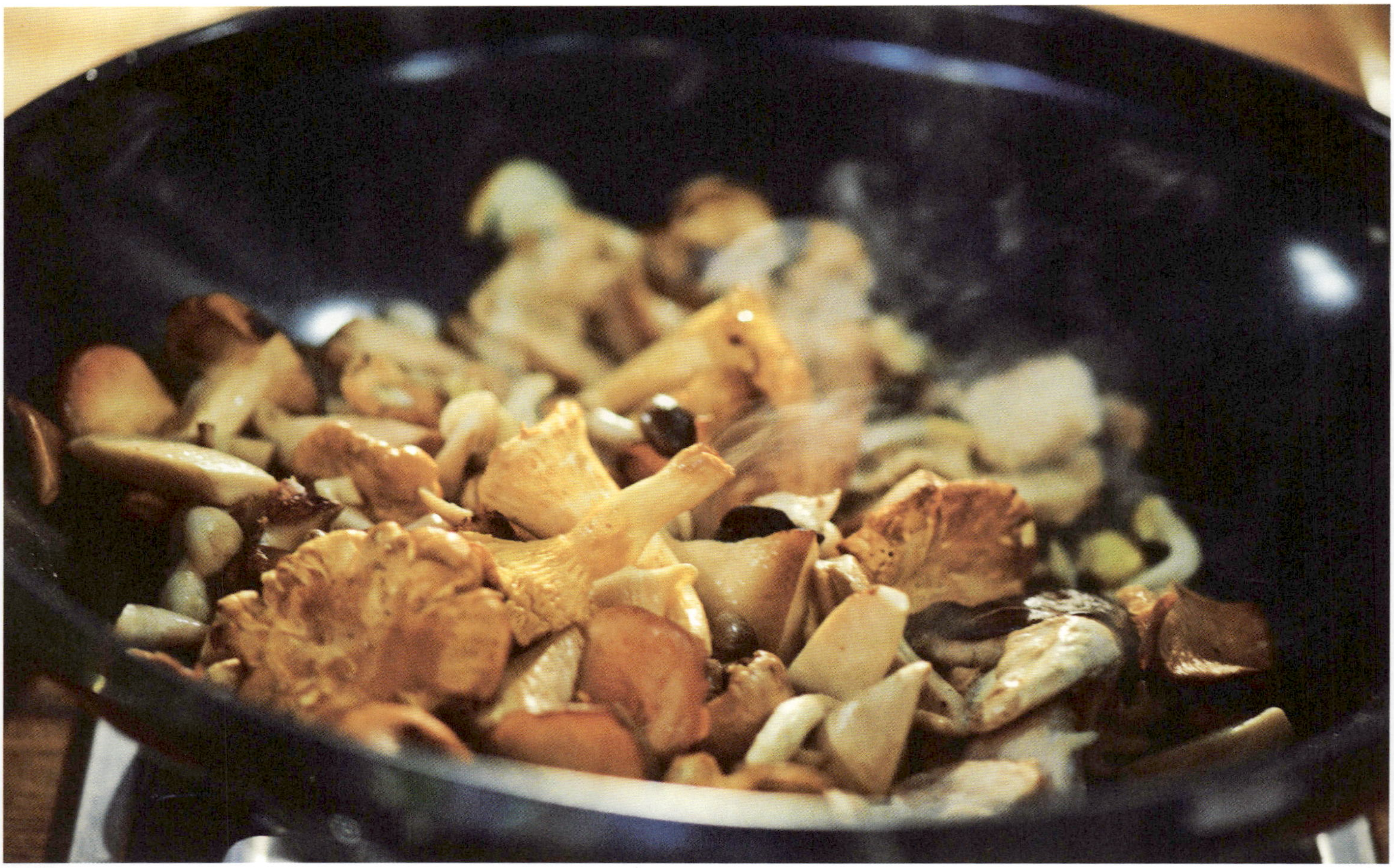

Mushroom Ragout on Peasant Bread

Ingredients (serves 4)

3 garlic cloves
1 red onion
2 cups red wine
sugar
2 tablespoons soy sauce
2 tablespoons mirin (or 1 tablespoon sugar)
1 1/2 pounds mixed, cultivated mushrooms (shiitake, oysters, flamingos, white mushrooms, king oysters, almond mushrooms, Namekos)
4 tablespoons olive oil
salt and pepper
1–2 tablespoons lemon juice
4 slices peasant bread
2 tablespoons vegetable oil, neutral in taste
2 tablespoons butter
3 scallions

1. To make the stock, peel and dice the garlic and red onion. Heat the red wine with garlic, onions and 2 tablespoons of sugar in a pot and reduce to about 1 cup. Season with soy sauce and mirin.
2. Clean the mushrooms and cut into bite-sized pieces. Heat the olive oil in a large pan and sauté the mushrooms for 3–4 minutes. Pour in the stock and bring to a boil until it thickens. Season with salt, pepper and lemon juice.
3. Toast slices of bread in a pan in 2 batches with 1 tablespoon of oil and 1 tablespoon of butter until golden brown. Wash the scallions and cut into fine slices.
4. Spread the mushroom ragout on the slices of bread and sprinkle with chopped scallions before serving.

Preparation time: 45 minutes

TIP: This dish can be varied by serving with fried or poached eggs.

Green Chickpea Salad with Fried Halloumi

Ingredients (serves 4)

- 1 green bell pepper
- 1/2 small cucumber
- 1 heart of romaine lettuce
- 2 scallions
- 2 green apples
- 1 can chickpeas (15 ounces net weight)
- 2/3 cup whole-milk yogurt
- 2 tablespoons lemon juice
- 3 tablespoons olive oil
- sugar
- salt
- 1/2—1 green chili pepper
- 1/2 pound halloumi cheese (see note)

1. Cut the bell pepper into quarters, remove the seeds and then dice the flesh. Peel the cucumber, cut it in half and remove the seeds with a teaspoon. Finely dice the cucumber. Cut the heart of romaine lettuce lengthwise into 1/2-inch wide strips. Wash and spin dry. Wash the scallions and cut into thin slices.

2. Wash the apples, cut both in half and take out the cores. Cut one apple into fine slices and dice the other. Drain the chickpeas in a sieve and rinse them off in cold water. Mix with the apples, peppers, cucumbers, scallions and lettuce.

3. Blend the yogurt with lemon juice, 1 tablespoon of olive oil and 1 pinch of sugar until smooth. Add salt to taste. Chop the chili pepper into thin rings and mix in. Toss the lettuce with the dressing.

4. Cut the halloumi into 1/2-inch slices. Heat 2 tablespoons of olive oil in an oven-proof pan and fry the cheese on all sides for 1—2 minutes. Serve the halloumi with the salad on plates.

Preparation time: 35 minutes

HALLOUMI is a fried cheese from Cyprus, Greece or Turkey that you can find in the dairy aisle of the grocery store or at special stores. Depending on the brand, some cheeses are extremely salty, so they don't need any salt added to them after frying. You can cut halloumi in slices in advance and place them in cold water for 1 hour if too salty.

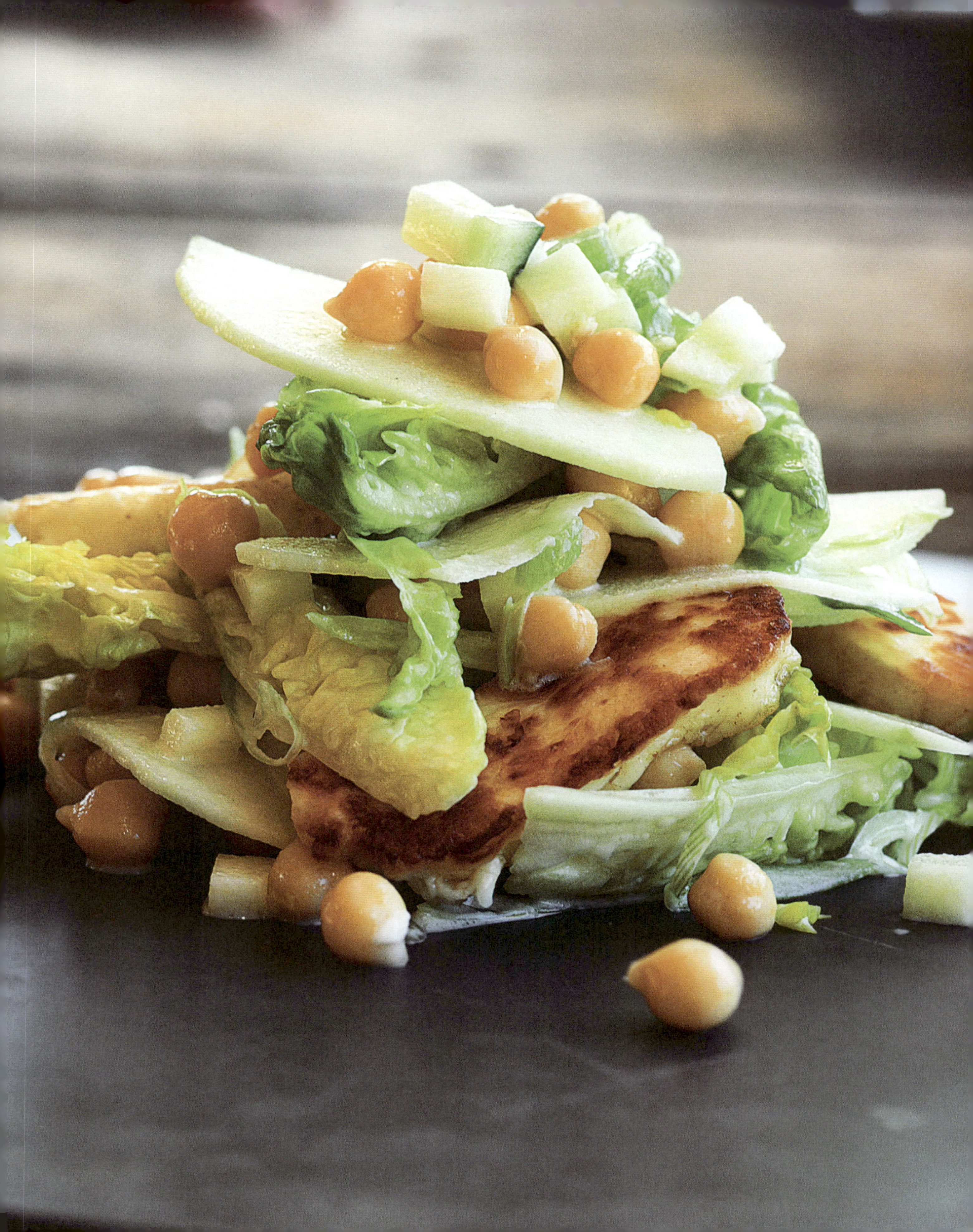

SMOKEY AROMAS

The sweet "woody" smell of smoke works well with garlic cloves, corn on the cob, potatoes in their skins, tofu, eggs and cheese. If you can smoke in your garden or on your porch, you should try using a wok:

Cover the inside of the wok and its lid with tin foil. Place 3/4 of an inch of smoking flour on the bottom of the wok (available in most fishing and sporting goods stores). Cover a round grill rack with tinfoil and perforate it. Place the grill rack on the wok base. Place the food to be smoked on the grill rack, put on the lid and turn on the stove until the flour begins to smoke. Carry the wok from the cooker outside. (Be careful! Hot!) Let the food smoke for 10—25 minutes, depending on how intense you want the smoky flavor to be.

ONLY SMOKE OUTSIDE PLEASE!

You can introduce fine smoky aromas into a well-aired vegetarian kitchen with a few tricks – and completely without smoke:
SMOKE SALT (also **HICKORY SALT**) is smoked salt or salt that has had smoke flavor added to it. It is awesome in ketchup, in herb butter for corn on the cob, in farmers' stews or sauces and dips. **PIMENTON DE LA VERA** is a fine powder made from smoked, sweet paprika, which has a very intense flavor used in chili sin carne, vegetable casseroles, sauces and soups.
SMOKED TOFU can pass on its fine aroma to fried vegetables, stews, soups and sauces.
GRILLING, of course, is the main way to get delicious smoky aromas. You can buy woodchips, chunks and pellets to mix under the coals in the camping department of home improvement stores or in sporting goods stores. To intensify the taste, you can close the lid of the grill for a few minutes.

just in case →

201

Pea Soup with Smoked Garlic

We all know pea soup – we expect it to contain ham or bacon. And although we don't want that for green cuisine, we don't want to miss out on the delicious spicy flavor that pork imparts. Smoked garlic is the solution: it gives the soup that extra kick and is similar to the smoky flavor of bacon.

Ingredients (serves 6)

1 Spanish onion
6 garlic cloves
4 1/2 tablespoons butter
2 1/2 cups green split peas
2 bay leaves
8 1/2 cups vegetable stock
2 1/2 tablespoons smoked wood dust
1/2 organic lemon
2 stems marjoram (if dried, 2 teaspoons)
2 stems summer savory (if dried, 2 teaspoons)
salt and pepper
1 bunch arugula

1. Peel and finely dice the onion and 1 garlic clove. Melt half of the butter in a pot and sauté the onion, garlic and peas. Add bay leaves and pour in the vegetable stock. Cover and let it simmer for 1 hour, stirring occasionally.
2. Meanwhile, place tinfoil on the inside of a wok. Wrap the lid of the wok in tinfoil, too. Put the smoked wood dust into the wok. Place a rack over the bottom half of the wok and the remaining unpeeled garlic cloves on top. Heat the closed wok on high until the dust begins to smoke. Put the wok outside and smoke the garlic for 25 minutes with the lid on.
3. Blend the soup with a hand blender until mostly smooth, but you can still see bits of peas. Finely grate the lemon peel. Chop the herbs. Add it all to the soup and bring to a boil. Season the soup with salt, pepper and 1 dash of lemon juice.
4. Peel the smoked garlic and cut into thin slices. Let the remaining butter boil up in a pan and fry the garlic in it until light brown. Add washed and cleaned arugula and allow it to wilt. Season with salt and pepper and serve with the soup.

Preparation time: 1 hour and 15 minutes

VARIATIONS: If you don't want to do the smoking yourself, you can buy canned smoked garlic in selected shops or online. If you like your soup a little thicker, you can add potato or carrot cubes to the peas and cook them together.

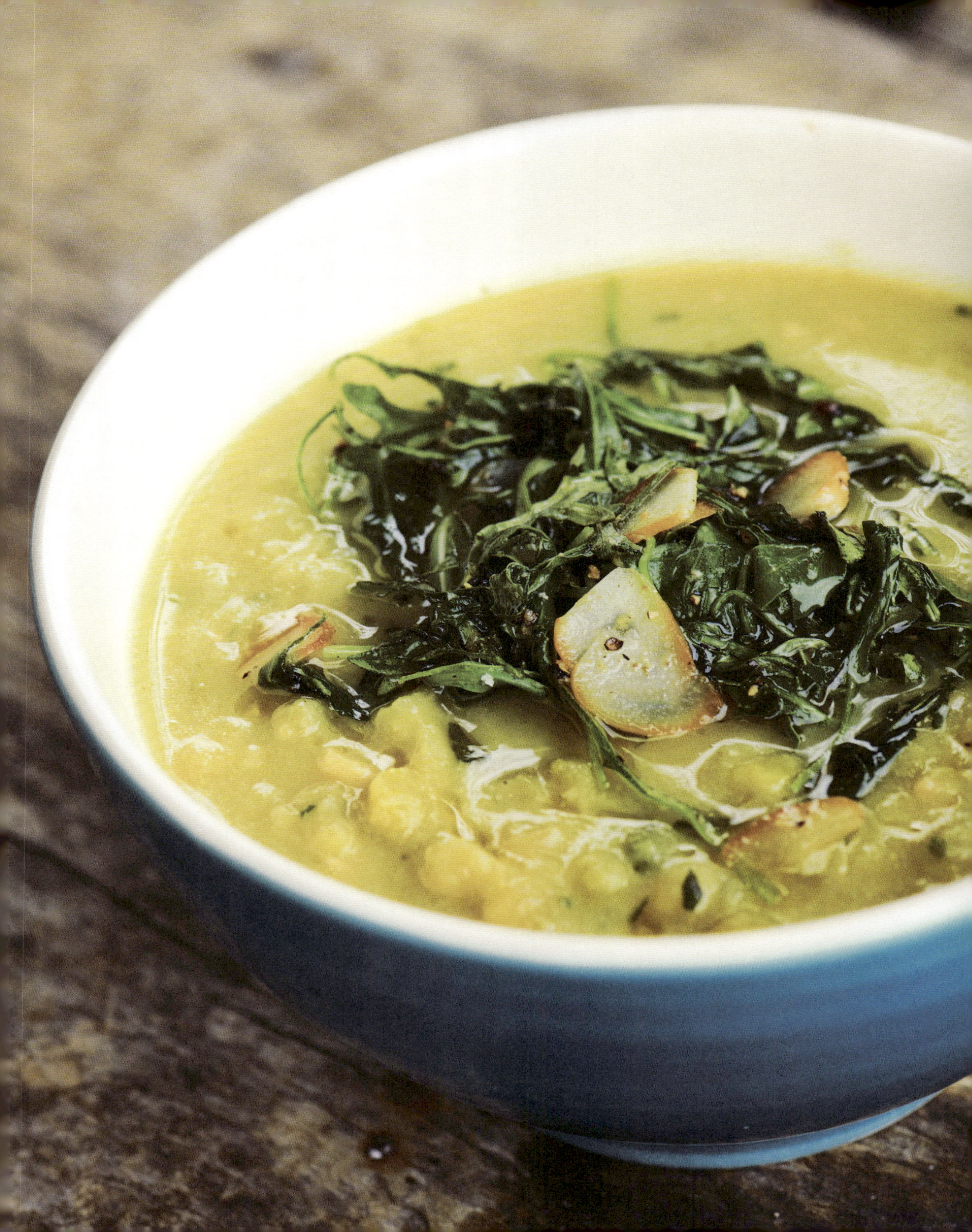

1

3

fantastic

2

X3 CARROTS: VERY TASTY

Carrots and baby carrots are available all year round. They taste best when bought locally between late summer and winter. In those months of the year they have the best flavor and are sweet, regardless of whether they are eaten grated and raw or gently boiled, sautéed or stewed.

1 Carrot Nut Purée

Roughly chop **1/2 cup of walnuts** and toast them with **1/2 tablespoon of butter** in a pan. Peel **2 1/4 pounds of carrots** and cut into fine slices. Peel and dice **2 shallots**. Put **2 tablespoons of butter, 1 tablespoon of sugar** and shallots into a pot and sauté. Add the carrots and caramelize them. Pour in **1/2 cup of apple juice** and steam for 15 minutes in a covered pot. Purée with a hand blender until smooth. Mix in **1—2 tablespoons of crème fraîche**, walnuts and **1—2 teaspoons of walnut oil**. Season with **salt, pepper** and **nutmeg**.

2 Carrot Salad with Pear and Smoked Almonds

Peel **1 pound of carrots** and slice them into strips lengthwise with the peeler. Pull off the leaves from **4 stems of flat leaf parsley**. Chop **2 tablespoons of smoked almonds**. Mix **2 tablespoons of lemon juice** with **2 tablespoons of pear or apple juice, 1 tablespoon of honey** and **4 tablespoons of olive oil**. Season with **salt** and **pepper**. Cut **1 small pear** into thin slices. Mix the salad dressing with carrot, pear juice and parsley. Serve sprinkled with smoked almonds.

3 Carrot Soup with Apricots and Pine Nuts

Peel **1 1/4 pounds of carrots** and cut them into thin slices. Peel **2 ounces of shallots** and dice them. Heat **3 tablespoons of oil** and **2 tablespoons of butter** in a pot and sauté the shallots and carrots. Pour in **3 1/2 cups of vegetable stock**. Cook the vegetables until soft for 15 minutes in a covered pot. Toast **2 tablespoons of pine nuts** in an ungreased pan until golden brown and then chop them. Slice **6 dried apricots** into fine strips and add half of them to the soup. Purée with a hand blender and season to taste with **salt, pepper** and **1—2 tablespoons of lemon juice**. Sprinkle with a few **parsley leaves, 1 tablespoon of olive oil,** the pine nuts and the rest of the apricot slices and serve.

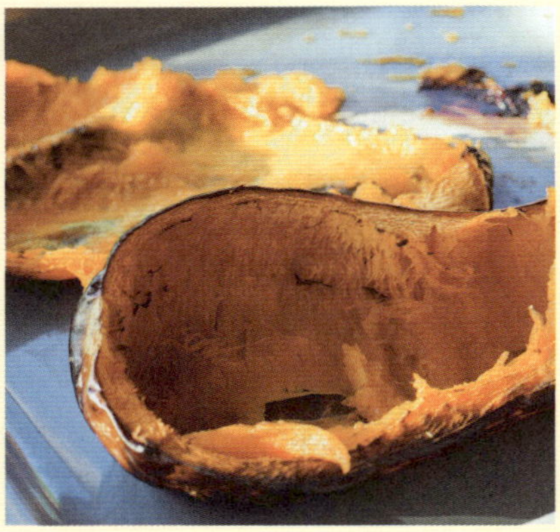
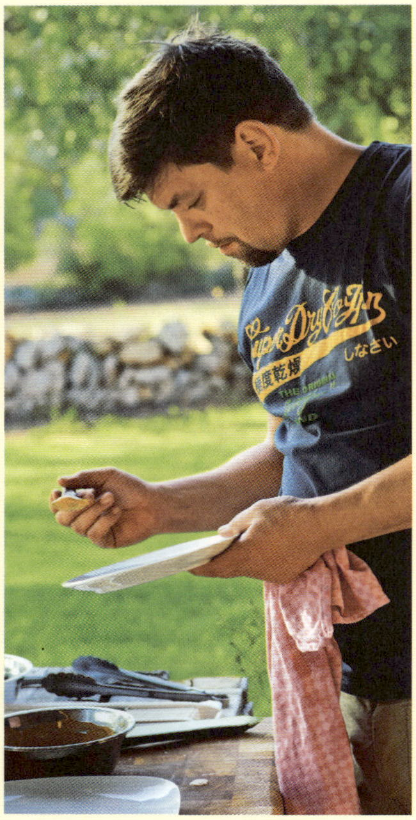
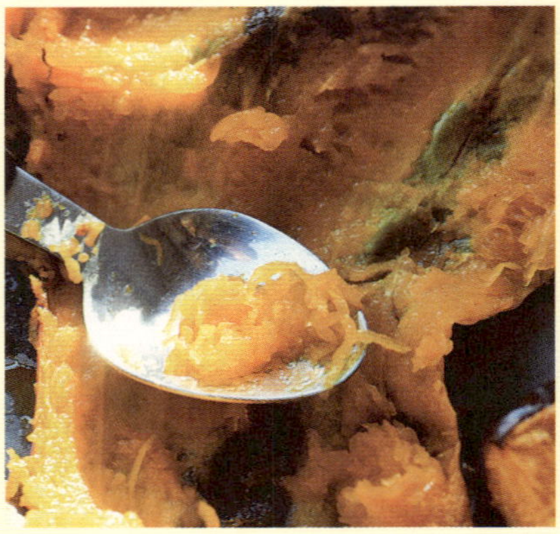
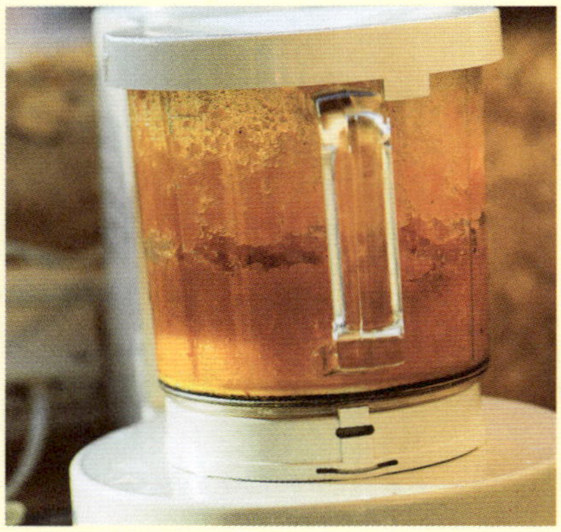
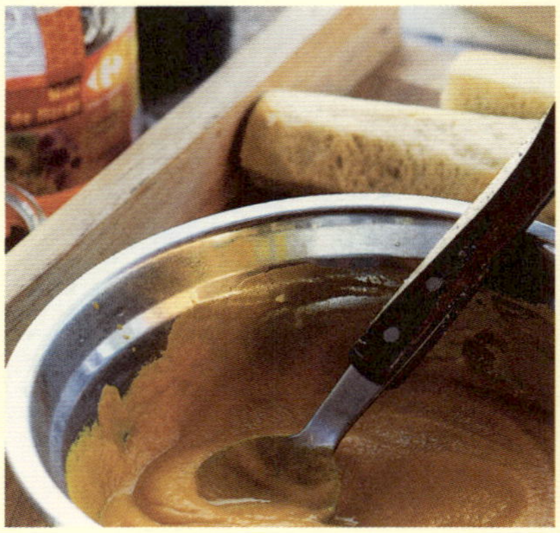
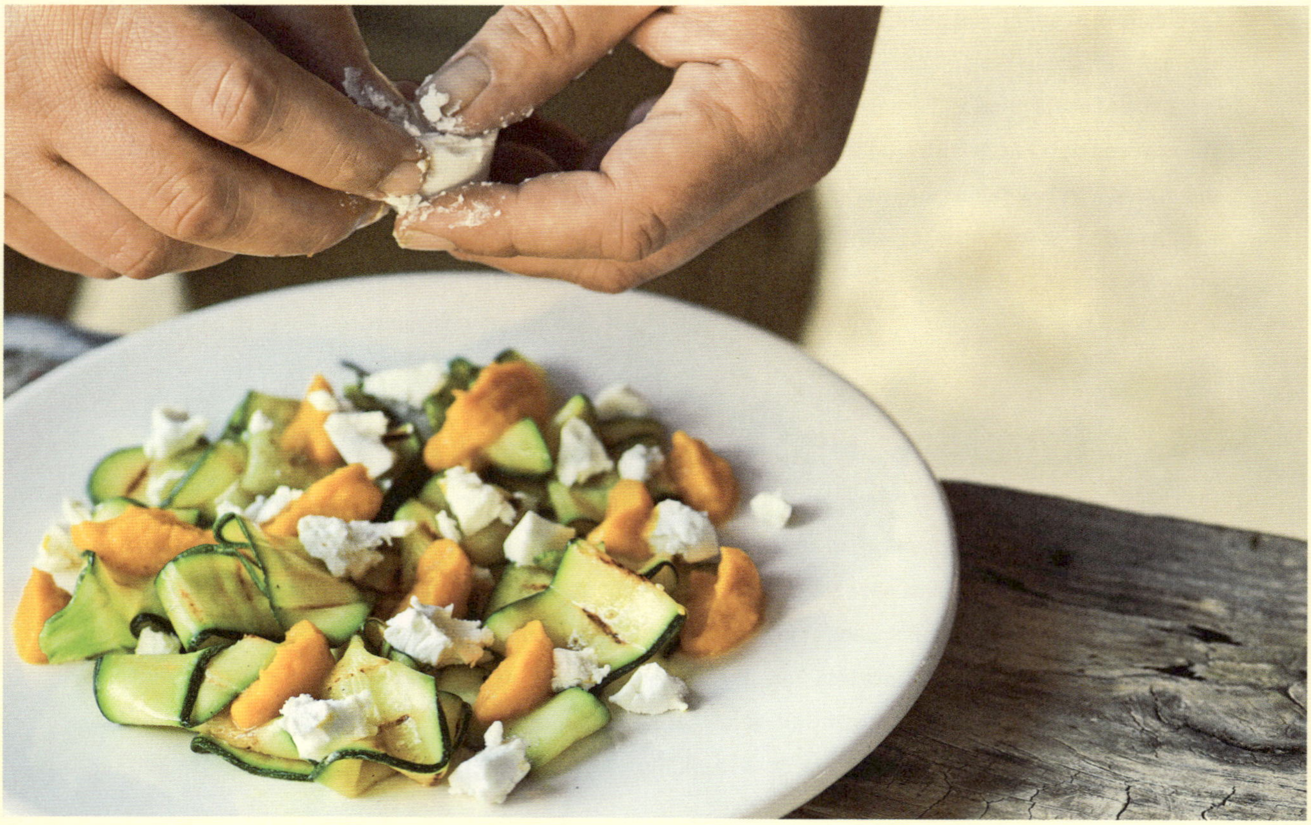

Squash Purée with Grilled Zucchini and Goat Farmer Cheese

Ingredients (serves 4)

3 pounds butternut squash
2 tablespoons ground almonds (or grated Parmesan)
lemon juice
salt and pepper
sugar
4 small zucchini
2 tablespoons olive oil
4 tablespoons pumpkin seeds
2 tablespoons honey
4 round goat cheese (picandou)
pumpkin seed oil

1. Cut the squash in half. Scrape out the seeds with a teaspoon and reserve. Preheat the oven to 350°F and bake for approximately 45 minutes until soft on a baking tray on the second rack to the bottom.

2. Scrape the squash from its skin with a spoon and purée it in a blender with the ground almonds until creamy and smooth. Season with 1 dash of lemon juice, salt and 1 pinch of sugar. Heat it all up and then keep it warm.

3. Cut the zucchini lengthwise into thin slices. Mix with olive oil and grill in a grill pan in portions. Season with salt and pepper.

4. Chop the squash seeds and warm them in an ungreased pan, add the honey and remove from the heat.

5. Heat up the plates and arrange the zucchini on them. Place small spoonfuls of purée on the zucchini (serve the rest of the purée separately). Sprinkle the dish with crumbled goat cheese and the pumpkin seeds. Add a few drops of pumpkin seed oil and serve immediately.

Preparation time: 1 hour and 10 minutes

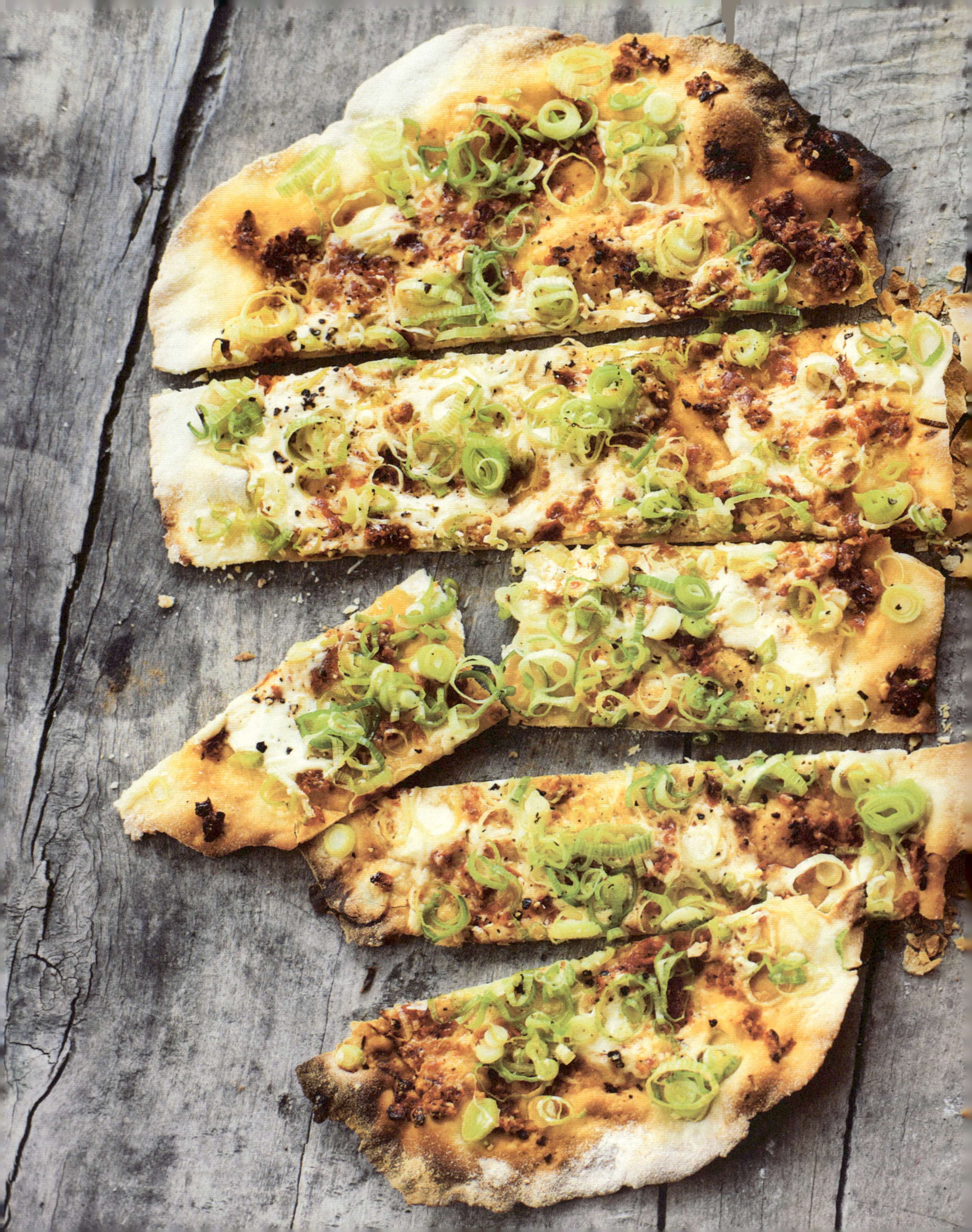

Tarte Flambée "Italiano" with Leek

Ingredients (serves 4)

1 teaspoon active dry yeast
sugar
2 cups flour
1/2 cup buttermilk (room temperature)
8—10 tablespoons olive oil
salt
1—2 garlic cloves
3 ounces sundried tomatoes
1 teaspoon dried oregano
8 tablespoons grated Parmesan
1 cup sour cream
1 leek

1. Dissolve the yeast together with 1/2 teaspoon of sugar in 2 tablespoons of lukewarm water. Sift flour into a bowl and press a hollow into the middle. Add the yeast and mix in some flour from the edge of the bowl. Add buttermilk, 2 tablespoons of olive oil and 1 teaspoon of salt. Knead the dough (it is alright if it's firmer than pizza dough). Let rise in a warm place for 2 1/2 hours.

2. Divide the risen dough into 4 pieces and roll them out until they are very thin. Place each one on a separate piece of floured parchment paper and cover with cling wrap until you are ready to use them.

3. Preheat the oven on the highest possible temperature, with a baking sheet on the bottom rack.

4. Peel the garlic and purée together with the dried tomatoes, 8—10 tablespoons of olive oil, oregano, 1/2 teaspoon of sugar and the Parmesan. Stir sour cream well until smooth.

5. Wash the leek and cut it into thin slices. Mix with a pinch of sugar, some salt and a little bit of olive oil.

6. Remove cling wrap from the dough and evenly spread on the tomato paste, sour cream and leek. One after the other, let the tartes slide from the baking paper on to the hot baking sheet in the oven. Bake until golden brown about 5 to 8 minutes.

Preparation time: 30 minutes (+ 2 1/2 hours for dough to rest)

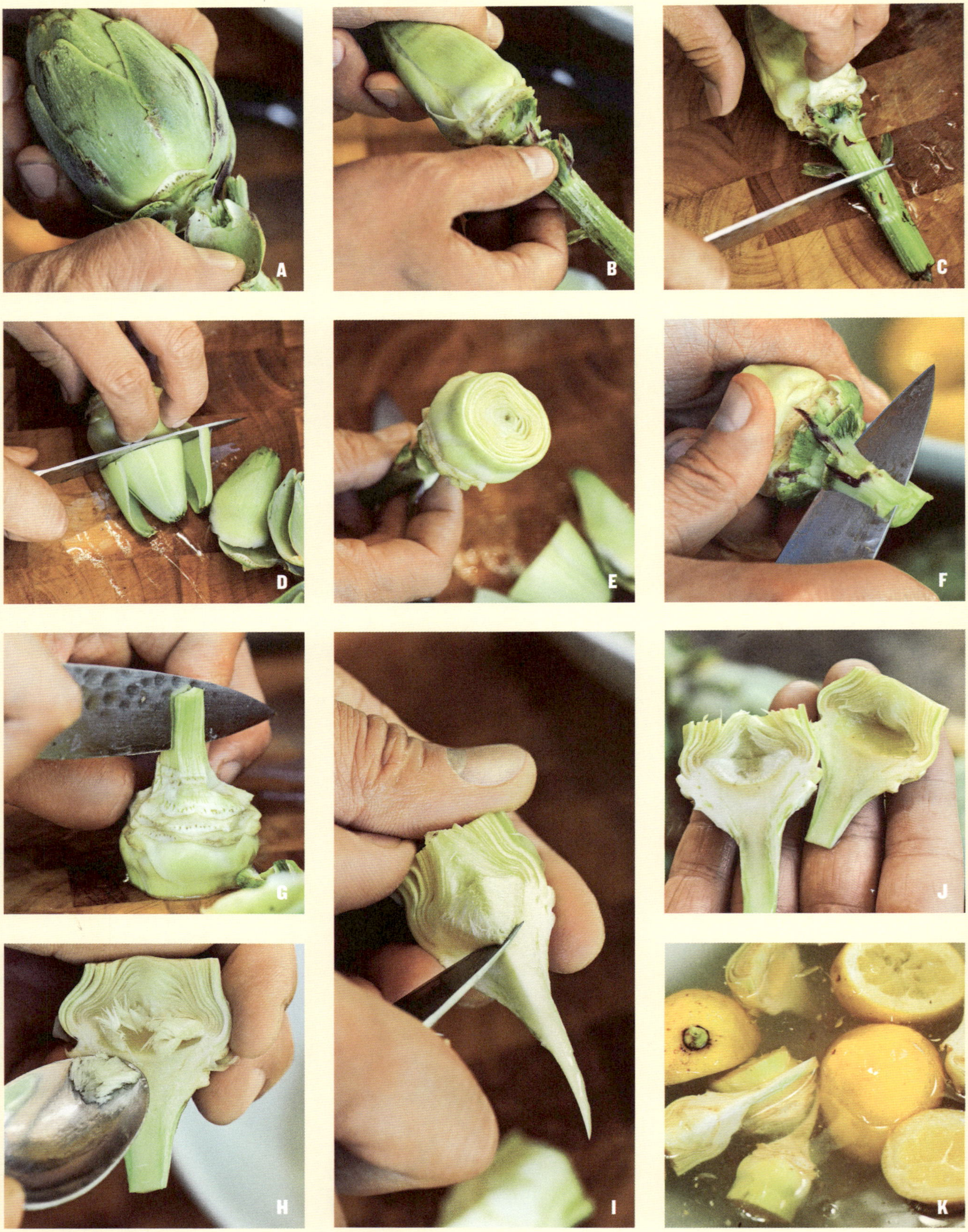
A
B
C
D
E
F
G
H
I
J
K

Cleaning Artichokes

Artichokes can be tricky to handle, but they are worth the trouble!

Ingredients (serves 4)

1 organic lemon
12 baby artichokes

1. Mix cold water with lemon juice in a bowl. Remove the outer hard green leaves of the artichoke (A) until you get to the light yellow petals (B). Briefly dunk the artichoke into the lemon water. Cut the stem a little (C).
2. Cut the artichoke horizontally in half (D, E), throwing away the petals you have cut off. Then dunk the cut sides of the artichokes in lemon water. Peel the stem (F).
3. Slice the artichokes lengthwise (G). Scrape out the choke with a teaspoon (H, J). Put the cleaned artichoke halves back into the lemon water.
4. You can also quarter the artichokes and remove the choke with a knife (I). Put the cleaned artichoke halves back into the lemon water (K).
5. Once you have prepared artichokes like this, you can fry them, boil them or eat them raw cut into thin slices, as it says in the recipe on page 212.

Preparation time: 35 minutes

INFORMATION: Freshly prepared, fat-headed artichokes taste so much better than the processed varieties you find in the grocery store that come in a jar, soaked in vinegar. For beginners, I would recommend the delicate baby artichokes. You can tell they are fresh when the outer leaves and long stem are firm. If the stem bends easily, then the artichokes are dried out. They taste best in early summer.

Artichoke Salad *delicate blossom meets fine oil*

Ingredients (serves 4)

12 baby artichokes
1 organic lemon
8 tablespoons olive oil
4 tablespoons freshly squeezed lemon juice
salt and pepper
1/2 red onion
1/2 a head of red oak leaf lettuce (or arugula)
4 stems parsley
2 ounces of Parmesan

1. Wash the artichokes in lemon water (see description page 210). Mix the olive oil with lemon juice. Season with salt, 1 pinch of sugar and pepper.
2. Cut the cleaned artichokes into thin slices and lay them in the vinaigrette. Peel the onion and cut into thin slices. Wash, rinse and spin the lettuce dry.
3. Rip the lettuce into bite-sized pieces, pull off the parsley leaves and mix both in with the artichokes. Season with salt and pepper. Slice the Parmesan into chunks and sprinkle over the salad.

Preparation time: 35 minutes

VARIATIONS: The salad also tastes great if you replace 1–2 tablespoons of olive oil with smoked olive oil or walnut oil. 1–2 teaspoons of sesame oil give the salad an Asian-inspired taste. Instead of using Parmesan, the salad can be served with sliced mountain cheese, mild sheep's cheese or smoked scamorza.

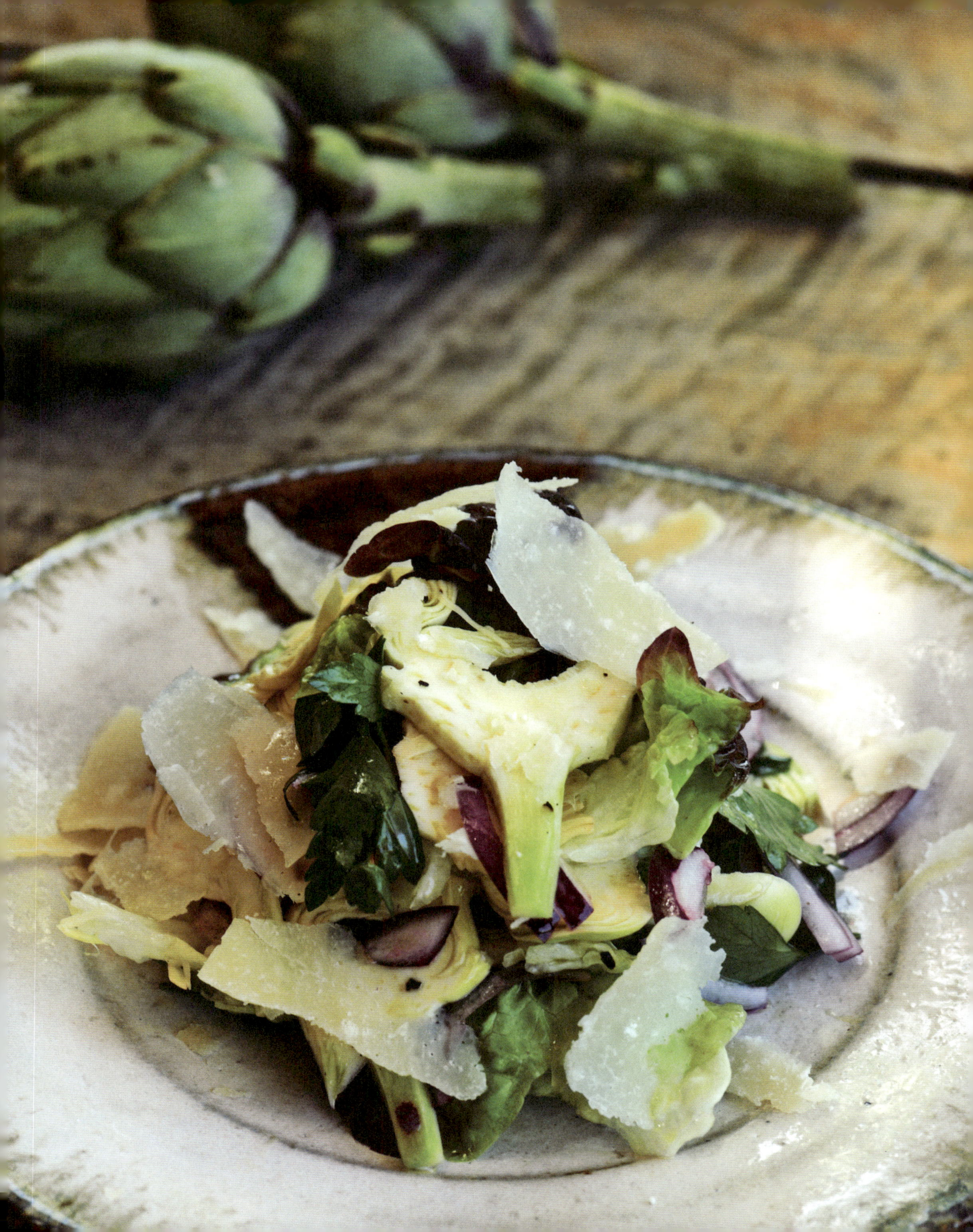

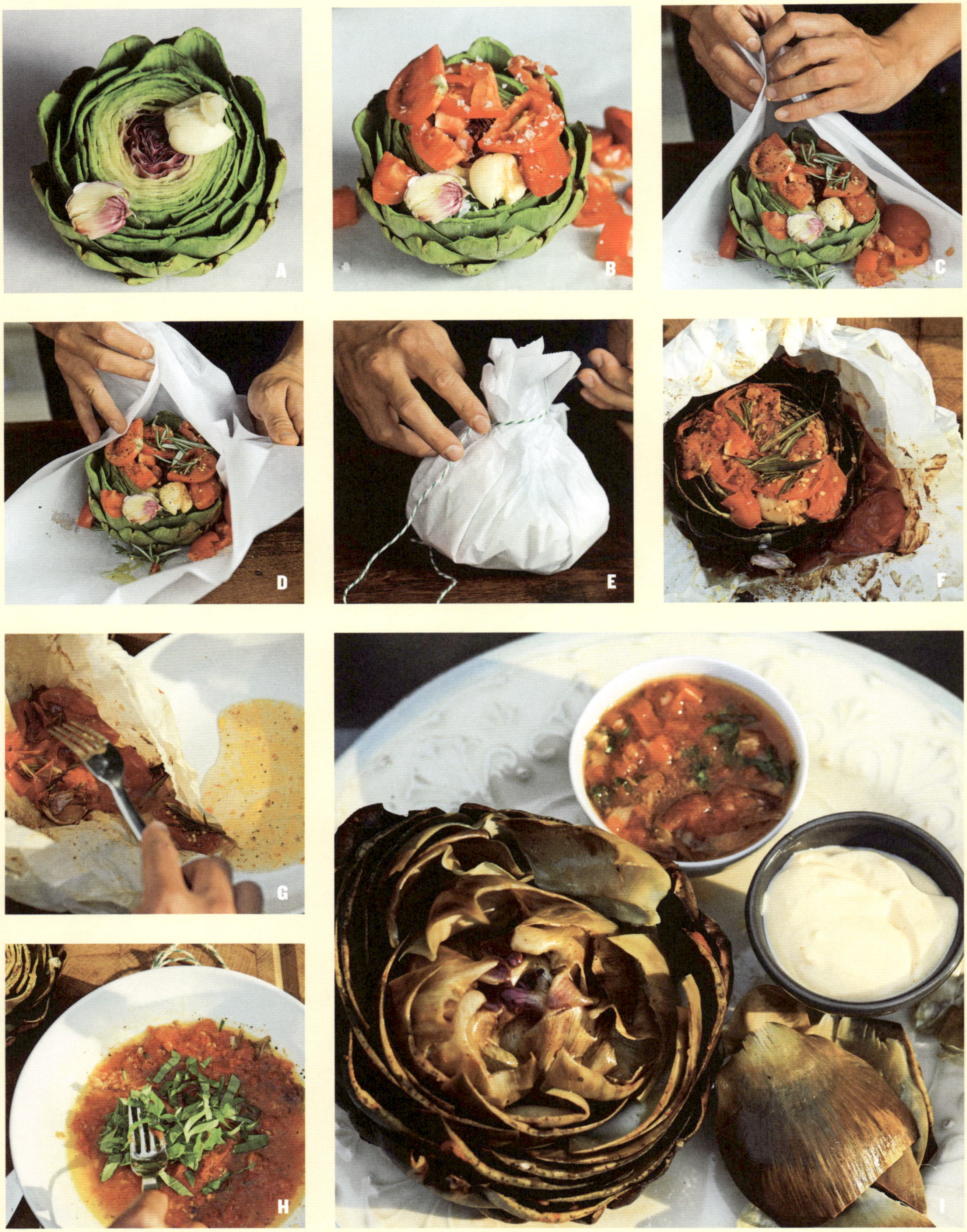
A
B
C
D
E
F
G
H
I

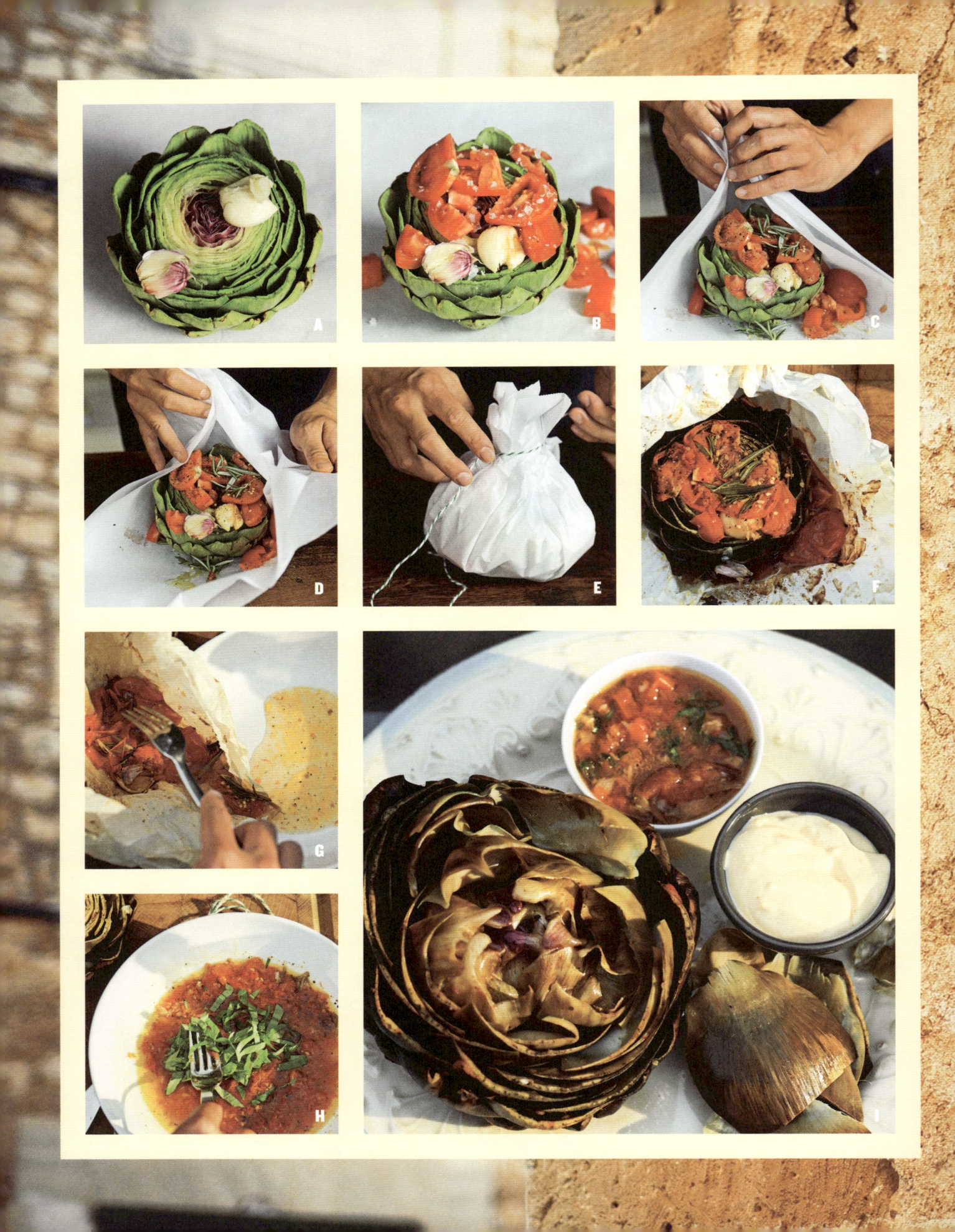

Baked Artichokes with 2 Dips

Ingredients (serves 4)

4 pieces parchment paper, 24 x 18 inches)
2 tomatoes
5 garlic cloves
2 artichokes
2 dried chili peppers
2 stems rosemary or thyme
salt and pepper
6 tablespoons olive oil
kitchen twine
1/4 cup whole milk
sugar
1/2 cup neutral vegetable oil
1—2 teaspoons tomato ketchup
1 teaspoon grated organic lemon peel
1—2 teaspoons white wine vinegar
4 stems basil

1. Lay 2 sheets of parchment paper on top of each other. Wash the tomatoes and cut into slices. Peel 4 garlic cloves and crush them. Wash the artichokes and let them drain, then cut the upper quarter off and break off the stem. Place the artichokes in the middle of the parchment and cover with tomatoes, garlic, chili peppers and herbs (A). Season each with salt and pepper and drizzle with 2 tablespoons of olive oil (B).
2. Fold the ends of the parchment paper into the middle (C, D) and tie together with twine (E). Preheat the oven to 350°F. Place both packages into an oven-proof dish and cook on the middle rack for 90 minutes until done.
3. In the meantime, peel the remaining garlic and put into a high-sided container together with the milk. Season with salt and a pinch of sugar. While blending with a hand blender, gently pour in the vegetable oil and mix until a creamy mayonnaise forms. Fold in the ketchup and the grated lemon peel.
4. Remove the artichokes from the oven and move them from the parchment to the plates (F). Pour the cooking liquid into a bowl (G). Mash all the ingredients with a fork (H), add the rest of the olive oil and season to taste with salt, pepper, vinegar and 1 pinch of sugar.
5. Pull off the basil leaves, dice and mix them in. Serve the artichokes with mayonnaise and the tomato dip (I).

Preparation time: 1 hour and 40 minutes

Marinated Green Beans with Scamorza-Toast

Ingredients (serves 4)

- 1/4 pound smoked scamorza
- 1 large egg
- 2/3 cups heavy cream
- salt and pepper
- 4 slices peasant bread
- 1 pound green beans
- 1/2 red onion
- 1—2 tablespoons red wine vinegar (or white wine vinegar or cider vinegar)
- 7 tablespoons olive oil
- 1 teaspoon fresh thyme leaves
- 1/3 pound date or cherry tomatoes
- sugar

1. Finely grate the scamorza and whisk with the egg and cream with a hand blender until smooth and creamy. Season with salt and pepper. Cut the slices of bread in half and immerse in the scamorza cream in a bowl. Let soak for 10 minutes.

2. Clean the green beans and boil in salted water for 7—8 minutes until just tender. Drain the beans and rinse in cold water. Dry on paper towels.

3. Peel the onion and cut into fine slices. Mix with vinegar, 4 tablespoons of olive oil and thyme leaves. Mix the beans with the vinaigrette. Cut the tomatoes in half and stir in. Season with salt, pepper and 1 pinch of sugar.

4. Heat the remaining oil in a non-stick pan and fry the drained pieces of bread on each side for 2—3 minutes until golden brown. Arrange the bread on a plate with the beans.

Preparation time: 30 minutes

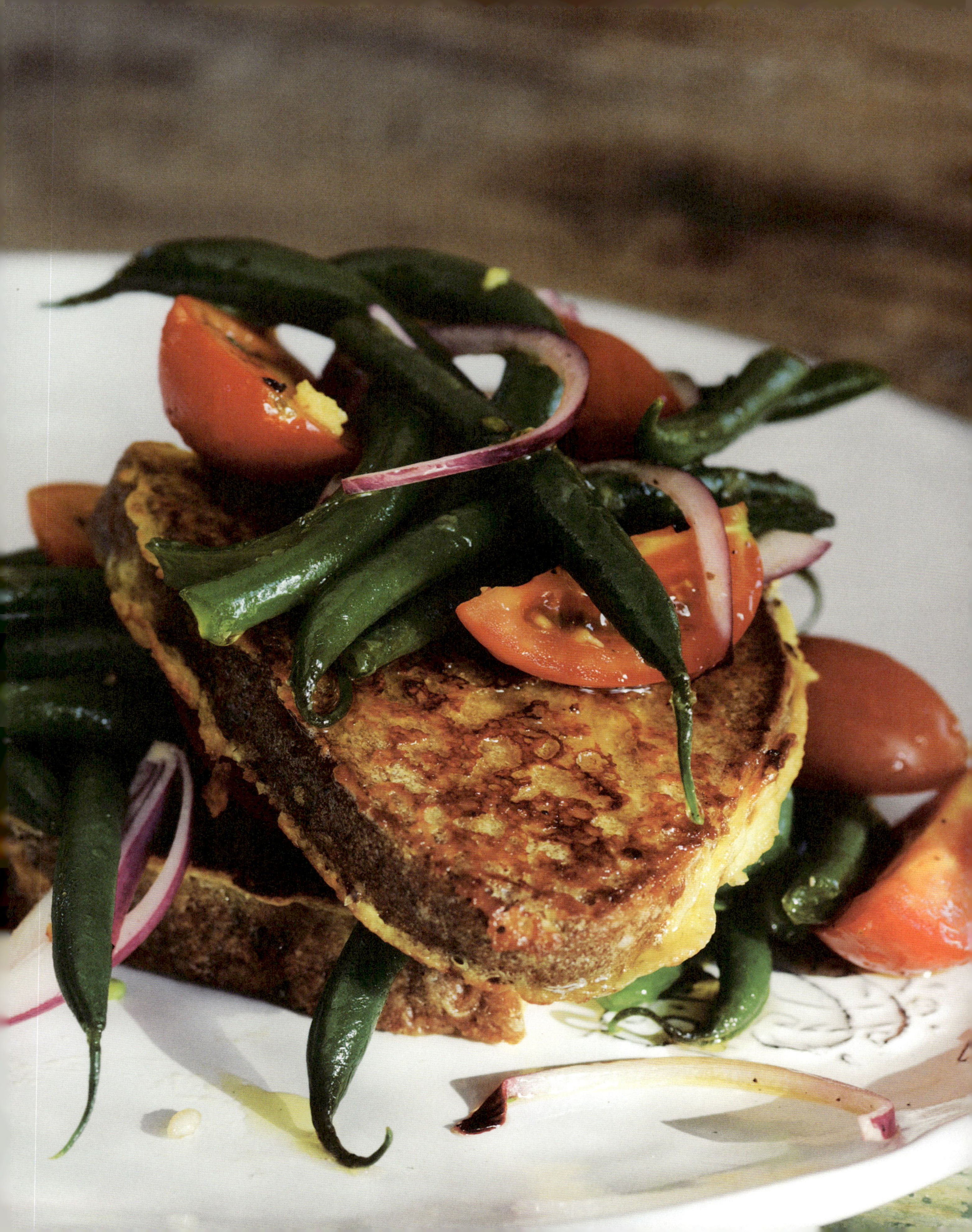

Soba Noodle Salad with Miso Dressing

Ingredients (serves 4)

2 large eggs
salt and pepper
1 scallion
2–3 tablespoons miso paste
2–3 tablespoons white wine vinegar
2 tablespoons sunflower oil
sugar
1/2 pound soba noodles (see note)
1 heart of romaine lettuce
1/2 small red onion

1. Cook the eggs in boiling water for 12 minutes. To make the dressing, wash the scallion and cut into fine slices. Mix with the miso paste, 1 cup of water, vinegar and oil. Season with salt and pepper.
2. Cook the soba noodles according to the package instructions, drain and rinse under cold water. Drain again.
3. Wash the lettuce, spin it dry and cut it into small pieces. Peel the onion, chop into very small pieces and mix with the lettuce. Cool the eggs in cold water, peel and chop them. Mix the lettuce with the noodles and, just before serving, add the dressing. Arrange on the plate with chopped egg and serve immediately.

Preparation time: 25 minutes

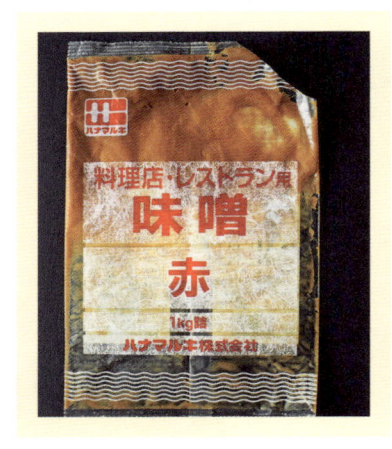

SOBA NOODLES are Japanese buckwheat noodles. Traditionally, they are served separately with hot or cold soup, or with all kinds of side dishes, depending on the season. Soba noodles can symbolize various things in the Japanese culture: long life, happiness in times of turmoil or change. It is Japanese tradition to eat soba noodles as the last meal of the year on New Year's Eve and they are a popular gift to take to house warming parties. Itadakimasu (Bon appetit!).

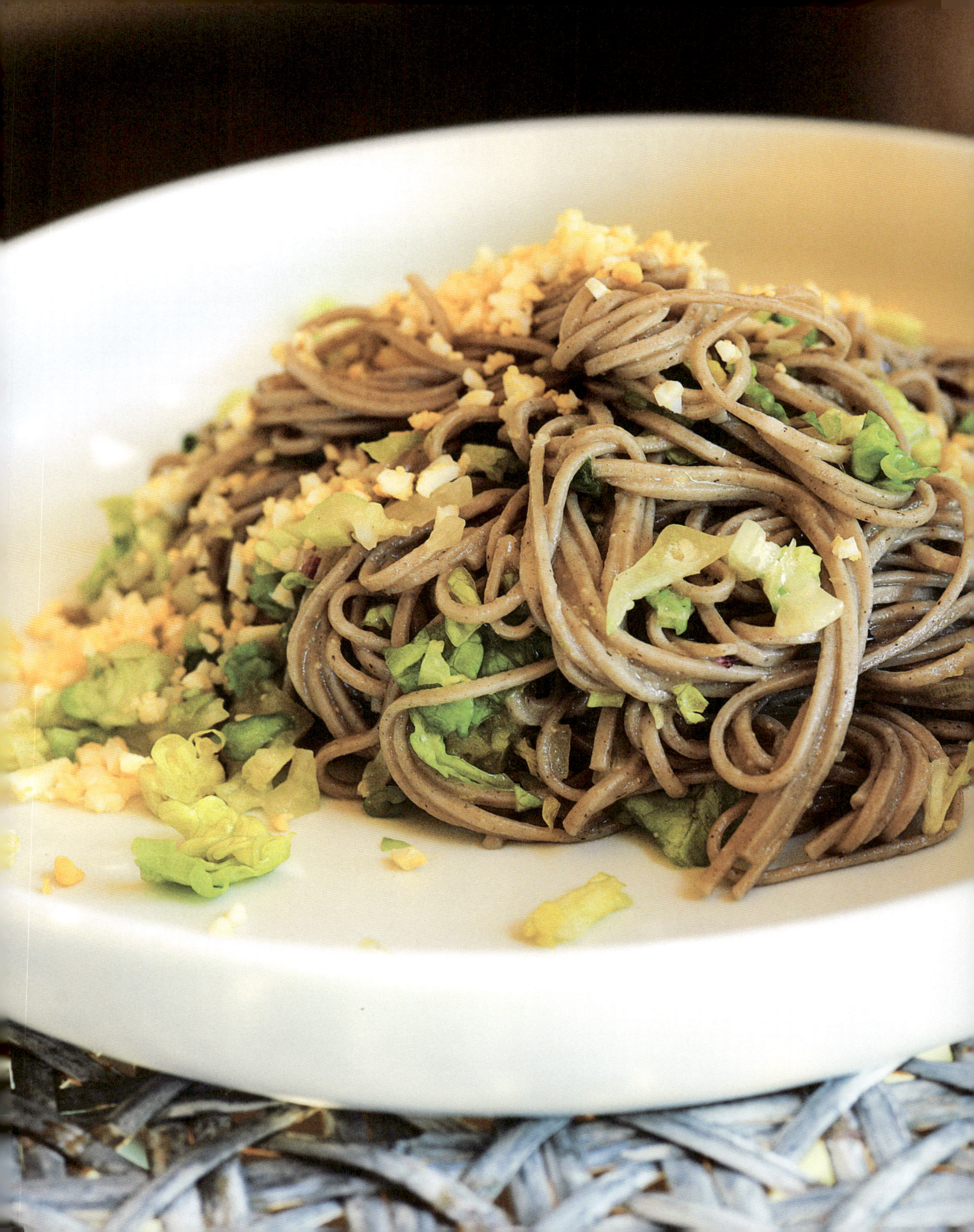

Jerusalem Artichoke and Lentil Salad

Ingredients (serves 4)

- 1/4 cup beluga lentils
- 1 pound Jerusalem artichokes (also known as sunchokes – see note)
- 6 tablespoons olive oil
- salt and pepper
- 1/2 cup organic pear juice
- 2 tablespoons sherry vinegar (or white wine vinegar or cider vinegar)
- 1 tablespoon honey
- 1 tablespoon spicy mustard
- 3 tablespoons sunflower oil
- 1/2 red onion
- 1/2 head of garden lettuce

1. Boil lentils in unsalted water for 15 minutes. Peel the Jerusalem artichokes, lay them in a bowl of water and set aside. Cut the bulbs into 1/2-inch cubes and sauté for 2—3 minutes in a pan with 3 tablespoons of olive oil on a medium heat. Season with salt and pepper.
2. Drain the lentils and whisk with the pear juice, vinegar, honey, mustard, sunflower oil and 3 tablespoons of olive oil until smooth. Season with salt and pepper.
3. Peel the onion and cut into thin slices. Wash the lettuce and spin it dry. Arrange the Jerusalem artichokes on a plate with the lettuce and drizzle with the lentil vinaigrette.

Preparation time: 25 minutes

JERUSALEM ARTICHOKE is the sweet root of species of sunflower and comes from Native American cuisine. The potato-like root does not contain any carbohydrates and, due to its high insulin content, it is approved for a diabetic diet. You can even buy jerusalem artichoke syrup to use as a natural sweetener.

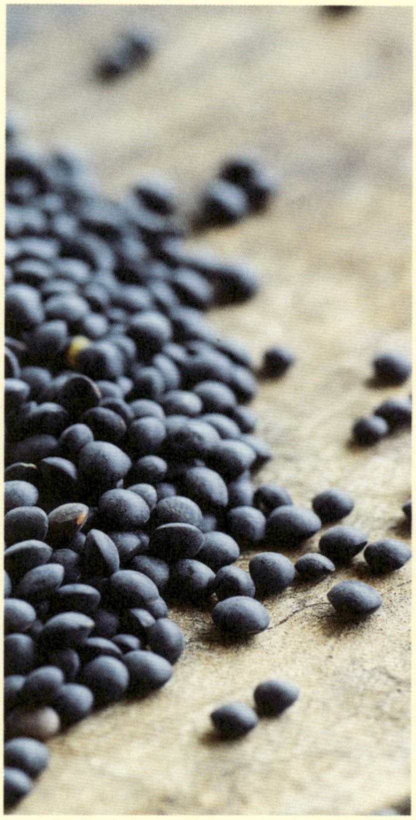

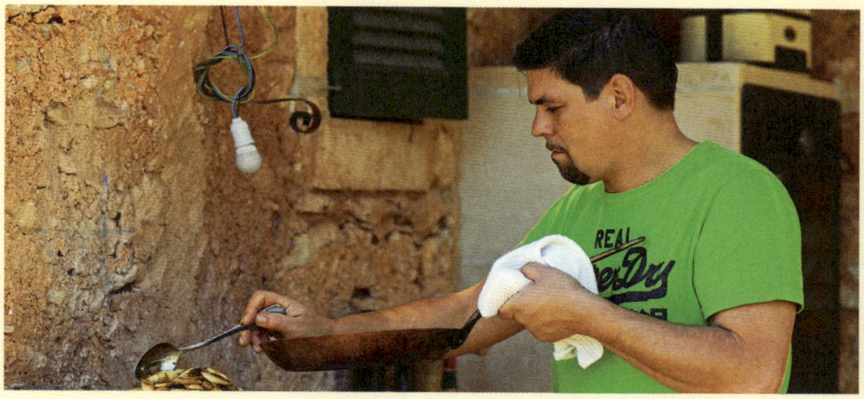
REAL

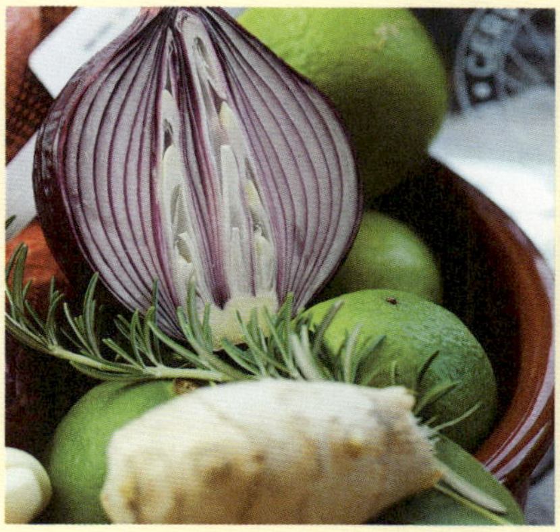

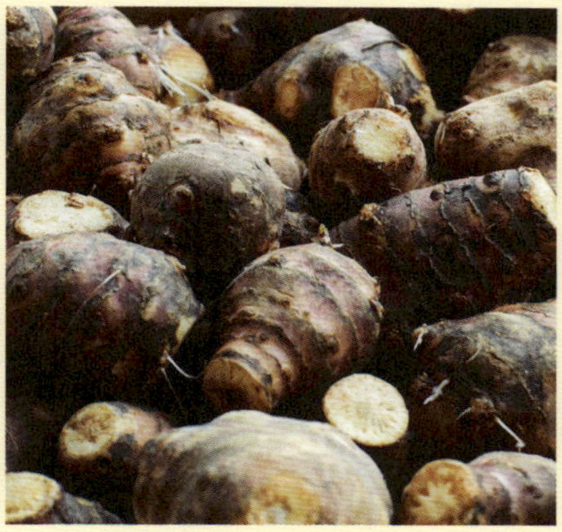

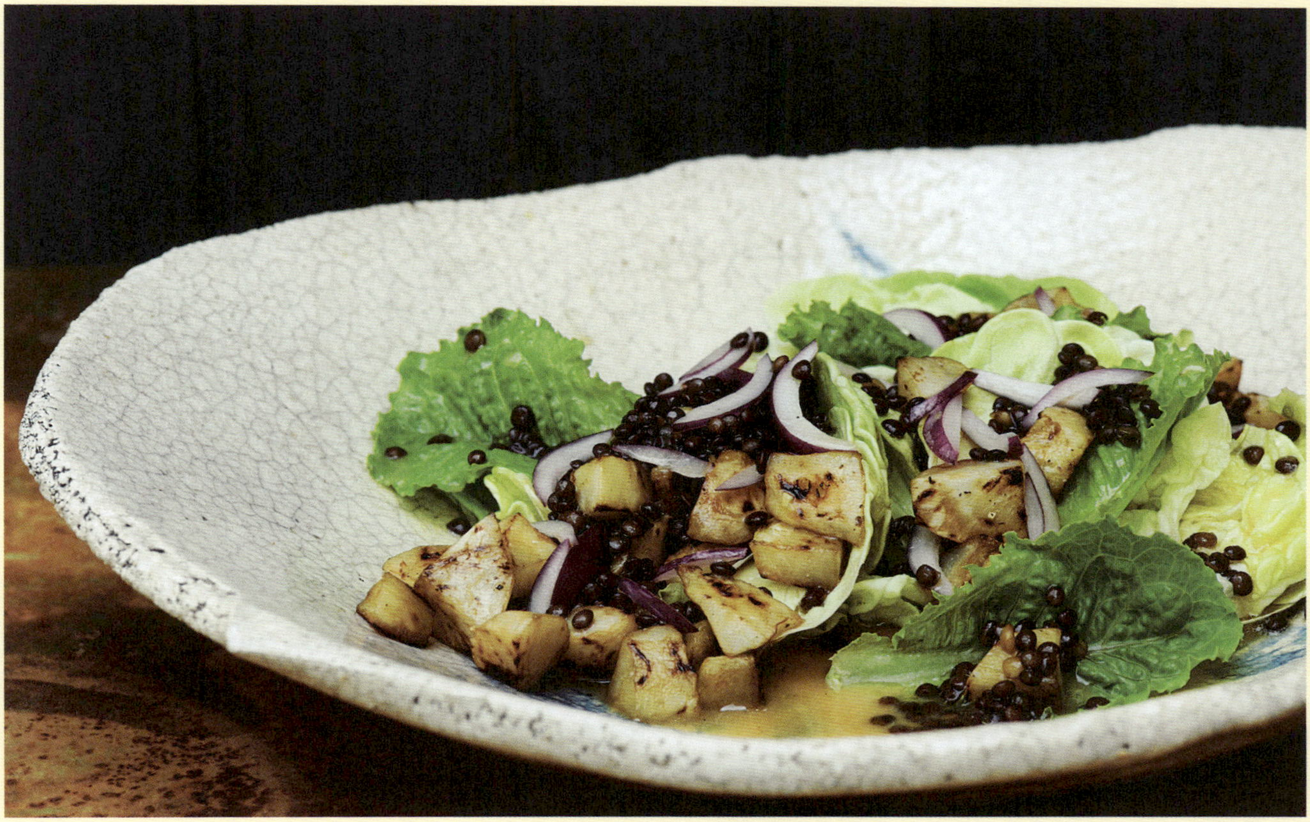

SALT MIXTURES

Salt is probably the most important type of seasoning we have to cook with. It used to be a form of currency – today it makes for good business. The funny thing is that salt is actually a simple mineral that consists of 95—98% sodium chloride – at least your palate can't tell the difference in price. However, there is a difference in flavor between unrefined and industrially refined salt. What is interesting from the cooking standpoint is salt's consistency, shape and purity level.

TABLE SALT is produced by condensing the water extracted from stone salt. Neutral tasting additives have an anti-caking effect. Some kitchen salts have iodine and fluoride added to them. This type of salt is the most common one.

SEA SALT is obtained when sea water in solar houses or shallow pools is evaporated. It is milder than table salt. Rough sea salt is perfect for salt crusts or as a savory base for cooking larger pieces of vegetables. It is really good for bringing out the flavor in dishes and is ideal for making salt mixtures.

FLEUR DE SEL is an extremely fine sea salt whose name means "salt flower." It is an ultra-thin layer on the surface of the ocean that forms only on hot days when there is no wind and has to be harvested by hand. Sophisticated, crisp fleur de sel shouldn't be used until after cooking the food. It would be a waste to cook with fleur de sel. It can mostly be found in Mediterranean regions. The salt gardens of the French Atlantic coast are famous for their high quality.

It's very easy to make **SALT MIXTURES** yourself. Salt binds flavors together. If you store the salt mixture in an airtight container, it keeps for much longer. You can grind spices such as fennel seeds, black pepper, chili flakes and aniseed in a mortar and use them as aromatic compounds. But you can also use fresh ingredients such as finely grated lemon or orange peel from organic fruit, freshly chopped rosemary, lemon thyme, or bay leaves to make unique salt mixtures. Homemade salt mixtures in pretty jars make great presents.

GOOD TO KNOW: The most famous salt mixture comes from Japan. To make gomasio, you take sesame seeds and toast them without fat in an ungreased pan, then mix them with salt in a ratio of 7:1 (seeds to salt).

Salt-Baked Beet Salad

Ingredients (serves 4)

- 3 3/4 cups rough sea salt
- 6 small beets with leaves
- 1 organic lemon
- 4 stems rosemary
- 6 waxy potatoes (red or new potatoes)
- salt and pepper
- 1–2 tablespoons white wine vinegar
- 4 tablespoons olive oil
- 2 stems dill
- 4 cornichons
- 2 shallots

1. Mix the sea salt with 4 tablespoons of water. Spread half of that onto the bottom of an ovenproof dish. Cut off the beet leaves and set aside.

2. Wash the beets thoroughly and lay on the bed of salt (B). Cut off the lemon peel in strips and lay it over the beets with the rosemary (C). Cover with the rest of the salt (D). Preheat the oven to 400°F. Bake for 1 hour and 15 minutes on the second rack from the bottom.

3. While the beets are cooking, wash the potatoes thoroughly and boil them in their skins for about 15–20 minutes in salted water until just tender. Rinse under cold water, peel and immediately cut into thick slices. Place the slices into a bowl and drizzle with white wine vinegar and 2 tablespoons of olive oil. Season with salt and pepper and the dill leaves. Cut the cornichons lengthwise into thin slices. Peel and dice the shallots. Mix both with the potatoes.

4. Take the beets out of the oven and crack open the salt crust. Remove the beets, allow to cool, peel and then cut into wedges. Turn them around in a bowl with 1 tablespoon of cornichons water and 1 tablespoon of olive oil. Drain and mix carefully with the potatoes. Fold in a few tender beet leaves (E). Season the salad with salt and pepper.

Preparation time: 1 hour and 30 minutes

A

B

C

D

E

1
2
3

FLAVOR ALL-ROUNDERS: MELONS X 3

It really doesn't matter whether it is sugar, honeydew, watermelon, cantaloupe, cavaillon or Galia: if they are perfectly ripe and chilled, melons in the summer are delicious, honey-sweet refreshments. But melons are capable of more! Prepared as a vegetable, they demonstrate a completely new flavor: stewed, grilled or spiced, cooked melons are a delicious discovery.

1 Melon Curry

Cut **1 2/3 pounds of watermelon and cantaloupe flesh** into bite-sized pieces. Peel **1 red onion** and cut into wedges. Heat **4 tablespoons of olive oil** in a pot, dust the melons and onions with **1 teaspoon of curry powder** and sauté for 2 minutes. Pour **1 can of peeled tomatoes (28 ounces net weight)** through a sieve (catch and save the tomato juice for later use). Chop the drained, peeled tomatoes and add to the melons. Simmer on medium heat for 10 minutes, uncovered. Chop **3 stems of cilantro** and fold in. Season the curry with **salt.**

2 Cold Honeydew Melon Basil Soup

Peel **1 large honeydew melon,** cut in half and remove the seeds. Dice the flesh and place on a plate in the freezer for 1 hour. Then in a blender, finely blend the melon with the **juice of 1 lime and 1 orange, 3 tablespoons of olive oil** and **2 stems of basil.** Season with **salt** and pour servings into bowls. Cut **2 basil leaves** into fine strips and sprinkle over the soup. Serve with **a few drops of olive oil** and **a little pepper.**

3 Grilled Melon

Peel **1 cantaloupe,** cut in half, remove the seeds and cut into eight pieces. Dip the wedges in **2—3 tablespoons of olive oil** and lay on the grill. Grill each side for 2 minutes. Season with **salt** and **chili flakes.** Serve garnished with a few washed **arugula leaves.**

Crisp Celery Root with Ginger Pepper Cherries

Ingredients (serves 4)

- 1/2 pound sweet cherries
- 1 celery root
- salt and pepper
- 2 large eggs
- 2/3 cup flour
- 3/4 pound breadcrumbs
- oil
- 3/4 inch fresh ginger
- 1 stem basil
- 3 tablespoons butter

1. Wash the cherries, remove the pits and set aside. Peel the celery root and cut into 1/2–3/4-inch slices. Cook the celery in a large amount of boiling salted water for 1 minute. Rinse under cold water, drain and sprinkle with salt.

2. Whisk the eggs, season slightly with salt. Dip the celery in the flour, shake off and then dunk into the egg. Drain and coat with breadcrumbs.

3. Cover the bottom of a pan with oil and sauté the celery "escalopes" over medium heat on both sides. Drain on paper towels. Season with salt and keep warm.

4. Peel the ginger and cut into wafer-thin strips. Pull off the basil leaves. Heat butter in another pan until it froths and turns light brown. Stir in 1 pinch of salt and the cherries and then the ginger and basil. Season with pepper and serve with the celery "escalopes."

Preparation time: 35 minutes

》 The favorite dish of unsuccessful hunters! 《

TIP

Cherries go very well with cheese,
grilled vegetables or crunchy salads.

Tofu Sprout Salad with Prune Dip

Ingredients (serves 4)

- 10 pitted dried soft prunes
- 2 garlic cloves
- juice of 1 lime
- juice of 1/2 lemon
- 4 tablespoons soy sauce
- 1 chili pepper
- salt and pepper
- 3—4 tablespoons rice vinegar (or white wine vinegar)
- 1/2 pound soy bean sprouts
- 1/2 pound firm tofu
- 1/2 pound shiitake mushrooms
- 5 tablespoons neutral vegetable oil
- 2 hearts of romaine lettuce

1. To make the prune dip, in a blender or food processor, blend together the prunes, 1 peeled garlic clove, lime juice, lemon juice, 5 1/2 tablespoons of water, 2 tablespoons of soy sauce, chili pepper, a pinch of salt and 2 tablespoons of rice vinegar until smooth.
2. Cook the sprouts in boiling salted water for 20 seconds, rinse in cold water and drain in a sieve. Chop the sprouts into small pieces. Drain the tofu and chop into approx. 1/2-inch cubes. Peel and dice the rest of the garlic. Clean and chop the mushrooms.
3. Heat 3 tablespoons of oil in a pan and fry the tofu on all sides for 3—4 minutes until golden brown. Pour in the rest of the soy sauce. Remove the tofu from the pan.
4. Put the rest of the oil in the pan and heat. Sauté the mushrooms for 2 minutes. Add the sprouts and the tofu. Take off the heat and season with salt, pepper and 1—2 tablespoons of rice vinegar.
5. Wash and rinse the lettuce and pull off the leaves. Cut the tender lettuce hearts into fine strips. Spread the tofu mixture onto the leaves and sprinkle with lettuce strips. Serve with the prune dip.

Preparation time: 45 minutes

yummmmy! YUMMY! yummmmy!

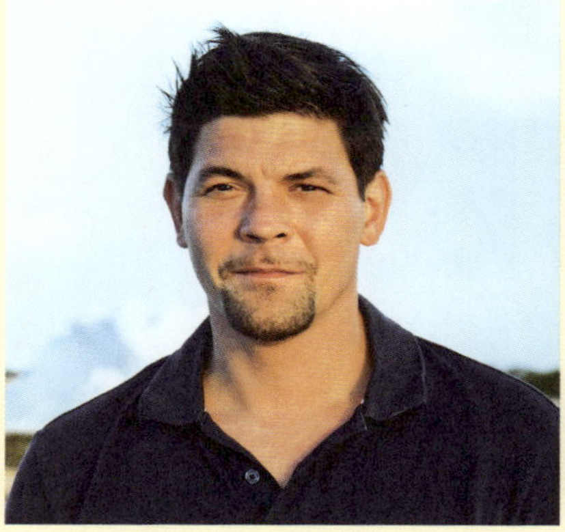
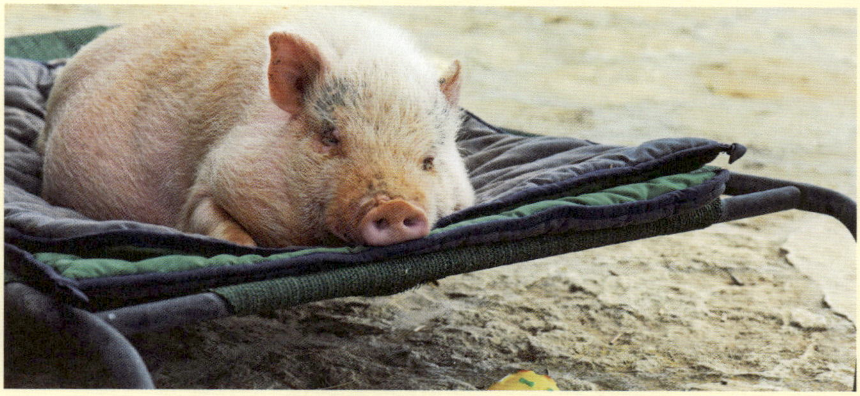
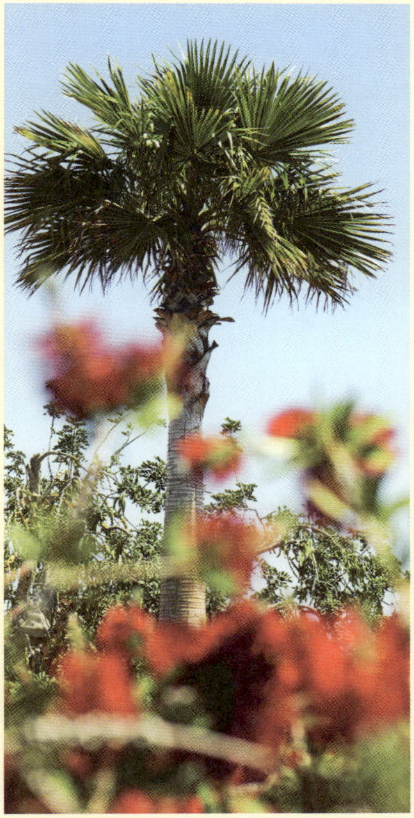
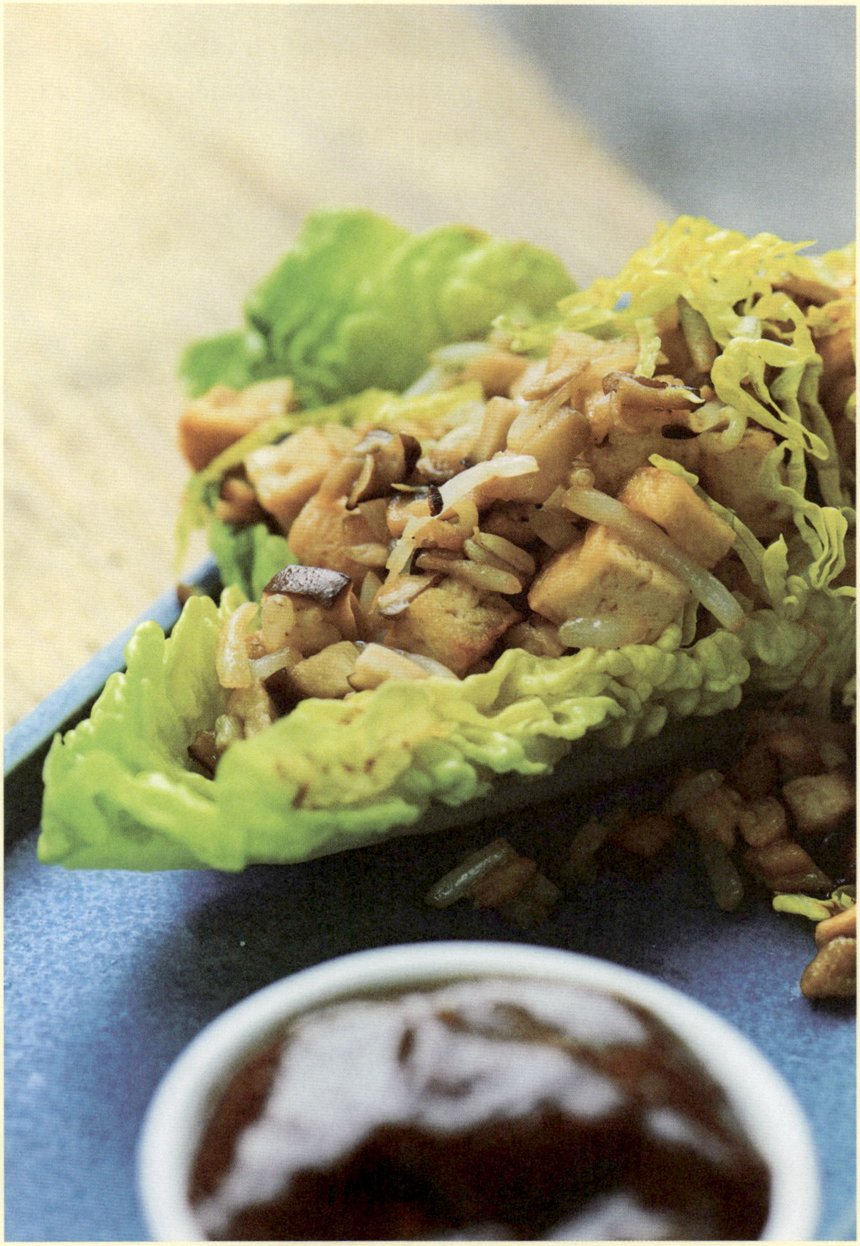
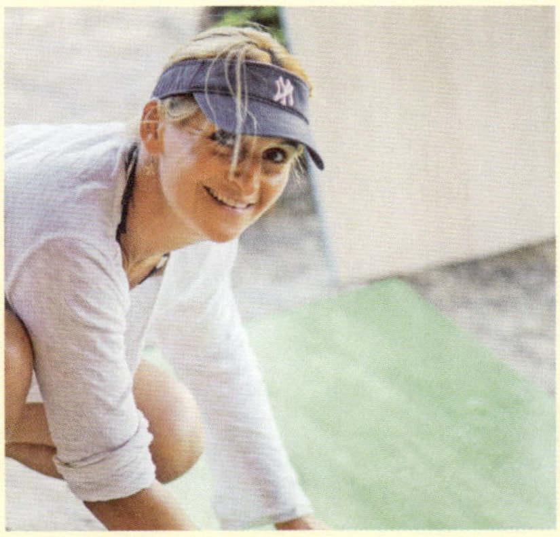

PESTO & VEGETABLE PASTES:

How to get quick flavor!

Mashed or finely grated vegetables, fresh or dried herbs, nuts, spices and olive oil – that's all you need to create countless spice pastes. These can be varied again with garlic, grated cheese, capers and hot peppers. There are as many possible combinations as uses for spice pastes: they pump up flavors in vegetable dishes, they taste good on their own with pasta or as a homemade spread on fresh bread (fresh cheese and pesto on bread is a favorite). Fast food in the best sense!

PESTO is a classic among herb pastes and can be made with relatively few ingredients. The most popular pesto is the green pesto alla Genovese (meaning originally from Genoa), made with 2—3 bunches of basil, 2—3 tablespoons of toasted pine nuts, 1—2 cloves of garlic, 1/4—3/4 cup of strong grated Parmesan cheese and some olive oil. These ingredients are mixed together to form a creamy paste. My recipe for classic pesto and three other variations are on pages 120/121. It's worth experimenting with and it's really easy: swap the herbs, use other nuts, a special kind of oil, leave out the cheese or use some other kind of hard cheese. That makes for a completely new culinary experience every time! The French version of "pesto" is called "pistou" and crowns the famous vegetable noodle soup "soupe au pistou."

CURRY PASTES are a little more work than the quick pestos. They come in countless flavors in well-stocked grocery stores or ethnic shops. But it's worth making your own curry pastes: overall they have more flavor, you can decide how spicy you want them to be and you know what's in them. You should always fry curry pastes before adding them to other dishes so that they release their full aromas. Curry pastes can be preserved by frying them, letting them cool down, and then putting them into airtight jars topped with a layer of oil. Store the jars in the fridge.

For quick flavor, green cuisine also has **HARISSA,** a piquant paste from North Africa that contains chili peppers, garlic, cumin and coriander.

Tim's green curry paste

Toast **1 TEASPOON OF CORIANDER AND CUMIN SEEDS** in a pan. Let the mixture cool before grinding it finely in a mortar. Wash **4 STEMS OF LEMON GRASS** and remove the outer leaves. Cut the light-colored inside piece into fine slices. Peel and chop **4 CLOVES OF SMOKED GARLIC** and **3 SHALLOTS.** Roughly chop **1 CUP OF CILANTRO** with its tender stems. Peel **3 INCHES OF GALANGAL** (alternatively **GINGER**) and cut it into pieces. Chop **2–3 CHILI** and **8 KAFFIR LIME LEAVES.** In your food processor or with a hand blender, purée all of these ingredients together with the **JUICE OF 1 ORGANIC LIME, 2–3 TABLESPOONS OF PALM OR BROWN SUGAR, 1 TEASPOON OF SOY SAUCE, SALT, 2 TABLESPOONS OF WATER** and **4 TABLESPOONS OF OIL.**

Green Jungle Curry

Ingredients (serves 4—6)

- 3 shallots
- 1 sweet potato
- 1/4 pound mushrooms
- 1/3 pound baby corn
- 1/4 pound sugar snap peas
- 1 small yellow zucchini (or green)
- 1/2 cup cherry tomatoes
- 4 scallions
- 1 organic lime
- 1/2 pound water chestnuts, fresh or canned
- 1 small eggplant
- 1 red chili pepper
- 2 cups coconut milk, unsweetened
- 1 cup vegetable stock
- 3 tablespoons peanut oil
- 6—8 tablespoons homemade green curry paste (see page 233, or 2—4 tablespoons ready-made curry paste)
- 6 kaffir lime leaves
- 6 stems Thai basil
- 6 stems cilantro

1. Peel the shallots and cut into thin slices. Peel the sweet potato, cut lengthwise and then across in approximately 1/4-inch slices. Clean the mushrooms and quarter or half them depending on their size. Wash the baby corn and sugar snap peas and cut in half. Wash the zucchini and cut lengthwise into 1/4 inch slices.
2. Wash the cherry tomatoes and cut in half. Wash the scallions and cut into 1 1/2-inch long pieces. Wash the lime and quarter it. Rinse off the water chestnuts and slice them. Wash the eggplant and dice into 3/4 inch pieces. Diagonally slice the chili pepper.
3. Warm the coconut milk and vegetable stock in a small pot.
4. Heat the peanut oil in another pot and sauté the shallots. Add the curry paste and cook for 1—2 minutes. Add the sweet potatoes and cook for 2—3 minutes, stirring constantly. Add the kaffir lime leaves and coconut milk stock and bring to a boil. Throw in the zucchini and eggplant and cook for 5 minutes on medium heat. Add the mushrooms and water chestnuts and cook for another 3—4 minutes. Add the cherry tomatoes, baby corn, sugar snap peas and scallions and cook for 2—3 minutes. Season with salt and 1 pinch of sugar.
5. Pull off the herb leaves and add to the curry with the lime quarters and the chili pepper. Serve with jasmine rice.

Preparation time: 60 minutes

NOTE: Consistency is a very important factor in Asian dishes. All the vegetables should be al dente after cooking. Since the different vegetables require different cooking times, I recommend keeping the vegetables in separate bowls before cooking as they do in Asian-Chinese takeouts.

TIP: If you prefer a thicker sauce, you can thicken it with cornstarch dissolved in a little water.

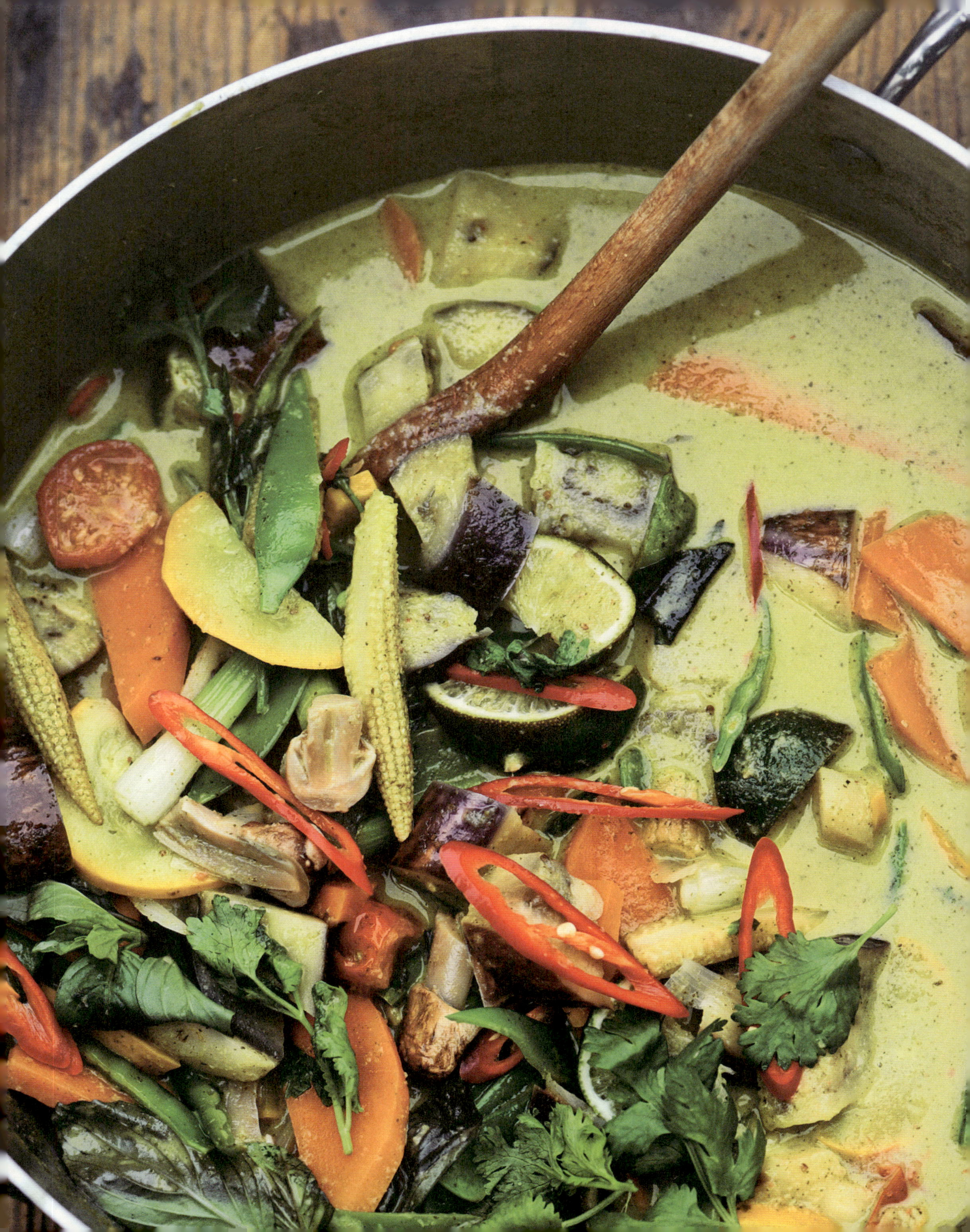

Crunchy Bananas with Quick Green Tomato Chutney

The chutney is easy to make and tastes good cold, too!

Ingredients (serves 4)

3 scallions
2 garlic cloves
6 green tomatoes (or unripe RAF tomatoes, see note)
1 green chili pepper
3 tablespoons olive oil
1 teaspoon black mustard seeds
1 tablespoon curry leaves (available in Asian shops, or 2 bay leaves)
2 organic limes
3 tablespoons brown sugar
1/2 cup apple juice
salt
12 small (or 4 large) green, unripe bananas
2 cups breadcrumbs
2 tablespoons mild curry powder
2 large eggs
3/4 cup flour
frying oil

1. Wash and chop the scallions. Peel the garlic and chop into small pieces with the tomatoes and chili. Heat olive oil in a pot with the mustard seeds and the curry leaves. Add the chili and garlic and sauté them. In a bowl, grate the lime peel and mix with the sugar and then add to the sauté. Fold in the tomatoes and the scallions. Deglaze with juice from the limes and the apple juice. Allow to reduce and thicken and then season with salt. Set aside.

2. Peel the bananas. Cut the large bananas into three pieces. Mix the breadcrumbs with curry powder. Whisk the eggs. Toss the bananas in flour, shake them off and cover them in egg. Turn them over in the breadcrumbs and be sure the crumbs are sticking.

3. Heat the oil in a pot or in the deep fryer to 350°F. Fry the bananas for 3—4 minutes until golden brown. Drain on paper towels and serve with warm chutney and basmati or jasmine rice.

Preparation time: 35 minutes

RAF TOMATOES are one of the oldest types of tomatoes in the world. They originated in Almeria in Andalusia, Spain. They get their strong flavor from their native chalky soil and salty water.

GREEN TOMATOES are often tomatoes picked before they ripen, usually harvested in fall. Connoisseurs like them especially for their sour taste. Some other types of tomatoes are becoming more and more popular, such as the green sweet cherry tomato called "Green Zebra" (yellow and green striped), "Evergreen" (green flesh tomato) and "Green Grape" (green cocktail tomato).

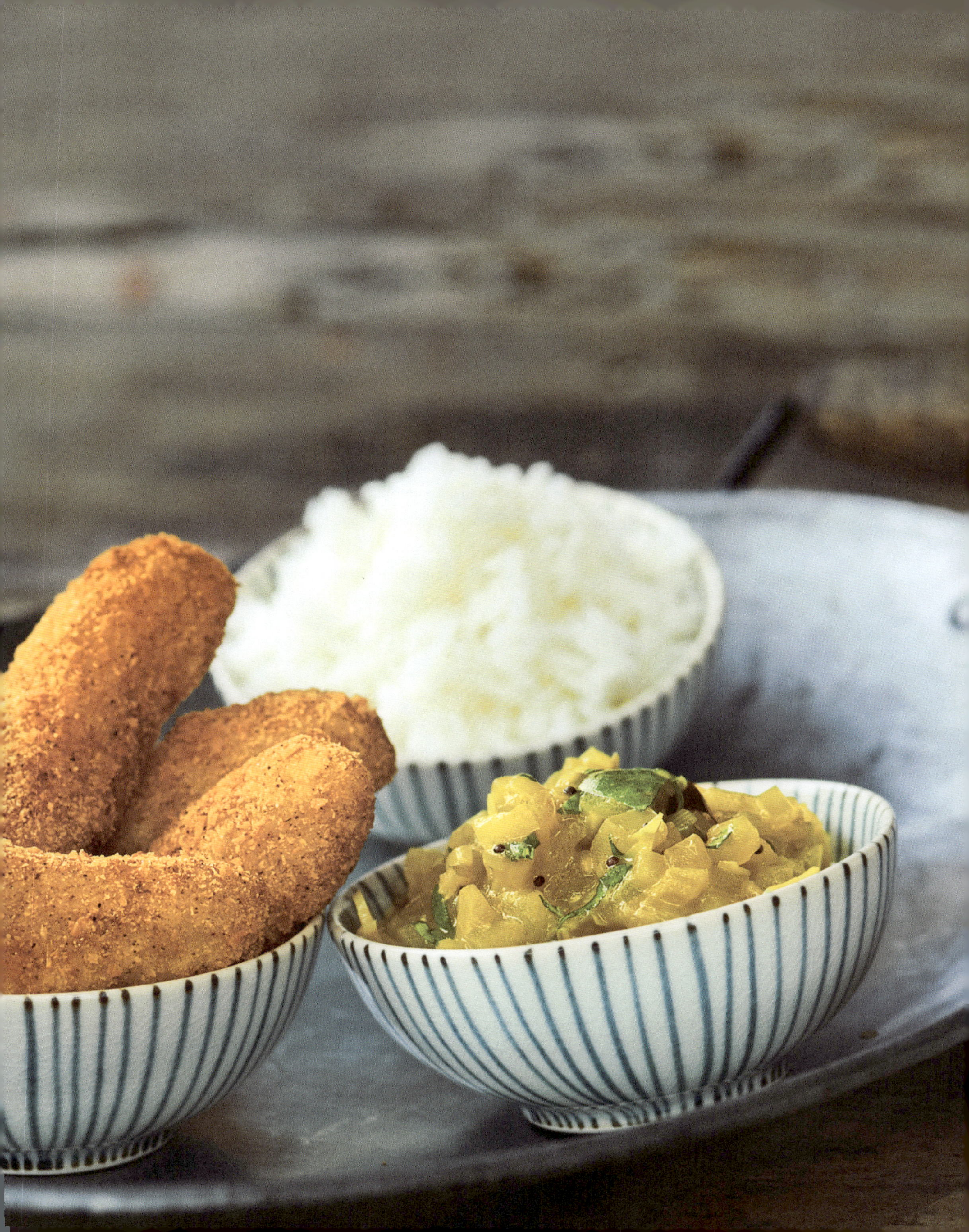

Amalfi Lemon Salad with Ricotta Cakes

Ingredients (serves 4—6)

1 organic Amalfi lemon (2/3 pound, see note)
10 tablespoons olive oil
2/3 pound russet potatoes
salt and pepper
1 pound radish
1 bunch dill
3 tablespoons lemon juice
1/2 cup ricotta cheese
2 large eggs, separated
1 large egg yolk
1/2 cup flour

1. Wash the Amalfi lemon thoroughly and pat dry. Thinly slice the entire lemon (A) and mix with 4 tablespoons of olive oil (B). Cover and leave to absorb the olive oil for 2 hours.
2. In the meantime, peel the potatoes, cut into halves or quarters, depending on their size. Cook in salted boiling water for 20 minutes or until soft. Let them cool to lukewarm temperature.
3. Peel and roughly grate the radishes. Mix with 2 tablespoons of olive oil. Pluck off the dill tips. Mix the lemon slices and radishes with dill and lemon juice.
4. Mash the potatoes with a potato press twice (or grate with a fine grater). Add the ricotta and the egg yolks to the potato mixture. Add flour, salt and pepper and mix well.
5. Whisk the egg whites with a pinch of salt and fold into the potato ricotta mixture.
6. Heat up the remaining olive oil in a nonstick pan. Spoon the potato ricotta mixture and fry in small portions over medium heat until golden brown on each side (C). Drain on paper towels (D) and serve immediately with the lemon salad (E).

Preparation time: 40 minutes (+ 2 hours steeping time)

AMALFI LEMON: These lemons do not taste particularly sour, but fruity and fresh. The taste unfolds in the combination of the fruit pulp and peel. You cut them into very thin slices and eat them with the peel. The white skin of an Amalfi lemon doesn't taste bitter, but rather sweet. You can't compare the taste of Amalfi lemons to the ones you find in grocery stores. If no Amalfi lemons are available, you may substitute grapefruit. Peel the grapefruit, making sure to remove all of the white skin.

TIP If you like, you can add some finely chopped sundried tomatoes to the potato batter.

A

B

C

D

E

Nasi Goreng

Ingredients (serves 4)

4 tablespoons light soy sauce
1 tablespoon honey
1 teaspoon sambal oelek (Indonesian chili paste; or chili sauce)
6 shallots (approx. 2/3 cup)
3 garlic cloves
1 celery stick
1/2 cup white cabbage
1 carrot
1 green chili pepper
1—2 tomatoes
2 large eggs
6 tablespoons peanut oil
2 1/2 cups day-old steamed rice
4 stems Thai basil (or 2 stems basil)
4 stems cilantro
4 tablespoons fried onions

1. Mix the soy sauce with the honey, sambal oelek and 3 tablespoons of water. Peel the shallots and cut into fine slices. Peel and dice the garlic. Wash the celery stick and cut into strips. Wash the white cabbage and cut into thin slices. Peel the carrot, cut into half lengthwise and into thin stripes again lengthwise. Dice the chili.

2. Take the cores out of the tomatoes and dice. Whisk the eggs. Heat up 3 tablespoons of oil in a large nonstick pan and add the carrot and the cabbage and fry for 2 minutes (stirring constantly). Add the celery, shallots, chili and garlic and sauté for another 2—3 minutes. Put the vegetables from the pan into a bowl.

3. Heat the rest of the oil in a pan, add the eggs and allow to thicken, stirring all the time. Add rice and sauté with the scrambled eggs for 2 minutes. Add the spicy sauce and continue frying until all the liquid has evaporated or has seeped in. Fold in the vegetables and tomatoes and sauté for another minute. Chop the Thai basil and cilantro and mix them in. Serve sprinkled with fried onions.

Preparation time: 25 minutes

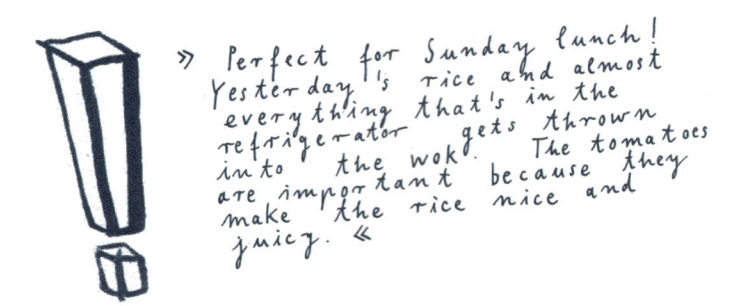

» Perfect for Sunday lunch! Yesterday's rice and almost everything that's in the refrigerator gets thrown into the wok. The tomatoes are important because they make the rice nice and juicy. «

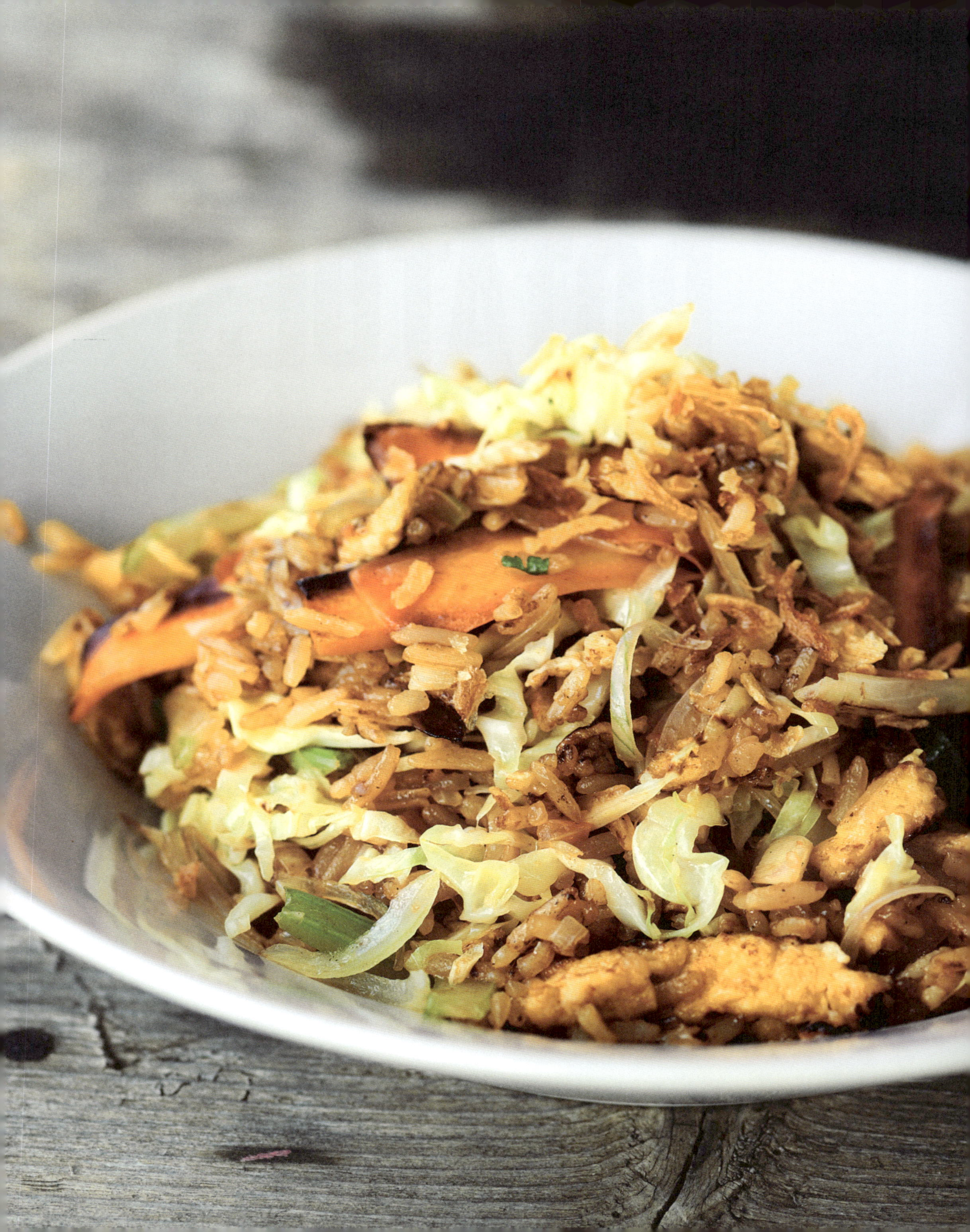

FOUR
SPUDS FOR PEOPLE IN A HURRY
POTATOES

1. Fried Potatoes on the Fly

Peel and cut **1 1/3 pounds of waxy potatoes** into approximately 1/2-inch cubes. Heat **6 tablespoons of olive oil** in a large nonstick pan and sauté the potatoes for 20 minutes on a medium heat. Add **2 stems of rosemary** and sauté for another 2 minutes. Season with **salt** and serve.

2. Potato and Fried Onion Purée

Peel **1 1/3 pounds of potatoes,** cut in half and boil until soft in **salted water.** Peel **1 Spanish onion,** cut into strips and fry until golden brown in **3 tablespoons of olive oil.** Drain the potatoes and mash with **6 tablespoons of butter.** Season with **salt** and **1 pinch of freshly grated nutmeg.** Fold in the cooked onions.

You can buy potatoes locally. It is worth finding out what types of local potatoes are available where you live and which ones taste the best—from the small, aromatic early potatoes served in spring and summer to the tasty late potatoes served in fall and in winter.

3 Quick Potato Salad

Thinly slice **1 2/3 pounds of cooked potatoes**. Bring **1 cup of vegetable stock** with **4 tablespoons of white wine vinegar, 4 tablespoons of olive oil, 2 teaspoons of sugar** and **1 teaspoon of medium-hot mustard** to a boil and pour over the potato slices. Mince **1 bunch of chives** and add them. Mix everything together, stirring occasionally and then allow to cool. The potato salad will absorb all the liquid.

4 Tex-Mex Potatoes

Grind **1 teaspoon of black peppercorns, 1 teaspoon of dried oregano, 1 teaspoon of cilantro seeds, 1 teaspoon ground sweet paprika** and **1/2 teaspoon of cumin seeds** with **1 tablespoon of coarse salt, 1/2 teaspoon of sugar** in the mortar and mix with **5 tablespoons of olive oil**. Cut **1 2/3 pounds of small waxy potatoes** (e.g. new potatoes) in half and mix with the spiced oil. Preheat the oven to 425°F and bake until crisp in an ovenproof dish on the middle rack for 30 minutes. Drizzle with **1 tablespoon of honey** and return to the oven for another 5 minutes.

Classic Potato Gratin

"The classic potato gratin we know from French restaurants is not made very often anymore and, if so, only as a side dish. I think that if you make a potato gratin with a bit of creativity, you don't need anything else."

Ingredients (serves 4—6)

- 1 2/3 pounds waxy potatoes
- 3 1/2 tablespoons butter
- 1 garlic clove
- 2 cups heavy cream
- 2 cups milk
- nutmeg
- salt

1. Peel the potatoes and put into cold water. Brush the inside of an ovenproof dish with 2 teaspoons of butter. Drain the potatoes and cut into thin slices, making sure to maintain the potatoes' shape. Then press the slices apart, arrange them in the shape of a fan and place in the dish.

2. Peel the garlic, cut in half and bring to a boil with heavy cream, milk and 3 tablespoons of butter. Season with 1 pinch of nutmeg and quite a bit of salt. Remove the garlic and pour the milk over the potatoes.

3. Preheat the oven to 400°F and bake until golden brown on the second rack from the bottom for 40 minutes.

Preparation time: 60 minutes

VARIATIONS: The gratin cream can also be cooked and its flavor enhanced with the following:

- 1 teaspoon freshly chopped rosemary or thyme
- 2—3 finely chopped sundried tomatoes
- 1—2 tablespoons minced black olives
- 1 teaspoon dried and roughly chopped porcini or morels

You can replace a few of the potatoes with:

- thinly sliced celery root
- zucchini slices
- grilled eggplant slices

10 minutes before the dish has finished cooking, you can sprinkle the gratin with a little blue cheese, freshly grated Gruyére, fontina or Parmesan.

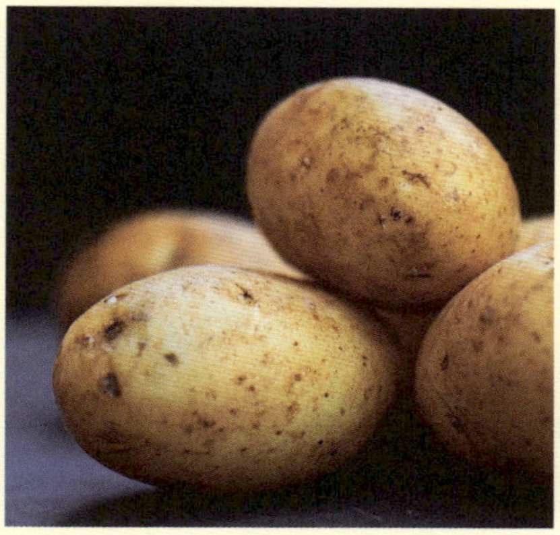
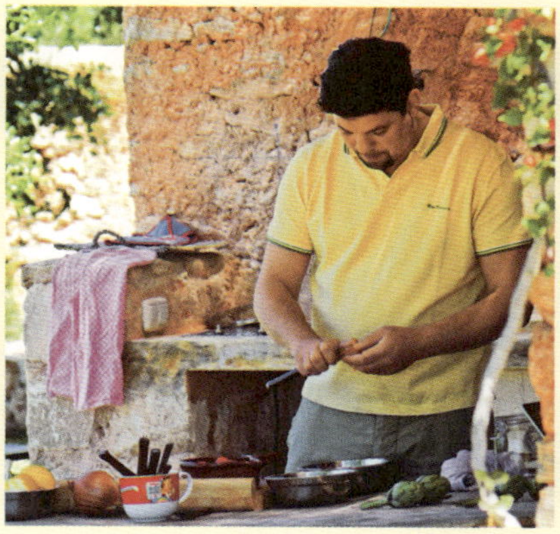
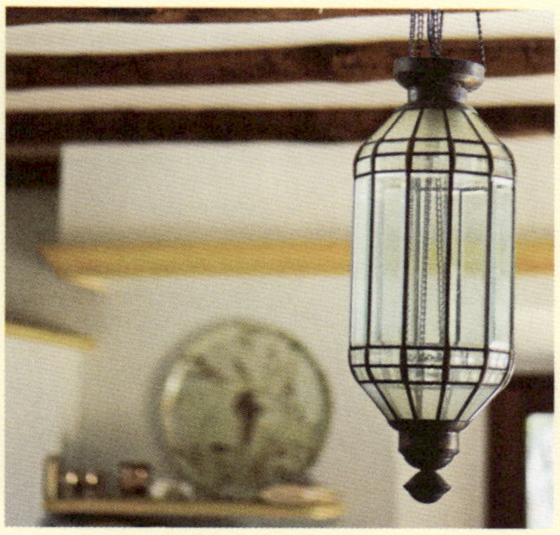
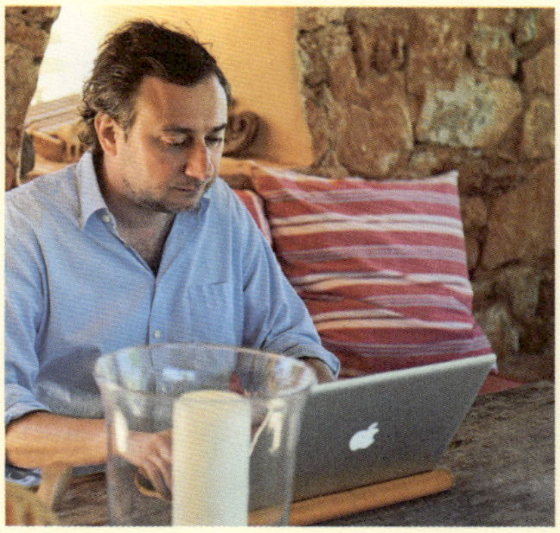
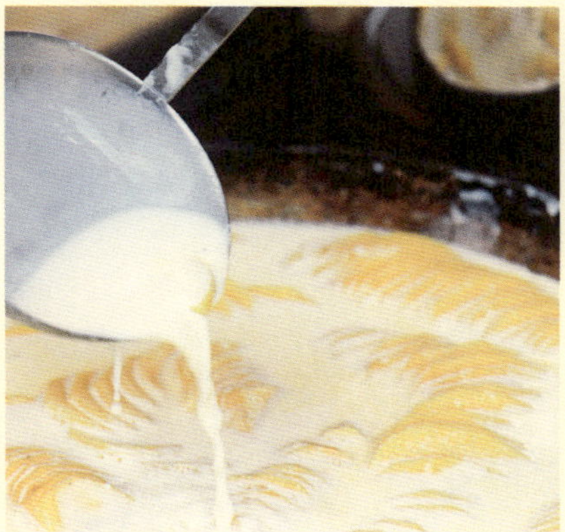
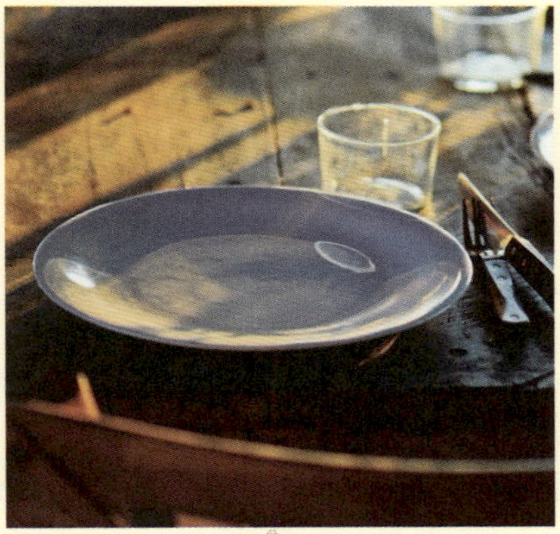
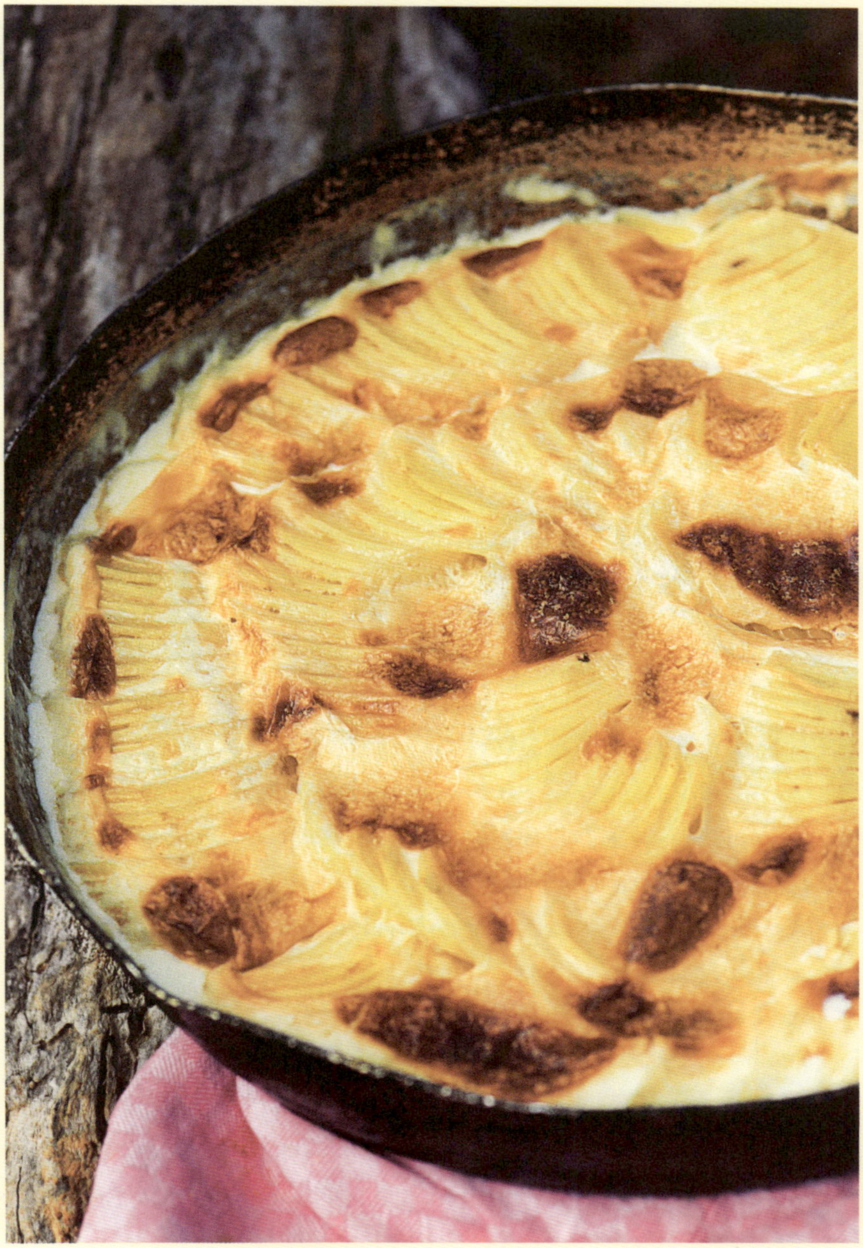

MUSHROOMS x 4
AND BON APPÉTIT!

1. Asian Shiitake Antipasti

Mix together **3 tablespoons of water** with **3 tablespoons of soy sauce**, **2–3 teaspoons of white wine vinegar**, **1 teaspoon of sesame oil**, **2 tablespoons of olive oil** and **1–2 teaspoons of sugar**. Dice **1 washed scallion**, **1 peeled garlic clove**, **1 green chili pepper** and **2 stems of cilantro** and fold in. Cut **1 pound shiitake mushrooms** into thick slices and fry until golden brown in **4 tablespoons of hot oil** in a large pan for 3–5 minutes. Season with **salt** and arrange on a platter. Serve drizzled with the spicy sauce while still warm.

2. Porcini Carpaccio

Cut **4 porcini** into very thin strips and arrange on plates. Cut **1 celery stick** into fine slices and place over the mushrooms. Drizzle with **1–2 teaspoons of lemon juice** and **1 tablespoon of argan oil**. Season with **salt** and **pepper**.

Mushrooms are the meat of the green kitchen: they have incredible aromas (chanterelles, morels and porcini), they are versatile (oyster mushrooms and white mushrooms), and they are firm to the bite (king oysters). Confusing these mushrooms with poisonous varieties is the only thing that could spoil your enjoyment. Considering this, it's better to focus on cooking and leave sourcing the mushrooms to the experts.

3 Mushroom "Groestl"

Wash **2/3 pound of mixed mushrooms**. Cut them and **2/3 pound of boiled potatoes** into thick slices. Heat **6 tablespoons of olive oil** in a large pan, add potatoes and mushrooms. Before stirring, let fry for 2—3 minutes and then continue for another 6—8 minutes, stirring every now and then. Cut **5 sundried tomatoes** into thin strips. Wash **1 scallion** and cut into thin rings. Pull off the leaves from **2 stems of marjoram**. Peel **1 garlic clove** and cut into slices. Throw everything into the pan and sauté for another minute. Season with **salt** and **pepper**.

4 Oyster Mushrooms "Viennese"

Put **2/3 pound of oyster mushrooms** and **4 tablespoons of flour** into a plastic bag and shake. Take the mushrooms out and dust them off. Peel and dice **1 garlic clove**. Chop **4 stems of parsley**. Cover the bottom of a pan with **oil** and heat. Fry the mushrooms in batches until golden brown. Dry on paper towels. Season with **salt** and **pepper**. Pour off the oil and melt **1 1/2 tablespoons of butter** in the pan. Add garlic and parsley and let it all boil up. Season with **salt** and pour over the mushrooms. Serve with **4 organic lemon wedges**.

Gnocchi with Porcini Mascarpone Cream

Ingredients (serves 4)
- 1 1/3 pounds waxy potatoes
- salt and pepper
- 6 tablespoons semolina
- 2/3 cup flour
- nutmeg
- 2 egg yolks (large eggs)
- olive oil
- 1/2 cup white port wine
- 2/3 cup vegetable stock
- 3 tablespoons ground dried porcini
- 2/3 cup mascarpone
- lemon juice
- 1—2 tablespoons freshly grated Parmesan
- 1 cup cress

1. Boil the potatoes with their skins on in salted water for 25 minutes. Drain and let them dry off in a preheated oven at 325°F (convection: 280°F) on the second rack from the bottom for 20 minutes. Then peel the potatoes, squeeze them through a potato ricer twice and allow to cool.

2. Add the semolina, flour, salt and 1 pinch of freshly grated nutmeg to the potatoes and mix gently. Add the egg yolks and mix with a wooden spoon to form a smooth dough.

3. Divide the potato dough into 4 equal pieces. On a floured surface, roll out the pieces so they are approximately 10 inches long (A) then cut these into 1/2-inch pieces (B). Roll the pieces over the prongs of a fork and gently press them with your thumb to shape into gnocchi (C, D).

4. Boil the gnocchi in lots of simmering salted water for 2—3 minutes (E, F). Take out with a skimmer and lay aside on a slightly oiled platter.

5. Boil the port with the vegetable stock and porcini flour. Whisk in the mascarpone and bring to a boil again. Season the sauce with salt, pepper, 1 pinch of nutmeg and 1 dash of lemon juice.

6. Add the gnocchi to the sauce and let them steep in it for 2 minutes (H). Fold in the Parmesan and sprinkle cress over it. Serve drizzled with a little olive oil (I).

Preparation time: 1 hour and 15 minutes

VARIATIONS: If you prefer, you can add green peas or pieces of green asparagus to the gnocchi water and cook it for 2—3 minutes. You can then fold them into the gnocchi sauce.

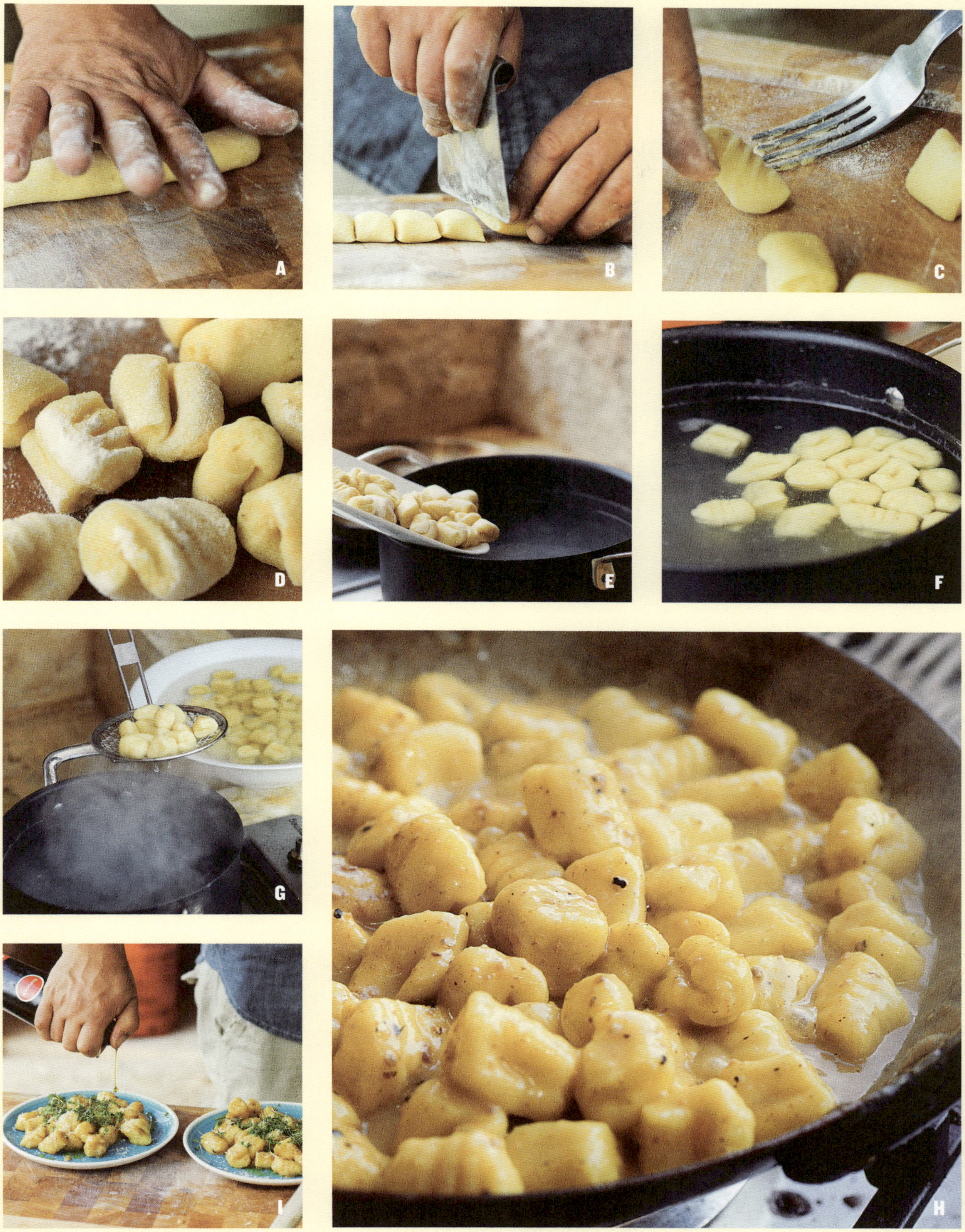
A
B
C
D
E
F
G
H
I

1

2

3

PRETTY QUICK X3: CABBAGE

Peppery, spicy heads of cabbage are in peak season during the fall and winter: red cabbage, white cabbage and curly kale taste best when it is freezing cold outside. Kale actually needs the first frost to fully develop its sweet, earthy aroma. The only exception is the tender, nutty, pointed cabbage used in summer salads and in quick and light cabbage recipes. You can purchase them from May right through to December.

1 Coleslaw

Cut **1 small head of pointed cabbage (approximately 1 pound, or substitute white or savoy cabbage)** into fine strips and knead until soft with **1 teaspoon of salt**. Wash **1/3 pound of kohlrabi** and **1/3 pound of carrots**, grate them coarsely and mix together. Mix in **2 tablespoons of olive oil** and **3/4 cup of creamy yogurt**. Dice **8 dried apricots** and add to the salad. Season to taste with **1—2 tablespoons of lemon juice, salt, pepper** and **1—2 pinches of sugar**.

2 Sautéed Red Cabbage with Balsamic Vinegar

Chop **1 pound of red cabbage** into fine strips. Heat up **5 tablespoons of olive oil** in a pan and sauté the red cabbage and **4 tablespoons of unsalted pistachios** for 5 minutes. Season with **2 tablespoons of sugar**. Pour in **4 tablespoons of balsamic vinegar** and cook for 2 minutes. Add **salt** and **pepper** to taste. Cut **a few stems of chives** into little rolls and mix together. Serve the salad lukewarm.

3 Cabbage Squares

Boil **1/2 pound of pappardelle** (Italian ribbon noodles) in salted water according to the instructions on the packaging. Remove the core of **1 small pointed cabbage (approximately 1 pound)**. Tear the leaves into bite-sized pieces. Cut **4 king oyster mushrooms** lengthwise into slices. Sauté the cabbage and mushrooms in **6 tablespoons of olive oil** with **1/2 teaspoon of crushed caraway seeds** until golden brown. Roughly chop the leaves of **4 stems of tarragon** and mix with the hot, drained pasta. Fold in with the vegetables. Season with **salt, pepper, 1 pinch of sugar** and a **few drops of lemon juice**.

CABBAGE

A

B

C

D

E

F

Savoy Cabbage and Pasta Strudel

Ingredients (serves 4—6)

- 1 2/3 cups flour
- 1/3 cup fine soft wheat semolina plus a little extra to work with
- 3 egg yolks (large eggs)
- 1 large egg
- 2 tablespoons olive oil
- salt and pepper
- 1 3/4 pounds savoy cabbage
- 3 tablespoons oil
- 1 1/2 inches fresh ginger
- 4 stems thyme
- 1 tablespoon flour
- 3 cups vegetable stock
- 2 cups heavy cream
- 1/2 organic lemon
- sugar
- butter
- 1 cup sour cream
- 1/2 bunch chives minced

1. Mix the flour and semolina. Add 2 egg yolks, 1 whole egg, 2—3 tablespoons of water and olive oil. Season with 1 pinch of salt and knead for 5 minutes into a smooth noodle dough. Wrap it in cling wrap and put it in the refrigerator to cool.

2. Wash the savoy cabbage, remove the core and cut into strips. Season with salt and boil in a pot for 12 minutes on medium heat. Peel and dice the ginger, pull off the thyme leaves and add both to the savoy cabbage. Dust with flour and fold the flour in. Pour in 1 2/3 cups of vegetable stock and cream. Simmer, uncovered, until it thickens. Finely grate the lemon peel, juice the lemon and add the zest and the juice to the cabbage. Season with salt, 1 pinch of sugar and pepper. Let it cool for 45 minutes.

3. Whisk 1 egg yolk until smooth. On a surface dusted with semolina, roll out the pasta dough until it's very thin (A). Spread the cold savoy cabbage mixture on the dough and leave an edge of approximately 3/4 inch (B). Brush the edges with egg yolk (C). Roll the dough into a sausage shape (D).

4. Cut the dough into pieces of 1 1/2—2 inches. Brush the inside of an ovenproof dish with butter and place the pieces into the dish with their cut edges face up next to each other (E). Pour in the remaining vegetable stock until only approximately 1/8 inch of the pieces are visible above the stock.

5. Preheat the oven to 400°F (convection not recommended) and bake on the second rack from the bottom for 40 minutes. Serve sprinkled with sour cream and minced chive.

Preparation time: 1 hour and 45 minutes

Minestrone
Spoonable vegetables

Ingredients (serves 6)

- 1 cup dried porcini
- 2 ripe tomatoes
- 1 garlic clove
- 1 onion
- 3 cloves
- 4 bay leaves
- 1/4 pound Parmesan rind (or 2 ounces Parmesan in one piece)
- 1 small savoy cabbage
- 1 1/2 cups carrots
- 2 stems leeks
- 1/2 pound green beans
- 10 cherry tomatoes
- 1 1/3–1 3/4 pounds vegetables according to taste (see note)
- salt
- freshly ground black pepper
- 6 slices sourdough bread
- 1 1/4 cups freshly grated parmesan
- olive oil

1. Mince the porcini in the food processor with the tomatoes and the peeled garlic clove. Put everything into a large pot. Pour in 10 1/2 cups of water and bring to a boil. Peel the onion, cut in half and roast in an ungreased pan until the cut sides are almost black. Add onions to the soup, then add the cloves, bay leaves and Parmesan rind. Simmer gently.

2. Wash the cabbage and cut into thin slices. Peel the carrots and cut into slices, wash the leek and cut into rings, wash the beans and cut them into thirds. Cut the cherry tomatoes in half. Wash the rest of the vegetables, cut into bite-sized pieces and add everything to the soup. Simmer the soup for 30 minutes. Season with salt and freshly ground pepper.

3. Sprinkle the slices of bread with a little freshly grated Parmesan. Drizzle with olive oil and toast under the broiler until golden brown. Distribute the rest of the Parmesan in warm bowls. Add the soup and drizzle with olive oil and serve with the bread.

Preparation time: 60 minutes

MINESTRONE is a very popular vegetarian dish in Italy that makes great use of leftovers. You make a tasty base for the soup with dried porcini, tomatoes, roasted onions and seasoning. You should have cabbage, leeks, carrots, beans and tomatoes in the minestrone and from there you can add any other kind of vegetables; for example, zucchini, green or white asparagus, brussel sprouts, kohlrabi, mushrooms and pieces of potato. You can also add soup noodles. Crispy Parmesan bread and your best olive oil make the leftover dish a feast!

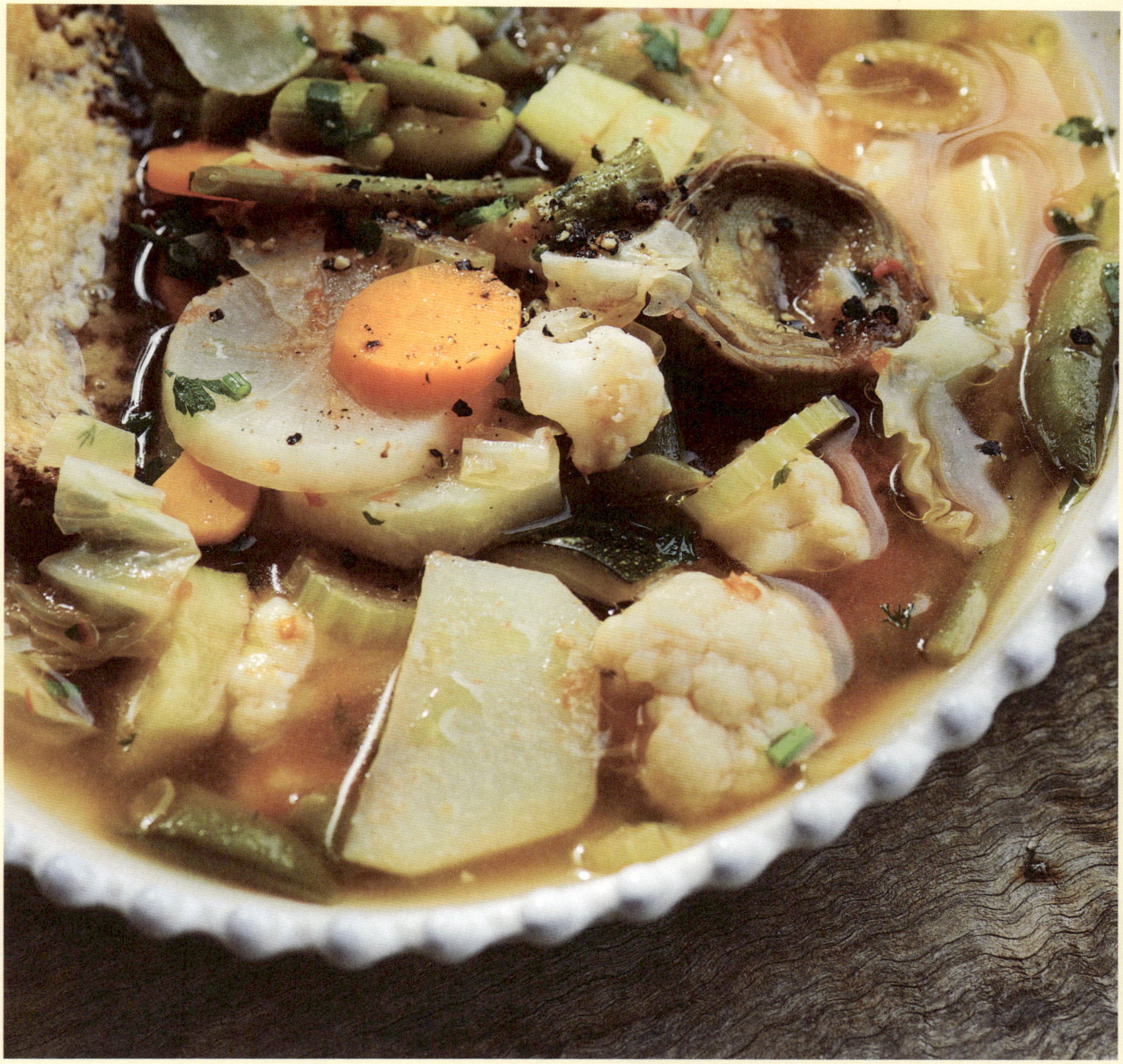

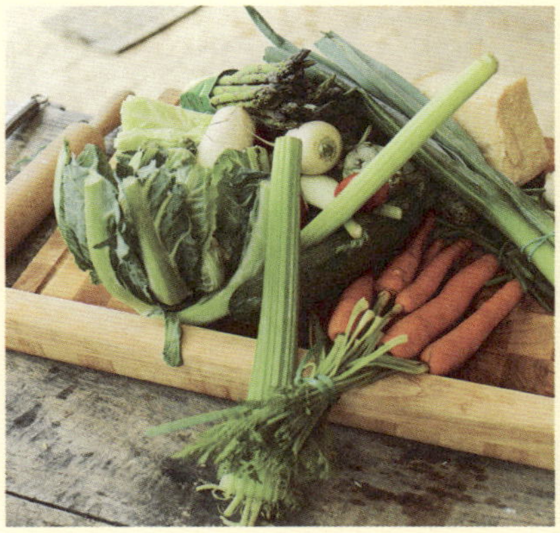

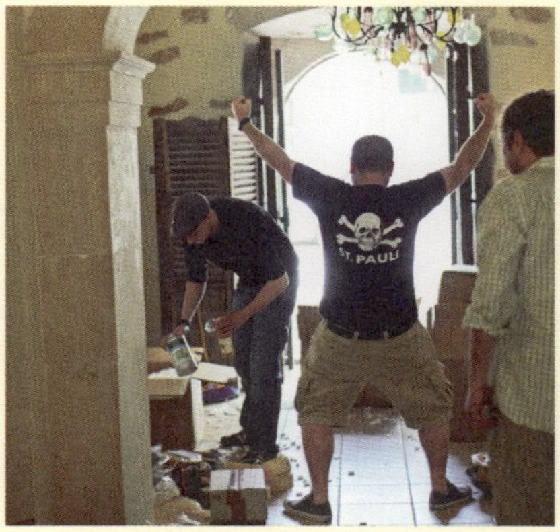
ST. PAULI

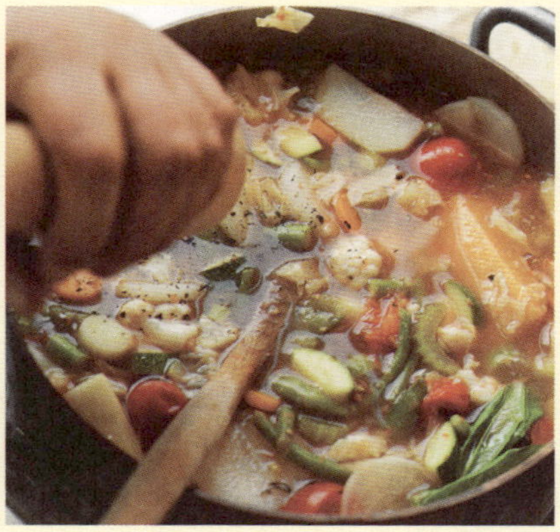

Index A—Z

A

Ajvar 68
Amalfi Lemon Salad with Ricotta Cakes 238
Artichoke Salad 212
Artichokes from the Oven with 2 Dips 215
Asian Crumbs 79
Asian Radish with Crispy Tempeh 117
Asian Shiitake Antipasti 246
Asparagus Salad with Cilantro and Mango 158
Asparagus with Tarragon Tomato Zabaglione 161
Avocado Spread 59
Avocado with Goat Cheese and Passion Fruit Dressing 59

B

Bagna Cauda with Veggie Nibble 16
Baked Beans 40
Baked Potato with Salsa Verde 62
Beet Purée with Poached Eggs and Horseradish Bread Salad 18
Beet Tabouleh 50
Bell Pepper Antipasti 145
Bell Pepper Ketchup 145
Bell Pepper Pastilla 92
Bell Pepper Tortilla 145
Black Salsify "à la Crème" 126
Broccoli Cannelloni in a Spicy Tomato Sauce 98
Burrata with Sweet Tomatoes and Fennel 27

C

Cabbage Squares 251
Carrot Salad with Pear and Smoked Almonds 205
Carrot Soup with Apricots and Pine Nuts 205
Carrot with Carrot Vinaigrette, Cottage Cheese and Daikon Cress 153
Cauliflower Soup 108
Cauliflower with Polish Salsa 108
Chanterelle Ricotta Tart "Filo!" 113
Chickpea Mousse 45
Chickpea Soup with Fried Sauerkraut 43
Chickpea and Fennel Salad with Apricots and Oranges 142

Classic Basil Pesto 121
Cleaning Artichokes 211
Coconut Relish 45
Cold Cucumber Soup 46
Cold Honeydew Melon Basil Soup 227
Coleslaw 251
Cooled Bell Pepper Soup with Melon 155
Corn and Coconut Soup with Lime 173
Creamed Spinach 190
Creamy »Cassoulet« with 3 Types of Beans and Savory Crumbs 81
Creamy Sauerkraut Lasagne with Gruyère 37
Crisp Celery Root with Ginger Pepper Cherries 228
Crunchy Bananas with Quick Green Tomato Chutney 236
Cucumber Nectarine Salsa 61
Cucumber Salad 47
Curry Crumbs 78

E

Eggplant and Bok Choy "Asian Style" 71
Eggplant Carpaccio 68
Eggplant Vinaigrette 68

F

Focaccia with Grilled Vegetable Salsa 130
Fried Cauliflower with Sesame 108
Fried Noodles "Take away!" 66
Fried Potatoes on the Fly 242

G

Gnocchi with Porcini Mascarpone Cream 248
Goat Cheese Calzone with Tomato Salsa and Deep-Fried Capers 24
Gravy 103
Greek Salad with Cucumbers "Sous-vide" 49
Green Asparagus Croquettes with Blood Orange Mayonnaise 141
Green Chickpea Salad with Fried Halloumi 198
Green Jungle Curry 234
Green Olive Pesto with Macadamia Nuts and Orange 120
Green Ratatouille with Sweet Stewed Chicory 122
Grilled Asparagus with Parmesan Vinaigrette 159

Grilled Asparagus with Parmesan-Polenta and Pine Nut Gravy 104
Grilled Beets with Balsamic Vinegar, Oranges and Olive Oil 183
Grilled Melon 227
Grilled Scallions 178
Guacamole Panamericana 58

H

Hazelnut Vinaigrette 194
Home Fries for 2 64
Hot Bell Pepper Pan "Juliška" 73

I

Iced Cream of Asparagus with Yogurt 159
Igor's Tomato Soup 24

J

Jerusalem Artichoke and Lentil Salad 220

K

"Knoepfle" with Dried Tomatoes and Garlic Cream 55

L

Lamb's Lettuce Salad with Fried Eggplants and Sweet Chestnut Purée 32
Lentil Date Salad 44
Lentils with Stewed Parsley Root 138

M

Mallorcan Coca with Rhubarb 166
Mango Pepper Salsa 60
Marinated Green Beans with Scamorza-Toast 216
Matthias' P'amb Oli 177
Melanzane 68
Melon Curry 227
Middle Eastern Crumbs 79
Minestrone 254
Mozzarella with Pea Vinaigrette 136
Mozzarella with Watercress Pomegranate Vinaigrette 75
Müller Marquard Mälzer Salsa 61
Mushroom "Groestl" 247
Mushroom Ragout on Peasant Bread 197
Mushroom Risotto with Gorgonzola 125

N

Nasi Goreng 240
Noodle Soup "Dashi" 31

O

Olive and Thyme Crumbs 78
Onion Rings 178
Onion Tarte 94
Oyster Mushrooms "Viennese" 247

P

Pan-Fried Flatbread with Lentils, Coconut and Chickpeas 44
Pasta for Gals 21
Pasta Paella 107
Pasta with Grated Fennel Tomato Sauce 149
Pea Pasta 136
Pea Purée 136
Pea Soup with Smoked Garlic 202
Peach Zucchini Salad with Mozzarella Dressing 168
Peperonata French Fries 82
Pineapple Apple Salad with Celery and Red Lentils 156
Pommes Anna with Sautéed Onions and Hazelnut Crust 186
Porcini Carpaccio 246
Porcini with White Bean Mousse, Spinach and Hazelnut Vinaigrette 194
Potato and Fried Onion Purée 242
Potato Celery Purée with Buttered Green Vegetables 162
Potato Gratin, Classic 244
Pot-Roasted Radicchio with Warm Tomato Fig Salad and Smoked Cheese 87
Pretzel Dumplings with Crème Fraîche, Tomatoes and Horseradish 192

Q

Quick Potato Salad 243
Quick Sauerkraut with Grapes and Walnuts 128
Quick Stewed Cucumbers 47

R

Ragù "Especial" 96
Raw Cauliflower Salad 108

S

Saffron Potato Risotto with Cauliflower and Pine Nuts 35

Salt-Baked Beet Salad 224

Salt 'n Pepper Corn 173

Sautéed Asparagus 158

Sautéed Corn 173

Sautéed Red Cabbage with Balsamic Vinegar 251

Savoy Cabbage and Pasta Strudel 253

Savoy Fondue with Bread, Stock and Swiss Cheese 111

Sesame Spinach Salad 190

Shallots from the Oven 178

Smoked Almond Pesto 120

Soba Noodle Salad with Miso Dressing 218

Soft-Boiled Eggs in Green Sauce 135

Special No. 1 (Very Hot) 84

Spinach Bruschetta 190

Squash Purée with Grilled Zucchini and Goat Farmer Cheese 207

Squash Risotto with Morels and Almonds 174

Steamed Silk Tofu with Carrot Butter 118

Summer Rolls 91

T

Tagliatelle with Chanterelles and Cherries 171

Tarte Flambée "Italiano" with Leek 209

Tex-Mex Potatoes 243

The Best Oven Tomato Sauce Ever 24

Tim's Crunchy Burger with Ginger Shallots 147

Tofu Sprout Salad with Prune Dip 230

Tomato Pistachio Pesto with Couscous 121

Tomato Salad "Extra Virgin" 24

Tomato Salad with Almond and Caper Vinaigrette 189

Tzatziki 46

W

Warm Harz Cheese "with Music" and Bouillon Potatoes 181

Z

Zucchini with Eggplant Vinaigrette 68

Vegetables, Legumes & Fruit
– an overview of our starring roles:

Apple

Green Chickpea Salad with Fried Halloumi 198

Pineapple Apple Salad with Celery and Red Lentils 156

Artichokes

Artichoke Salad 212

Artichokes from the Oven with 2 Dips 215

Cleaning Artichokes 211

Minestrone 254

Avocado

Avocado Spread 59

Avocado with Goat Cheese and Passion Fruit Dressing 59

Avocado with Grapefruit Caramel and Farmer Cheese 56

Guacamole Panamericana 58

Beets

Beet Purée with Poached Eggs and Horseradish Bread Salad 18

Grilled Beets with Balsamic Vinegar, Oranges and Olive Oil 183

Salt-Baked Beet Salad 224

Bell Pepper

Ajvar 68

Bell Pepper Antipasti 145

Bell Pepper Ketchup 145

Bell Pepper Pastilla 92

Bell Pepper Tortilla 145

Cooled Bell Pepper Soup with Melon 155

Focaccia with Grilled Vegetable Salsa 130

Green Chickpea Salad with Fried Halloumi 198

Green Ratatouille with Sweet Stewed Chicory 122

Hot Bell Pepper Pan "Juliška" 73

Mango Pepper Salsa 60

Pasta Paella 107

Peperonata French Fries 82

Special No. 1 (Very Hot) 84

Black Salsify

Black Salsify "à la Crème" 126

Bok Choy

Eggplant and Bok Choy "Asian Style" 71

Broccoli

Broccoli Cannelloni in a Spicy Tomato Sauce 98

Fried Noodles "Take away!" 66

Pasta for Gals 21

Cabbages

Cabbage Squares 251

Chickpea Soup with Fried Sauerkraut 43

Coleslaw 251

Creamy Sauerkraut Lasagne with Gruyère 37

Eggplant and Bok Choy "Asian Style" (bok choy) 71

Minestrone (savoy, pointed cabbage) 254

Nasi Goreng (white cabbage) 240

Quick Sauerkraut with Grapes and Walnuts (white cabbage) 128

Sautéed Red Cabbage with Balsamic Vinegar 251

Savoy Cabbage and Pasta Strudel 253

Savoy Fondue with Bread, Stock and
   Swiss Cheese (savoy cabbage) 111

Summer Rolls (red cabbage) 91

Tim's Crunchy Burger with Ginger Shallots (chinese cabbage) 147

Carrots

Bagna Cauda with Veggie Nibble 16

Carrot Nut Purée 205

Carrot Salad with Pear and Smoked Almonds 205

Carrot Soup with Apricots and Pine Nuts 205

Carrot with Carrot Vinaigrette, Cottage Cheese and Daikon Cress 153

Coleslaw 251

Fried Noodles "Take away!" 66

Gravy 103

Minestrone 254

Nasi Goreng 240

Ragù "Especial" 96

Special No. 1 (Very Hot) 84

Steamed Silk Tofu with Carrot Butter 118

Summer Rolls 91

Cauliflower

Cauliflower Soup 108

Cauliflower with Polish Salsa 108

Fried Cauliflower with Sesame 108

Raw Cauliflower Salad 108

Saffron Potato Risotto with Cauliflower and Pine Nuts 35

Celeriac, Celery Root

Crisp Celery Root with Ginger Pepper Cherries 228

Gravy 103

Green Ratatouille with Sweet Stewed Chicory 122

Lentil Date Salad 44

Nasi Goreng 240

Pineapple Apple Salad with Celery and Red Lentils 156

Porcini Carpaccio 246

Potato Celery Purée with Buttered Green Vegetables 162

Ragù "Especial" 96

Special No. 1 (Very Hot) 84

Chickpeas

Chickpea Mousse 45

Chickpea Soup with Fried Sauerkraut 43

Chickpea and Fennel Salad with Apricots and Oranges 142

Green Chickpea Salad with Fried Halloumi 198

Corn

Corn and Coconut Soup with Lime 173

Creamy Cheese Polenta with Chanterelles 101

Green Jungle Curry 234

Grilled Asparagus with Parmesan-Polenta and Pine Nut Gravy 104

Salt 'n Pepper Corn 173

Sautéed Corn 173

Cress

Beetroot Purée with Poached Egg and Horseradish Bread Salad 18

Carrot with Carrot Vinaigrette, Cottage Cheese and Daikon Cress 153

Gnocchi with Porcini Mascarpone Cream 248

Mozzarella with Watercress Pomegranate Vinaigrette 75

Soft-Boiled Eggs in Green Sauce 135

Cucumbers

Cold Cucumber Soup 46

Cucumber Nectarine Salsa 61

Cucumber Salad 47

Greek Salad with Cucumbers "Sous-vide" 49

Green Chickpea Salad with Fried Halloumi 198

Green Ratatouille with Sweet Stewed Chicory 122

Quick Stewed Cucumbers 47

Summer Rolls 91

Tzatziki 46

Eggplant

Ajvar 68

Eggplant and Bok Choy "Asian Style" 71

Eggplant Carpaccio 68

Eggplant Vinaigrette 68

Green Jungle Curry 234

Lamb's Lettuce Salad with Fried Eggplants and Sweet Chestnut Purée 32

Melanzane 68

Fennel

Bagna Cauda with Veggie Nibble 16

Burrata with Sweet Tomatoes and Fennel 27

Chickpea and Fennel Salad with Apricots and Oranges 142

Pasta with Grated Fennel Tomato Sauce 149

Green Asparagus

Bagna Cauda with Veggie Nibble 16

Green Asparagus Croquettes with Blood Orange Mayonnaise 141

Grilled Asparagus with Parmesan Vinaigrette 159

Grilled Asparagus with Parmesan-Polenta and Pine Nut Gravy 104

Potato Celery Purée with Buttered Green Vegetables 162

Special No. 1 (Very Hot) 84

Green Beans, White Beans

Bagna Cauda with Veggie Nibble 16

Creamy "Cassoulet" with 3 Types of Beans and Savory Crumbs 81

Marinated Green Beans with Scamorza-Toast 216

Minestrone 254

Peach Zucchini Salad with Mozzarella Dressing 168

Potato Celery Purée with Buttered Green Vegetables 162

Kohlrabi

Coleslaw 251

Minestrone 254

Steamed Silk Tofu with Carrot Butter 118

Leek

Chickpea Soup with Fried Sauerkraut 43

Gravy 103

Minestrone 254

Tarte Flambée "Italiano" with Leek 209

Lentils

Jerusalem Artichoke and Lentil Salad 220

Lentil Date Salad 44

Lentils with Stewed Parsley Root 138

Pineapple Apple Salad with Celery and Red Lentils 156

Mango

Asparagus Salad with Cilantro and Mango 158

Mango Pepper Salsa 60

Melon

Cold Honeydew Melon Basil Soup 227

Cooled Bell Pepper Soup with Melon 155

Grilled Melon 227

Melon Curry 227

Mushrooms

Asian Shiitake Antipasti 246

Cabbage Squares 251

Chanterelle Ricotta Tart "Filo!" 113

Creamy Cheese Polenta with Chanterelles 101

Eggplant and Bok Choy "Asian Style" (shiitakes) 71

Gnocchi with Porcini Mascarpone Cream 248

Gravy 103

Green Jungle Curry 234

Mallorcan Coca with Rhubarb 166

Minestrone 254

Mushroom "Groestl" 247

Mushroom Ragout on Peasant Bread 197

Mushroom Risotto with Gorgonzola (mixed mushrooms) 125

Noodle Soup "Dashi" 31

Oyster Mushrooms "Viennese" 247

Pasta Paella 107

Porcini Carpaccio (porcini) 246

Porcini with White Bean Mousse, Spinach and Hazelnut Vinaigrette (porcini) 194

Pumpkin Risotto with Morels and Almonds 174

Ragù "Especial" (mixed mushrooms) 96

Special No. 1 (Very Hot) (dried shiitakes) 84

Tagliatelle with Chanterelles and Cherries 171

Tim's Crunchy Burger with Ginger Shallots (king oysters) 147

Tofu Sprout Salad with Prune Dip 230

Onions

Coconut Relish 45

French Fries á la Anna with Sautéed Onions and Hazelnut Crust 186

Grilled Scallions 178

Onion Rings 178

Onion Tarte 94

Potato and Fried Onion Purée 242

Potato Celery Purée with Buttered Green Vegetables 162

Shallots from the Oven 178

Warm Harz Cheese "with Music" and Bouillon Potatoes 181

Parsley Root

Fried Noodles "Take away!" 66

Lentils with Stewed Parsley Root 138

Peas

Mozzarella with Pea Vinaigrette 136

Pasta for Gals 21

Pasta Paella 107

Pea Pasta 136

Pea Purée 136

Pea Soup with Smoked Garlic 202

Potatoes

Amalfi Lemon Salad with Ricotta Cakes 238

Asparagus with Tarragon Tomato Zabaglione 161

Baked Potato with Salsa Verde 62

Croquettes from Green Asparagus with Blood Orange Mayonnaise 141

Fried Potatoes on the Fly 242

Gnocchi with Porcini Mascarpone Cream 248

Green Jungle Curry 234

Home Fries for 2 64

Iced Cream of Asparagus with Yogurt 159

Minestrone 254

Mushroom "Groestl" 247

Peperonata French Fries 82

Pommes Anna with Sautéed Onions and Hazelnut Crust 186

Potato and Fried Onion Purée 242

Potato Celery Purée with Buttered Green Vegetables 162

Potato Gratin, Classic 244

Quick Potato Salad 243

Saffron Potato Risotto with Cauliflower and Pine Nuts 35

Salt-Baked Beet Salad 224

Tex-Mex Potatoes 243

Warm Harz Cheese "with Music" and Bouillon Potatoes 181

Radishes

Asian Radish with Crispy Tempeh 117

Bagna Cauda with Veggie Nibble 16

Rhubarb

Majorcan Coca with Rhubarb 166

Salads

Artichoke Salad (curled lettuce) 212

Avocado with Goat Cheese and Passion Fruit Dressing (arugula) 59

Avocado with Grapefruit Caramel and Farmer Cheese (arugula) 56

Bagna Cauda with Veggie Nibble (hearts of romaine) 16

Cooled Bell Pepper Soup with Melon (hearts of romaine) 155

Creamy Cheese Polenta with Chanterelles (frisee lettuce) 101

Eggplant Carpaccio (arugula) 68

Green Chickpea Salad with Fried Halloumi (hearts of romaine) 198

Green Ratatouille with Sweet Stewed Chicory (chicory) 122

Grilled Melon 227

Jerusalem Artichoke and Lentil Salad 220

Lamb's Lettuce Salad with Fried Eggplants and
   Sweet Chestnut Purée 32
Lentils with Stewed Parsley Root 138
Pea Pasta (arugula) 136
Pea Soup with Smoked Garlic (arugula) 202
Pot-Roasted Radicchio with Warm Tomato Fig Salad and
   Smoked Cheese 87
Smoked Cheese (radicchio) 87
Soba Noodle Salad with Miso-Dressing (hearts of romaine) 218
Summer Rolls (iceberg lettuce) 91
Tofu Sprout Salad with Prune Dip 230

Snap Peas & Peas in the Pot

Bagna Cauda with Veggie Nibble 16
Fried Noodles "Take away!" 66
Green Jungle Curry 234
Potato Celery Purée with Buttered Green Vegetables 162

Spinach & Spinach Salad

Creamed Spinach 190
Mallorcan Coca with Rhubarb 166
Pasta for Gals 21
Porcini with White Bean Mousse, Spinach and
   Hazelnut Vinaigrette 194
Pretzel Dumplings with Crème Fraîche, Tomatoes and Horseradish 192
Sesame Spinach Salad 190
Special No. 1 (Very Hot) 84
Spinach Bruschetta 190

Sprouts

Eggplant and Bok Choy "Asian Style" 71
Noodle Soup "Dashi" 31
Special No. 1 (Very Hot) 84
Summer Rolls 91
Tofu Sprout Salad with Prune Dip 230

Squash

Squash Purée with Grilled Zucchini and Goat Farmer Cheese 207
Squash Risotto with Morels and Almonds 174

Tomatoes

Artichokes from the Oven with 2 Dips 215
Asparagus with Tarragon Tomato Zabaglione 161
Baked Beans 40
Broccoli Cannelloni in a Spicy Tomato Sauce 98
Burrata with Sweet Tomatoes and Fennel 27
Creamy Sauerkraut Lasagne with Gruyere 37
Crunchy Bananas with Quick Green Tomato Chutney 236
Goat's Cheese Calzone with Tomato Salsa and
   Deep-Fried Capers 24
Greek Salad with Cucumbers "Sous-vide" 49
Green Jungle Curry 234
Guacamole Panamericana 58
Hot Bell Pepper Pan "Juliška" 73
Igor's Tomato Soup 24
Marinated Green Beans with Scamorza-Toast 216
Matthias' P'amb Oli 177
Melon Curry 227
Minestrone 254
Mozzarella with Pea Vinaigrette 136
Nasi Goreng 240
Pasta with Grated Fennel Tomato Sauce 149
Pot-Roasted Radicchio with Warm Tomato Fig Salad and
   Smoked Cheese (radicchio) 87
Pretzel Dumplings with Crème Fraîche, Tomatoes and Horseradish 192
Ragù "Especial" 96
Spinach Bruschetta 190
Tim's Crunchy Burger with Ginger Shallots 147
Tomato Pistachio Pesto with Couscous 121
Tomato Salad "Extra Virgin" 24
Tomato Salad with Almond and Caper Vinaigrette 189

Watercress

Cucumber Salad 47
Mozzarella with Watercress Pomegranate Vinaigrette 75

White Asparagus

Asparagus Salad with Cilantro and Mango 158
Asparagus with Tarragon Tomato Zabaglione 161

Fried Asparagus 158
Grilled Asparagus with Parmesan Vinaigrette 159
Iced Cream of Asparagus with Yogurt 159

White Beans

Baked Beans 40
Creamy "Cassoulet" with 3 Types of Beans and Savory Crumbs 81
Porcini with White Bean Mousse, Spinach and
  Hazelnut Vinaigrette 194

Zucchini

Focaccia with Grilled Vegetable Salsa 130
Green Jungle Curry 234
Green Ratatouille with Sweet Stewed Chicory 122
Minestrone 254
Peach Zucchini Salad with Mozzarella Dressing 168
Squash Purée with Grilled Zucchini and
  Goat Farmer Cheese 207
Zucchini with Eggplant Vinaigrette 68

Seasonal

It feels like all types of vegetables are available all year round and most of the Green Box recipes can be enjoyed all year round. However, vegetables from local producers taste best of all when they are in season. And that's how it should be. Here is our little cooking recommendation:

Spring

Artichoke Salad 212
Artichokes from the Oven with 2 Dips 215
Asparagus Salad with Cilantro and Mango 158
Asparagus with Tarragon Tomato Zabaglione 161
Bagna Cauda with Veggie Nibble 16
Cleaning Artichokes 211
Cold Honeydew Melon Basil Soup 227
Creamy "Cassoulet" with 3 Types of Beans and Savory Crumbs 81
Green Asparagus Croquettes with Blood Orange Mayonnaise 141
Grilled Asparagus with Parmesan Vinaigrette 159
Grilled Asparagus with Parmesan-Polenta and Pine Nut Gravy 104

Iced Cream of Asparagus with Yogurt 159
Majorcan Coca with Rhubarb 166
Potato Celery Purée with Buttered Green Vegetables 162
Sautéed Asparagus 158
Soft-Boiled Eggs in Green Sauce 135
Special No. 1 (Very Hot) 84
Steamed Silk Tofu with Carrot Butter
Three Salsas 60/61

Summer

Amalfi Lemon Salad with Ricotta Cakes 238
Asparagus Salad with Cilantro and Mango 158
Bagna Cauda with Veggie Nibble 16
Baked Potato with Salsa Verde 62
Burrata with Sweet Tomatoes and Fennel 27
Chanterelle Ricotta Tart "Filo!" 113
Chickpea and Fennel Salad with Apricots and Oranges 142
Coleslaw 251
Cooled Bell Pepper Soup with Melon 155
Creamy "Cassoulet" with 3 Types of Beans and Savory Crumbs 81
Croquettes from Green Asparagus with Blood Orange Mayonnaise 141
Crunchy Bananas with Quick Green Tomato Chutney 236
Goat Cheese Calzone with Tomato Salsa and Deep-fried Capers 24
Greek Salad with Cucumbers "Sous-vide" 49
Green Jungle Curry 234
Green Ratatouille with Sweet Stewed Chicory 122
Grilled Asparagus with Parmesan-Polenta and Pine Nut Gravy 104
Grilled Beets with Balsamic Vinegar, Oranges and Olive Oil 183
Grilled Melon 227
Iced Cream of Asparagus with Yogurt 159
Igor's Tomato Soup 24
Matthias' P'amb oli 177
Melon Curry 227
Mozzarella with Pea Vinaigrette 136
Mozzarella with Watercress Pomegranate Vinaigrette 75
Mushroom Risotto with Gorgonzola 125
Pasta with Grated Fennel Tomato Sauce 149
Pea Pasta 136
Pea Purée 136

Peach Zucchini Salad with Mozzarella Dressing 168

Pesto x 3 120/121

Potato Celery Purée with Buttered Green Vegetables 162

Pot-Roasted Radicchio with Warm Tomato Fig Salad and Smoked Cheese 87

Three Salsas 60/61

Salt 'n Pepper Corn 173

Soft-Boiled Eggs in Green Sauce 135

Special No. 1 (Very Hot) 84

Squash Purée with Grilled Zucchini and Goat Farmer Cheese 207

Squash Risotto with Morels and Almonds 174

Steamed Silk Tofu with Carrot Butter

The Best Oven Tomato Sauce Ever 24

Tomato Salad "Extra Virgin" 24

Fall

Avocado with Goat Cheese and Passion Fruit Dressing 59

Avocado with Grapefruit Caramel and Farmer Cheese 56

Beet Tabouleh 50

Cabbage Squares 251

Chanterelle Ricotta Tart "Filo!" 113

Greek Salad with Cucumbers "Sous-vide" 49

Green Ratatouille with Sweet Stewed Chicory 122

Grilled Beets with Balsamic Vinegar, Oranges and Olive Oil 183

"Knoepfle" with Dried Tomatoes and Garlic Cream 55

Lamb's Lettuce Salad with Fried Eggplants and Sweet Chestnut Purée 32

Lentils with Stewed Parsley Root 138

Mushroom "Groestl" 247

Mushroom Ragout on Peasant Bread 197

Mushroom Risotto with Gorgonzola 125

Pea Soup with Smoked Garlic 202

Pineapple Apple Salad with Celery and Red Lentils 156

Porcini Carpaccio 246

Porcini with White Bean Mousse, Spinach and Hazelnut Vinaigrette 194

Pot-Roasted Radicchio with Warm Tomato Fig Salad and Smoked Cheese 87

Pretzel Dumplings with Crème Fraîche, Tomatoes and Horseradish 192

Salt-Baked Beet Salad 224

Sautéed Red Cabbage with Balsamic Vinegar 251

Savoy Cabbage and Pasta Strudel 253

Savoy Fondue with Bread, Stock and Swiss Cheese 111

Squash Purée with Grilled Zucchini and Goat Farmer Cheese 207

Squash Risotto with Morels and Almonds 174

Tagliatelle with Chanterelles and Cherries 171

Winter

Black Salsify "à la Crème" 126

Cabbage Squares 251

"Knoepfle" with Dried Tomatoes and Garlic Cream 55

Lentils with Stewed Parsley Root 138

Pea Soup with Smoked Garlic 202

Quick Sauerkraut with Grapes and Walnuts 128

Salt-Baked Beet Salad 224

Sautéed Red Cabbage with Balsamic Vinegar 251

Savoy Cabbage and Pasta Strudel 253

Savoy Fondue with Bread, Stock and Swiss Cheese 111

Corn and Coconut Soup with Lime 173

Gnocchi with Porcini Mascarpone Cream 248

All Year Round

Ajvar 68

Asian Radish with Crispy Tempeh 117

Asian Shiitake Antipasti 246

Baked Beans 40

Beet Puree with Poached Eggs and Horseradish Bread Salad 18

Bell Pepper Antipasti 145

Bell Pepper Ketchup 145

Bell Pepper Tortilla 145

Broccoli Cannelloni in a Spicy Tomato Sauce 98

Capers 24

Carrot Salad with Pear and Smoked Almonds 205

Carrot Soup with Apricots and Pine Nuts 205

Carrot with Carrot Vinaigrette, Cottage Cheese and Daikon Cress 153

Cauliflower Soup 108

Cauliflower with Polish Salsa 108

Chickpea Mousse 45
Chickpea Soup with Fried Sauerkraut 43
Coconut Relish 45
Cold Cucumber Soup 46
Creamed Spinach 190
Creamy Sauerkraut Lasagne with Gruyère 37
Crisp Celery Root with Ginger Pepper Cherries 228
Crumb Variations 78/79
Cucumber Salad 47
Eggplant and Bok Choy "Asian Style" 71
Eggplant Carpaccio 68
Eggplant Vinaigrette 68
Focaccia with Grilled Vegetable Salsa 130
Fried Cauliflower with Sesame 108
Fried Noodles "Take away!" 66
Fried Potatoes on the Fly 242
Gravy 103
Grilled Scallions 178
Guacamole Panamericana 58
Hazelnut Vinaigrette 194
Home Fries for 2 64
Hot Bell Pepper Pan "Juliška" 73
Jerusalem Artichoke and Lentil Salad 220
"Knoepfle" with Dried Tomatoes and Garlic Cream 55
Lentil Date Salad 44
Minestrone 254
Mozzarella with Pea Vinaigrette 136
Nasi Goreng 240
Noodle Soup "Dashi" 31
Onion Rings 178
Oyster Mushrooms "Viennese" 247
Pan-fried Flatbread with Lentils, Coconut and Chickpeas 44
Pasta for Gals 21
Pasta Paella 107
Pea Pasta 136
Pea Purée 136
Peperonata French Fries 82
Pesto x 3 120/121
Pommes Anna with Sautéd Onions and Hazelnut Crust 186

Potato and Fried Onion Purée 242
Potato Gratin, Classic 244
Quick Potato Salad 243
Quick Stewed Cucumbers 47
Ragù "Especial" 96
Raw Cauliflower Salad 108
Saffron Potato Risotto with Cauliflower and Pine Nuts 35
Sautéed Corn 173
Sesame Spinach Salad 190
Shallots from the Oven 178
Soba Noodle Salad with Miso-Dressing 218
Spinach Bruschetta 190
Tarte Flambée "Italiano" with Leek 209
Tex-Mex Potatoes 243
Three Salsas 60/61
Tim's Crunchy Burger with Ginger Shallots 147
Tofu Sprout Salad with Prune Dip 230
Tzatziki 46
Warm Harz Cheese "with Music" and Bouillon Potatoes 181

Easy Recipes!
Even inexperienced cooks will easily manage these:

A
Ajvar 68
Asian Crumbs 79
Asian Radish with Crispy Tempeh 117
Asian Shiitake Antipasti 246
Asparagus Salad with Cilantro and Mango 158
Avocado with Goat Cheese and Passion Fruit Dressing 59

B
Bagna Cauda with Veggie Nibble 16
Baked Beans 40
Baked Potato with Salsa Verde 62
Bell Pepper Ketchup 145
Bell Pepper Tortilla 145
Black Salsify "à la Crème" 126

C

Cabbage Squares 251

Carrot Nut Purée 205

Carrot Salad with Pear and Smoked Almonds 205

Carrot Soup with Apricots and Pine Nuts 205

Carrot with Carrot Vinaigrette, Cottage Cheese and Daikon Cress 153

Cauliflower Soup 108

Cauliflower with Polish Salsa 108

Chickpea Mousse 45

Chickpea Soup with Fried Sauerkraut 43

Chickpea and Fennel Salad with Apricots and Oranges 142

Classic Basil Pesto 121

Coconut Relish 45

Cold Cucumber Soup 46

Coleslaw 251

Corn and Coconut Soup with Lime 173

Creamed Spinach 190

Crumb Variations 78/79

Cucumber Nectarine Salsa 61

Cucumber Salad 47

Curry Crumbs 78

E

Eggplant and Bok Choy "Asian Style" 71

Eggplant Carpaccio 68

Eggplant Vinaigrette 68

F

Fried Cauliflower with Sesame 108

Fried Potatoes on the Fly 242

G

Gravy 103

Green Chickpea Salad with Fried Halloumi 1 98

Green Olive Pesto with Macadamia Nuts and Orange 120

Grilled Asparagus with Parmesan Vinaigrette 159

Grilled Beets with Balsamic Vinegar, Oranges and Olive Oil 183

Grilled Melon 227

Grilled Scallions 178

Guacamole Panamericana 58

H

Home Fries for 2 64

Honeydew Melon Basil Cold Soup 227

Hot Bell Pepper Pan "Juliška" 73

I

Igor's Tomato Soup 24

J

Jerusalem Artichoke and Lentil Salad 220

L

Lentil Date Salad 44

M

Mango Pepper Salsa 60

Matthias' P'amb Oli 177

Melanzane 68

Melon Curry 227

Middle Eastern Crumbs 79

Minestrone 254

Mozzarella with Pea Vinaigrette 136

Mozzarella with Watercress Pomegranate Vinaigrette 75

Müller Marquard Mälzer Salsa 61

Mushroom "Groestl" 247

O

Olive and Thyme Crumbs 78

Onion Rings 178

Onion Tarte 94

Oyster Mushrooms "Viennese" 247

P

Pan-Fried Flatbread with Lentils, Coconut and Chickpeas 44/45

Pasta with Grated Fennel Tomato Sauce 149

Pea Pasta 136

Pea Purée 136

Peach Zucchini Salad with Mozzarella Dressing 168

Pesto x 3 120/121

Pineapple Apple Salad with Celery and Red Lentils 156

Porcini Carpaccio 246

Porcini with White Bean Mousse, Spinach and Hazelnut Vinaigrette 194
Potato and Fried Onion Purée 242

Q
Quick Sauerkraut with Grapes and Walnuts 128
Quick Stewed Cucumbers 47

R
Raw Cauliflower Salad 108

S
Salt 'n Pepper Corn 173
Sautéed Asparagus 158
Sautéed Corn 173
Sautéed Red Cabbage with Balsamic Vinegar 251
Savoy Fondue with Bread, Stock and Swiss Cheese 111
Sesame Spinach Salad 190
Smoked Almond Pesto 120
Soba Noodle Salad with Miso Dressing 218
Special No. 1 (Very Hot) 84
Spinach Bruschetta 190
Squash Purée with Grilled Zucchini and Goat Farmer Cheese 207

T
Tex-Mex Potatoes 243
The Best Oven Tomato Sauce Ever 24
Three Salsas 60/61
Tomato Pistachio Pesto with Couscous 121
Tomato Salad "Extra Virgin" 24
Tomato Salad with Almond and Caper Vinaigrette 189
Tzatziki 46

W
Warm Harz Cheese "with Music" and Bouillon Potatoes 181

Quick!
Easy to make everyday recipes that take between 10 to 30 minutes to cook are in the overview. Can someone set the table already?

10 Minutes
Asian Crumbs 79
Asian Shiitake Antipasti 246
Chickpea Mousse 45
Classic Basil Pesto 121
Cold Cucumber Soup 46
Creamed Spinach 190
Curry Crumbs 78
Fried Corn 173
Green Olive Pesto with Macadamia Nuts and Orange 120
Grilled Melon 227
Honeydew Melon Basil Cold Soup 227
Middle Eastern Crumbs 79
Mozzarella with Pea Vinaigrette 136
Olive and Thyme Crumbs 78
Porcini Carpaccio 246
Raw Cauliflower Salad 108
Sesame Spinach Salad 190
Smoked Almond Pesto 120
Tomato Pistachio Pesto with Couscous 121
Tomato Salad "Extra Virgin" 24

15 Minutes
Asparagus Salad with Cilantro and Mango 158
Avocado with Goat Cheese and Passion Fruit Dressing 59
Carrot Salad with Pear and Smoked Almonds 205
Eggplant Vinaigrette 68
Fried Cauliflower with Sesame 108
Grilled Beets with Balsamic Vinegar, Oranges and Olive Oil 183
Grilled Scallions 178
Guacamole Panamericana 58
Pasta with Grated Fennel Tomato Sauce 149
Pea Pasta 136
Quick Stewed Cucumbers 47
Tzatziki 46

20 Minutes
Carrot with Carrot Vinaigrette, Cottage Cheese and Daikon Cress 153
Chickpea and Fennel Salad with Apricots and Oranges 142
Coconut Relish 45

Coleslaw 251
Cooled Bell Pepper Soup with Melon 155
Matthias' P'amb Oli 177
Oyster Mushrooms "Viennese" 247
Pineapple Apple Salad with Celery and Red Lentils 156
Sautéed Asparagus 158
Sautéed Red Cabbage with Balsamic Vinegar 251

25 Minutes

Bagna Cauda with Veggie Nibble 16
Black Salsify "à la Crème" 126
Carrot Nut Purée 205
Carrot Soup with Apricots and Pine Nuts 205
Cauliflower Soup 108
Cauliflower with Polish Salsa 108
Corn and Coconut Soup with Lime 173
Cucumber Nectarine Salsa 61
Cucumber Salad 47
Eggplant and Bok Choy "Asian Style" 71
Grilled Asparagus with Parmesan Vinaigrette 159
Hazelnut Vinaigrette 194
Jerusalem Artichoke and Lentil Salad 220
Lentil Date Salad 44
Mango Pepper Salsa 60
Melon Curry 227
Müller Marquard Mälzer Salsa 61
Mushroom "Groestl" 247
Nasi Goreng 240
Noodle Soup "Dashi" 31
Pasta for Gals 21
Porcini with White Bean Mousse, Spinach and
   Hazelnut Vinaigrette 194
Quick Potato Salad 243
Salt 'n Pepper Corn 173
Soba Noodle Salad with Miso Dressing 218
Spinach Bruschetta 190
Steamed Silk Tofu with Carrot Butter 118
Tomato Salad with Almond and Caper Vinaigrette 189

30 Minutes

Asian Radish with Crispy Tempeh 117
Bell Pepper Antipasti 145
Bell Pepper Tortilla 145
Chickpea Soup with Fried Sauerkraut 43
Creamy Cheese Polenta with Chanterelles 101
Fried Noodles "Take away!" 66
Fried Potatoes on the Fly 242
Green Ratatouille with Sweet Stewed Chicory 122
Home Fries for 2 64
Marinated Green Beans with Scamorza-Toast 216
Potato and Fried Onion Purée 242
Pot-roasted Radicchio with Warm Tomato Fig Salad
   and Smoked Cheese 87
Tagliatelle with Chanterelles and Cherries 171
Tim's Crunchy Burger with Ginger Shallots 147

Having Guests!

Whether you're inviting people for a posh dinner or throwing a huge party: you will find recipes here that are suited to creating a full menu and/or party recipes that you can easily adjust and prepare according to the number of guests you are expecting.

Party

Artichokes from the Oven with 2 Dips 215
Asian Shiitake Antipasti 246
Bagna Cauda with Veggie Nibble 16
Baked Beans 40
Baked Potato with Salsa Verde 62
Bell Pepper Ketchup 145
Burrata with Sweet Tomatoes and Fennel 27
Chickpea Mousse 45
Coconut Relish 45
Coleslaw 251
Corn and Coconut Soup with Lime 173
Focaccia with Grilled Vegetable Salsa 130
Green Jungle Curry 234
Grilled Asparagus with Parmesan Vinaigrette 159

Grilled Melon 227

Guacamole Panamericana 58

Igor's Tomato Soup 24

Jerusalem Artichoke and Lentil Salad 220

Lentil Date Salad 44

Majorcan Coca with Rhubarb 166

Matthias' P'amb Oli 177

Minestrone 254

Mozzarella with Watercress Pomegranate Vinaigrette 75

Onion Tarte 94

Pan-Fried Flatbread with Lentils, Coconut and Chickpeas 44/45

Pasta with Grated Fennel Tomato Sauce 149

Pea Soup with Smoked Garlic 202

Peach Zucchini Salad with Mozzarella Dressing 168

Pesto x 3 120/121

Pineapple Apple Salad with Celery and Red Lentils 156

Quick Potato Salad 243

Ragù "Especial" 96

Salt 'n Pepper Corn 173

Shallots from the Oven 178

Tex-Mex Potatoes 243

Three Salsas 60/61

Tomato Salad "Extra Virgin" 24

Tomato Salad with Almond and Caper Vinaigrette 189

Menue

Artichoke Salad 212

Artichokes from the Oven with 2 Dips 215

Asparagus with Tarragon Tomato Zabaglione 161

Avocado with Goat Cheese and Passion Fruit Dressing 59

Carrot Salad with Pear and Smoked Almonds 205

Carrot Soup with Apricots and Pine Nuts 205

Carrot with Carrot Vinaigrette, Cottage Cheese and Daikon Cress 153

Cauliflower Soup 108

Chanterelle Ricotta Tart "Filo!" 113

Chickpea Soup with Fried Sauerkraut 43

Cold Cucumber Soup 46

Cooled Bell Pepper Soup with Melon 155

Creamy "Cassoulet" with 3 Types of Beans and Savory Crumbs 81

Creamy Cheese Polenta with Chanterelles 101

Crisp Celery Root with Ginger Pepper Cherries 228

Crunchy Bananas with Quick Green Tomato Chutney 236

Eggplant and Bok Choy "Asian Style" 71

Eggplant Carpaccio 68

Goat Cheese Calzone with Tomato Salsa and Deep-Fried Capers 24

Gravy 103

Greek Salad with Cucumbers "Sous-vide" 49

Grilled Asparagus with Parmesan-Polenta and Pine Nut Gravy 104

Grilled Beets with Balsamic Vinegar, Oranges and Olive Oil 183

Hazelnut Vinaigrette 194

Honeydew Melon Basil Cold Soup 227

Iced Cream of Asparagus with Yogurt 159

Mozzarella with Pea Vinaigrette 136

Mushroom Risotto with Gorgonzola 125

Onion Tarte 94

Porcini Carpaccio 246

Porcini with White Bean Mousse, Spinach and Hazelnut Vinaigrette 194

Potato Gratin, Classic 244

Pretzel Dumplings with Crème Fraîche, Tomatoes and Horseradish 192

Salad from Beetroot Baked in Salt 224

Spinach Bruschetta 190

Squash Purée with Grilled Zucchini and Goat Farmer Cheese 207

Squash Risotto with Morels and Almonds 174

Tarte Flambée "Italiano" with Leek 209

After-work drink

As in every cookbook before this one, there were lots of motivated, helping hands on board. They cut, stirred, cooked, baked, washed, measured and thought up recipes, developed, shopped, designed, drew and took photos.

What I really have to emphasize again is the unique team spirit and the will of each and everyone to do their utmost to reach our mutual goal. You have my greatest respect for that. You can be truly proud of your achievements, because what you have done is simply sensational!

Thanks to **MARCEL STUT**, **MATTHIAS HAUPT**, **STEVAN PAUL** (also known as the "protractor" among the recipe writers), **ANJA LAUKEMPER**, **TINA HILSCHER**, **BERND BRINK**, **LUCAS BUCHHOLZ**, **RINAH LANG** (whose illustrations made the book so wonderfully lively), **CRISSI VELTEN**, **FELIX CORDES** und **KATRIN HEINATZ**. And of course thanks are due to **STEFFI** from Cafe C'an Gelat, who was our very own post office. Special thanks go to **RALF BOS** for his punctual monster grocery deliveries.

I thought up the majority of the recipes and ideas for the book in my second home, on the island of Majorca. It is no secret that this island means a lot to me. This is not only because of the beautiful markets, the fantastic food and the great weather – it's the people who make this place so special to me. That's why I would like to dedicate this book to all the good friends I was lucky to get to know there and who welcomed me into their families with open arms and hearts.

Muchas Gracias **STEFFI** and **BERNADO**, **PEP**, **KATI**, **PEP JUNIOR** and **SEBASTIAN SOLIVELLAS** and **THEIR FAMILIES**, **DITA** and **JOCKEL**, **JUAN**, **JUAN-FRANCESCO** and so many more.

Additionally I need to mention and thank those who made all of this possible: your help and support give me the freedom and the time to get involved in so many wonderful projects – with my heartfelt thanks to **NINA**, **MY FAMILY**, **TOM**, **FRANK**, **OLLI**, **BORIS**, **FRED**, **PATRICK**, **ROSARIO**, **HEIDE** and, of course, all the others from the **BULLEREI CREW**.

Last but not least, I would like to thank my publishers, in particular **MONIKA KÖNIG** and her team around **CORNELIA HANKE** and **INA HOCHBACH**. What you have in your hands right now is the fifth cookbook we have produced together. Thanks for your incredible patience and your courage to keep on going down this road with me.

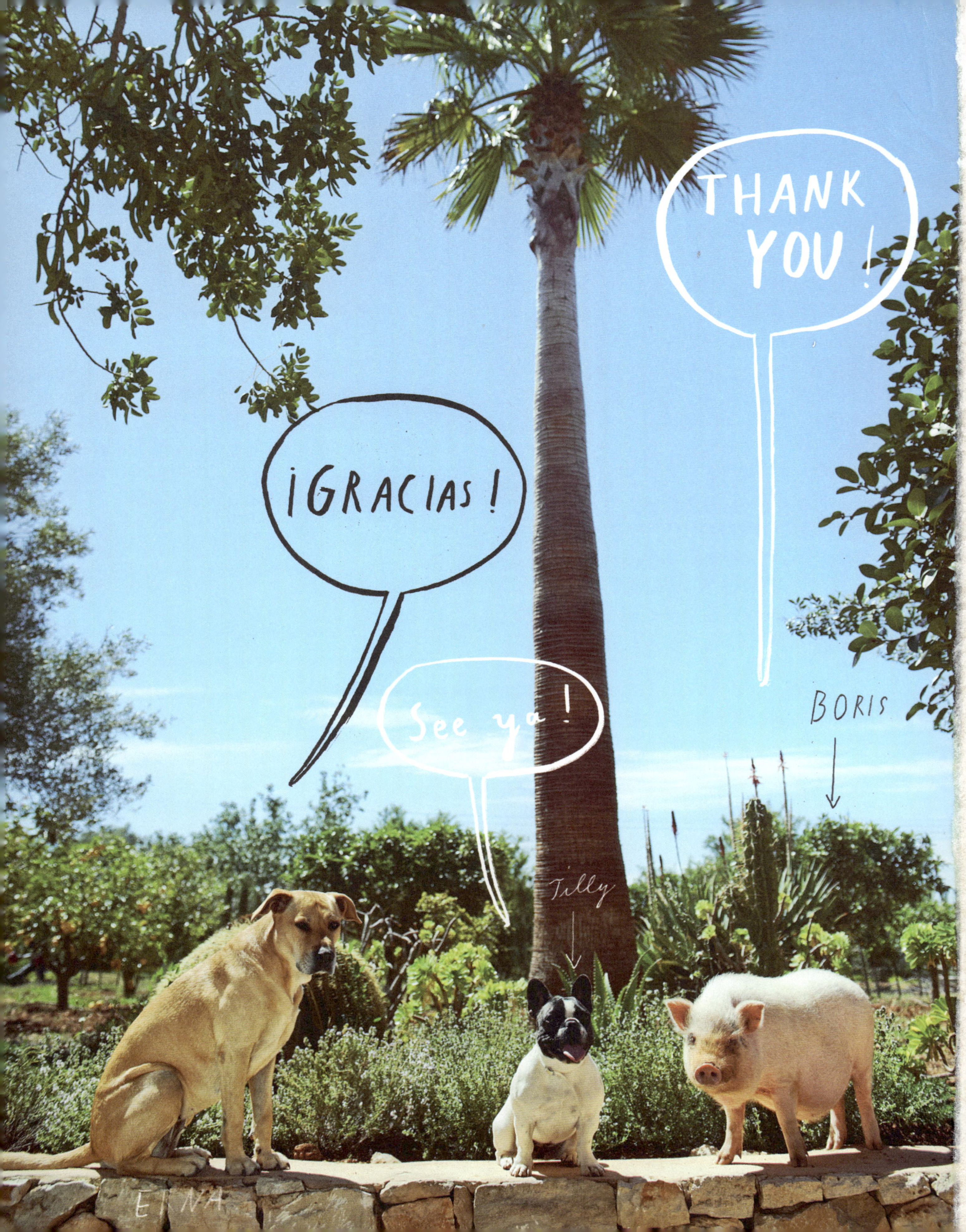
THANK YOU!
¡GRACIAS!
See ya!
BORIS
Tilly

BOX

Ooooh : delicious! very delicious.

Box

cool
sharp

♡ parsley

Lemon

sour
YES.

tasty!

chives
SORREL

GARLIC

CRESS   sage